AFRICAN THEOLOGY

AFRICAN THEOLOGY

A Critical Analysis
and Annotated Bibliography

Josiah U. Young III

Bibliographies and Indexes in Religious Studies, Number 26

G. E. Gorman, *Advisory Editor*

GREENWOOD PRESS
Westport, Connecticut • London

BT
30
.A438
Y68
1993

Library of Congress Cataloging-in-Publication Data

Young, Josiah U. (Josiah Ulysses)
    African theology : a critical analysis and annotated bibliography
/ Josiah U. Young.
        p.   cm.—(Bibliographies and indexes in religious studies,
    ISSN 0742-6836 ; no. 26)
    Includes bibliographical references and index.
    ISBN 0-313-26487-2 (alk. paper)
    1. Theology, Doctrinal—Africa, Sub-Saharan—History—20th
century.   2. Theology, Doctrinal—Africa, Sub-Saharan—History—20th
century—Bibliography.   3. Africa, Sub-Saharan—Religion.
4. Africa, Sub-Saharan—Religion—Bibliography.   I. Title.
II. Series.
    BT30.A438Y68   1993
    230'.0967—dc20   92-38979

British Library Cataloguing in Publication Data is available.

Library of Congress Catalog Card Number: 92-38979
ISBN: 0-313-26487-2
ISSN: 0742-6836

First published in 1993

Greenwood Press, 88 Post Road West, Westport, CT 06881
An imprint of Greenwood Publishing Group, Inc.

Printed in the United States of America

The paper used in this book complies with the
Permanent Paper Standard issued by the National
Information Standards Organization (Z39.48-1984).

10 9 8 7 6 5 4 3 2 1

To my parents, Josiah and Jacqueline;
and to the African youth who
are struggling for a better day.

Contents

Foreword

Black people regard theology which claims to be just theology, i.e. to be universal as particularistic, i.e. white, because the historical experience of people whose skin is a different colour, finds no echo there.

-Theo Witvliet

African theology is very much alive and active. It is at a time of excitement and ferment. The new is emerging, ideas and perspectives that will enrich not only Africa and the African Church but world Christianity. The Church universal will do well to follow the debate.

-M.M. Veigh

Many people with scholarly, professional or personal interests in the religious life of man have more than passing familiarity with black theology, having read James Cone's *Black Theology and Black Power* (1969) and the alternative position of Deotis Roberts developed most substantially in *Liberation and Reconciliation: A Black Theology* (1971). Since its origins in the mid-1960s, black theology has attracted a great deal of interest not only among black people of North America but also among students of liberation theology, who see Cone, Roberts and others as exponents of one school of this wider movement.

These same people would be likely, if given a list of names that included Desmond Tutu, Allan Boesak, Engelbert Mveng, Charles Nyamiti and John Mbiti, to link them with Cone and Roberts——simply a group of Africans who expound an African version of American black theology. The relationship between African and black theology is a clear one: "black theology, African theology and Asian Christian theology are cultural theologies in the sense that they are concerned with the recovery and preservation of their indigenous traditions and history."[1] That is, (American) black theology and African theology are each contextual theologies in their own right; they are both cultural theologies, but arising from, and responding to, different cultures.

Thus black theology arises from the experience of black Americans, and from the response to that experience of such leaders as Martin Luther King and Malcolm X.

---

[1] James Evans, Jr. *Black Theology: A Critical Assessment and Annotated Bibliography.* Bibliographies and Indexes in Religious Studies, 10 (Westport, Conn.: Greenwood Press, 1987), 14.

> Black theology's focus on the central theme of liberation represents our commitment to both Martin and Malcolm, martyrs who freely gave their lives for the freedom of our people. Together Martin and Malcolm remind us that there can be no freedom for black people unless it is derived from the particularity of our cultural history (Malcolm) and which also moves beyond itself to embrace the freedom of all people (Martin).[2]

This "moving beyond itself to embrace the freedom of all people" has occurred most visibly in South Africa, which approximately two decades ago adopted American black theology as yet another weapon in its arsenal against apartheid, which in so many ways resembles the social and political culture of the American ghetto. "Originating in America in the late 1960s, this kind of theology was imported to South Africa in the early 1970s by the Black Theology Project of the University Christian Movement."[3] By 1977 South African black theology had its own equivalent of Cone's *Black Theology and Black Power*——Allan Boesak's *Farewell to Innocence* (Maryknoll, N.Y.: Orbis Books)——and its own martyrs in place of Martin Luther King.

But the transposition of black theology from Harlem to Soweto is not the totality of African theology. Indeed, some might even say that black theology in South Africa is not truly African theology, although in our view African black theology has developed an ethos and a response to the South African situation that does indeed give it a uniquely African expression. The classic perception of African theology, articulated by, among others, Kwesi Dickson in *Theology in Africa* (Maryknoll, N.Y.: Orbis Books, 1984), suggests that a truly African theology is founded on the resources of *traditional* African culture, not just as a response to social and political inequalities imported from the West. It must establish the cultural continuity between the traditional religions of Africa and the religion of the Hebrews as articulated in the Old Testament; to the extent that it does this *only*, African theology differs significantly from black theology. It differs also in temporal terms, having pre-dated black theology as a self-conscious method of theological reflection by two decades. African theology's earliest modern expression was in 1946 with the publication of Placide Tempels' *La Philosophie bantoue*, and within a decade African theology was being discussed from Paris to Nairobi. "In 1955 a group of African and Haitian priests studying in Rome met to discuss the problem of relating the Christian message to the life and thought of their people. The term 'African Theology' was...used by M. Hebga at this discussion..."[4]

Students of African culture may well see in this development an echo of, and indeed even clear links with, the *négritude* movement of the 1930s, which gradually developed a following in Africa through the work of, among others, Léopold Senghor. In Paris during the 1930s *négritude* was essentially an awakening of universal black consciousness, an awareness that African heritage and traditions united black peoples around the world. Within Africa *négritude* seemed to manifest itself as a more indigenous movement; in Gerald Moore's view

> ...this comes up in the insistence on African Socialism as the programme of political and social action. And what goes with that——the attempt to feed into a new synthesis, into a new culture (a neo-African culture...) all

---

[2]Ibid., 60.

[3]Mokgethi Motlhabi, "Introduction." In *The Unquestionable Right to Be Free: Black Theology from South Africa*, ed. by Itumeleng J. Mosala and Buti Tlhagale (Maryknoll, N.Y.: Orbis Books, 1986), vii.

[4]Justin Ukpong, "Theological Literature from Africa." *Concilium* 199 (1988): 68.

those elements of African traditional civilization which are felt to be of absolute validity for the coming world in which Africa will pour its riches into a common pool.[5]

Having developed this idea during his discussion of the poetry of Senghor, Moore then worries aloud about this because of Senghor's "...profound Christian piety, because of his concern with reconciliation, because of his desire always to make the initial gesture of resentment, the gesture of bitterness, and, at the end of the poem, to bring everything to a harmonious conclusion."[6] The irony of this in the present context cannot go unnoticed; Senghor seems an ideal anthropomorphism for African theology, combining as he does profound Christian beliefs with a passionate advocacy of the validity of Africanness as a cultural vehicle for expressing those beliefs.

Négritude is but one manifestation of the move towards cultural autonomy within Africa that began in 1940s; African theology is another. This theology is, in a sense a type of evangelization involving translation of the Christian message into a form that can be readily assimilated by the peoples of Africa. It is the theological counterpart to decolonization, permitting indigenous peoples to discover their own ways of responding to the Christian kerygma. It thus represents the attempt from within Africa to move away from a Eurocentric expression of this kerygma, and from abstract statements of dogma, to an African expression of the Christian truth. It is not an attempt to fashion Christ into an African (just as British theology should not be seen as an attempt to fashion Christ into a comfortable middle class shopkeeper) but an attempt to show Christ as present in African history, culture and society. African theology represents, in other words, Africa's efforts at contextualizing theology. As such, it recognizes that the socio-political and historical contexts determine the way in which Africans answer questions about God's role in the playing out of human existence. This means that exegesis of the biblical message is accompanied by an equally important analysis of the social and cultural context in which the indigenous church tradition exists.

Given its links with black theology and other liberation theologies, and because it relies on theories of explanation developed by social scientists as well as theologians, our understanding of African theology is often characterized by confusion and misunderstanding——witness the tendency noted above for African theology to be viewed as just another manifestation of black theology. It is as much because of this, as for the stimulating new insights to be gained from an encounter with African theology, that we approached Dr. Josiah U. Young III, Professor of Systematic Theology at Wesley Theological Seminary in Washington, D.C., to prepare a volume that would document the developments and trends in African theology. In a sense this compilation complements James Evans' earlier volume in the series, *Black Theology: A Critical Assessment and Annotated Bibliography*. That earlier work, with some two dozen references to African theology, merely scratched the surface of this unique manifestation of theological contextualization. Furthermore, in the five years that have elapsed since the publication of Evans, African theology has experienced a blossoming of interest and of quality scholarship.

Clearly the time is ripe for a selective and carefully structured bibliographic introduction to the theology of and from Africa. In this volume Dr. Young offers us just such a work. Of particular note are the analytical chapters in Part One, which present a challenging and lucid discussion of inculturation/acculturation and religio-cultural/social

---

[5]Gerald Moore, "The Politics of Negritude." In *Protest in African Literature*, ed. by Cosmo Pieterse and Donald Munro (London: Heinemann Educational Books, 1969), 36.

[6]Ibid.

analysis as ways of understanding the main schools in African theology, termed "old guard" and "new guard." Also, the summary of African black theology very ably describes its antecedents in American black theology and subsequent contextualization in Africa. For ease of reference these themes are carried into the annotated bibliography, which in four chapters offers a guide to the most significant African theological literature of recent decades.

In this well-crafted volume Dr. Young presents a detailed bibliographic survey that is both accessible to the student and useful to the scholar. Those unfamiliar with African theology could do no better than to begin by reading the essays in Part One; more advanced students and scholars will find much value in the bibliography, which usefully draws comparisons and makes connections that many other commentators have missed. This work is commendable not only for its broad treatment of the various aspects of African theology but also for its logical arrangement and clear assessment of the most important publications in the field. In short Dr. Young's compilation sets a high bibliographic standard for any future work on African theology and is another welcome addition to Bibliographies and Indexes in Religious Studies.

The Revd Dr. G. E. Gorman FLA FRSA
Advisory Editor
Charles Sturt University - Riverina

Preface

As an African-American, who is drawn to the continent of my ancestors, I have been very edified by my work on this bibliography. It is not definitive, but I hope that it is instructive. The work has been arduous, but I have enjoyed the opportunity to deepen my interest in African theology——a theology from an exploited and diseased continent. I especially value what I have learned from the francophone theologians, particularly as embodied in the *Association oecuménique des théologiens africains* (AOTA). They, I have found, are among the most creative and courageous African theologians. Indeed, they comprise the majority of the theologians that I have dubbed the "new guard." In a continent where people are abused at a most alarming rate, their commitment to liberation and insightful explorations of the meaning of African culture define an option for the poor that goes to the heart of liberation theology. Indeed, African theologians have deepened my resolve to contest the pigeonholing of liberation theology as a "new"——and somewhat dispensable——"trend." With African theologians, I hold that *theology* must address injustice, and theologians must be close to the misery of its victims, if they are to have credibility in light of Christianity's dominant emblem——the Cross.

I must thank Gary Gorman, editor of the series and Marilyn Brownstein and George Butler, both of Greenwood Press, for their patience. I also thank Sallie Cuffee, who helped with twenty-eight of the annotations I have complied. Suzette Randolph, who helped with the typing, has been of tremendous help, as has Tim Adamson, who did the title index for me. Thanks are also due to Professor Larry Stookey for his critical review of the manuscript. Howertine Duncan provided immediate assistance when I needed to track down bibliographic information.

I thank my wife, Pamela Monroe; she has improved the narrative chapters significantly, making them far more readable than they would have been without her critical eye. Our son, Josiah Monroe Young, has also been patient. I have had to spend too many weekends "grinding away" on this project. I greatly appreciate his sweet disposition and gracious respect of my calling.

Introduction

The term "African theology" can be misleading. One might well argue that African theology, like European theology, does not exist.[1] There is no *one* African theology, but distinct works by Africans and broad groupings, such as the old guard, the new guard and black theology. (I will say more about these groupings later.) These nuances are lost in the abstraction, "African theology." Still, one cannot abandon the descriptive term. As I will show in more detail later, the term itself signifies an *otherness* that edifies Christian thought. That is, African theology has emerged from the "underside of history" and signifies that Africans have broken away from Eurocentric theologies which virtually ignore the legacies of slavery and colonization that afflict African people.

Critical tools Africans use to facilitate their break from Eurocentric thought are social analysis and religio-cultural analysis. These analyses, as defined within the Ecumenical Association of Third World Theologians (EATWOT) and *l'Association oecuménique des théologiens africains* (AOTA), help one examine issues related to African theology.[2] The Africans make up a sizable portion of EATWOT, which was founded by Africans, Asians, and Latin Americans in the recognition that First World theologians are not equipped to produce theologies relevant to the oppressed of the Third World.

Indeed, I cannot envisage a comprehensive bibliography on African theology without annotations that explore pertinent historical and socioeconomic contradictions, i.e., social analysis. Neither can I envisage a bibliography that does not give equal weight to religio-cultural analysis. In order to facilitate an understanding of these terms, I will for the remainder of this introduction briefly discuss them, as well as the groupings of African theology to which I have just referred——that is, the old and new guards and black theology.

---

[1]Many Third World theologians find that the term "European theology" is an apt term when one considers the problem of Eurocentricity--the intransigence of which is observed in the "periphery" by the oppressed.

[2]See 002-003; 344, 352, 371, 427-428; 435, 437-438; 456, 458, 505.

Social and Religio-cultural Analysis: A Plumbline for a Study of African Theology

Aware of the larger contradictions between the First and the Third Worlds, one focuses in social analysis on the "smaller" contradictions of a country, which involve economic and social discrepancies among the bourgeois elite, the workers, and the peasants. In examining contradictions in this way, theologians set in bold relief the issues related to the liberation of the oppressed——principally the workers and the peasants, and especially their children. "Liberation," which inspires social analysis, signifies Africans' faith that God is on the side of the oppressed rather than the side of the oppressors, who represent slavery, colonialism and the alienation each have wrought in Africa.

Much of religio-cultural analysis focuses on africanization, which involves inculturation and acculturation. Inculturation——a generic term descriptive of Asian as well as African realities——is a process that attempts to make Christianity relevant and meaningful to autochthones, who refuse to forsake their traditional religions.[3]   One often discusses inculturation in terms of horticultural metaphors: one grafts Christianity to an African stock, or roots Christianity in African soil so that faith yields African produce.[4]   I understand acculturation——also a generic term——as the *spontaneous* force that africanizes Eurocentric missionary Christianity among the peasants and the workers. Acculturation makes Christianity African in a process that de-europeanizes Christian faith. One observes this grassroots process within the African independent churches, which are integral to the study of African theology.[5]   Indeed, the independent churches exemplify that africanization involves acculturation as well as inculturation.

Among   the   BaKongo   influenced   regions   of   Zaire,   for   instance, "Kimbanguism"——an example of an independent church——represents an African Christianity precisely because of the preponderance of things African in its expression.[6] Inculturation is at work too, however. Here inculturation signifies the christianization of traditional BaKongo religion, but does not obfuscate the acculturative force of ancestral values. In short: without inculturation, African *theology* is not Christian; without acculturation, Christian theology is not *African*.

I have found a paradigm of the reciprocity of acculturation and inculturation in the work of Mercy Oduyoye (a noted feminist and a member of the new guard). She writes that acculturation pertains to the efforts of "Africans to use things African in their practice of Christianity"; "inculturation [refers to] the manifestation of changes that have come into

---

[3]Contiguous with the stone and iron ages, yet with a dynamism revealing its own impetus to historical development, African traditional religions have persisted despite and in conjunction with Christianity and Islam——so-called world religions whose early histories are also part of Africa's own history. In fact, certain Africans argue that African theology pertains primarily to the gods of so-called "pagan" people, such as the Yoruba, the Dogon and the BaKongo——African civilizations with religious structures as sophisticated as any "world religion."

[4]Inculturation is related to two other terms, indigenization and *adaptation*. Both terms refer to efforts to divest Christianity of its Eurocentric accoutrements, in order to place it in African garb.

[5]On the independent churches, see 008, 026, 046, 051, 063, 064, 077, 141, 142, 143, 144, 183, 184, 185, 186, 192, 198, 199, 206, 207, 208, 224, 225, 227, 228, 235, 239, 240, 248, 251, 258, 259, 265, 266, 267, 268, 269, 272, 274, 275, 278, 285, 290, 296, 307, 316, 317, 321, 322, 325, 326, 330, 332, 333, 346, 356, 360, 363, 394, 412, 430, 431, 450, 451, 452, 458, 462, 495, 499, 546, 554, 555, 581, 585, 590, 592.

[6]On the BaKongo, see 150, 185; 198-199. On Kimbanguism see 185, 199, 208, 263, 330.

the African way of life as a result of the Christian faith."[7] An *African* Christianity, then, emerges from the acculturative power of African tradition, which resists alien values as significant themes of the Christian story modify, enrich and regenerate autochthonous values. The problem here involves the tension between christianization and africanization: who decides whether an expression is Christian and when africanization sublates christianization? This problem——which I will explore in more detail in Chapter Three——is significant and illuminates issues related to both social and religio-cultural analyses, as well as distinctions in African theology.

The Old Guard, The New Guard and Black Theology

The distinction between the old and new guards is not one of the "young Turks" and the aging relics. The distinction between them, rather, is one of theological orientation, though one can find elements of the new guard in the old, and the old, in the new. Generally, the old guard has focused on religio-cultural analysis, with little, if any, social analysis. Here their emphasis has been on inculturation rather than acculturation. That is, they have sought to christianize elements of African culture rather than embrace the africanization of Christianity. The old guard, moreover, has argued that liberation theology pertains only to the southern part of the continent, though their struggling, and barely emergent, nations were regressing under the same scepter that has been disabling black South Africans, who are still saddled by racial injustice (the legacy of apartheid).

The new guard, on the other hand, is committed to both social analysis and a religio-cultural analysis in which inculturation is complemented by acculturation. Like black South African theologians, the new guard swells the ranks of liberation theologians. For both groups, the way of liberation is integral, not epiphenomenal, to Christian identity. Black South African theology is the counterpart of black North American theology and is distinguished by social analyses that have focused on the contradictions of apartheid. Religio-cultural analysis is a factor too, particularly given the acculturative force of the South African independent churches.

Having defined the terms pertinent to this study, I should now say a few words about the layout of *African Theology: A Critical Analysis and Annotated Bibliography*. Part One of the text consists of four chapters. In Chapter One, I give a synopsis of the historical background of African theology, with a focus on outstanding historic figures. Both space and time dictate that the historical discussion be brief and sketchy. (I must reiterate here the limits of my historical discussion; I focus on the English-speaking context. I note for the record, however, that developments in French-speaking Africa are just as intriguing.)[8] Chapter Two focuses on the old guard; and Chapter Three, on the new guard. I devote Chapter Four to a summary of black South African theology.

The annotated bibliography, Part Two of the text——which covers the period from about 1955 to 1992——serves the narrative chapters. The bibliography is divided into the following headings: "History and Social Analysis"; "African Traditional Religion and Religio-Cultural Analysis"; "African Theology: The Old and New Guards"; "Black South African Theology." Although outstanding African theologians are noted throughout, the reader should not expect a full listing of their published works. I have chosen only those sources that exemplify the import of social and religio-cultural analyses, and the "types"

---

[7] See 458.

[8] See, for instance, Barthélemy Adoukonou, *Jalons pour une théologie africaine: Essai d'une herméneutique chrétienne du Vodun dahoméen. Tome I: Critique théologique.* (Paris: Éditions Lethielleux, 1980), 91-110. See also 288.

of African theology. Nonetheless, the works cited——609 in all——adequately represent the various voices of African theology. They are gleaned from disparate resources: volumes of collected essays; books by single authors; and journals (especially the *Journal of African Theology* and *Bulletin de théologie africaine*). Most of the sources have been published in Africa, the United States, or Great Britain; and most are in English, though a good many are in French. While other bibliographies will likely undertake different methods of compilation, I am content that this one comprehensively introduces one to the depth and scope of African theology.

Part I

AFRICAN THEOLOGY: A CRITICAL ANALYSIS

1

Ancestors of
African Theology

African theology is part of the history of Christianity in Africa and is the legacy of outstanding African Christians. These ancestors of African theology appear throughout the history of Christianity in Africa, which is commonly discussed in terms of three phases.

The First Phase

The first phase, related to the patristic period and extending for the most part until the seventh century, places one initially in the context of the first century C.E. Legend has it that the Apostle Mark brought the gospel to Alexandria in the first century. Although Alexandria was then the hub of a latinized Egypt, it was no less an African context. Its Africanness is to be seen, in part, in the Coptic culture familiar with the cryptic art of mummification, resistant to hellenization and integral to the Monophysite christology extant today and different from the Western and the Eastern churches. What is more, several theologians seminal for an appreciation of Christian thought were Africans. These Africans may not have been blacks——i.e., Congo-Kordofanian——but so-called Caucasian Berbers and so-called Afro-Asiatic, Hamitic people.[1] In the East, such Africans were Alexandrians: Clement (third century), Origen (185-254) and Athanasius, the "black dwarf" (296-373). The Carthaginians were in the West: Tertullian (160-220), Cyprian (200-258) and Augustine (354-430). Augustine, Bishop of Hippo, a Numidian of Berber stock, is one of the greatest theologians in the history of the church. Related to him were the Donatists——Christian Berbers, schismatics, fiercely resistant to Rome and guardians of an Africanity not unlike the African independent churches today. In the fourth century, Axum——northeastern Ethiopia——was christianized under the leadership of the warrior king, Ezana. Axumite Christianity is the forerunner of the Ethiopian Orthodox Church of today. Monophysite like its Coptic sibling to the North, this Ethiopian church is one of the oldest forms of Christianity and bears an essential relationship to African theology, as it is a paradigm of the africanization of Christianity (acculturation). King Ezana conquered neighboring Nubia and christianized it. The main centers of Nubian Christianity were Nobadia, Maukuria and Alwa, of which little is

---

[1]African theology today, which is the focus of this bibliography, pertains primarily to the so-called Negroid people below the Sahara who are said to constitute a different race from the Berbers, the Hamites and the Busmanoids. While talk of different races is always specious, the Christianity of the first phase did not spread significantly, if at all, to Black Africa. (The impressive Savannah states of the medieval period were fairly Islamicized though.)

known. With the exception of Nubia and the Monophysites of Egypt and Ethiopia, the Christianity of the first phase was extinguished by Islam in the seventh century. The Nubians were overcome by Muslims in the fourteenth century.

The Second Phase

In the fifteenth century, thanks to the Roman Catholic Portuguese, Christianity re-emerged in Africa. The Portuguese rounded the Cape of Good Hope, traveled North through the Indian Ocean and set up posts on the coastal areas, as they could not as yet penetrate the interior.

A significant area under Portuguese influence was the Congo. The Portuguese set up churches there with the blessing of the powerful BaKongo, christianized regent, Affonso Mbemba a Nzinga. The son of Nzinga became a Catholic bishop, consecrated in Europe in the early sixteenth century.[2]

As important as the royal family is a charismatic figure, Dona Béatrice, also known as Kimpa Vita.[3] She indicates that the phenomena of the African independent churches stretch back to the dawning of the eighteenth century. Dona Béatrice is not unlike her BaKongo kinsman, Simon Kimbangu, who came after her in the twentieth century. Kimbangu is the founder of the L'Eglise de Jésus Christ sur la terre par le prophète Simon Kimbangu (EJCK), one of the largest and most significant African independent churches.[4]

The founder of the so-called Antonian sect, Béatrice thought herself to be the reincarnation of St. Anthony, who allegedly came to her as she lay gravely ill. Given certain nuances of BaKongo religion, one can *imagine* why Béatrice could take on St. Anthony's identity. The acculturative force of BaKongo values were such that Catholic hagiography was made to serve a BaKongo imperative.

BaKongo have believed that the cosmos is made up of the realms of the living (*ntoto*) and the dead (*mpemba*). As white is the color of *mpemba*, as in white clay, BaKongo often thought that Europeans were their ancestors, who had found a novel way to cross the watery threshold between the living and the dead.[5] Indeed, for the BaKongo, the boundary between the living and the dead is a river, *kalunga*. On their sides of *kalunga*, the living and the dead engage in the activities proper to them. When the sun shines for the living, the moon shines for the dead, and vice versa. Human beings, BaKongo believe, pass through both realms in a perpetual cycle. The living had been the ancestors of yesterday; and the dead are, in some sense, the unborn of tomorrow.

Thus, all "turn in the path" that is the ellipse of *ntoto* and *mpemba*——the trajectory of the rising and setting sun. The fact, then, that Dona Béatrice saw herself as the reincarnation of St. Anthony is accounted for by BaKongo values, in which the living are the reincarnated dead.

Béatrice was highly critical of Catholic practices, undoubtedly aware of the complicity of the priests in the slave trade and the defeat the BaKongo people. Although she was critical of the priests, she claimed to be Christian. Her interpretation of Christianity not only entailed her claim that she embodied Anthony, but that she was an

---

[2]Peter Forbath, *The River Congo. The Discovery, Exploration and Exploitation of the World's Most Dramatic River* (New York: E.P. Dutton, 1979).

[3]Ibid.

[4]On Kimbangu, see 185, 199, 208, 263, 330.

[5]See 150, 185, 198-199.

exemplar of the Virgin Birth as well.[6]   Steeped in the ancestral ways of the BaKongo, Béatrice exhorted her kinfolk to expect the restoration of the ancient BaKongo kingdom tragically divided and in ruins due to the wars of the seventeenth and eighteenth centuries. The BaKongo regent, King Pedro IV, had her burned alive in 1706, and her movement was arrested.

By the end of the eighteenth century, there was no Christianity anywhere in Black Africa to speak of.   Portuguese preoccupation with the slave trade; the paucity of African priests; the absence of African seminaries; the waning influence of Catholicism as an imperial force in Europe; and the small number of missionaries, made even smaller by African disease——all took their toll on the Christianity of the second phase.

The Third Phase

The Christianity of the third phase took root and flourished in West Africa largely because Africans themselves played a seminal role in the planting of Christianity there.[7] These Christians, ancestors of African theology, include Samuel Crowther, James Holy Johnson and Edward W. Blyden. Discussion of them requires an appreciation of Great Britain during the rise of the Industrial Revolution, which made slavery a less viable economic mode——a fact that facilitated the abolitionism that burgeoned there.

Tied to Christian mission, abolitionism led, in the latter part of the eighteenth century, to the manumission of slaves in England and the founding of a British colony in Africa, Sierra Leone, the principal city of which was Freetown. By the 19th century, Freetown had become a seminal, urban context for the gathering of African people——ex-slaves, recaptives, creoles, etc.[8] Under the patronage of missionary societies, such as the Church Missionary Society (CMS), Freetown was characterized by an ethos in which British philanthropy, bound to mission and abolition, undertook to train African people to become exemplars of Anglo-Saxon civilization (nearly synonymous with capitalism and Eurocentric, Christian piety). A historic example of that practice was Fourah Bay College, founded by the CMS and championed by British abolitionists such as Henry Venn, Thomas Buxton and William Wilberforce. An illustrious prodigy of Fourah Bay was Samuel Crowther. He was a Yoruba sold into slavery as a consequence of the civil wars of Yorubaland. Subsequently recaptured by the Royal Navy and relocated in Sierra Leone, Crowther became the leading example of the African leadership Venn hoped would

---

[6]Forbath, *The River Congo*. According to Forbath:

> [Béatrice] claimed Saint Anthony was the second God, who held the keys to heaven and was eager to restore the Kongo kingdom. She herself..."[w]as in the habit of dying every Friday," in imitation of the passion of Christ, and going up to heaven to "dine with God and plead the cause of the Negroes, especially the restoration of the Kongo" and being "born again on Saturday." She imitated the Virgin as well, and when she had a son she told [a priest] "I cannot deny that he is mine but how I had him I do not know: I know however that he came to me from heaven." She preached that there was a fundamental difference between whites and blacks, saying the former "were originally made from a certain soft stone called fama" while the latter "came from a tree called musenda," and her followers wore garments made from the bark of that tree (a species of fig). (See pp. 138-139.)

[7]Events relevant to this period took place as well in East Africa. Southern Africa, during the nineteenth century, was also an important context for an appreciation of this third phase. Missionaries such as Jahannes Vanderkemp, Robert Moffat and John Phillip come to mind in that regard. Particularly outstanding among the missionaries of Southern Africa was the explorer David Livingstone, the first White to traverse the continent from points between the Atlantic and the Indian oceans. Following the Zambezi river and bound to proclaim the Word "beyond every other man's line of things," Livingstone was more explorer than missionary.

[8]See 026, 042, 051, 112.

proliferate by way of a missiology that planned for its own demise. Venn described this *"euthanasia* of a Mission," in his essay, "Minute upon the Employment and Ordination of Native Teachers."[9] (Venn, a white Protestant, had a white Catholic priest as his colleague in this regard——Monseigneur Marion Brésillac, who sought to nurture an African clergy in old Dahomey.)[10] Crowther became *the* Bishop of an enormous area in West Africa, wrote a pioneering vocabulary of the Yoruba language and displayed sensitivity to what is now called inculturation. Like the old guard, Crowther recognized the depth of the structure of traditional religion and thought a vital missiology should be astute enough to root itself in that structure by the conservative translation of Christian values into traditional idioms.

According to Crowther, missionaries should be ever mindful that

> Christianity does not undertake to destroy national assimilation; where there are any degrading superstitious defects, it corrects them; where they are connected with politics, such connection should be introduced with due caution and in all meekness of wisdom, that there may be good and perfecting understanding between us and the powers that be....[Africans'] mutual aid clubs should not be despised, but where there is any connection with superstition they should be corrected and improved after a Christian model....Their religious terms and ceremonies should be carefully noticed; a wrong use made of such terms does not depreciate their real value, but renders them more valuable when we adopt them in expressing scriptural terms in their right senses and places, though they have been misapplied for want of better knowledge.[11]

Toward the end of his life, his episcopacy was undermined by the CMS.

Another forerunner of the old guard was Bishop James Holy Johnson.   A contemporary of Crowther, a Yoruba and a denizen of the environs of Sierra Leone, Johnson became a leading figure in the history of the West African Church and a leading cultural nationalist. Johnson thought that Christianity is

> intended for and is suitable for every race and Tribe of people on the face of the Globe.   Acceptance of it was never intended by its Founder to denationalise any people and it is indeed its glory that every race of people may profess and practice it and imprint upon it its own native characteristics, giving it a peculiar type among themselves without losing anything of its virtue. And why should not there be an African Christianity as there has been a European and an Asiatic Christianity?[12]

Johnson's strong support of an africanized Christianity is as significant as Crowther's legacy in the study of African theology.

---

[9]C.P Groves, *The Planting of Christianity in Africa, Vol. 2, 1840-1878* (London: Lutterworth Press, 1954), 217. See 042.

[10]See Adoukonou, *Jalons*, 95-102.

[11]See Jesse Page, *The Black Bishop: Samuel Adjai Crowther* (New York: Fleming H. Revell, 1908), 299-300. Also see annotations 109; 087, 145, 328, 346, 356, 357, 360, 480.

[12]See Ayandele, *Holy Johnson: Pioneer of African Nationalism* (New York: Humanities Press, 1970), 304. Also see 007. See also, 087, 136, 346.

While Johnson's and Crowther's legacies are to be appreciated in the context of Sierra Leone, Edward Blyden's legacy takes one back to the development of Liberia. Liberia, not unlike Sierra Leone, was founded under the auspices of whites. As members of the American Colonization Society (ACS), they wished to reduce the number of non-slaves in North America more than they wished to uplift African people. And the African-Americans these whites sponsored——the Americo-Liberians who colonized Liberia——were oppressively unsympathetic to the values and mores of the Africans.[13] Blyden, however, was a notable exception in that regard. Blyden also exemplified the role African-Americans have played in African theology's development.[14]

Born in St. Thomas, Virgin Islands, but spending most of his life in West Africa, Edward Blyden is considered to be the ancestor of a Pan-Africanism that remains a central feature of African theology. Indeed, Blyden——allegedly of Igbo descent——presaged *négritude* as well as African personality, notions that still make their way into African theology.[15] He even may be said to have anticipated much that was later meant by "African socialism," or *ujamaa*.[16] Blyden, moreover, used the phrase African theology in the latter part of the nineteenth century——long before it became the clarion call of the African church. In the words of Blyden's principal biographer, Hollis Lynch, Blyden hoped "that Liberia would give the lead to the rest of Africa by creating 'new forms representing the African idea...African literature with the smell of Africa upon it...African freedom, African thought, and *African theology*' [emphasis added]."[17]

Blyden asserted that blacks

> were created with the physical qualities which distinguish [them] for the glory of the Creator, and for the happiness and perfection of humanity; and that in [their] endeavors to make [themselves] something else, [they] are not only spoiling [their] nature and turning aside from [their] destiny, but [they] are robbing humanity of the part [they] ought to contribute to its complete development and welfare...[18]

His perspective is similar to the hope one finds today among African theologians. Blyden, however, like Crowther and Johnson, thought that European civilization would be, in the final analysis, providential, if for no other reason than that it allegedly brought true religion and empirical know-how to the continent. As the next chapter will show, however, the notion of true religion remained far too Eurocentric. And, as the third chapter will show, the transfer of technological know-how——much of it obsolete——has tended to accentuate the structural disparity between Africa and its former colonial masters.

Much has been left unsaid regarding this third and seminal phase in the development of African theology. Still, attention to the forces and events that produced the ancestors——

---

[13]See 028-029; 054; 126-127.

[14]See 027, 028-029; 042, 063, 094, 111, 112, 122, 126-127.

[15]On *négritude* see 114-115; 340, 353, 475, 511; on African personality see 016-018; 081-082. See also note 16, Chapter 2.

[16]See 098-099; 102-106; 108, 114.

[17]Hollis Lynch, *Edward Wilmot Blyden: Pan-Negro Patriot* (New York: Oxford University Press, 1970), 165. See also 016-018, 081-082.

[18]Ibid., 215. See 081. See also 016-018.

Crowther, Johnson and Blyden——sum up the salient issues of the period and bring one to the dawning of the twentieth century in which African theology became a formal discourse.

2

The Old Guard:
The Christianization of
Aspects of African
Traditional Religion and
the Myth of Independence

After the Berlin Conference and World War I, Great Britain and France, ruling the largest amount of African territory, emerged as the superior colonial powers.[1] In the wake of World War II, Britain and France lost power due to the hegemonic rise of the United States and found it expedient to supervise the reform of their colonial systems by way of "devolution"——the incremental promotion of the elite to ostensible control of the colonial state.[2] This devolution led to what is called independence——a myth the African elite has tended to promulgate.[3]

The elite, who led the nationalistic movements for independence, were educated, for the most part, in mission schools and often pursued higher education abroad in their metropoles. The old guard has been part of this elite, who have inherited the colonial states and upheld the cultural nationalism that owed more to westernization than to popular culture.[4]   An example of such nationalism is *négritude*[5]——a Pan-African idiom developed in francophone Africa and its diaspora. *Négritude*, a form of *cultural* nationalism, is often associated with the writings of the West Indian, Aimé Césaire and the African, Léopold Senghor.[6] One sees the relation of *négritude* to the old guard in the

---

[1]See 004, 020, 037, 124.

[2]See 092, 124. Not all elites were captive to the West. Jomo Kenyatta, Kwame Nkrumah, Sekou Toure were socialized like the African pseudo-bourgeoisie, but hardly made the ideological choice for a pro-Western, pro-capitalist position.

[3]See 055.

[4]The reference to popular culture indicates that other forces, such as trade unionism, were integral to the demise of olden colonialism. That is, workers and peasants, nearer to the bottom of colonial society than the elite——and therefore viscerally connected to traditional culture——also sought to end colonial rule. One thinks of the Maji Maji rebellion in Tanzania, the Mau-Mau in Kenya, or the struggles of PAIGG whose resistance has been defined by Amilcar Cabral (see 023-024). In addition, one also thinks of the rise of the independent churches——and their prophets, John Chilembwe, Simon Kimbangu, William Wade Harris, Josiah Oshitulu, etc.——that represent resistance to colonialism. On the independent churches, see note 5, Introduction.

[5]See note 14, Chapter 1.

[6]See 114-115.

seminal *Des prêtres noirs s'interrogent*,[7] which was published in 1956——the year prior to the "independence" of the Gold Coast.[8] The book, containing pioneering essays on the relation of African culture and history to Christianity, is seminal because it marks a formal emergence of African theology. In *Des prêtres noirs s'interrogent*, black priests asserted: "For too long, others have thought about our problems for us, without us and even despite us. The African priest must also say what he thinks about his church and his country in order to advance God's kingdom [my translation]."[9]

African priests were attuned to the shortcomings of *négritude*, in that they agreed that it, like the word Africa itself, is a generic term given to imprecision.[10] Still, they would not abandon *négritude*. According to these priests, all black countries, and by implication Africans in predominately white countries, are bonded together.[11] As Marcel Lefebvre, who wrote the *Lettre-Préface* to *Des prêtres noirs*, explains:

> It is true that it is dangerous to speak of Africa generically [*de parler l'Afrique en général*] and those who are honest and prudent do so less and less, for each African country has its idiosyncracy [*a son cachet*], its originality, its personality. But these nuances may be recognized as a substratum, common to all black countries——there is among them a common factor, common situations, common reflexes, which should be reflected upon and defined. *Négritude*, despite its tendency to provoke ethereal and gratuitous ratiocination, itself expresses this one reality, or rather, a complex of realities, that boil up from the bottom of the soul of all blacks, from the singular fact that they are blacks, that is, placed ethnically

---

[7]A. Abble, *et al.*, *Des prêtres noirs s'interrogent* (Paris: Les Éditions du Cerf, 1956). See 294, 303, 329, 353, 370, 415, 416, 464, 475, 500, 511.

[8]The independence of the Gold Coast is considered to be the watershed mark in Africa's struggle to abolish olden colonialism. Soon to become Ghana after 1957 and led by Africa's favorite son, Kwame Nkrumah——see 096-101——,the "independence" of the Gold Coast foreshadowed the rapid devolution of independence onto the majority of Black African "states."

[9]See *Des prêtres noirs*, 16.

[10]See *Des prêtres noirs*. Marcel Lefebvre writes:

> We often speak of *négritude*, and use the word Africa here, for a practical reason——a generic term is necessary. Ordinarily, *négritude* signifies all the black countries (Cameroon, Senegal, Guinea), [even, to a certain extent,] those in far away America, as is the case with Haiti. What is the import of these words [négritude and Africa] in their *ampleur*, their elasticity, and their imprecision? The question itself indicates one has already undertaken a consideration of *négritude*. One discovers that it is sometimes more charged with emotion than objective content. *Négritude* has conjured up a poetic theme quite conducive to myriad, more or less sincere, tragic or lyric variations. Indeed, the word Africa itself will be passed through the sieve and be submitted to the assault of the same critique [my translation]. (See pp. 16-17.)

[11]It would appear that the Pan-Africanism to which the priests refer in terms of *négritude* is confined to Black countries like Haiti. Yet a few of the articles in this volume refer to North American Blacks as part of the "generic" Africa. For instance Meinard Hebga in his essay, *"Christianisme et négritude"*——see 353——writes of the uncanny sublimity of the spirituals and the blues:

> Wagner imitates the roar of God's thunder at the last judgement, as do Fauré and Perosi. Blacks have not a single monumental work; but is anything more penitent, more poignant than Negro American blues? Has one ever been gripped by a holy fear at the sudden explosion (*d'une sainte frayeur à éclatement soudain*) of a Negro spiritual: *Steal away to Jesus*, or *My Lord What a Morning*? (See p. 201.)

This Pan-Africanism, this *négritude*, pertains to the totality of the Diaspora.

in a socially and psychologically determined situation. In fact, in our encounters with blacks of other countries, we have tended to value the commonality that we share rather than what differentiates us [my translation].[12]

Indeed, the appeal to *négritude* indicates that African theology is emergent from a Pan-African perspective.

One also sees *négritude* at work in the old guard theology of Vincent Mulago, specifically his *Un visage africain du christianisme: L'union vitale bantu face à l'unité vitale ecclésiale*, published in 1962.[13] Mulago, a contributor to *Des prêtres noirs*, also indicates that African theology is a Pan-African discourse. According to Mulago, the African church should not be ashamed of her blackness. Indeed, *négritude*, he asserts, has made a contribution to the edification and enrichment of the totality of the body of Christ.[14]

Another way to examine the relation of cultural nationalism to African theology is in terms of "African personality"——a concept developed in anglophone Africa. Whereas *négritude,* in francophone Africa, has been expressed through a certain Roman Catholic consciousness, African personality, in anglophone Africa, has been expressed through a certain Protestant consciousness.[15]

The idiom, African personality, is, as I have noted, attributed to Edward Blyden; and although its precise meaning is elusive, I have found that Alex Quaison-Sackey——former Permanent Representative of Ghana to the United Nations——has provided the most substantial discussion I have come across so far. According to Quaison-Sackey, writing during the immediate aftermath of Ghana's "independence," African personality signifies the African's attempt

> to understand who he is, whence he came; and since he knows that no personality can be fully and effectively realized except in the open air of freedom and independence, he wishes not only to obtain these conditions for himself but to recover what his ancestors once had achieved before they finally succumbed, through conquest, bribery, treachery, and bad faith, to European power. Yet he knows, too, as a result of colonial domination, that his struggle to attain a personality, an individuality, and the equality, dignity and respect that accompany it, is more difficult for him than for peoples of other colors——and largely because the white man has needed to depict him as, in effect, subhuman in order to justify his own cruelty and rapacity.[16]

---

[12]*Des prêtres noirs*, 17.

[13]See Vincent Mulago, *Un visage africain du christianisme: L'union vitale Bantu face à l'unité vitale ecclésiale* (Paris: Présence Africaine, 1962). See also 417. For other works by Mulago, see 415-421.

[14]Mulago, 227. See 417.

[15]It may rightly be argued that the relationship between anglophone theology and African personality is less direct than that between négritude and the francophone theology. Discussion of "African personality" is no less important because of that. Without an appreciation of the relation of the idiom to African theology, the Pan-African implications of the latter become less clear. What also becomes less clear is how "African personality," often petty-bourgeois in orientation, accounts for the narrowness of African theologies that precluded the relevance of the praxis of liberation for most of Black Africa.

[16]Alex Quaison-Sackey, *Africa Unbound. Reflections of an African Statesman* (New York: Frederick A. Praeger, 1963), 39-40.

African personality made its way into seminal old guard texts, such as Bolaji Idowu's *Towards an Indigenous Church* published in 1965.

Idowu, in defining indigenization——i.e., acculturation and inculturation——indicates the relation of African personality to anglophone theology in asserting

> that the Church in Nigeria should be the Church which affords Nigerians the means of worshipping God as Nigerians; that is, in a way which is compatible with their own spiritual temperament, of singing to the glory of God in their own way, of praying to God and hearing His holy Word in idiom which is clearly intelligible to them. She should be a *corporate personality*, personally discerning what is the will of God for herself and responsible for all requisite steps taken in fulfilling it [emphasis added].[17]

Although Idowu defines indigenization in terms of Nigerian nationalism, his *Towards an Indigenous Church* has Pan-African implications; it has been recognized as a model of the quest for African theology.[18]

The notion of African personality is also at work in *Biblical Revelation and African Belief*, edited in part by Kwesi Dickson, and published in 1969 under the auspices of the All Africa Conference of Churches.[19] John Mbiti, well-noted among the old guard, who contributed to that volume, discusses "African personality" in his seminal *African Religions and Philosophy*.[20] As with *négritude*, he treats the idiom very critically.

Indeed, critics have asserted that *négritude*——and by implication African personality——is but a bourgeois game played by the African elite, a game embarrassingly akin to the game whites themselves play in regard to Africa. Allegedly, *négritude* is meant to amuse Westerners captive to the notion of the noble savage. As such, it is out of touch with the dynamic liberation struggles of the African people.

New guard theologian, Jean-Marc Éla, points out, for instance, that *négritude* is very much akin to white Westerners' preoccupation with a pristine Africa. That Africa, he asserts, is only an illusion. The real Africa——*une Afrique en ébullition*——is in dire straits. Nonetheless, writes Éla, the white *ethnologues* invade the villages of the bush, in quest of a paradise (*un monde intact et pur, ayant échappé au "péché originel" de la "civilisation"*). According to Éla, these Europeans appear, index cards in hand, ready to conquer "virgin territory," un-trod as yet by whites, expecting to discover the authentic African. Éla asserts that this attitude, this *négritude*, refuses to examine the contradictions

---

[17]Idowu, *Towards an Indigenous Church*, 11. See 356.

[18]See 356, 458.

[19]Regarding *Biblical Revelation and African Belief*, see 179, 241, 286, 343, 357, 381. Despite the argument that the notion of "African personality" had little to do with African theology in English speaking contexts, Kwesi Dickson indicates the contrary. In his *Theology in Africa*——see 327——Dickson sums up developments in African theology pertinent primarily to the contributions of the old guard. In noting the necessity for the emergence of views I have typified in terms of the new guard, he argues convincingly for the criticalness of religio-cultural analysis. In doing so, he indicates the epistemological significance of "African personality." He calls this selfhood. He writes: "Selfhood has not been realized by the Church in Africa, which is not surprising, for without the achievement of national selfhood in the sense of the practice of that kind of life-style which exhibits a keen awareness of the values in African religio-cultural traditions, selfhood in the Church could hardly become a reality." (See p. 85.) For a sampling of Dickson's other works, see: 322-327.

[20]See 200.

between the rural and urban areas. He tells us that these bush people's villages are not, essentially, living museums of traditions and folklore, but constitute a place not unlike like Golgotha (*le lieu du calvaire d'un peuple*).[21]

In a way somewhat different from Éla, Barthélemy Adoukonou also finds that *négritude* is an alienated discourse. If Africa, explains Adoukonou, can discover its culture only in and through a radically alienated and pathetic history, Africans themselves must insist on asking whether the note of danger, violence, subversion, is inextricable from *la Beauté Noire*. In this regard, Adoukonou appeals to the thought of Stanilas Adotévi, who has written a significant critique of *négritude*.[22] According to Adoukonou, Adotévi wishes to add an essential caveat to "Black is beautiful"——"a categorical imperative of terror: The Negro must become dangerous [*Le Nègre doit devenir dangereux*!]."[23]

Négritude, nonetheless, is related to African traditional religion, the study of which was the central feature of the old guard's focus on inculturation. The leader of the old guard's study of African traditional religion is John Mbiti. Mbiti has done outstanding work on traditional religion, but his critics have serious reservations about it.
They charge that he examines African concepts of God by way of an outline derived from systematic theology. Here, Africans' God(s)——i.e., their views on Supreme Being——are construed in terms of a dogmatic, Christian delineation of divine attributes.[24] The disparity of his approach with that which he examines renders his christianizing agenda too transparent.

Critics have also criticized Mbiti's survey approach. That is, Mbiti has discussed African traditional religions in terms of specific themes: God, the ancestors, sacrifice, *rites de passage*, witchcraft, religious specialists. These, according to one source, "present little more than superficial catalogues of examples extracted in Frazerain fashion from concrete socioreligious contexts. For the most part they concentrate upon 'beliefs' without giving due recognition to the sociocultural and ritual fabric within which they are imbedded."[25]

African philosophers, in addition, have pointed out that Mbiti has done traditional religion (and African philosophy) a disservice by asserting that the totality of African traditional religion can be understood in terms of *Zamani*——a Swahili word meaning "past."[26] According to Mbiti, *Zamani* is an ontology that focuses on the past, without diminishing the significance of the present, and virtually precludes the future. The future is but an extension of the present, or reincarnated past. For Mbiti, African traditional religion——the essence of which is *Zamani*——is two dimensional, cyclical and sucked backward into a spiraling void where the ancestors are no longer remembered by name. *Zamani*, explains Mbiti, "is the graveyard of time, the period of termination, the dimension in which everything finds its halting point."[27]

---

[21]See Éla, *L'Afrique des villages* (Paris: Editions Karthala, 1982), 11. See 336.

[22]See Stanislas Spero Adotévi, *Négritude et négroloques* (Paris: Union Générale d'Éditions, 1972).

[23]See Barthélemy Adoukonou, *Jalons pour une théologie africaine: Essai d'une herméneutique chrétienne du Vodun dahoméen. Tome I: Critique théologique* (Paris: Éditions Lethielleux, 1980), 31. See also 288.

[24]See 009, 136, 157, 162, 221, 223, 239, 279.

[25]Benjamin Ray, *African Religions: Symbol, Ritual, and Community* (Englewood Cliffs: Prentice-Hall, 1976), 13-14. See 239.

[26]See 176, 223, 279.

[27]Mbiti *African Religions and Philosophy* (New York: Anchor Books, 1970), 29. See 200.

The essential backward orientation of African religion is *too* precarious and should, argues Mbiti, be redeemed by the dynamism of a Christian eschatology that, unlike *Zamani*, is teleological. He seeks not to uproot *Zamani* but to edify it in Christian terms. (I will say more about this later.)

Mbiti's interest in the christianization of *Zamani* is paradigmatic of the old guard's reproduction of the work of European missionaries such as Wilhelm Schmidt, Edwin Smith, Placide Tempels, and Geoffrey Parrinder.[28] These European scholars were among the first to study African traditional religion through an anthropological perspective that Mbiti calls "sympathetic." Still, their work was skewed by assumptions that Christianity is the ultimate religion.

Mbiti has been especially edified by Parrinder and asserts that Parrinder's *African Traditional Religion*[29] is *the* "pioneer work." Mbiti basically "africanized" Parrinder's survey approach——the leitmotif of which has been the assumption that traditional religion has been little more than a *praeparatio evangelica* (preparation for the gospel: *pierres d'attente*).[30] Bolaji Idowu also reveals the influence white missionaries have had on the old guard; he uses Wilhelm Schmidt's argument that African traditional religion had been monotheistic. Schmidt——a Catholic priest who worked among the Pygmy people of Central Africa early in the twentieth century——thought Africans had lost a primitive monotheism. In his view, Africans, over time, fell——as it were——into polytheism; they regressed culturally.[31] Taking over Schmidt's view, Idowu claims: "The Supreme Being of the primitive culture is a genuinely monotheistic Deity, described as Father, Creator, eternal, completely beneficent, ethically holy, and creatively omnipotent."[32]   Given Idowu's intention to christianize traditional religion, his African God, like Schmidt's, is perhaps a projection of a Christian doctrine onto African realities.

Another example of Christian projection is Idowu's definition of Yoruba religion as a "diffused monotheism"——a term derived from Evans-Pritchard's work among the

---

[28]On Schmidt see 179, 244. On Smith see 254-255; 200. The missionary perspective Smith represents can also be seen in *African Ideas of God*, which he edited. See 156, 163, 170, 172, 173, 229, 264, 281. On Tempels see 261-262. On Parrinder see 229-231.

[29]See 230.

[30]For an indication of how Mbiti has been influenced by Parrinder, see 200-204. Perhaps one cannot fault Mbiti, and others of the old guard, for undertaking the study of African traditional religion with commitment to the notion of the ultimacy of Christianity. This is particularly so given their attempts to find Christian meaning in non-Christian religion. What is unacceptable, essentially, is the disingenuousness of their presentation of African traditional religion. By no means, then, were the old guard and their White predecessors "objective" regarding African traditional religion. (While it is likely that the subject-object dichotomy intrinsic to Western knowledge has a certain epistemic value, the pretense to objectivity is always exposed by the subjectivity involved in so-called objective judgments.) Nor were they especially sensitive to the possibility that true theology lay outside dogma and within the independent churches where God could be more profoundly at work in an alterity for which the West has no analogue. In other words, to quote Hendrikus Berkhof: "Systemization is elimination. And the price for refusing to eliminate [the unpredictability of God's initiative] is the forfeiture of systematic transparency."

[31]See Roger Schmidt, *Exploring Religion*, 2nd ed. (Belmont, California: Wadsworth, 1988). Schmidt explains that Father Wilhelm Schmidt (1868-1954) "found belief in creator deities or what are referred to as 'high gods' to be common among nonliterate people. Thus, the contention that belief in a supreme being evolved only in conjunction with monarchies——one God and one king——was discredited by tribal [sic] peoples who believed in a high God but who had no political model for their belief. Father Schmidt speculated that a primordial monotheism may have been humankind's first conception of deity and that animism, ancestral spirits, and polytheism were devolutionary rather than progressive." (See p. 42.)

[32]Kwesi Dickson and Paul Ellingworth, eds., *Biblical Revelation and African Belief* (Maryknoll, N.Y.: Orbis Books, 1969), 18. See 179

Nuer.[33] Nuer——as well as Pygmy——however, are far too dissimilar from Yoruba, linguistically and culturally, perhaps even "racially," to serve as a model for Yoruba religion. Scholars, in addition, have critiqued Pritchard's notion that Nuer religion can be interpreted in terms of Western categories, such as monotheism and sin. Indeed, one scholar asserts that Evans-Pritchard's *Nuer Religion* is " a desperate attempt to fit Nuer thinking into Judeo-Christian theology, [which] is completely without foundation."[34] Despite this critique, Idowu has very usefully explored the traditional Yoruba conception of God in his *Olodumare: God in Yoruba Belief.*[35] Unfortunately, Idowu concludes *Olodumare* with the assumption that Yoruba religion must wane in the presence of Christianity. (Less of this Christian triumphalism is found in Idowu's *African Traditional Religion*, another book that indicates how analysis of African traditional religion served as a propaedeutic to African theology.)[36]

Like Idowu, Vincent Mulago also reveals the old guard's assimilation of Eurocentric scholarship.[37] Mulago has been influenced by Placide Tempels, a Belgian, Roman Catholic priest and missionary, who worked among the Baluba of the Belgian Congo (Zaïre).

Whereas the focus of Mbiti's African philosophy has been *Zamani*, that of Tempels' Bantu philosophy was *force vitale*. *Force vitale* conveys the sense of the Aristotelian "Great Chain of Being"; all entities participate in a vital force with a potency proportionate to their position in an ontological hierarchy. Humans, then, can conjure more force than lower primates, and so forth. The African philosopher, Tshiamalenga Ntumba, asserts that Temples's method may be called that of sympathy——which is not edifying because it is comprised of superficial assessment and half truths.[38] That is, Tempels assumes there is a certain parity between European consciousness and Bantu culture——a highly diversified phenomenon resistant to sweeping generalization.

According to Tshiamalenga Ntumba, moreover, the fact that the Baluba are especially attuned to "force" does not mean that they equate force with Being. An ontology, Tshiamalenga Ntumba asserts, is not to be construed on the basis of an epiphenomenon, such as force. Moreover, "force," for the Bantu, argues Tshiamalenga Ntumba, is different from what Europeans call Being. In the West, Being is utterly transcendent and only opposed to nothingness; in Africa *force vitale* is one among many "penultimate" phenomena.[39]

---

[33]See 164.

[34]Luc de Heusch, *Sacrifice in Africa: A Structuralist Approach*. Translated by Linda O'Brien and Alice Morton (Blommington: Indiana University Press, 1985), 12. See 158.

[35]See 177.

[36]See 178.

[37]See 417. For other works by Mulago, see: 415-421.

[38]See 209. According to Ntumba, Tempels method "appears to be simply that of sympathy (*Einfühlung*) and correspondence with the Baluba of Shaba——rapid equations, superficial and comprised of hasty generalizations. Now it is clear that if sympathy can suggest a hypothesis, Tempels' is not at all well-founded [my translation]." (See p. 178.)

[39]See 209. He writes:

> Thus, one cannot logically draw the conclusion that force equals being for the Baluba simply because they are particularly attentive *à la "force,"* which is supposed to be immanent in all things. An ontology is not constituted on the basis of an interpretation of its affects (*comportements*). In reality, the identification of *la force Bantou* with being construed in

Tempels' paternalism is also a problem for Tshiamalenga Ntumba.[40]   Indeed, "paternalistic" describes the Europeans whose work has been paradigmatic for the old guard. That they have subscribed to such paternalism illumines the irony of the African elites' alienation from the African culture they seek to vindicate. Indeed, for Tshiamalenga Ntumba, Tempelsians, such as Vincent Mulago, have distorted vital African realities by examining them through Eurocentric lenses (*succombant ainsi à une simple projection 'eurocentriste'*).

That many of the elite were unaware of such distortion is undoubtedly true, but no less problematic. Vincent Mulago's intentions, for instance, have not been identical with Tempels'. Yet his notion of *union vitale bantu* is a reproduction of Tempels' notion of force——the Bantu's "imperishable aspiration towards the strengthening of life." Indeed, Mulago credits Tempels with facilitating his own work in *Un visage africain du christianisme*, in which he focuses on the Bantu of Bushi, Rwanda and Burundi.[41] Himself a Catholic priest, Mulago begins *Un visage* with a definition of *adaptation*. Like inculturation, *adaptation* is defined in terms of the incarnation.[42]   For Mulago, in addition, *adaptation* entails discernment of what, in Bantu religion, can be purified or extirpated by the gospel.[43]

What is salvageable for Mulago is the Bantu sense of community, *la participation*, which is the essence of Bantu religion.   More ontological than sociological, *la participation*, also called *union vitale*, unites members of an ethnic group——both the living and the dead.

Western terms is impossible simply because force, among the Bantu, is a well-determined concept and in opposition to others, while being, in Western tradition, is a notion that transcends all determination, opposed only to nothingness. Finally, the equation, being = force, must be considered as a simple invention, as a mere *construction tempelsienne*——for nowhere does a bantu-luba text either express [the equation] or permit one to contrive such [my translation]. (See pp. 178-179.)

[40]See Placide Tempels, *Bantu Philosophy* (Paris: Presence Africaine, 1959). He writes: "The Bantu can be educated if we take as a starting point their imperishable aspiration towards the strengthening of life. If not they will not be civilized. The masses will flounder, in even greater numbers, in false applications of their philosophy; that is to say, in degrading 'magical' practices; and meanwhile the others, the *évolués*, will make up a class of pseudo-Europeans, without principles, character, purpose, or sense." (See p. 120, and annotation 261.) And so Tempels penned his *Bantu Philosophy* as a foundation of the benevolent, colonial pedagogy he envisioned. Tshiamalenga Ntumba's critique of Tempels's paternalism——i.e., his so-called, and very much absent, Bantu philosophy——is as follows: "It is not at all surprising...that Tempels thinks it necessary to resort to an *instrumentarium conceptuel* derived rom Western philosophies and languages. Tempels animus is that of his own philosophy——and not that of *la philosophie traditionnelle bantoue*. Tempels has *constructed* a philosophy; he has not *reconstructed* the Bantu's [my translation]. (See p. 179.)

[41]Vincent Mulago, *Un visage africain du christianisme: L'union vitale bantou face à l'unité vitale ecclésiale* (Paris: Présence africaine, 1962). See 417.

[42]See 417. Quoting Catholic doctrine, he writes: As *Christ assumed a true human nature*, the Church too has the fullness of what is authentically human, and it is for a her a source of supernatural life. The Church lives and develops globally (*se développe dans tous les pays du monde*), and each country makes a contribution to her life and development [my translation; emphasis added]." (See p. 26.)

[43]See 417. He writes: The Church's paradoxical mission is the continuation of that of its divine Founder. She is the mystic Body of Christ, and must also incarnate herself and transfigure all she touches, giving to all a new *valeur*. The praxis of mission (*l'acte missionnaire*) will thus consist of the discernment of what may be purified [and] what is essentially opposed to the evangelical spirit [my translation]." (See p. 29.)

For Mulago, *la participation* corresponds to *l'unité ecclésiale* (oneness of the church).[44] If *la participation* is God's gift of creation to the Bantu, then the *unité ecclésiale* is God's gift of himself——Christ, the gift of redemption as well as salvation. According to Mulago, then, the gift of salvation and redemption sanctifies what is valuable in traditional Bantu religion. He thanks Tempels for awakening him to the fact that Bantu culture is undergirded by a philosophy that explains the logic, coherence and unity of Bantu civilization.[45]

Toward African Theologies

Having studied African traditional religion, the old guard, such as Mulago and Mbiti, set out to further africanize Christianity in terms of African theologies. (Mulago's *Un visage* may in fact be said to be an early example of such "africanized" theology.)

As one studies their pioneering work in African theology, however, he discovers that they did not really africanize Christianity. They *christianized* select elements of African traditional religion——a process, for all intents and purposes, little different from what they did in their studies of African traditional religion.

The old guard's approach to theology has been determined by European systematic theologies——i.e., dogmatic or symbolic theologies. They assumed that aspects of African traditional religion could be paired with aspects of Christian doctrine.[46] The juxtaposition constituted early attempts at African theology.

One might well understand the juxtaposition as follows:

ancestors	Communion of Saints
initiation	sacraments
witchcraft	atonement
divinities	Christ as mediator
Zamani	eschatology

---

[44]See 417. Mulago explains the correspondence as follows: "The life-connection that grounds the unity of Bantu communities and individuals, this *communication–participation vitale* through vital means——this quest for increase, surplus, *d'enrichissement ontal*——finds a response and a sublime and transcendent realization in Christ's Church. She is also a living community, in which the vital principle is participation in trinitarian life, humanized (*humanisée*) in the Word of God made man. Such participation is never achieved here below, and tends constantly toward greater growth through its resemblance to the Son of God, Founder of the clan descended from heaven——the Church. (See p. 161.)

[45]See 417. More precisely, Mulago writes: "The grand value of Father Temples' hypothesis, for us, is that he aroused an appropriate reaction and awakened the consciences of as many Africans as Westerners to Bantu values hidden under the trappings of *la primitivité*. We add to this primordial and incontestable merit the veracity of the greater part of ethnological observations, which are appreciated only if it is admitted that a certain philosophy——logically elucidated, coherent and unified——undergirds Bantu practices and institutions [my translation]." (See p. 156.)

[46]One should note that African theology involved not only the analogy between African traditional religion and systematic theology. The Bible and the African independent churches have also been sources for African theologies. As I have noted——see note 5, Introduction——African independent churches emerged from the dynamic, acculturative encounter between traditional worldviews and Christianity. These churches greatly emphasize healing and prayer. Although the African independent churches reveal theologies far more African than the academic theologies of the elite, they were not, as a rule, central to the epistemology of the old guard. The old guard has tended to think that independent churches have been unsophisticated prototypes of the africanization of Christianity. The old guard, in addition, saw no political significance in these churches——a view indicating their complicity in the obfuscation of neocolonial contradictions.

Here, traditional reverence for the ancestors is christianized in terms of the communion of saints. Initiation——that is, specific modes of *rites de passage*——is brought under the authority of the sacraments, particularly baptism. The traditional, almost paranoid, fear of witches and other malevolent forces are christianized by way of atonement theories, such as the Classic Theory (*Christus Victor*). The faith that Christ is the mediator between God and humankind christianizes the intercessory role of the divinities (though with the intent to negate the divinities).

In his *Creative Evangelism*, the late Harry Sawyerr, who had been the elder statesman of the old guard, provides a more detailed example of how the old guard went about relating the aspects of traditional religion to Christian doctrine. For Sawyerr, much of African traditional religion signifies an archaic neurosis that leads "the pagan to improvise his own solutions...sometimes invoking the aid of God. The Christian, on the other hand, turns his attention towards God in total surrender to the will of God."[47] The ancestors are redeemable, however, if they are reappropriated in terms of the communion of saints. First, though, the ancestors have to be "de-africanized," i.e., demythologized. Contrary to traditional belief, Sawyerr asserts that the ancestors cannot effect changes related to life and death. Only God can. From Sawyerr's perspective, then, the traditional view of the ancestors——which demands that sacrifices be made to them——is idolatrous. For Sawyerr, Christian ecclesiology corrects such idolatry and is thus as iconoclastic as it is salvific.

According to Sawyerr, Africans must ask God to liberate their ancestors from the cul-de-sac of paganism. (For Sawyerr, the salvific power of the Christian God is so extensive as to effect the conversion of the pre-Christian dead.) Freed from primitive religion, desacralized, but converted eschatologically, the ancestors would be christianized posthumously. In no case must libation be poured to them, for that would be a regression to benightedness.

John Mbiti provides another example of how the old guard went about relating aspects of traditional religion to Christian doctrine. As indicated earlier, Mbiti has sought to christianize the notion of *Zamani*. In his *New Testament Eschatology in an African Background*, he clarifies his analogy between traditional African "deteriology" and Christian teleology, with a focus on his own people, the Akamba of Kenya.[48] As noted, Mbiti holds that Africans, i.e., Akamba, are orientated toward the past; yet they also attach great significance to the present. The present, which Akamba call *mituki*, constitutes the "nowness" of time that extends into the immediate past and the sudden future (which are but the extended present).

Time, nonetheless, is essentially retrogressive and is to be understood in terms of *tene*, the Akamba (kikamba) word for *Zamani*. *Tene*,

> is the dimension into which all phenomena sink, History according to Akamba...conception, is a movement from the *mituki* dimension, from the now period to the *tene* period. History moves "backward" from the now moment to that period beyond which nothing can go.[49]

---

[47]Harry Sawyerr, *Creative Evangelism: A New Encounter with Africa* (London: Lutterworth, 1968), 77. See 476.

[48]See 397.

[49]Mbiti, *New Testament Eschatology in an African Background* (London: Oxford University Press, 1971), 28. See 397.

"Death," according to Mbiti, "is therefore, a process of removing a person from the *mituki* of his being...until he eventually disappears into the remote *tene*."[50] Thus, the ancestors——no longer remembered by name after three generations——fade into oblivion. There is no future to speak of——no teleology, no forward movement, no progress. The Akamba worldview is a bit necrophilic. "Or to put it another way," writes Mbiti, "God does not recreate what at death has begun to disintegrate. There is no teleology in African Eschatology; what there is might be called 'deteriology'."[51]

Christian eschatology, by contrast, is three-dimensional, historical and orientated to the future. Still, argues Mbiti, this eschatology has an essential two-fold, temporal dimension (to which the Akamba worldview is analogous). "The Church," explains Mbiti, "lives between two eschatological termini: the Cross and the Parousia."[52] There in the middle, so to speak, between the two termini, Christians experience salvation as a present reality. In Mbiti's ecclesiology, eternal life, won by Christ——wholly obedient to the Father——is made known to the believer in the present, through the work of the Holy Spirit. In the present, the past (crucifixion) and the future (eternal life) merge in the promise of the resurrected Christ, who, given an understanding of the Trinity, is God and pneumatically here. Thus, one need not, for Mbiti, focus on the future to convey the Christian faith. One may focus on the present; not, however, the necrophilic past (as in *tene*).

Unfortunately, asserts Mbiti, the missionaries evangelized the Akamba with a near exclusive focus on the futuristic dimensions of Christian faith. Given their conception of the future, claims Mbiti, Akamba had no option but to expect the imminent end of the world——as if the parousia would occur in the *near future*. Disappointed by its continual delay, the first generation of christianized Akamba became disillusioned with Christianity——thinking it fraudulent.

Inculturation, that is the christianization of *tene and mituki*, asserts Mbiti, requires that Akamba, two-dimensional time be reinterpreted in terms of the "dimensionless" present. Here one attains, pneumatologically, the certainty of eternal life in Christ. For Mbiti, then, a three-dimensional eschatology is not indispensable. A two-dimensional eschatology, he argues, can be edifying and is eminently biblical. Akamba——by virtue of their sense of *mituki*——are uniquely suited to appreciate that the nuance of New Testament time "has been realized in the historical present of the Church, and what is to be consummated at the parousia."[53]

In sum, the old guard sought to expose continuities and discontinuities between African traditional religion and Christian faith. Favoring a theological agenda grounded explicitly in a cultural problematic, the old guard gave little attention to political problems of a new colonial Africa. They held on to the view that most of Black Africa was "independent"; a focus on liberation was deemed unnecessary.

This is so despite the fact that things began to fall apart again. As Chinua Achebe points out in his novel, *Things Fall Apart*, olden colonialism broke down the centers of traditional authority and caused, as a result, many unsettling changes in traditional

---

[50]Ibid., 29-30.

[51]Ibid., 139.

[52]Ibid., 45.

[53]Ibid., 182.

contexts.[54]   Now the Africa caught in the grip of neocolonialism discovered once again that the center——the "independent" state——could not hold.

The old guard gave little, if any, serious attention to: the Congo crisis, which included the assassination of Patrice Lumumba and the rise of Mobutu; the fall of Nkrumah's Ghana, which marks a turning point in the undermining of revolutionary Pan-Africanism; the assassination of Amilcar Cabral; the proliferation of micro-nationalism, i.e., the civil wars between Nigeria and Biafra and the Tutsi and Hutu of Burundi; the horror of African fascism; and the rising indebtedness of the continent to its colonial masters and the United States.[55]   All have taken their toll and constitute the death pangs of a diseased continent. The old guard, in addition, gave little attention to the similarities between "tribalism," as a species of racism, and apartheid. Neither did the old guard realize that the totality of Black Africa——and not just South Africa——suffers from the massive pauperization of peasants and workers; the agglutination of a power elite; and the covert manipulation by the Western bloc.

One should wonder why the old guard, theologians of a continent as troubled as Latin America, failed to make the praxis of liberation the way and theme of African theology. But, for the most part, as the dialogues between African and African-American theologians show, the old guard's consensus was that liberation theology belonged in Southern Africa alone.[56]   Indeed the old guard failed to address the myth of independence.

---

[54]See 132.

[55]On the Congo crisis see 078-079; 098. On Pan-Africanism see 038, 092, 099-101; on Cabral see 023-025; on micro-nationalism see 032-033; 040, 074. On African fascism see 053, 071.

[56]See 606.

3

The New Guard:
The Africanization of
Christianity and the Reality
of Neocolonialism

Beyond "Solidity": A Vision of a New Africa

Wole Soyinka, a Noble Prize winning novelist and vehement critic of "independence," writes often on the crisis of neocolonial Africa. Having been incarcerated for his opposition to the civil war between Nigeria and Biafra, he defines the crisis in terms of the legacy of the Berlin Conference:

> What God (white man) has put together, let no black man put asunder. The complications of neo-colonial politics of interference compel one to accept such a damnable catechism for now, as a pragmatic necessity. Later perhaps, the black nations will themselves sit down together, and, by agreement, set compass and square rule to paper and reformulate the life-expending, stultifying, constrictive imposition of this divine authority. What is clear, miserably clear is that a war is being fought without a simultaneous programme of reform and redefinition of social purpose. A war of solidity; for solidity is describing a war which can only consolidate the very values that gave rise to the war in the first place, for nowhere and at no time have those values been examined. Nowhere has there appeared a programme designed to ensure the eradication of the fundamental iniquities which gave rise to the initial conflicts.[1]

Although they may not have a program——on the scale of the Partition of Africa——the new guard seeks to eradicate the neocolonial state of things that Soyinka describes. They are not resigned to "pragmatic necessity." The new guard, such as Jean-Marc Éla, Engelbert Mveng, Eboussi Boulaga, Barthélemy Adoukonou and Mercy Oduyoye, do not seek solidity.[2] They seek——as does Soyinka——a new Africa, not a neocolonial one where old contradictions persist in pernicious guise.

One might mark the emergence of the new guard in terms of the formation of the Ecumenical Association of Third World Theologians (EATWOT) in Dar Es Salaam,

---

[1]Wole Soyinka, *The Man Died* (New York: The Noonday Press, 1972), 181.

[2]On Éla see 334-341; on Mveng see 432-440; on Boulaga see 305-307; on Adoukonou see 288. On Oduyoye see 452-459.

Tanzania, 1976. There, African theologians, as well as other Third World theologians, issued a "Final Statement." They wrote:

> We call for an active commitment to the promotion of justice and the prevention of exploitation, the accumulation of wealth in the hands of a few, racism, sexism, and other forms of oppression, discrimination, and dehumanization....[T]his...means being committed to a lifestyle of solidarity with the poor and...and involvement in action with them....in their struggle for liberation.[3]

The new guard became more visible at the Pan-African Conference of Third World Theologians, also held under the auspices of EATWOT, which met in Accra, Ghana in 1977. In Ghana, African theologians asserted that "African theology must...be *liberation* theology.... We stand against any form of oppression because the Gospel of Jesus Christ demands our participation in the struggle to free people from all forms of dehumanization."[4]

One discovers the new guard in yet another organization, *l'Association oecuménique des théologiens africains* (AOTA)——a Pan-African organization that came into being with the founding of *Bulletin de théologie africaine* in 1979.[5] AOTA seeks to: unify African Christians; promote African theology; and help African churches challenge their socioeconomic contexts. AOTA is another revelation of the new guard's commitment to the liberation of the poor.

Indeed, their commitment to an Africa beyond solidity——a liberated Africa——brings to mind Amilcar Cabral's definition of re-Africanization.[6] Cabral explains that re-Africanization——which is not unlike Soyinka's "redefinition of social purpose"——is a process alienated elite must undergo in order to divest themselves of the bourgeois culture of the colonizers. In re-Africanization, the elite experience "a spiritual reconversion" in which they are edified by the grassroots where African culture is dynamic and real——not at all the reified and static *négritude* of the alienated elite. African culture, explains Cabral, "is nourished by the living reality of the environment and rejects harmful influences as much as any kind of subjection to foreign cultures."[7] Entailing, then, social and religio-cultural analyses, re-Africanization is not unlike the new guard's vision of liberation. With Cabral, the new guard recognizes that, "if imperialist domination has the vital need to practice cultural oppression, national liberation is necessarily an *act of culture.*"[8] Re-Africanization, then, is that process which allows one to make an option for the African poor——whom Éla calls *l'Afrique "d'en-bas"* (the underside of Africa).[9]

The new guard, in its commitment to the underside, struggles with the fact that

---

[3]Sergio Torres and Virginia Fabella, eds. *The Emergent Gospel* (London: Geoffrey Chapman, 1978) 270.

[4]Kofi Appiah-Kubi, and Sergio Torres, eds. *African Theology en Route* (Maryknoll, N.Y.: Orbis Books, 1979), 194.

[5]See note 2, Introduction.

[6]On Amilcar Cabral, see 023-025.

[7]Amilcar Cabral, *Unity and Struggle: Speeches and Writings of Amilcar Cabral*, with an introduction by Basil Davidson and biographical notes by Mário de Andrade (New York: Monthly Review Press, 1979), 143. See 024.

[8]Ibid.

[9]See 339.

Africa, since "independence," has regressed. Illiteracy is on the rise in Africa——such that over fifty per cent of the African people will be illiterate by the year 2000. The continent, on the whole, no longer grows its own food and can no longer manage the traditional problems of drought and desertification.

Africa has the highest infant mortality rate in the world——black babies die from measles and diarrhea, as well as from famine. Indeed, the problem of infant mortality might be called infanticide, since misplaced political priorities, due to corruption and conflicts among the élite, make infant care expendable.   Other health care problems——such as the horrific AIDS epidemic——also show that Africa is dying.

Jean-Marc Éla's social analysis reveals that the lack of adequate health care is a pernicious ramification of neocolonialism. Focusing on his context, Cameroon, Éla argues that the health of today's peasants——like those of yesterday——is of little value. True to form, not even the children, who suffer from chronic malnutrition, receive proper medical attention.[10] (Ironically, under olden colonialism, they were cared for, apparently in order to pay taxes upon reaching adulthood.) Only the elite receive proper medical attention.

The perniciousness of neocolonialism can be seen further in other manifestations of the miserable life of the poor. Their rural misery, for instance, is due, in part, to the neocolonial preference for the cities. Services are directed toward the urban areas because the elite are there. One can see the priority given to the urban elite in terms of education.

The elite send their children to Europe, "but millions of men and women are left in a situation where they are unable to write their names or interpret the road signs [signaux] of urban life."[11]   Indeed, the peasants are deprived of a pedagogy that would equip them to deal with everyday problems. According to Éla, this

> indifference of the powerful regarding the cultural needs of the peasants is
> quite surprising as one recognizes more and more...that illiteracy is one of
> the causes of the economic failure of underdeveloped countries.   That is
> why literacy campaigns have had as their objectives not only a better
> comprehension of the surrounding world and participation in civic life, but
> the immediate amelioration of [the peasants'] level of life and the
> augmentation of production [my translation].[12]

Éla argues that literacy will take hold in Africa only as the peasants organize in conjunction with a re-Africanized elite. These re-Africanized intellectuals recognize that true liberation struggles——i.e., de pays d'Afrique où l'indépendance n'a pas été octroyée par les anciennes métropoles——have not been about devolution.[13] In countries where there was revolution——such as in Guinea Bissau[14]——the peasants and intellectuals found themselves together in the bush, shoulder to shoulder, coude à coude fraternel. Thus Éla

---

[10]See Éla, "Luttes pour la santé de l'homme et Royaume de Dieu dans l'Afrique d'aujourd'hui," *Bulletin de théologie africaine* 5,9 (janvier-juin 1983): 65-84. See 338. Here, Éla quotes a manual defining medical practices in colonial Dahomey: "The white man needs palm oil and the palm tree does not grow in his cold country, he needs cotton, maize and so forth....If the blacks die, who will climb the palm tree, who will make the oil, who will carry it in the factories? The administration is supported through taxes, if black babies do not survive, who will pay them [my translation]? (See p. 64.)

[11]Éla, *L'Afrique des villages* (Paris: Éditions Karthala, 1982), 55. See 336.

[12]Ibid.

[13]Ibid., 226. On devolution, see 124.

[14]See 023-025.

makes a case for an option for the underside of Africa where a vital social analysis develops in conjunction with peasant realities.

Engelbert Mveng has also made the underside of Africa the focus of African theology. His social analysis identifies levels of indigence. One must distinguish ideological poverty (*pauvreté idéologique*), from real poverty (*pauvreté réelle*.) Ideological poverty is a Western, misanthropy that feeds on the real poverty of the masses exploited for political ends.[15] Ideological poverty, argues Mveng, is the immorality of the *réelle*, both of which are integral to a commerce responsible for black misery. Yet another, but more insidious, form of poverty is "anthropological poverty" (*pauvreté anthropologique*)——the theme of black misery. *Pauvreté anthropologique* negates blacks' fundamental rights in demolishing African institutions, civilizations, religions. Denying blacks the right to exist, to love, to hope, anthropological poverty, is the insidious structure of a massive conspiracy that seeks to oppress Africa. It reaches even into the Diaspora.[16] This anthropological poverty was barely addressed by the old guard, who did not focus on the struggle for liberation or make the underside the subject of African theology. For the re-Africanized new guard theologians, though, such as Mveng and Éla: "One understands why, in such [an African] context, the only theology and the only spirituality possible are those of liberation [my translation]."[17]

As the most alienating poverty is anthropological, the struggle for liberation necessarily involves religio-cultural analysis——what Barthélemy Adoukonou calls *une théologie de la réappropriation culturelle critique*.[18] For the new guard, religio-cultural analysis has nothing to do with "a disquisition on local curiosities, folklore, or peculiarities of a lifestyle that have disappeared or are barely surviving."[19] Religio-cultural analysis——as Frantz Fanon reminds us——"has never the translucidity of custom."[20] Rather, as new guard theologian, Eboussi Boulaga, explains, religio-cultural analysis studies the people's dynamic struggle to overcome alienation.

As a vital, radical, political expression, religio-cultural analysis reveals that culture "reacts, mobilizes, and creates antibodies [that resist] aggression from without."[21] Culture resists the forces that perpetuate black misery and equips the poor——and the re-Africanized intellectual——to relearn the contexts that constitute African reality. In that

---

[15]See Engelbert Mveng, "Récent développements de la théologie Africaine." *Bulletin de théologie africaine* 5,9 (*janvier-juin* 1983): 137-144. Mveng explains that ideological poverty can only be a *commerce vulgaire qui utilise comme matière première la pauvreté réelle des sans-voix à des fins politiques*. (See p. 141.) See also annotation 437.

[16]Ibid. A more precise rendering of Mveng's definition is as follows: Integral to Black misery, making its way through such misery to the negation of our fundamental rights, our cultures, our religions, *pauvreté anthropologique* demolishes our institutions and our civilizations; it denies our right to existence, to love, to hope, it accompanies the massive conspiracy perpetrated by those interested in Africa. This form of misery particularly afflicts the Black race in Africa, the U.S., the Caribbean and Latin America [my translation]." (See p.141.)

[17]Ibid, 141.

[18]See Adoukonou, 33 (note 23, Chapter 2); and annotation 288.

[19]Eboussi Boulaga, *Christianity without Fetishes* (Maryknoll,N.Y.: Orbis Books, 1984), 57. See also annotation 307.

[20]See 034.

[21]Boulaga, 77. See 307.

way, African reality "'learn[s] itself and 'regain[s] control of itself in the face of and because of an adversity."[22]

An example of this learning process is found in Jean-Marc Éla's analysis of the adversity of the Cameroonian peasants, forced to turn a profit at the expense of their culture. In the brink of the Sahel, he writes,

> in that tropical region where farmers reap but one harvest a year, where sowing is always difficult, and where women and children live in a state of chronic famine, thousands of peasants are being forced to pull up millet that is just sprouting and to plant cotton in its place. In societies where millet is the staple, that deed forced upon landless peasants is a veritable dagger in the heart. It is all done so quietly, under the watchful eye of the agricultural monitors employed by a large development company investing in cash crops.[23]

Here, Éla describes the situation of cultural and social alienation that sets the context for re-learning African reality. In the Sahel, the peasants are not only alienated from modes of subsistence, but also from the religious values of millet itself. In returning to more traditional values——namely those related to subsistence and the cosmological significance of millet——the peasants recognize that their lives have not at all been improved by so-called national development.

The pervasiveness of infant mortality under the present neocolonial system is unprecedented. Indeed, the peasants recognize that infant mortality is due as much to alienation from traditional values and the flaws of the present system as to the need for improved technology.[24] In valorizing their culture, in re-Africanizing themselves, then, they attain a resolve to better their situation. They focus on the quest for fecundity——a leitmotif of traditional culture. Éla, himself re-Africanized by peasants' struggles, has thus begun to theologize in accordance with African realities——in accordance with Adoukonou's assimilation of *l'Africanisme du dedans*.[25] For instance, in regard to his critique of health care, which I have discussed earlier, he produces a theology which asserts that the present system is a contradiction of the Kingdom of God (*Royaume de Dieu*). According to Éla: "It would be absurd to separate radically the Kingdom of God

---

[22]Ibid., 79.

[23]Éla, *African Cry* (Maryknoll,N.Y.: Orbis Books, 1986), v. See annotation 340.

[24]Éla, "Luttes pour la santé de l'homme et Royaume de Dieu dans l'Afrique d'aujourd'hui." See note 10 above and annotation 338. In his own words:

> Perhaps the infant mortality rate should be examined as a ramification of agricultural modernization, which takes the form of economic and cultural colonization. Here, peasants procure wages to the extent that "traditional" life is debased by: *l'enseignement*, the institutions and projects; the dislocation of agrarian economies, singly by incitation to cultures of exportation; the insufficiencies of agronomical research; the weaknesses of *politiques de prix* and the infrastructures. Those factors explain underproductivity as much as the peasants' mentality. [Indeed], socioeconomic, cultural and political realities purveyed by the surrounding world are far more responsible than peasant communities. From this perspective, one must recognize——in a society in which *la monoculture industrielle* evinces its inability to respond to problems related to health and nutrition——the demagoguery in the *reprise* of slogans such as *la santé pour tous* [my translation]. (See p. 67.)

[25]See Adoukonou, note 18 above.

from the struggles for justice——as if the reign of God were situated in another world, indifferent to the disorders of this world in which we live [my translation]."[26]

For Éla, the church itself is often guilty of such separation, and thus alienated from God's Kingdom. He argues that the African Catholic church is too dependent on the Vatican, which itself exacerbates the economic exploitation of the peasantry. The peasants are dependent upon a European priesthood that, exported from Rome, has little understanding or appreciation of African realities. The priests are also in very short supply——a problem that deprives the peasants of the Eucharist, since only priests may consecrate the elements of bread and wine.[27] "This dependence is no less obvious," asserts Éla, "when we examine the elements of the Eucharistic rite itself." The Roman rite, he explains, is captive to symbols that have no meaning for the African. That is:

> Current religious practice involves the African Christian in a cultural universe having no link with the real life of African communities. The symbolism of the Eucharist escapes the savanna people or the forest people because the meaning of wheat bread and grape wine in European culture escapes them.[28]

The imported products are also costly and in short supply.

The Eucharist would be far more edifying, in the Sahel, if the elements were millet and nut beer as opposed to bread and wine. Millet and nut beer are hallowed symbols of a people's spirituality as well as their life-sustaining stables. They signify God's bounty and the procreative values of fecundity. The use of imported elements, for Éla, then, means that God's Kingdom has yet to be announced.

What better way to inculturate Christian faith than by way of millet and nut beer? The people grow these things and to consecrate them in Holy Communion is to cultivate a Christianity rooted in African humanity. Then, argues Éla,

> Jesus Christ [would appear] as God with a peasant's black face and hands toughened by labor under the burning sun. Humanity [would thus be] linked to the God of Revelation through its quest for food, and nothing can come between work and prayer.[29]

Indeed, Éla, in his religio-cultural analysis, makes an argument for inculturation and acculturation. (Recall my discussion of this in the introduction.) Inculturation would take place as the Africans receive the Eucharist with an understanding of the salvation Christ brings. Acculturation would take place as Africans use traditional stables as symbols of the body and blood of Christ.

Mveng, in his *L'art d'Afrique noire: Liturgie cosmique et langage religieux,* also shows us how acculturation and inculturation work together in new African theology. For

---

[26]Éla, "Luttes pour la santé de l'homme et Royaume de Dieu dans l'Afrique d' aujourd'hui," 83.

[27] Éla, *African Cry.* He writes: "Let us note that the unconditional submission to a theological schema that makes the priest the necessary minister of the Eucharist condemns the little communities on which much pastoral concern is currently concentrated to live in dependence on foreigners. It is a schema productive of a privileged class of clerics who preside at the Eucharist; consequently, the churches of Africa, unable to afford the cost of the years of training for the priesthood, must rely on aid from without. This aid will be twofold, human and economic." (See p. 2.)

[28]Ibid., 5.

[29]Éla, *My Faith as an African* (Maryknoll, N.Y.: Orbis Books, 1988), 8. See 341.

the most part, the text represents a form of religio-cultural analysis more in keeping with the new guard than the old, though it is, in part, reminiscent of the method of the old guard.[30] Mveng, in what I think is a novel and very edifying approach, seeks to plant Christianity deep within African soil.

According to Mveng, African soil, i.e., Bantu culture, yields three acculturative poles ready to support Christianity: God, the world and humanity. Humanity and the world form a dialectic, the points of which are: the *cosmological* (structure and expression of the world) and the *anthropological* (structure and expression of humanity). For Mveng, this dialectic structures humans' creative, free initiative, an initiative that humanizes the world and corresponds to the image of God (*imago Dei*). God, argues Mveng——with an appeal to general revelation——has created the world in such a way that humankind is divinized through the exercise of this initiative.[31] The exercise of this initiative, asserts Mveng, constitutes a spirituality, the chief characteristic of which is prayer. Prayer reveals that the African's spirituality is theological. One cries to God in order to defeat the forces that lead to death. For Mveng, the Africans' cosmic symbolism——reflective of their prayer-life——signifies salvation from all that would block life in all abundance. This African soteriology is most profoundly communicated through African art.

African art entails drumming, i.e., polyrhythm; the patterns of textiles; representations of fauna; sculpture——all of which function as a religious language. African art, moreover, has its laws constituted by *la poétique Bantou*.[32] These laws are the monad, the dyad, and the triad——i.e., *masculinité, féminité, fécondité*. These principles are structural: ontological and anterior to ethical determination. Through these laws, the African realizes his/her destiny as a mode of liberation.[33]

---

[30]See his *L'art d'Afrique noire: liturgies cosmique et langage religieux* (Yaounde: Éditions CLE, 1974), and 432 of this bibliography. Mveng suggests the influence of Tempels in his work, for instance. That is, he asserts that the African is preoccupied with force *qui renforce sa Vie, se situe sur l'échelle dialectique qui montre vers Dieu.* (See p. 20.) Such a notion of the humans' desire to fortify their life in accordance with their position in a hierarchical structure is not unlike Temples notion of *force vitale*.

Mveng also subscribes here to the notion that African traditional values can be understood in terms of sin:

> While biblical sin is not pagan sin, it is no less important to underline that, in Africa, the idea of a rupture with God has undergird mythology, and yesterday's provisional proclamation [of such a rupture] is made clear in confident Christian invocation [my translation]. (See p. 18.)

Consistent with the method of the old guard, then, Mveng was influenced by an alienated discourse——i.e., Tempels' *Bantu Philosophy*——and subscribed to the notion that African traditional religion has been little more than a preparation for the Gospel.

[31]Ibid., 40.

[32]Ibid. He writes: "*La poétique Bantou*——we mean by this the laws of the creative genius of our culture——can not...in any sense be construed as an aesthetics. Aesthetics, contrived as spectacle and satisfying concupiscence, expresses the passivity of humans' sensorial system before reality. (*L'esthétique traduit la passivité du système sensoriel de l'homme devant le réel construit en spectacle et servi en nourriture pour sa concupiscence.*) *La poétique*, has to do with human spontaneity that, constituted in liberty, rises up against natural determinism. (*La poétique, elle, se situe au moment où la spontanéité de l'homme se dresse contre le déterminisme de la nature et se constitue en liberté.*) (See p. 94.)

[33]Ibid.; he writes: "At the start, man appears as *Monad*——objective given, condemned to indetermination. In the second moment, man is *Dyad*——he is *man-woman*——moment of conscience as well as liberty. In discovering his/her structure man chooses or rejects it, and in that way constitutes himself/herself/ in liberty. Essentially free, man makes himself responsible. Responsible for himself in his double dimension, man makes himself personal [my translation]." (See p. 76.)

The triad, fecundity, signifies that life issues forth from the monad and the dyad. Fecundity is the *raison d' être* of Bantu art, and expresses a synthesis integral to human destiny. In passing from monad to dyad to triad, Africans become creators of themselves as well as of society. As we have seen, this ability to create is a God-given liberty, corresponding to the image of God (*imago Dei*). Becoming Father-Mother-Infant, monad, dyad triad, the African is God's expression of the triumph of life. *Il est fécondité* ("he/she is fecundity").[34]   For Mveng, then, analysis of autochthonous prayer, and its cosmic symbolism, is part of the acculturative field that makes Christianity African rather than European. His commitment to inculturation is nonetheless intense. In fact, true religious language, for Mveng, is Christian. A true religious symbol, for him, can only be Christian since Christianity is God's total response to humankind's quest for meaning and purpose. (*Un symbole authentiquement religieux ne peut être que chrétien, car le Christianisme est la réponse totale de Dieu à l'appel de l'homme total.*)[35]

Regarding what makes African culture Christian (inculturation), Mveng, not unlike Éla and Adoukonou, defines an africanization of the Cross (acculturation). The Cross provides another example of how the use of things African de-europeanizes Christianity.[36] So even in his commitment to inculturation, Mveng evinces the significance of acculturation. Mveng notes that the crests of traditional initiation masks "often carry the symbol of the cross inscribed in a circle."[37]

The cross signifies the four quarters of the world——*le cercle, la totalité.* One might say that the cross is a liminal symbol.[38] That is, all thresholds converge in a *communitas*[39] in which progenitors and progeny are one. Indeed, the living and the dead——the visible and the invisible——intersect in the form of the cross.

For Mveng, the Cross, interpreted through the African worldview he has defined, realizes Africans' most precious religious insight. Life vanquishes death. Here, Africanity is more than a stepping stone to Christianity, more than a preparation for the gospel; it is an indispensable spirituality fructified in Christ. For Mveng the God of creation is the God of redemption. From a trinitarian perspective, the God of creation enters into the cosmos

---

[34]Ibid., 76.

[35]Ibid., 30.

[36]For Éla, too, the dominant theme of African spirituality is the victory of life over death. Like Mveng, Éla believes that Christianity edifies that struggle by way of the Cross. The Cross is the supra-symbol——what Adoukonou understands to be the U-Topos——that makes sense of African traditional religion. Still, Éla, Mveng and Adoukonou understand the Cross in African terms. Éla explains that the cross is a crossroads symbol, the intersections of which comprise a liminality, for all thresholds converge into Christ's body in whom the totality of existence and being attain meaning. Adoukonou——see his *Jalons pour une théologie africaine: Essai d'une herméneutique chrétienne du Vodun dahoméen*——understands the Cross in relation to Vodun. He explains that the Dahomean Kings upheld a sealed calabash containing *la Divinité Vodun. Ce mystère 'tenu caché depuis les siècles en Dieu'*" is now revealed: it is the mystery of Christ crucified. On the title page of his *Jalons pour une théologie africaine*, a picture of the Cross is being "watered" by the now open calabash. Each of the two sections pour fluid, as in libation, over each side of the Cross, where the vertical and horizontal meet. Adoukonou explains that the picture symbolizes an image of an "African Easter", which is *la raison d'être* of African theology. (*Nous avons en symbole une image de cette Pâque africaine qu'est appelé à être la théologie africaine.*)

[37]Mveng, 30.

[38]See 272-274.

[39]On *communitas*, See 272-274.

in order to redeem it. The incarnation and the resurrection negate the death that had returned ineluctably in African traditional religion.[40]

Mveng and Éla——as well as Boulaga and Adoukonou——show clearly how religio-cultural analysis and social analysis are integral to the new guard theology of liberation. They evince how the new guard differs from the old. Yet another way to see that difference is through the new guard's solidarity with the black theologians of South Africa. (Recall my discussion of this in the introduction.) According to Éla there is no essential difference between apartheid and the neocolonialism that plagues most of the black continent.[41] According to Mveng, in addition, the "anti-Christianity" practiced in South Africa makes it the quintessential place for theological reflection.[42] I turn now then to a discussion of black theology.

---

[40]He writes: "Life's triumph had always before it the ineluctable return of death. At bottom, the vital cycle closed us in nature's prison. This is why the fecundating mystery of life is eternally that of a hypostatic reality in the *plotinien* sense of the word——a reality on the axis of Life, at the extraordinary level of a one-of-kind participation [*Voilà pourquoi le mystère fécondant de la Vie reste à jamais une réalité 'hypostatique" au sens plotinien du mot, sur l'axe de la Vie, au seul niveau de la participation ponctuelle*]. In order to ascend the ladder [of vital being] more than a man is necessary——a divine Redeemer [*Pour remonter l'échelle, il faudra plus qu'un homme: un Rédempteur divin*]." (See pp. 113-114.)

[41]See 339.

[42]See 439.

4

The Black Theology
of South Africa:
Sibling of the New Guard

Distinctions between black South African theology and the new guard are of degree, not kind. The prophetic synthesis of liberation and africanization define the work of both groups oppressed by racial and economic injustices and in touch with traditional values. Still, black theology must be studied in its own context. Apartheid, the allegedly defunct white supremacist doctrine of the separation of the "races," has been, as Mveng points out, unique. Supported by the neocolonial matrix——the United States, Great Britain and fortress Europe[1]——the legacy of apartheid demands an analysis endemic to Southern Africa.

Under apartheid, the black majority——i.e., the so-called Bantu——have been fourth class citizens. They constitute the lowest caste——that below Asians and "coloreds," all of whom are under the rule of whites, both the English-speaking and Afrikaner minorities. Blacks, though in the majority, have had no vote, provide the cheap labor and suffer, in the townships and homelands, the most impoverished conditions.[2]

The Transatlantic World of Black Theology

Although black theology is peculiar to the southern part of the continent, it has been essentially influenced by the black theology of the United States. If black South African theology is the sibling of the new guard, it has another sibling in North America. Across the Atlantic, black North American theology emerged from the experiences of an African people who——not unlike black South Africans——have suffered three centuries of white supremacist rule. The more immediate context of this black theology was the decade of the 1960s, in which the Civil Rights movement and the Black Power movement represented African-American outrage at their historic mistreatment.[3] Black Power rhetoric——a

---

[1]On "fortress Europe," see, Jan Neder Veen Pieterse, "Fictions of Europe," *Race & Class* 32,3 (January-March 1991): 3-10.

[2]See 118.

[3]By the mid sixties, Black pastors became impatient with the integrationist path of the Civil Rights Movement and turned to the Black nationalist path of the Black Power Movement. The integrationists, such as Martin Luther King, Jr., held that Whites would eventually include Blacks in American institutions——such that Blacks would be first rather than second class citizens. Black nationalists, such as Malcolm X, however, held——and still hold——that Whites *can* never include Blacks in a way proportionate to their numbers——hence Blacks were to maintain strong, separate institutions in order to achieve social, economic and political power despite Whites.

species of black nationalism——spoke profoundly to the disappointment and cynicism of the black poor.[4]

The theologian who has best expressed the Christian implications of Black Power is James Cone. At the dawning of black theology in South Africa, Cone's work was endorsed essentially because it suited the values of the Black Consciousness Movement——the South African counterpart of the Black Power movement. Cone's first two books, *Black Theology and Black Power* and *A Black Theology of Liberation*, were especially significant for black South African theologians. Capturing the rage of the Black Power period, Cone hurled a re-interpretation of the gospel at whites. For James Cone, true Christianity was nearly identical with the "de-honkification" of theology. "Honky," an insulting term for whites, was tantamount to what the Black Consciousness Movement meant by "whitey."

The Black Consciousness Movement is heir to the legacies of South Africans such as Anton Lembede and Robert Sobukwe. As champions of African nationalism and founders of the Pan-Africanist Congress (PAC), Lembede and Sobukwe helped lay the foundations of values that differ from those of the African National Congress (ANC). Both congresses——and especially the ANC——are leading black organizations in the struggle for racial and economic justice. The PAC, however, eschews the nonracialism of the ANC in favor of an ideology that heightens the differences between the white settlers and the black autochthons. In a vein similar to the PAC, the rallying cry of the Black Consciousness Movement——as it emerged from the South African Student Organization (SASO)——has been "Black man, you are on your own!" The dictum signifies blacks' rejection of the ambivalent role white liberals have played in the anti-apartheid movement.

White liberals came to lead the anti-apartheid movement in the aftermath of the banning of the ANC and the PAC in the early sixties. They did so moderately; they have gained much from apartheid and had little incentive to jeopardize their privileges. As Steve Biko, the martyred leader of Black Consciousness, pointed out, liberals assumed that the system had integrity apart from the racist intransigence of Boers (Afrikaners) at the top.[5] And so liberals would do little to alter social arrangements——and blacks would remain divested of land and power.

The path to liberation, argued Biko, required blacks to cleanse themselves of liberalism and its Christian expressions. Blacks were to re-define the Christianity of white missionaries in terms of black theology, which

> seeks to relate God and Christ once more to the black man and his daily problems. It wants to describe Christ as a fighting god, not a passive god who allows a lie to rest unchallenged. It grapples with existential problems and does not claim to be a theology of absolutes. It seeks to bring back God to the black man and to the truth and reality of his situation.[6]

---

[4]Black outrage at the impediments to integration erupted into urban riots across North America in the middle sixties. Sensitive to and expressive of such rage, Black clergy and theologians began to question King's position and gravitate toward that of Malcolm X. They realized——as did Malcolm X and, later, Martin King——that legislation passed as a result of the Civil Rights Movement could do little to affect the structural problems that have deprived African-Americans of economic power and social respectability.

[5]See 013-015.

[6]Steve Biko, "Black Consciousness and the Quest for a True Humanity, in *The Challenge of Black Theology in South Africa*, ed. by Basil Moore (Atlanta: John Knox Press, 1973), 43. See 013.

The situation, however, is not a monolith. It has nuances that indicate that black theology signifies a matrix more than a context.

Black Theology and the Implications of Black Consciousness

Black theology is split along ideological lines. One line is consistent with the trajectory of the Black Consciousness Movement (BCM) that stands in the PAC tradition. Theologians in that tradition——consistent with the values of the Azanian People's Organization (AZAPO) and the National Forum (NF)——would re-name South Africa, Azania. (Undoubtedly, they are not the only ones who envision majority rule in terms of Azania.)

AZAPO and the National Forum——in distinction from the ANC and the United Democratic Front (UDF), which are also connected to the BCM——have serious reservations regarding the non-racialism of the historic *Freedom Charter*. As black theologian, Bonganjalo Goba, explains, the National Forum, for instance, "is inclined to a Pan-Africanist ideology reflecting an exclusive kind of nationalism and a strategy that excludes whites as participants in the revolutionary process."[7] Such ideology is reflected in the work of the black theologian, Takatso Mofokeng, for whom black and white reconciliation, and the non-racialism it implies, are premature goals in that they dissimulate the blacks' right to the land. As Mofokeng explains:

> Black people have been dispossessed of their land which is the basic means
> of all production and subsistence as well as a source of power. They have
> been turned into dispossessed workers whose only possession is their labour
> power. By identifying black people as workers [black] theologians have
> lifted our struggle beyond civil rights to human rights, from an exclusive
> struggle against racism to a social and national revolution.[8]

Contrary to those who assert that nationalism in black theology constitutes racism in reverse, Mofokeng eschews racism in his valorization of human rights.

Indeed, his contention that "non-racialism" is a political, and thus ideological, idiom——which dissimulates the *human rights* of the black oppressed——is not a racist argument. The black oppressed, the majority, are, essentially, the nation; and the equation, African nationalism = racism, appears specious. The critical questions that challenge such speciousness for Mofokeng are: how does one define and live a black theology that is itself the dynamic fruit of the liberation struggle? How will this struggle serve the humanizing agenda of black people? For Mofokeng, such questions are integral to the struggle for Azania.

Another line of black theology is drawn from the camps of the African National Congress (ANC) and the United Democratic Front (UDF). Here, given the vilification of blackness in South Africa, Black Consciousness is a prerequisite for a democratic vision defined in terms of non-racialism. Blackness is a metaphor: *all* who love freedom and seek justice in South Africa are "black" by virtue of their identification with those who suffer most from the lack of basic freedoms.

---

[7]Bonganjalo Goba, "The Black Consciousness Movement: Its Impact on Black Theology." In *The Unquestionable Right to be Free: Black Theology from South Africa*, ed. by Itumeleng J. Mosala and Buti Tlhagale, 57-70 (Maryknoll,N.Y.: Orbis Books, 1986) See annotation 550.

[8]Takatso Mofokeng, "Black Theological Perspectives, Past and Present." In *We Are One Voice: Black Theology in the USA and South Africa*, ed. by Simon Maimela and Dwight Hopkins, (Braamfontein: Skotaville Publishers, 1989), 109. See also annotation 568.

Alan Boesak, for example, a leading black theologian in the non-racialist traditions of the ANC and the UDF, asserts that affirmation of the cultural and chromatic particularities of black people is the *a priori* of the struggle for racial and economic justice. For Boesak, then, Black Consciousness is indispensable for the realization of non-racialism as a political goal. He explains that "blackness is an awareness, an attitude, a state of mind. It is a bold and serious determination to be a person in one's own right."[9] Many "Negroid" people, he argues, are not black; and many Caucasians, by virtue of their love for justice, are.

Blackness is also a metaphor for Christ because it is analogous to his true humanity——God's incarnation as an oppressed Jew. Boesak writes:

> As in the Old Testament, the God who comes to us in Jesus the Messiah is the God who takes sides. He is neither indifferent nor aloof. He sides with the poor and the weak, prefers to speak of himself as a "servant," becomes "a friend of publicans and sinners." His own background is that of the much despised *am ha'aretz*——the poor of the land. He is the Oppressed One whose life reflects so much of the life of oppressed people.[10]

So in Boesak's theology, the Oppressed One's life clarifies the meaning of the lives of black Africans: they in their suffering correspond to his historic reality. What is more, the Oppressed One is defined in terms of a Reformed christology that divests blackness of racist connotation and makes it a symbol of true humanity.

According to Boesak, oppressors partake of true humanity as they overcome their contempt of the oppressed. The oppressed do so as they shake off both their internalization of the oppressors' contempt and their hatred of the oppressor. For Boesak, then, the liberation of the oppressed involves the liberation of the oppressor; and both modes of liberation are integral to reconciliation between blacks and whites.

Toward that end, black power is theologically justifiable as both oppressed and oppressor would attain liberation through the empowerment of blacks. For Boesak, black power mandates that whites accept "blacks *as black persons*, and give themselves in service to [blacks]."[11]   Thus, black power is a creative theological element as it fosters reconciliation.

Black power is destructive, however, if it entails the apotheosis of blackness, which deforms black consciousness and precludes reconciliation. For Boesak, one avoids that deformity as he/she remains under critical scrutiny of the Word of God. The Word of God, for Boesak, hovers above all ideology; and black theology "should continue to cultivate self-critical reflection under the Word of God within the situation of blackness."[12]

For Itumeleng Jerry Mosala, however, a leading theologian in the UF and AZAPO traditions, Boesak's notion of the Word of God is naive. With Mosala, one returns to the nationalist path of black theology.

---

[9]Alan Boesak, *A Farewell to Innocence: A Socio-Ethical Study on Black Theology and Power*, (Maryknoll, N.Y.: Orbis Books, 1977), 27. See 517.

[10]Ibid., 43.

[11]Alan Boesak, *Black and Reformed: Apartheid, Liberation and the Calvinist Tradition* (Maryknoll, N.Y.: Orbis Books, 1984), 15. See 520.

[12]Boesak, *Farewell to Innocence*, 121.

According to Mosala, "universal abstract starting points derived presumably from the biblical message will not work for a biblical hermeneutics of liberation."[13] The Bible is made up of disparate sources——a disparateness that disallows the notion of *the* Word of God. No *one* Word of God, Mosala argues, constitutes *the* meaning of Scripture; yet black theologians such as Boesak

> write of the 'biblical message' rather than the 'biblical messages' (plural); the 'biblical God' rather than the 'biblical Gods'; the 'biblical right' rather than 'biblical rights.'[14]

What Boesak does not see, asserts Mosala, is that "the story of the oppressed [hidden in the Bible] has been stolen by the oppressors [who basically compiled and edited the Bible] and is being used as an ideological weapon against the oppressed in subsequent histories."[15] According to Mosala, Boesak unwittingly uses the oppressors' stories and thus weakens his position. Such reification of biblical complexity, implies Mosala, is almost comic.

Boesak, for instance, assumes that the meaning of Gen. 4:16——in which Cain murders his brother, Abel, and is cast from the land——is that

> oppressors shall have no place on God's earth. Oppressors have no home. Oppressors do not belong to, are not at home in God's objectives for this world. They have gone out of bounds. They have removed themselves from the world. Cain did not only break his relationship to the land, but also his relationship to God.[16]

Mosala writes: *"Kgakgamatso! Mohlolo! Isimanga!* 'What a miracle!' Africans would say."[17] Not only is Boesak's claim empirically unverifiable, but, ironically, upholds the inequities of the monarchy by slandering Cain, who is the hero of the oppressed. Boesak, argues Mosala, unwittingly appeals to the story that denigrates the oppressed. That is: "Cain the tiller of the soil must be seen to represent the freeholding peasantry who became locked in a life-and-death struggle with the emergent royal and latifundiary classes, represented in the story by Abel."[18]

Indeed, the story of Cain and Abel indicates that the Bible is a product of social conflicts. Today's bourgeoisie, however, asserts Mosala, protects itself by discrediting a perspicaciousness that would expose those biblical contradictions. Nonetheless, the perspective of the poor, argues Mosala, is discovered only by way of a radical ideological suspicion (of which the work of Norman Gottwald is an example). Here, one reads the Bible backwards: the poor question the text in the recognition that it lacks clear presentation of the perspective that corresponds to their own. In that way they pose "the

---

[13]Mosala, *Biblical Hermeneutics and Black Theology in South Africa*, (Grand Rapids: Wm. B. Eerdmans Publishing Company, 1989), 26. See annotation 578.

[14]Ibid., 28.

[15]Ibid., 34.

[16]Boesak, *Black and Reformed*, 140.

[17]Mosala, 34.

[18]Mosala, 35-36.

questions of which the texts are answers, the problems of which they are solutions."[19] In that way the poor produce liberating meaning from a liberated Bible.

To the extent that Boesak's exegesis obfuscates the socioeconomic struggle hidden in the Bible, it is alienated from "the black working-class and poor peasant culture" that should be the "materialist-hermeneutical starting point" of *black* theology.[20] "In the context of the Azanian/South African black struggle for liberation the working-class [subvert]...the normal criteria of biblical interpretation in favor of an organically black working-class hermeneutics——as shown, for example, in their preaching——[which] represents at least an ideological break with biblical criticism."[21]

The black oppressed, for Mosala, stand as the hermeneutical lenses through which the Bible is read in opposition to the white ruling elite, the African "tribal" lords and the pseudo-black bourgeoisie——all of whom have a stake in racist capitalism in South Africa. The black oppressed, moreover, hold the key to re-Africanization[22]——a term that here calls to mind National Forum sensibilities. That is, the more one eschews bourgeois mores the more he/she undergoes "a spiritual reconversion" that facilitates commitment to the oppressed——the black masses. Re-Africanization, in this sense, signifies an ecclesiology that recognizes the revolutionary potential of the independent churches——churches that often signify values inimical to racial and economic injustices.

Whether one subscribes to the views of Boesak or Mosala, few can deny the correctness of Mveng's assertion that South Africa today——a land of inestimable misery, indigence and violence——is the place to witness the theological imperative for justice. Indeed, black theology swells the cry of the entire continent, itself afflicted by a terrible *pauvreté anthropologique*.

---

[19]Mosala, 192.

[20]Mosala, 26.

[21]Mosala, 66.

[22]See 024.

5

Epilogue: Always Something New Out of Africa

The African-American scholar and activist, W.E.B Du Bois, wrote in 1914:

> "*Semper novi quid ex Africa*" cried the Roman consul; and he voiced the verdict of forty centuries. Yet there are those who would write world history and leave out this most marvelous of continents. Particularly today, most men assume that Africa lies far afield from the centers of our burning social problems...[1]

Indeed, African theology substantiates the claim that there is always something new out of Africa and that this something has to do with "our burning social problems." And it is unfortunate that Dr. Du Bois' disappointment with the fact that most people tend to neglect Africa is true even today. Nowhere in the world of Christian theology, with the exception of the African Diaspora, is there anything like African theology.

The newness of African theology involves the integration of Christian faith and so-called paganism. Although one may well argue that Christianity has always been reinterpreted in terms of a certain paganism, Africa's cultures bring a new dimension to this fact. As the histories of chattel slavery in the Americas and of colonialism in Africa reveal, African traditional values, so integral to African theology, were in most cases thought to be a signs of deep-seated deprivation. The christianization of the African people was thought to be providential, as it would uproot and replace "heathen" licentiousness. Yet this "heathenism" indicates that the salvation Christian faith promises is exceedingly broad and very diverse. And so Africa leads the way in correcting the alienation wrought by slavery and colonization: *Ex Africa semper aliquid novi*.

The proliferation of the African independent churches, the work of the old and new guards, and black South African theologians——all evince that new theologies regarding Christ and culture are emerging. In drawing out the Christian implications of African traditional religion, African theologians teach us something quite profound regarding the retroactive and proleptic implications of the Christian gospel. The Christian God is far more gracious, and salvation far more comprehensive, than Eurocentric missionaries knew. And so theologians, such as Barthélemy Adoukonou, have brought forth a new method and a new hermeneutic. In Adoukonou's work, an Afrocentric exegesis has emerged from the threshold where traditional religion and Christ meet. In a innovative way, we are edified

---

[1] W.E.B. DuBois, *On the Importance of Africa in World History* (Harlem, New York: Black Liberation Press, 1978), 15.

by Adoukonou's forging of a hermeneutic circle with a two-fold center: i.e., *Vodun et Christique*.[2] In years past——and even today——nothing more antithetical to Christianity than "voodoo" could be envisaged. Yet, Africa shows us in an unprecedented way, that oxymoron yet provides a dissonance through which the devout discover new possibilities regarding their faith in an Incarnate God.

The newness that African theology brings to faith involves the issue of liberation as well as culture. (As Cabral has shown us, the struggle for liberation is necessarily an "act of culture" since the deadliest imperialist's blow hammers autochthonous civilization.)[3] Indeed, dynamic cultural resistance and the struggle for liberation cannot be torn asunder insofar as the socioeconomic and political oppressions of African people have involved the sabotage and negation of their ancestral and contemporary humanity. In revealing the global dimensions of the economic and racial injustices that prevail, African theology is redefining a Christian imperative for justice and peace——an imperative that demands human liberation and the survival of diverse cultures.

Engelbert Mveng's definition of *pauvreté anthropologique* is most edifying in that regard. Here the denial of the right to exist——to love and to hope——defines the tragedy of infant morality. And Jean-Marc Éla's strong social analysis brings this horrible truth to the world's attention, a truth of an impoverished continent. In light of Éla's work, Mveng's argument that the focus of African culture has been fecundity is all the more profound. Indeed, the traditional focus on fecundity is decisive today for an appreciation of the fullness of life the gospel promises. Because of the work of theologians like Adoukonou, Mveng, and Éla, it should no longer be possible to talk about liberation theology without a substantial focus on Africa.

---

[2] See his *Jalons pour une théologie africaine: Essai d'une herméneutique chrétienne du Vodun dahoméen*; annotation 288. Adoukonou gives us an indication of this hermeneutic as he writes about the way in which the African theologian bypasses the page where one finds the relation between *Paul-Onésime-Philémon* in order to focus on that pericope where *le Crucifié*——clairvoyantly explaining the meaning of his death, *donnant par avance l'exégèse de sa mort*——informs his disciples that he is Lord. According to Adoukonou, that exegesis is analogous to the ritual disassociation one finds in Vodun. The phenomenon in which the divinity rides the devotee in Vodun is not unlike the hypostatic union of the Second Person with Jesus. That is, God is like *la figure de l'Autre chevauchant l'adepte du Vodun*. And this God——as *l'autre présent en Jésus Crucifié*——lovingly emptied himself until death on the Cross. Hence, Adoukonou arrives *à clore cercle herméneutique à double foyer: Vodun et Christique*. (See p. 59.)

[3]See 024.

Part II
ANNOTATED BIBLIOGRAPHY

6

History and Social Analysis

001   Aidoo, Thomas Akawasi.   "Ghana: Social Class, the December Coup, and the Prospects for Socialism." *Contemporary Marxism: Proletarianization and Class Struggle in Africa* 6 (Spring 1983): 142-165.

Aidoo's essay indicates the social analysis of the new guard. According to Aidoo, "What emerged after Ghana's independence in 1957 was a nationalist government headed by a petty bourgeoisie that was given to a kind of socialist ideal called Nkrumahism, Consciencism and African Socialism" (p. 146-147).   See 038, 054; 096-099.   This socialism was only ostensible: Ghana became dominated by "petty bourgeois class interests."   National development, he argues, would have been facilitated by a focus on peasant realities, which have not been attractive to Western investors.   Nonetheless, these realities "if encouraged and developed, could form a basis for local accumulation of capital for a self-reliant national development" (p. 146).   In his focus on the peasantry, Aidoo brings Jean-Marc Éla to mind. See 334-341.

002   Andriamanjato, Richard.   "From Abidjan '69 To Lusaka '74." In *The Struggle Continues: Lusaka 1974*, 68-73. Nairobi: All Africa Conference of Churches, 1975.

A succinct summary of the developments of the All Africa Conference of Churches (AACC) from its inception in 1969 to its meeting in Lusaka.   See 066, 316-317. According to Andriamanjato, the AACC is essentially committed to the liberation of the African people.   Indeed, his essay indicates that the call for liberation was characteristic of African theology before EATWOT's Pan-African caucus convened in 1977.   See Chapter 3 of this bibliography; and 003, 137, 322, 423, 434, 503.

003 Ankrah, Kodowo E. "Church and Politics in Africa." In *African Theology en Route*, ed. by Kofi Appiah-Kubi and Sergio Torres, 155-161. Maryknoll, N.Y.: Orbis Books, 1979.

African Theology en Route is a historic document in that it represents: the historic conference held in Accra, Ghana in 1977; the Pan-African nuances of EATWOT; the new guard perspective that emerged from this historic conference.   See 002.   Ankrah, representing Uganda, examines the troubled history that has produced African theology. He argues that Christian missionaries are not unlike colonial mercenaries as both sought to undermine African self-determination. Today, reveals Ankrah, self-determination is still in danger and must be held in tension with "flag independence"——i.e., neocolonialism. In his definition of neocolonialism Ankrah quotes Kwame Nkrumah: "'the essence of neocolonialism is that the State which is subject to this, is, in theory, independent and has all the outward trappings of international sovereignty.   In reality its economic system and

thus its political policy is directed from the outside'" (p. 156).   See 092, 097, 100.
Ankrah wonders where the church stands in regard to "flag independence"?   According to
Ankrah, an element in the church refuses to deal with the question, having assumed that
politics are impertinent to "the 'gospelling' of the Word of God."   Not unlike Jerry
Mosala——see 572-578——Ankrah holds that the kerygma has been crusted with the sallow
mold of the status quo.   For Ankrah, the church has tended to preach peace without its
necessary counterpart——justice.   Nonetheless, notes Ankrah, theologies, equipped with
a social analysis that refuses to conceal contradictions, are demanding justice, as well as
peace.   Indicating, then, the perspective of new guard theologians, Ankrah argues
persuasively for an African theology of liberation.

004 Austin, Dennis.   *Politics in Africa*. 2nd ed. Hanover: University Press of New
England, 1984.
    Austin helps one study old guard theologians, who have been captive to the illusion
of independence and blind to the relevancy of liberation theology for Africa.   Austin's
thesis is that despite "independence," the colonial state remains.   Imperial powers still
extort the substance of development from the African "nations," thereby enriching the
metropolitan bourgeoisie.   *Politics in Africa* helps one appreciate the social analysis that
new guard theologians employ.   See 288, 334-341; 371, 382, 432-440; 452-459.

005 Axelsen, Diane.   "Philosophical Justification for Contemporary Social and Political
Values and Strategies." In *African Philosophy: An Introduction*, ed. by Richard A. Davis,
227-244. Lanham: University Press of America, 1984.
    Axelsen's essay leads one to question why the old guard gave so little attention to
radical African thinkers.   She argues that Kwame Nkrumah (see 096-101); Frantz Fanon
(see 034-035); Amilcar Cabral (see 023-025); and Julius Nyerere (see 102-106) are as
important as Plato, Marx and Sartre.   For Axelsen, these African philosophers define an
African ontology and an African anthropology and historiography, as well as the Pan-
African meaning of black culture.   According to Axelsen, moreover, "the theme of social
commitment runs through the work of all four men.   We should note, too, that they
directed their philosophical activity toward the goal of meeting urgent human needs" (p.
241).   Especially edifying here is the way in which the four struggled on behalf of Africa's
most precious resource——the children, dying today at the world's most alarming rate.
Her essay is a good discussion of the relation of culture to radical political theory and is
therefore a means of appreciating the work of the new guard.

006 Ayandele, E.A.   "Traditional Rulers and Missionaries in Pre-Colonial Africa." *Tarikh*
3,1 (1969): 23-37.
    An informative essay on the interaction of traditional authority and the missionaries.
See 009.

007 Ayandele, E.A.   *Holy Johnson: Pioneer of African Nationalism, 1836-1917*. New
York: Humanities Press, 1970.
    Like his *The Missionary Impact on Modern Nigeria*, Ayandele's biography of Holy
Johnson is a valuable source for an appreciation of the ancestors of today's African
theology.   See 009. James Holy Johnson, a Yoruba, was an Anglican priest and a leading
cultural nationalist of his day.   At the forefront of efforts to establish an independent
African church, he anticipated much of the discussion on inculturation current today.
Johnson desired "to see Christianity and pure scriptural morality deep-rooted in the African
soil" (p. 287).   He thought Christianity should be "de-europeanized"——africanized by the
acculturative force of the African personality.   See 087, 136.   (See discussion of African
personality in Chapter 2 of this bibliography.)

008   Ayandele, E.A.   "Address by Professor E.A. Ayandele, Principal, University of
Ibadan, Jos Campus, on Sunday, 31 August, 1975." In *Christianity in Independent Africa*,
ed. by Edward Fasholé-Luke, Richard Gray, Adrian Hastings and Godwin Tasie, 606-613.
Bloomington: Indiana University Press, 1978.

In a tenor very much like the new guard's, Professor Ayandele criticizes old guard
theologians alienated from "the African *milieu* in which they should expect the Christianity
of the Bible to be incarnate" (p. 606). Like new guard theologians, such as Éla (see 334-
341) and Oduyoye (see 452-459), Ayandele is edified by the independent churches. On
the independent churches, see 026, 227, 228, 234, 239, 240. According to Ayandele, the
independent churches are "held in irrational, uncharitable, and jaundiced contempt by the
more elitist Western-oriented churches" (p. 606). For Ayandele, the elitist churches offer
no moral leadership in the wake of the crises of the continent. The masses, he argues,
tend not to look to the elitist church for direction, but to African traditional religion (or the
independent churches). Ayandele asserts that Christian scholars alienated from the masses
assume that the meaning of African traditional religion is conspicuous. "Scratch the
African pastor and you would discover [however] that he has greater faith in the charms
and amulets he wears surreptitiously and in the 'witch-doctor' to whom he pays nocturnal
visits than in the Holy Bible and Jesus Christ" (p. 612). The pity, for Ayandele, is that
many Christians fail to see that Christianity and African traditional religions are not
adversaries. Biblical Christianity, he argues, is not deprived of its salvific power when it
is africanized. See 041. To substantiate his assertion, Ayandele concludes his address by
quoting Bishop James Holy Johnson——an eminent ancestor of African theology. See 007.

009   Ayandele, E.A. *The Missionary Impact on Modern Nigeria, 1842-1914*. Burnt Mill:
Longman Group, 1981.

The Missionary Impact on Modern Nigeria helps one appreciate the historical
background of African theology, particularly in regard to the third phase (see Chapter 1
of this bibliography). According to Ayandele, traditional rulers supported missionaries as
a foil for their political aspirations. The issue, for most, was not spiritual conversion, but
political expediency. (He also shows how Islam hampered the spread of Christianity in
Nigeria.) Despite the political agenda of the kings, colonialism took hold on Africa——a
development contrary to traditional aspirations. Here, colonialism was facilitated by
British and French missionaries who paved the way for colonial infrastructures. Yet,
Ayandele reveals that missionaries also influenced the rise of West African nationalism.
See 049. In this regard, he discusses seminal figures such as: Bishop Crowther (see 057-
058, 109); Edward Blyden (see 016-018, 057-058, 081-082); and James Johnson (see 007,
057-058). All are important forerunners of African theology.

010   Azikewe, Nnamdi.   "A Denunciation of European Imperialism." In *The Africa
Reader: Independent Africa*, ed. by Wilfred Cartey and Martin Kilson, 69-77. New York:
Vintage Books, 1970.

Azikewe has been a leading Nigerian nationalist (Igbo) and was the first President
of Nigeria. His essay amplifies the issues that burgeoned into a continent-wide movement
for the end of olden colonialism. Of particular interest here is his correct identification of
the role Africa played in the two great World Wars, which were catalysts of the
decolonization movement. The essay is not only a fine sample of the literature of African
nationalism. It is also a fine paradigm of the social analysis that examines the
contradictions of colonial history.

011   Barongo, Yolamu.   "Alternative Approaches to African Politics." In *Political Science
in Africa: A Critical Review*, ed. by Yolamu Barongo, 138-154. London: Zed Press, 1983.

An example of the social analysis and historical perspective of the new guard: Barongo argues that colonial contradictions must be defined in terms of the "material base of [African] countries." According to Barongo, "this base is characterized by a severe shortage of material resources, the result of a long history of imperialist exploitation and contemporary manipulations of the dependent nations by the international capitalist system" (p. 151). See 110, 120. These contemporary manipulations continue essentially because the African bourgeoisie (the *elite*) staff inherently un-democratic structures left over from olden colonialism. See 004. These, by design, *cannot* stabilize the political economy. For Barongo, social analysis of that problem requires "the political economy approach, which employs class-analysis as its major methodological guide, accompanied by an analysis of historical variables" (p. 151). According to Barongo, such an approach is superior to the "approaches formulated by so-called Africanists who invariably tend to view African politics through concepts developed in the static tradition of Western bourgeois scholarship" (p. 151). See 120. The social analysis Barongo commends is very much like that commended to us by new guard theologians, Jean-Marc Éla and Englebert Mveng. See 334-341; 432-440.

012 Benson, Mary. *Nelson Mandela*. London: Panaf Books, 1980.

This little book is a fine introduction to both the life of Nelson Mandela, and the freedom struggle of the African National Congress (ANC). No one studying black South African theology can afford to ignore the history of the ANC and the leadership of Mandela. See 085-086.

013 Biko, Steve. "Black Consciousness and the Quest for a True Humanity." In *The Challenge of Black Theology in South Africa*, ed. by Basil Moore, 36-47. Atlanta, Georgia: John Knox Press, 1973.

The Challenge of Black Theology in South Africa is a landmark text in the history of black South African theology. See 526, 527, 534, 556, 570, 579, 580, 582, 586, 587, 588, 590. Indeed, part of its historic value is that it includes an essay by Biko. According to Biko, black theology seeks to relate God and Christ to Africans and their struggles. Here Christ is a "fighting god," who emerges from a revolutionary hermeneutic——the fruit of ideological suspicion. "It is the duty therefore," writes Biko, "of all black priests and ministers to save Christianity by adopting Black Theology's approach and thereby once more uniting the black man with his God" (p. 43). Biko defines black theology partly in terms of traditional values that tend not to treat human beings as expendable objects. According to Biko, traditional Nguni culture——Biko himself was a !Xhosa——is focused on human needs and is essentially democratic. According to Biko, these so-called Bantu values must be at the heart of black theology. Biko also reveals another way in which Fanon (see 034-035) and Cabral (see 023-025) correctly define the revolutionary dimensions of African (i.e., black) culture. For Biko, black culture is dynamic since it sustains itself in creative responses to crises not addressed by the ancestors or the invading whites.

014 Biko, Steve. *I Write What I Like*. San Francisco: Harper & Row, 1978.

Steve Biko is as important as Mandela for an understanding of the social analysis that defines nuances of black theology. Indeed, Steve Biko and the Black Consciousness Movement (BCM) that he led——see 036, 039——were catalysts spawning the development of black theology in South Africa. *I Write What I Like* contains Biko's speeches and reflections on the black struggle for liberation in South Africa.

015 Biko, Steve. *Black Consciousness in South Africa*. Edited by Millard Arnold. New York: Vintage Books, 1979.

Like the text immediately above, this volume is a fine introduction to the principles and values of BCM. Especially valuable is the transcript of Biko's prison trial, which reveals his perspicacity and un-compromised goodwill. Since the values of BCM and Biko's legacy are seminal sources of black South African theology, this text is also necessary for a critical appreciation of the ideological matrix from which black South African theology is hurled at apartheid.

016 Blyden, Edward. *African Life and Customs*. London: C.M. Phillips, 1908.

Edward Blyden (1834-1912) was a leading black intellectual and Presbyterian minister. He emigrated to Liberia from the Americas and lived out the rest of his life as a West African. Multi-lingual and well-published, he is noted as the father of Pan-Africanism. He was the leading cultural nationalist of his day and one of the great ancestors of African theology. See 081-082; 116, 209. *African Life and Customs* reveals that Blyden is indeed a forerunner of African theologians, who study African traditional culture in the quest to africanize Christianity. Blyden envisioned "new forms representing the African idea...African literature with the smell of Africa upon it...African freedom, African thought, and African theology." Blyden is also credited with anticipating nationalistic movements, particularly that of *négritude*, which influenced the emergence of African theology. On *négritude*, see: 114-115; 353, 475, 511. He also anticipated the notion of the African personality——see 007——which holds that Africans possess a unique cultural genius. Supremely humanistic——inimical to the technological desecration of the earth——this genius would save the world from the deformed mores of Europe. Blyden influenced the thought of leading African politicians, such as Kwame Nkrumah (see 096-101), who in turn influenced the emergence of African theology insofar as he became a symbol of Africa's drive for "independence."

017 Blyden, Edward. *Christianity, Islam and the Negro Race*. London: Edinburgh University Press, 1967.

A compilation of Blyden's essays, *Christianity, Islam and the Negro Race* was noted, during the late nineteenth and early twentieth centuries, as evidence of the intellectual abilities of African people. Blyden explores issues related to the tension between christianization and africanization. The text is seminal in that it is an early——and still relevant——discussion of issues related to African theology. See 209.

018 Blyden, Edward. "Search for a Liberal Education for Africans." In *The Africa Reader: Independent Africa*, ed. by Wilfred Cartey and Martin Kilson, 42-56. New York: Vintage Books, 1970.

Blyden, in this excerpt from *Christianity, Islam and the Negro Race*, argues for a pedagogy that would equip African youth to serve in the struggle for Africa's redemption. Blyden's essay is another indication of his seminal role in establishing the rhetoric of African nationalism and Pan-Africanism. Blyden claims that Eurocentrism is an evil "to which Negroes are, everywhere in Christian lands, subjected, and which everywhere affects them unfavorably." He argues for an Afrocentric curriculum, central to which would be an *African* theology. See 016, 209.

019 Brown, E. "The Necessity of a 'Black' South African Church History." In *Relevant Theology for Africa*, ed. by Hans-Jurgen Becken, 79-125. Durban: Lutheran Publishing House, 1973.

Brown posits that a true history must embody the history of black Christians, particularly in terms of the development of black theology; but it must essentially reflect, in proper proportion, the history of "white theologies" of South Africa. For Brown the history of the church in South Africa involves the conflicts between the Afrikaners and their British "overlords," both of whom have had problematic relations with "the heathens [sic]." According to Brown, the hegemonic force of the English and the nuisance of the Bantu produced the Afrikaner nation. And the history of the South African church for Brown is essentially the history of a neo-Calvinism——the theological support of Afrikaner nationalism. For Brown, blacks enter South African history only after W.W. II. He asserts that Black Consciousness——see 013-015; 036, 039——reifies South African history in uncritically calling whites oppressors, regardless of their ideological perspective. Black theology, asserts Brown, plays a significant role in that reification, insofar as much of its historical vision is truncated due to its "frustrated thinking." According to Brown, black theology is more of a cultural ideology than a theology, which——he alleges——has little to do with the church. Still, Brown holds that black theology is indispensable for the revisionist tasks of historians, who seek to render the totality of South African Church history as far as possible.

020 Bureau, M.R. "Influence de la christianisation sur les institutions traditionnelles des ethnies côtières du Cameroun." In *Christianity in Tropical Africa: Studies Presented and Discussed at Seventh International African Seminar, University of Ghana, April, 1965*, ed. by C.G. Baëta, 165-181. London: Oxford University Press, 1968.

A monograph on the historic encounter between German missionaries and the coastal people of Cameroon: Bureau focuses on the tension (*le dialogue*) between missionaries' values and those of the Duala people. He examines two Duala institutions, the cult of the water spirits (*le culte des génies de l'eau*) and the dowry, or the prenuptial agreement *(le prix-de-la-fiancée)*. Bureau asserts that the first missionaries sought to uproot these institutions——a praxis which Eboussi Boulaga calls cruel and alienating (see 307). That praxis was legitimated and enforced by the military might of the metropoles, which, in the nineteenth century, paved the way for the missionaries. Now, however, after the events of W.W. II, the legacy of the missionaries is being modified. There is, as it were, a return to the sources of Africanity. *Il va* [the African scholar him or herself] *donc chercher à se poser lui-même en s'opposant au Blanc, selon la 'négritude'* (p. 179). Indeed, *Le Noir s'aperçoit qu'il n'a pas été 'blanchi' par le christianisme; la puissance du Blanc, il doit la conquérir lui-même, et par d'autres voies que celles qu'on lui avait proposées* (p. 178-179). Here, Bureau obviously refers to the *négritude* movement. See 114-115; 511.

021 Busia, K.A. *The Challenge of Africa*. New York: Frederick A. Praeger, 1964.

Busia, like Danquah——see 155——was a leading Ghanian intellectual and a leading member of the United Gold Coast Convention——the "evolutionist" party instrumental in retrieving Nkrumah from England in 1947. Busia was the president of Ghana for a short time after Nkrumah was disposed in 1966. See 038, 055; 100-101. Busia also discusses the importance of culture. Especially relevant is his discussion of "African personality" and *négritude*. Both precepts are integral to the study of African theology. See 007, 019, 114-115; 353-355, 475.

022 Busia, K.A. "Colonial Administration and Social Change in Ghana, 1900-1920's." In *The Africa Reader: Colonial Africa*, ed. by Wilfred Cartey and Martin Kilson, 108-114. New York: Vintage Books, 1970.

Another sampling of Busia's analysis of the movement for independence. He examines the way in which colonial rule undermined traditional authority. He focuses on the Ashanti and the notion of indirect rule: "Under the British administration the chief has become a subordinate authority. This is constantly in evidence in his relations with the police, the military, and other officials of the central government" (p. 1140.) On the Ashanti, see 153, 163, 242.

023 Cabral, Amilcar. *Return to the Source: Selected Speeches of Amilcar Cabral*, ed. by Africa Information Service. New York: Monthly Review Press, 1973.

Cabral's writings inform the social analysis of theologians such as Jean-Marc Éla (see 334-341) and Jerry Mosala (see 572-578). Cabral was the revolutionary theorist and Secretary-General of the African Party for the Independence of Guinea and the Cape Verde Islands (PAIGC). "Under his leadership, the PAIGC liberated three-quarters of the countryside of Guinea in less than ten years of revolutionary struggle." He was assassinated by the Portuguese in 1973. Cabral's legacy includes the valorization of the culture of the peasants. Indeed, Cabral asserted that the culture of the peasants heightens one's appreciation of the revolutionary potential of the oppressed——an exteriority (see 331) that intensifies commitment to the liberation struggle.

024 Cabral, Amilcar. *Unity and Struggle: Speeches and Writings of Amilcar Cabral*, with an introduction by Basil Davidson and biographical notes by Mário de Andrade. New York: Monthly Review Press, 1979.

The biographical notes reveal that the *négritude* movement made a seminal impact on Cabral. See 114-115, 511. Indeed, one might say that Cabral was a *négritude* poet early in his career. This fact sheds light on Cabral's immense contribution to the radical, religio-cultural analysis that makes its way into the work of the new guard. That is, his early attraction to the *négritude* movement is a clue to his on-going insights into the nationalistic significance of culture. In his essay, "National culture," also found in *Return to the Source*, Cabral explains that the people's land is a metonym of their culture; and both culture and land are part of the material base of precolonial and colonial contradictions. For Cabral, imperialism exacerbates precolonial contradictions in heightening the antipathy among ethnic groups, thereby playing one cultural nuance of the people against another one. When culture is manipulated in this way, the people are alienated from the land. Culture is liberating, however, when it valorizes the *Pan*-African values conducive to national liberation. For Cabral, then, "national liberation is necessarily an *act of culture*" (p. 143). According to Cabral, "re-Africanization" defines the praxis whereby the African elite, having been duped into an assimilation of the imperil culture, recognize the revolutionary potential of the workers and peasants. Peasants and workers are the visceral cultural tie to the land once held in contempt by the elite——a contempt that exacerbates the alienation in which colonialism thrives. In re-Africanization, the once alienated elite undergo "a spiritual reconversion...vital for their true integration in the liberation movement" (p. 145). That is, in seeking a more horizontal——i.e., democratic——structure, the elite recognize that the masses hold the key to the means of resistance. Indeed, the masses embody the essential difference of African people from their oppressors. This gives the masses incredible revolutionary power. See 023, 331, and 340.

025 Cabral, Amilcar. "Class and Revolution in Africa." In *Marxism: Essential Writings*, ed. by David McLean, 392-409. New York: Oxford University Press, 1988.

This essay is another example of the usefulness of Cabral's legacy to radical theologians——such as Jean-Marc Éla and Barthélemy Adoukonou (see 334-341; 288)——who critique the Eurocentric notion that Africa falls outside of history as it falls outside the paradigms of class struggle defined in Europe. For Cabral, the dynamism of history is related to "the level of productive forces," which is not ahistorical simply because it has not reached the class conflict of industrial nations. Like Cabral, new guard theologians argue that relevant social analysis must emerge from levels of African conflict——i.e., the tensions among diverse peasants and workers and their attendant modes of production; the tensions between a "re-Africanized" vanguard and the imperial bourgeoisie.

026 Clarke, Peter. *West Africa and Christianity*. London: Edward Arnold, 1986.
      Clarke's text is useful in the study of African theology as it provides historic
information on the development of Christianity in Africa. Chapter six, "The Rise,
Expansion and Impact of Independent Churches, 1890-1960," is a decent summary of the
independent churches——viewed by many as the only authentic contexts in which
Christianity is africanized. Clarke rightly concludes that these churches were "movements
of protest against the increasingly negative assessment of African capabilities made by
many European and American missionaries both black and white from the 1800s onward"
(p. 190). "These churches," writes Clarke, "were also a direct, conscious attempt to assert
the cultural and spiritual values and rights of Africans which missions were either unaware
of or chose to ignore" (p. 190). See 008. Chapter eight, "Developments in Christian
Relations with Islam and African Traditional Religions," is an edifying exploration of the
interaction of Christianity and African traditional religion——an exploration which goes
to the heart of an epistemological problem in African theology. (See the section of this
bibliography entitled "African Traditional Religion and Religio-Cultural Analysis.") The
critical question here is: has African traditional religion been distorted by African
theologians who, reproducing the methodology of European missionaries, tended to
interpret African traditional religion in terms of their commitment to Christianity? See
008, 136, 158 162, 221, 223, 239, 278. Clarke reveals the more progressive view that
African traditional religion——hardly the old relic giving way to Christian
eschatology——is a religion with its own integrity.

027 Cook, David.   "Church and State Zambia: The Case of the African Methodist
Episcopal Church." In *Christianity in Independent Africa*, ed. by Edward Fasholé-Luke,
Richard Gray, Adrian Hastings and Godwin Tasie, 285-304. Bloomington: Indiana
University Press, 1978.
      It has been shown that African-Americans played a seminal role in planting
Christianity in Africa. (See the discussion of Edward Blyden in Chapter 1 of this
bibliography.) Cook's essay, focusing on Zambia, enlarges an appreciation of the African-
American influence. He examines the role of the African Methodist Episcopal Church
(AME) there, a church founded by black North Americans. According to Cook, the AME
"entered the country in a context of pan-African feeling, and its leading members during
the movement towards independence contributed to, and were influenced by, the mounting
tide of nationalism in Zambia" (p. 285). Historically, the AME Church was a refuge for
Africans excluded from the white missionary bodies that maintained racism when Zambia
was Northern Rhodesia. The leading Bishop of the AME, Henry McNeal Turner——see
122——openly opposed white rule in Zambia as early as the dawning of the twentieth
century. His militancy attracted the Barostseland king, Lewanika, who facilitated the
inculturation of the African-America church in 1900. As a result, AME Christians were
banned from Northern Rhodesia by the British South Africa Company. "Christian
churches" writes Cook, moreover, "viewed the [AME] then rather as established churches
had viewed the Anabaptists in the sixteenth century and agreed with the ban" (p. 287).
The AME reentered the Zambian scene in the 1930s due to the efforts of African
nationalists; and it grew because of its independence from white control and closeness to
popular culture. The church also played a significant role in the burgeoning movement
toward independence. Indeed, Kenneth Kaunda——see 066-070; 191——was "a local
preacher and choir leader at the Lusaka church." As nationalism escalated, however, the
AME attempted to move to a position of neutrality. That development, coupled with the
white church's belated support of nationalism, explains the decline of the AME church in
the post-independence period. Now, notes Cook ironically, Zambians seek independence
from the African-American church.

028 Crummell, Alexander. *The Future of Africa*. New York: Scribner, 1962.
A collection of his essays. Like Blyden——see 016-018; 081——Crummell was an outstanding missionary, who lived in Liberia for twenty years before returning to the United States. See 094, 126. Crummell, despite his many virtues, exemplifies the peculiar American neurosis in which respect for the African heritage is handicapped by an infatuation with Eurocentric culture. Crummell's legacy, then, is not only useful in framing the historical background of African theology, but also clarifies, in part, why old guard theologians have produced what Eboussi Boulaga calls an alienated discourse. See 305-307. That is, certain African theologians have attempted to do African theology based upon ontologies and metaphysics that are essentially European. Their Eurocentrism is not unlike Crummell's "Anglophilia." See 063.

029 Crummell, Alexander. *Africa and America*. New York: Negro University Press, 1969.
Another compilation of Crummell's essays, and another indication of the genealogy of the old guard syndrome.

030 Davenport, T.R.H. *South Africa: A Modern History*. Toronto: University of Toronto Press, 1980.
Davenport's history of South Africa provides information on the country from which black South African theology emerged. The text is as informative in regard to the history of the whites as it is in regard to the history of black resistance. See 013-015; 036, 039.

031 Davidson, Basil. *The African Genius: An Introduction to African Social and Political History*. Boston: Little, Brown and Company, 1969.
Davidson explores the religio-cultural matrix so vital for an appreciation of the tension between acculturation and inculturation. See 061. More specifically, Davidson explores the richness of African traditional culture and suggests that Africa can liberate itself only to the extent that it reappropriates its ancestral values. Thus Davidson explores political culture, which is so much a part of the work of the new guard. See 033.

032 Davidson, Basil. *Can Africa Survive?* Boston: Little, Brown and Company, 1974.
Here Davidson probes the problems of an Africa caught in the grip of neocolonialism——the current matrix of African theology. He looks at the problems of underdevelopment and provides insight into its structural violence——i.e., the praxis which extracts wealth from Africa and yet to Africa gives nothing. Davidson offers indispensable insight into the myth of independence to which the old guard subscribed and which the new guard seeks to explode. See 288, 334-341; 432-440; 451-459.

033 Davidson, Basil. *Let Freedom Come: Africa in Modern History*. Boston: Little, Brown and Company, 1978.
No student of African theology can gain a comprehensive understanding of the matrix in which it is situated without a sense of the struggles of the Continent from the dawn of olden colonialism to the advent of neocolonialism. See 004. Basil Davidson's work is quite useful toward that end. *Let Freedom Come* is an excellent text revelatory of the African struggle for liberation.

034 Fanon, Frantz. *The Wretched of the Earth*. New York: Grove Press, 1968.
Fanon, a psychiatrist from Martinique, who participated in the Algerian revolution, establishes here a cultural and political paradigm that defines the insurrectionist values he deems necessary for the resistance to and abolition of colonialism in Africa. Particularly

edifying is the chapter, "The Pitfalls of National Consciousness." Here, Fanon lends substance to critics of the African theologians who correlate elements of traditional religion and (Eurocentric) theology too easily. See 008, 136, 305-307. That is, Fanon argues that the alienated African intellectual attempts to bend the realities of the dynamic culture of the African poor to theories of Africanity that, abstracted from the defunct practices of yesterday, exist in bourgeois thought only. According to Fanon:

> *Culture has never the translucidity of custom*; it abhors simplification. In its essence it is opposed to custom, for custom is always the deterioration of culture. The desire to attach oneself to tradition or bring abandoned traditions to life again does not only mean going against the current of history but also opposing one's own people....In an underdeveloped country during the period of struggle traditions are shot through by centrifugal tendencies. This is why the intellectual often runs the risk of being out of date [Emphasis added] (p. 224).

Indeed, as Éla points out——see 340——dynamic peasant culture and the reification of ancestral customs in the work of "*négritude*" intellectuals are not identical.

035 Fanon, Frantz. "The Intellectual Elite in Revolutionary Culture." In *The Africa Reader: Independent Africa*, ed. by Wilfred Cartey and Martin Kilson, 126-134. New York: Vintage Books, 1970.

Fanon makes a distinction between the "re-Africanized" intellectual (Cabral) and the alienated one. See 024. According to Fanon, African intellectuals, alienated from the masses, will incur the enmity of the peasants and the workers unless they extricate themselves from the "Greco-Latin pedestal." If, he admonishes, African intellectuals fail to come to this realization, fail to be enlightened by the acculturative force of "centrifugal tendencies," they will succumb to vulgar corruption. (It is fascinating to discover Fanon's affinity to Cabral in this essay. See 023-025.) Fanon holds that a re-Africanized intellectual——to use Cabral's term again——undergoes "a sort of *auto-da-fé*" in returning to the source. In returning to the source, to what Éla calls *l'Afrique "d'en-bas"*——that is, the underside of the colonial territory——the europeanized intellectual discovers the falseness of a Eurocentric orientation. See 339. He "lumpenizes" himself in

> the destruction of all his idols: egoism, recrimination that springs from pride, and the childish stupidity of those who always want to have the last word. Such a colonized intellectual, dusted over by colonial culture, will in the same way discover the substance of village assemblies, the cohesion of people's committees, and the extraordinary fruitfulness of local meetings and groupments (p. 129).

His essay sparks the questions: Did old guard theologians forget the poor, those who should benefit from "independence"? Did African theology——which, by implication, is what Fanon means by special disciplines——turn its back on the people's need for "*land and bread*"? A fortiori, did a certain snobbery toward the independent churches constitute the refusal to destroy idols.

036 Fatton, Robert. *Black Consciousness in South Africa: The Dialectics of Ideological Resistance to White Supremacy*. Albany: State University of New York Press, 1986.

Like Gerhart's and Lodge's texts——see 039, 075——Fatton's reveals the particularity of the black political thought of South Africa. Fatton focuses on the Black Consciousness Movement. Especially useful is chapter five, entitled "Black Theology." See 015.

037 Fetter, Bruce, ed. *Colonial Rule in Africa: Readings from Primary Sources*. Madison: The University of Wisconsin Press, 1979.

Fetter's "Introduction" to the primary sources compiled in *Colonial Rule in Africa* decently summarizes the history of colonial rule, from the Partition, i.e., the Berlin Conference, to the epoch of "Independence." Like Austin——see 004——Fetter argues that the continent "cannot easily escape the heritage of a century and a half of colonization" (p. 20). Among the informative documents following his introduction are excerpts from the Berlin Conference of 1884-85 and Fanon's *Les damnés de la terre*. See 034.

038 Fitch, Bob, and Mary Oppenheimer. *Ghana: End of an Illusion*. New York: Monthly Review Press, 1966.

Ghana: End of an Illusion provides insight into the context that continues to shape the theology of scholars such as Mercy Oduyoye (see 452-459), Kwesi Dickson (see 322-327), and John Pobee (see 468-469). The text is also a paradigm of the social analysis related to the work of those theologians. Fitch and Oppenheimer discuss the implications of the coup that toppled Nkrumah's Ghana. See 055, 100-101. Their analysis reveals the influence of Fanon——see 034-035——and furnishes insight into the contradictions of both Nkrumah's "revolutionary path" and the reactionary blocs allied against that path. Particularly insightful is their revelation that Nkrumah's party, despite its socialist rhetoric, acquiesced in the process through which the colonial state remains. See 001, 004. The authors suggest that the way out of this cul-de sac is through the "centrifugal force" of the peasants. See 034. They, in becoming guerrillas, will acquire the inventiveness that will promote growth and development. Their sense of the revolutionary power of the peasantry is not unlike Éla's. See 340, 336-337.

039 Gerhart, Gail. *Black Power in South Africa: The Evolution of an Ideology*. Los Angeles: University of California Press, 1978.

Gerhart notes the importance of black theology as an element of the Black Consciousness Movement. See 013-015; 036. She also provides insight into the political ideologies prevalent among leading black South African theologians, such as Jerry Mosala and Takasto Mofokeng. See 565-568; 572-578. While Gerhart heightens one's awareness of the history of black resistance in South Africa——from the founding of the African National Congress (ANC) to the Black Consciousness Movement (BCM)——she is very sympathetic to the Pan Africanist Congress (PAC). The PAC is a black nationalist organization traceable to the thought of Anton Lembede and Robert Sobukwe, both of whom were forerunners of the Black Consciousness Movement.

040 Graf, William. "African Elite Theories and Nigerian Elite Consolidation: A Political Economy Analysis." In *Political Science in Africa: A Critical Review*, ed. by Yolamu Barongo, 189-210. London: Zed Press, 1983.

Graf's essay facilitates social analysis within the context of Nigeria, an important context for the study of African theology. See 177, 210-220; 356-357; 358-360. According to Graft, both the Western supra-bourgeoisie and their "administrative superstructure" maintained traditional societies that were regularly sabotaged by the export of capital. What is more, the British policy of indirect rule is the prototype of neocolonialism and the progenitor of the Nigerian bourgeoisie. According to Graft, the Nigerian bourgeoisie, a faulted class——faulted because they do not own the means of production——is alienated from the masses. During the nationalist push for independence, this faulted elite, ironically, courted the masses. In the epoch of "independence," however, "the masses...had to be depoliticized rapidly in the service of...elite domination" (p. 193). Graf's discussion of these contradictions provides insight into the myth of independence, to which the old guard succumbed. In Nigeria, such contradictions led to vulgar corruption and civil war.

041   Gray, Richard.   *Black Christians and White Missionaries*. New Haven: Yale University Press, 1990.

Gray provides an edifying, historical interpretation of the African values that have divested Christianity of its Eurocentrism and made it uniquely African. He argues cogently that central Christian themes——the concept of evil for instance——are not so different from central themes of African religions. For Gray, then, it is wrong to conclude that the latter is to be extirpated if the former is to increase. He also examines the legacies of historic African Christians such as Lourenço da Silva, an African-Brazilian of the 17th Century who led black opposition to the slave trade. Lourenço argued that slavery was inherently anti-Christian. According to Gray: "For Lourenço and his fellow black Christians, the faith brought the hope of liberation, it demanded a commitment to the cause of the poor and the oppressed, and it involves an equality of treatment for 'any and every Christian'" (p. 7). For Gray, Lourenço is an early ancestor of black theology. Gray also examines the legacies of black Christians who emerged from historic Freetown. See 007, 009; 026, 042, 112. After an examination of Christianity and colonialism, Gray concludes his book with the chapter, "Christianity and Concepts of Evil in Sub-Saharan Africa." Here he reiterates his contention that Christianity and traditional religion are not nemeses. The notion that they are stems from an apotheosis of European cultures rather than the gospel. The gospel, like traditional religions, is concerned with the victory of life over death——to make an allusion to Engelbert Mveng (see 434-437). For Gray, there is a correspondence between the African preoccupation with modes of sacrifice——which negate the powers of evil——and Christ. According to Gray: "The message of the Cross and of the Resurrection are no more alien to Africa than any other part of the world."

042   Groves, Charles Pelam.   *The Planting of Christianity in Africa*. 4 vols. London: Lutterworth Press, 1948-1958.

Considered a classic in its field, Groves's work in four volumes is a detailed and comprehensive history of Christianity in Africa from the third to the twentieth centuries. The last volume is especially intriguing. It weaves the story of Christianity into the political ferment of the quest for independence. Here, Groves provides insight into the way in which theology is determined by socioeconomic factors which emerge from the matrix of political culture.

043   Haberland, E.   "Christian Ethiopia." In *The Middle Age of Africa History*, ed. by Roland Oliver, 7-12. New York: Oxford University Press, 1967.

Ethiopia's roots go back into the 4th Century and the Ethiopian Church is an enduring example of the longevity of African Christianity. Haberland highlights the historic, acculturative significance of the *Kebra Nagast*. He explains that the *Kebra Nagast* "is a collection of ancient oriental legends...tailored to suit the kingdom of Ethiopia and its dynasty" (p. 9). That is, the *Kebra Negast* is an *African* expression of Christianity by virtue of the preponderance of autochthonous values that dictate the meaning of Christianity in Ethiopia.

044   Hadjor, Kofi Buenor.   *On Transforming Africa: Discourse with Africa's Leaders*. New Jersey: Africa World Press, 1987.

Hadjor, a leading African journalist, tackles many of the problems with which the new guard is concerned——underdevelopment, exploitation of the peasants, corrupt leadership, African fascism, neocolonialism. He also reveals the significance of *Ghana: End of an Illusion*——see 038——and sings Fanon's praises. See 034-035. Hadjor writes that he "literally devoured 'Pitfalls of National Consciousness.'" See 034. Especially relevant to the problem of African theology is Hadjor's analysis of the African intellectual. He provides added insight into the alienation African theologians experience due to an intellectual and economic captivity to the West. Influenced by Antonio Gramsci's definition of "organic intellectual," Hadjor argues that the organic intellectual——who has opted for the underside—— develops "ideas that demystify the prevailing norms and values that obscure existing social relations." In that way, Hadjor implicitly critiques the old guard who claimed that liberation was irrelevant to African theology.

045 Hastings, Adrian. *Church and Mission in Modern Africa*. London: Burns & Oates, 1967.
Hastings provides valuable information regarding the relation of African Christianity to colonial and neocolonial realities. Here, he asserts that the future of the African Church rests with the elite. In subsequent works——see 046-047——he asserts that the future depends on the grassroots. One of his better insights, however, is his call for the declericalization of the historic church——a call echoed by new guard theologians. See 335.

046 Hastings, Adrian. *African Christianity*. New York: The Seabury press, 1976.
Hastings weaves together elements that heighten one's understanding of the relevant issues of African theology: the impact of the historic churches, the response of the independent churches and the socio-political background. Hastings's ability to illumine this matrix provides an invaluable introduction to the distinction between Christianity in Africa and African Christianity. *Christianity in Africa* signifies the spread of oppressive values that retard the development of the African continent. An *African Christianity* signifies a truly africanized faith that gives hope to the struggle for liberation. An African Christianity is revealed in the independent churches. See 008. "They have little of an explicit theology any more than has African traditional religion, but they have a praxis and a spirituality in which a theology is profoundly implicit. Their being is almost an irruption of African traditional religion integrally transmogrified by faith in Christ: the human situation is the same, the solution is different" (p. 54). Hastings's definition of African Christianity facilitates his critique of the theology of the old guard. For Hastings, the methodology of the old guard is too Eurocentric, not *African* at all. Also useful is Hastings's discussion of the distinction between the black liberation theology of South African and the old guard. He suggests that black South African theology may well be the most appropriate paradigm for theological reflection within the continent. The book concludes with a useful bibliographic essay.

047 Hastings, Adrian. *A History of African Christianity, 1950-1975*. New York: Cambridge University Press, 1979.
An indispensable source for those who wish to place African theology in recent historical framework. Hastings masterfully relates the historic churches, the independent churches, and the socio-political background to one another. Each chapter is divided into three categories: "Church and State"; "The Historic Churches"; and "Independence." "Church and State" sets the socioeconomic and political milieu, is edifying regarding the wider context of African theology, and informs those with interest in the historic and political problems of the continent. The sections focused on the "Historic Churches" provide valuable insight into the European missionaries and their African successors. The latter have tended to reproduce the alienation of European missiology. The sections focused on "Independence" offer valuable information on the genealogies of independent churches that are indispensable for an appreciation of the role of popular culture in African Christianity. See 046. Hastings concludes with the profound observation that as "the effective control of the Western churches declines, one has the strong impression that the model of historic Ethiopia increasingly prevails: village Christianity with very little superstructure had been present there all along together with much symbolic ritual now

making its way across the continent" (p. 274). See 043. Indeed, the creative new guard theologians are increasingly turning to the village in an effort to learn the meaning of a Christianity transformed by peasant values. See 336.

048 Hastings, Adrian. *African Catholicism: Essays in Discovery*. Philadelphia: Trinity Press International, 1989.

What is most pertinent is his discussion of African theology in Chapter 6. He notes the speciousness of the term "African theology," which——as I note in the introduction of this bibliography——can appear to be as sophistical as *European* theology. According to Hastings, though, African realities are such that the term itself is warranted for the moment. That is: "In its short-term contemporary situation, and as a short-term explicit reaction to, and escape from, the heavily European and white character not only of most missionary doctrine but of the whole mainstream of Christian theology in the recent past, it is appropriate as well as inevitable for Africans to pursue for a time an explicitly African or black theology" (p. 85). Nonetheless, Hastings appears to be uncomfortable with the specificity of black and African theologies——as if the conditions that gave rise to them were temporary. In that regard, he appears to have little use for the nationalist——i.e., Azanian——wing of black South African theology. See 565-568; 572-578. According to Hastings, in addition, black North American theology is "rather racialist." See 532-544. This unfair critique helps to explain why he renders the black theology of Mosala and Mofokeng invisible. See 565-568; 572-578. (One wonders how he views the theology of Jean-Marc Éla.) Nonetheless, Hastings discusses the special case of Archbishop Milingo——see 412——who constitutes for him a living paradigm of African Christianity.

049 Hodgkin, Thomas. *Nationalism in Colonial Africa*. New York: New York University Press, 1957.

Nationalism in Africa is considered to be a seminal study of African nationalism. Although dated, the text has enduring value as it identifies issues with which African theologians continue to wrestle. Particularly relevant are the chapters: "Prophets and Priests"; "Workers and Peasants"; and "Theories and Myths." Hodgkin holds——as does Mercy Oduyoye, see 458——that African Christianity has its own internal dynamism. He also asserts that the African independent churches——see 046——have political significance. That is, the hegemony of the independent churches is negating the cultural hegemony of Europe. *A fortiori*, one might say that insofar as a theology is *African*, it is political, for an African theology resists the export of European culture. Hodgkin's work has other implications for African theology. He argues that the elite often attempt to incorporate African customs, but in a bourgeois alienation from the peasants who embody the dynamism of culture. See 034-035. By implication, an African theology, if produced by an alienated elite, would reify the realities of the masses. According to Hodgkin, in addition, the nominal industrialization of the continent undermines the development of a radicalized proletariat. Still, Hodgkin notes that the workers, tied as they are to the matrix of peasant life, can extend the process of proletarianization and inject into traditional life a critical, if somewhat Western, orientation to political struggle. See 023-025.

050 Hofmeyr. J.W. "The Present Status of Church History in South Africa." In *African Church Historiography: An Ecumenical Perspective*, ed. by Ogbu Kalu, 28-38. Bern: Evangelische Arbeitsstelle Oekumene Schweiz, 1988.

Hofmeyr finds that "South African church historiography" is either superficial, glossing over the contradictions of a troubled nation, or too biased——told from the vantage point of *a* group. In order to overcome this chauvinistic situation, argues Hofmeyr, historians must be committed to scientific and academic standards, eschew ideology and acquiesce in the Word of God. One should compare Hofmeyr's argument with that of the black theologian, Jerry Mosala. See 572-578.

051 Idowu, E. Bolaji. "The Predicament of the Church in Africa." In *Christianity in Tropical Africa: Studies Presented and Discussed at the Seventh International African Seminar, University of Ghana, April, 1965*, ed. by C.G. Baëta, 417-440. London: Oxford University Press, 1968.

Idowu, one of the leading old guard theologians, notes the ferment over the place of the church in Africa. See 177-179; 256-257. He asserts that the relation of Eurocentric missiology to imperialism has caused nationalists to dismiss the church, though Idowu claims that the motives of certain missionaries were true to the gospel. He points out, in addition, that many of the missionaries of the 19th and early 20th centuries were black. Certain of these blacks were recaptives. (Recaptives were Africans who, in the 19th century, were liberated from slave ships in the coastal waters of West Africa by the British and American Navies. Resettled in contexts such as Sierra Leone and Liberia, recaptives associated Christianity with emancipation.) Black missionaries also promulgated a Christianity that later spread anglophone literacy, which strengthened African nationalism. See 006-007; 016-018; 027, 028-029; 042, 054, 057-058; 081-082. According to Idowu, white missionaries' historic attempt to plant Christianity by uprooting traditional culture led to the irruption of this culture in modified form in the independent churches. See 046. These churches deserve study and will perhaps be instructive in the quest for *African* hermeneutics.

052 Illif, John. *The African Poor: A History*. New York: Cambridge University Press, 1987.

Illif examines the precolonial, colonial and neocolonial contradictions that continue to produce the African poor. He proves that Africa, before European rule, was beset by massive poverty due to diseases, such as leprosy. Poverty was also a result of autochthonous racism, other bigotries, and unforeseen misfortune afflicting individuals.

053 Jackson, Robert, and Carl Rosberg. *Personal Rule in Black Africa: Prince, Autocrat, Prophet, Tyrant*. Berkeley: University of California Press, 1982.

Jackson and Rosberg reveal that the leaders who constitute authority in Africa command a vertical structure staffed by the elite. Insight into the machinations of the upper echelons of that structure sheds light on the context of the old guard. *Personal Rule in Black Africa* also reveals why the new guard is criticizing the inadequate leadership misleading the continent. Like certain of the new guard, Jackson and Rosberg claim that "most of Africa's rulers——soldiers and civilians alike——adopted practices of authoritarianism, with the consequence that national politics withered and a world of largely private power and influence emerged" (p. 2). Like Jean-Marc Éla, Jackson and Rosberg note that politics resembled an archaic feudalism in which a corrupt oligarchy "and a wider circle of elites...could only tenuously and unofficially represent the broader interest of social groups and classes" (p. 2). See 335-341. The chapter entitled "Tyrants and Abusive Rule" is of particular relevance to African theology. Theologians such as Éla and Boulaga are very critical of tyranny and decry the gross deterioration of human rights in Africa. Although many of these tyrants have fallen——Amin, Marcias, Bokassa——geopolitical tensions, neocolonialism and the attendant problems of underdevelopment make the continent vulnerable to continual tyranny.

054 Jacobs, Sylvia. "The Historical Role of Afro-Americans in American Missionary Efforts in Africa." In *Black Americans and the Missionary Movement in Africa*, ed. by Sylvia Jacobs, 5-30. Westport: Greenwood Press, 1982.

According to Jacobs, "The work of Protestant missionary societies in Africa began in 1737 when George Schmidt, of the Church of the United Brethren...went to South Africa as the first Protestant missionary" (p. 5). Jacobs then focuses on African-American missionaries, such as Lott Carey, Collin Teague and Daniel Coker, who pioneered the colonization of Liberia. See 016-018; 028-029; 057, 094, 126. Jacobs notes the crippling neurosis that afflicted African-American missionaries. See 028-029; 094, 126. She reveals that Africans, from their origins as Americans, have been ambivalent toward Africa. While they conceded their African heritage, they saw Africa as a context of benightedness. Nonetheless, she examines the fact that African-Americans were recalled from Africa by the white-controlled boards that sponsored them. Those whites feared that the rising black nationalism of the New World would inspire political struggle in Africa——which it did. Her essay gives further evidence of African-Americans' contribution to the development of Christianity in Africa and to African theology.

055   James, C.L.R.   "Colonialism and National Liberation in Africa: The Gold Coast Revolution." In *National Liberation in the Third World*, ed. by Norman Miller and Roderick Aya, 102-136. New York: The Free Press, 1971.
A succinct analysis of the movement toward "independence" in the Gold Coast (now Ghana). See 001, 021, 096-101. James illumines the problems that obstructed the Ghanian peoples' independence from Britain as well as the problems of "independence." For James, colonialism is legitimated through myths, as is resistance to colonialism. He notes that the African elite has legitimated its right to independence in terms of the Eurocentric myths that have oppressed them. See 023-025; 034-035, 120. The remedy to this blind alley, claims James, rests with the masses, who, far from the upper echelons in which European values are disseminated, carry the truly liberating myths. James's essay provides insight into the agenda of both the old and new guards.

056   James, C.L.R.   *Nkrumah and the Gold Coast Revolution*. Westport: Lawrence Hill and Company, 1977.
James, a leading intellectual of the African people and a socialist, provides insight into Nkrumah and his role in the Ghanaian struggle against imperialism. James's portrait of Nkrumah not flattering. See 096-101. Like Fitch——see 038——James argues that Nkrumah went wrong in alienating himself from the masses to whom he had been viscerally connected. Pushing too hard for development in accordance with Western models, Nkrumah, argues James, became too autocratic and thus contributed to the abortion of democracy and socialism in Ghana. See 053. According to James, Nkrumah's demise reveals that Africa "will go crashing from precipice to precipice unless the plans for economic development are part of a deep philosophical concept of what the mass of the African people need. That is where Nkrumah failed" (p. 188-188). See 001. *Nkrumah and the Gold Coast Revolution* is yet another source that facilitates critique of the old guard's captivity to the myth of independence.

057   July, Robert.   *The Origins of Modern African Thought*. New York: Frederick Praeger, 1967.
This book contains useful biographical information on ancestors of African theology, such as Edward Blyden (see 016-018), James Johnson (see 007) and Bishop Crowther (See 109). July also provides insight into the cultural nationalism that influenced the emergence of African theology. Particularly enlightening is July's discussion of the way in which much of African thought is plagued by a crippling contradiction——the push for independence is couched in Eurocentric terms and molded by Eurocentric values. Indeed, July provides insight into an epistemological problem characteristic of the work of the old guard.

058 July, Robert. *A History of the African People*. New York: Charles Scribner's Sons, 1980.

Students of African theology would do well to read a general history of Africa in order to get a sense of the vast space in which African theology is situated and the way in which that space and its people have been afflicted over time. See 030-032. July's volume is quite useful to this extent. Chapter 12 is especially pertinent to African theology. Here July notes the way in which Christianity took root in Africa due to the abolitionist movement——largely British——which led to the establishment of Freetown, Sierra Leone, a seminal context for the appreciation of historical roots of African theology. July discusses persons such as Henry Venn, Granville Sharp and Bishop Crowther. See 042, 109, 112.

059 Kalilombe, Patrick A. "The Presence of the Church in Africa." In *The Emergent Gospel: Theology from the Developing World. Papers from the Ecumenical Dialogue of Third World Theologians, Dar es Salaam, August 5-12*, ed. by Sergio Torres and Virginia Fabella, 22-30. London: Geoffrey Chapman, 1978.

This seminal volume contains the papers delivered at the ecumenical dialogue of Third World theologians at Dar es Salaam, Tanzania, August 5-12, 1976. See 089, 324, 352, 422, 447, 518, 529. The dialogue marks a critical moment in the establishment of EATWOT and marks the visibility of the new guard. According to Kalilombe——see 371-372——the African theologian's role is not clear until he/she has analyzed the role the church plays in Africa. He confines his analysis to the Roman Catholic Church in Malawi——his country. According to Kalilombe, this church was somewhat xenophobic as a result of its deprivileged position in the wake of the Enlightenment. It has tended to be afraid of diversity and to demand strict conformity to Vatican polity. Vatican II, however, modified that orientation in opening the church to diversity and inviting Third World Christians to make Christianity their own. According to Kalilombe, the sudden change in direction appeared somewhat disingenuous to the Malawian people. They, he asserts, wish to minimize the control of the Vatican in order to assume control of their ecclesial future. See 335, 340.

060 Kalu, Ogbu U. *Divided People of God: Church Union Movement in Nigeria: 1867-1966*. New York: NOK Publishers, 1978.

Kalu analyzes European missionaries' struggle to achieve ecumenicity in Nigeria and the way in which that struggle was carried out in spite of African realities. According to Kalu, moreover, the push for union dissimulated the desires for denominational hegemony. The africanization of the mission churches tended to reproduce that problem. Denominational tensions were carried into the postcolonial context and exacerbated by the ethnic and political enmity that exploded into civil war in 1966. Kalu's discussion of African theologians' attempt to construct ecclesiologies in relation to African traditional religion is particularly relevant. Kalu observes that these theologians did not study African traditional religion in its autonomous integrity, but in terms of their own Christian agenda. See 008, 136, 158, 162, 221, 223, 239, 278. Thus Kalu writes: "The recent acclaim of African theology is pregnant with confusion. Many are mistaking the study of [African traditional religion] as doing African theology" (p. 44). For Kalu, the two religions must be kept apart so that the incorporation of traditional idioms into Christian discourse is done critically and with precision.

061 Kalu, Ogbu U. "Church Unity and Religious Change." In *Christianity in Independent Africa*, ed. by Edward Fasholé-Luke, Richard Gray, Adrian Hastings and Godwin Tasie, 164-175. Bloomington: Indiana University Press, 1978.

Kalu reveals that church unity was a missionary strategy, the goals of which were to survive the natural harshness of the Continent——by huddling together——in order to win souls to Christ. See 061. Church unity was only ostensible, however, as nationalistic rivalries among denominations boiled just beneath the surface. Kalu reveals that Africans' response to church unity was complex. Many saw church unity as a euphemism for the continuum of the Berlin Conference. Others had so internalized denominationalism that they resisted even the pretense to ecumenism. On yet another level, reveals Kalu, missionaries of African descent argued that Christianity and European values were identical. Ecumenism from that perspective was but a stepping stone to europeanization. Kalu cites Alexander Crummell as an example of that view. See 028-029. Kalu also reveals that others saw "church union movement as an indigenization project (with all the wooly conceptions of indigenization)." (Indigenization involves the tension between acculturation and inculturation. See 051.) In order to explore the problem of church union in Africa with specificity, Kalu focuses on the neocolonial context of Nigeria——what he calls the Nigerian *débâcle*. Beneath preparations for the feting of Nigerian ecumenism lay acute interdenominational strife. This problem was but a microcosm of the larger reality that led to civil war. Kalu asserts that the "remarkable thing is that the situation in Nigeria is very typical of the rest of Africa" (p. 172). He notes that an exception here is Zaïre, where "Mobutuism," i.e., *authenticité*——see 302, 312, 367-368, 387——is brought to bear on ecclesial formations for the sake of union. Here, though, notes Kalu, quoting Milton, "we are faced——to put it mildly——with the dilemma of "the 'bounds of either sword.'" For Kalu, the awesome misery of the African poor should define the imperative for ecumenism. See 052, 128, 334-341.

062   Kalu, Ogbu U. "Church Presence in Africa: A Historical Analysis of the Evangelization Process." In *African Theology en Route*, ed. by Kofi Appiah-Kubi and Sergio Torres, 13-23. Maryknoll, N.Y.: Orbis Books, 1979

Kalu's essay was one of the papers delivered at the Pan-African Conference of Third World Theologians, Accra, Ghana, 1977. See 002, 003. In contrast to Hofmeyr——see 050——Kalu argues that historiography is dictated by ideology. If, then, one dimension of church history in Africa is Eurocentric, another, asserts Kalu, is Afrocentric——"what Africans thought about what was going on and how they responded" (p. 14). For Kalu, the history of African Christianity is comprehensive when it is interpreted in terms of popular culture——i.e., in terms of elements of African traditional religion. Indeed, Kalu, in that connection, succinctly notes the tension between acculturation and inculturation. According to Kalu: "Christianity must be traditionalized in African culture so that the dead wood in both will be destroyed and a new form can emerge" (p. 21).

063   Kalu, Ogbu U. "African Church Historiography: An Ecumenical Perspective." In *African Church Historiography: An Ecumenical Perspective*, ed. by Ogbu Kalu, 9-27. Bern: Evangelische Arbeitsstelle Oekumene Schweiz, 1988.

According to Kalu, church history is always written from an ideological perspective. "*Una Sancta*?," he writes. "It cannot be so when the ecclesiological map is like the shell of a tortoise!" For Kalu, much of African church historiography has serviced imperialism. The revisionists, mostly African nationalists, have attempted to correct that Eurocentric bias. Even they, however, have not overcome a certain Eurocentrism. See 055, 120. "The irony in nationalist historiography," writes Kalu, is that while condemning missionaries, the authors fail to see that their own people, the Africans, were the real agents who spread Christianity. Many of these agents would have worn Frantz Fanon's label, 'Black Skin White Mask' with much pride" (p. 16). See 034-035, 081-082, 094, 109, 112, 126-127. In that regard, Kalu notes the role of the African-

American, Alexander Crummell. See 028-029. Kalu argues that novelists and sociologists have been more useful than historians and theologians in rendering the true face of Africa. One of the novelists he notes is Chinua Achebe, specifically his *Things Fall Apart* and *Arrow of God*. See 132-133. In a way not unlike Sofola——see 494——Kalu argues that novelists are more knowledgeable of the nuances of traditional society. Novelists, then, best provide *African* perspectives on church history in Africa. According to Kalu, such history "is *not* the story of the role of white missionaries in cross-cultural mission." See 061. Rather, argues Kalu, such history is the account of African consciousness, such as that found in the African independent churches——see 008——particularly the Aladura. See 137, 183, 225, 227, 228, 234, 265-266, 398. *A fortiori*, church history in Africa, for Kalu, must be grounded in African traditional religions——not as prolegomena, but as integral elements of African Christianity.

064 Kamuyu-wa-Kang'ethe. "The Suppression of African Patriotism and Nationalism by the Mission Churches 1900-1950." In *African Church Historiography: An Ecumenical Perspective*, ed. by Ogbu Kalu, 157-179. Bern: Evangelische Arbeitsstelle Oekumene Schweiz, 1988.

With a focus on the Agikuyu people, the author seeks to substantiate his claim that the history of the mission church in Kenya is but the tragic tale of white racist enmity toward the liberation struggle of African people. The Agikuyu people concretely exemplify how African values can be a powerful means of resistance. According to Kamuyu-wa-Kang'ethe, Protestant mission is rooted in the legacies of John Wesley, Martin Luther and John Calvin. With respect to Luther, Kamuyu-wa-Kang'ethe focuses on the notion of divine authority and the civil authority that is its sword. Here civil authority restrains an essentially evil world through the civic use of the Law. For Kamuyu-wa-Kang'ethe, this Lutheran theology is a basic feature of Protestant mission. For the missionaries, the Africans, devoted as they were to "paganism"——i.e., the "evil" practice of clitoridectomy——disclosed the depth of the wickedness of humankind, *coram mundo*. According to Kamuyu-wa-Kang'ethe, however, the missionaries were not interested in the liberation of African women, but in the subjugation of African people. Female circumcision was used as a foil to legitimize the entrenchment of colonial rule. The Africans, though, also used the issue of circumcision as a foil. See 188-190. The issue not only gave impetus to cultural nationalism, but to the rise of independent churches as well. See 008. Of particular importance in that regard is the Karing'a group. According to Kamuyu-wa-Kang'ethe, "the Karing'a group can be considered a good case study of how churches in Africa can develop a new theology and forms of worship which would encompass aspects of African understanding of God, man, and the universe" (p. 175).

065 Karefa-Smart, John and Rena. *The Halting Kingdom: Christianity and the African Revolution*. New York: Friendship Press, 1959.

The Karefa-Smarts discuss: the significance of traditional culture; the relationship between Africa and the rest of the world; and the movements toward "independence." According to the Karefa-Smarts, African traditional culture is characterized by the close relationship between the visible and the invisible realms——a connection which accentuates community rather than individualism. They explore Africa's encounter with the world in terms of the histories of slavery and colonialism, which entail significant aspects of the annals of Christianity and Islam. With a focus on Ghana, the Karefa-Smarts discuss the rise of African nationalism——the movement towards "independence." See 001, 038, 054-055, 096-101. According to John and Karefa-Smart, the meaning of ecumenism must be expanded so that it includes the process of inculturation. See 061. They write: "The gospel must be announced in an African idiom if it is to be heard and taken to heart by Africans in their need of salvation" (p. 76). What is more, the authors argue that if "the church does not take root in African soil now, it will either grow into a deformed or dwarfed representation of what God intended it to be; or, worse, it will atrophy and die" (p. 79). The Karefa-Smarts also address the political turmoil of an Africa crossing the threshold between olden and neocolonialism. They note that African Christians are called "to come together at the cross, so that, as they search out solutions to their personal and social needs, they may, at the same time, be blessed with the insight, the spiritual resources, and the unfailing power that are required for full Christian obedience in a revolutionary situation" (p. 80).

066 Kaunda, Kenneth. "The Challenge of Our Stewardship in Africa". In *The Struggle Continues: Lusaka 1974, 65-67*. Nairobi: All Africa Conference of Churches, 1975.

    Kaunda exemplifies that African heads of state are involved in the struggle to define the meaning of Christianity in Africa. Here, Kaunda, the son of African missionaries and the president of Zambia——see 027——addresses the Third Assembly of the All Africa Conference of Churches. See 002, 316. He notes the political unrest of the period of "independence" and espouses a position not unlike that of Luther's notion of the "two kingdoms": "the Church is the custodian of moral supremacy in the State while Government is the custodian of justice" (Kaunda 170). See 064. He also discusses africanization, *qua* Zambianization, which, he explains, is not a racist praxis, but one that may make a contribution to world culture. Kaunda discusses world culture in terms of his definition of humanism——an orientation based on both Gandhi's definition of *satyagraha*, and Christian and socialist principles. See 068.

067 Kaunda, Kenneth. "The Challenge of Our Stewardship in Africa". In *Mission Trends No. 3: Third World Theologies. Asian, African and Latin American Contributions to a Radical, Theological Realignment in the Church*, ed. by Gerald Anderson and Thomas Stransky, 169-175. New York: Paulist Press; Grand Rapids: Wm. B. Eerdmans, 1976.

    See 066.

068 Kaunda, Kenneth. "Spirituality and World Community." In *African Christian Spirituality*, ed. by Aylward Shorter, 117-125. Maryknoll, N.Y.: Orbis Books, 1978.

    Here Kaunda explores his humanist philosophy, arguing that there is only one race——the human race. See 066. He cites South Africa as a context where humanism is not practiced. "Humanism," writes Kaunda, "harnesses the power of historical destiny, whilst *apartheid* is fighting against history, and it is a matter of record that those nations which have attempted to resist history have been swept aside." Kaunda asserts that humanism is a religious orientation that is catholic as it rings true to the best insights of the world's religions. For Kaunda, religion is edifying to the extent that it proclaims the dignity of humankind. He claims that respect of human rights is mandated by God, whose image human beings bear. See 362, 504.

069 Kaunda, Kenneth. "The Religious Phenomena of African-ness." In *African Christian Spirituality*, ed. by Aylward Shorter, 45-50. Maryknoll, N.Y.: Orbis Books, 1978.

    Africanness, argues Kaunda, is a spirituality deeply rooted in the African memory of "birth and death, harvest and famine, ancestors and the unborn" (p. 45). It is the cultivation of that memory, asserts Kaunda, that will produce *African* theology. See 191. Kaunda also recounts the biblical fundamentalism of his parents, which he finds edifying, though limited. As President of Zambia, he favors religious tolerance, which he defines in terms of Zambian Humanism. See 066.

070 Kaunda, Kenneth. *Kaunda on Violence*. Edited by Colin Morris. London: Sphere Books Limited, 1982.

Kaunda defines his African humanism——see 068——which is essential to his commitment to non-violence and revelatory of his Christian values. Yet Kaunda, having given himself over to hard social analysis regarding the liberation struggles of Zimbabwe, felt compelled to support the armed struggle there. Revealing a sobriety not unlike that of the new guard, Kaunda writes:

> Passive resistance may strengthen an oppressive authority if it diverts the people's righteous anger into easily controlled channels. On the other hand directed armed struggle, besides costing many lives, may set back the cause a long way by giving government the excuse to rid itself of its most dangerous opponents. According to *Ecclesiastes, to everything there is a season, and so it with resistance.* I believe there is a time to use the methods of passive resistance and a time to use those of armed struggle. And...discussion can only move forward if my critics allow that this is at least a tenable position which should be subjected to keen analysis rather than head shaking (p. 28-29).

Kaunda, a celebrated symbol of reconciliation, argues that the harshness of African realties may make it necessary to resort to violence——themes echoed by Frantz Fanon and new guard theologians such as Éla. See 034-035; 340.

071 Lamb, David. *The Africans.* New York: Random House, 1982.

Lamb offers recent statistics that reveal the decay of the African continent. He also gives specific examples of the fascism of despots such as Amin, Bokassa, Biyogo, Mobutu. See 053. Despite the contentions of the old guard, the text shows clearly that the struggle for liberation is very much relevant to so-called independent Africa. South Africa is not the only appropriate context for theologies of liberation. See 339, 439. One gets the impression, however, that Lamb is a bit biased toward the West and to capitalism. Useful, though, is Lamb's convincing discussion of the racist behavior of the Soviets in Africa.

072 Lee, Franz. "Dependency and Revolutionary Theory in the African Situation." In *Political Science in Africa: A Critical Review*, ed. by Yolamu Barongo, 178-188. London: Zed Press, 1983.

Although Lee's essay is pertinent to social analysis in African theology, he makes sustained reference to contradictions in Latin America. See 314-315. Heuristically, he allows one to see that Third World theologians oppose the same hegemonic blocs——i.e., capitalist imperialism or "neo-Stalinism." According to Lee, the cutting edge of theories resistant to imperialism is emancipatory praxis——the "necessity of empirical work to back theoretical questions." Without the appropriate revolutionary activism, revolutionary theories are useless abstractions, argues Lee. While "prolet-aryanism"——Eurocentric socialism——must be countered in terms of African realities, those realities must be transformed in revolutionary praxis, asserts Lee. Lee concludes his essay with the assertion that African underdevelopment is inextricable from the Western world's need for oil. *A fortiori*, he implies that social analysis in African theology must focus on contexts such as Nigeria and Angola. See 061, 319. Lee's essay heightens one's appreciation of the theology of the new guard, who also focus on the need for an *African* praxis. See 336-341, 437-439.

073 Lemarchand, René. "Patrice Lumumba." In *African Political Thought: Lumumba, Nkrumah and Toure*, ed. by W.A.E. Skurnik, 13-64. Denver: University of Denver, 1968.

Lemarchand's interpretation of Lumumba is less inspiring than that of the author of *Patrice Lumumba.* See 077. Lemarchand gives little attention to Machiavellian imperialism and the peoples' resistance to it in the form of their allegiance to Lumumba. The essay, however, discusses the traditional matrix from which Lumumba was spun.

Lemarchand explores the traditional values of the Batela to whom Lumumba was born, noting their history of resistance to Belgium. Given the theory and practice of Cabral, and the work of the theologian Jean-Marc Éla, one wonders whether Lumumba embodied values that were revolutionary precisely because they were contiguous with tradition. See 023-025; 338, 340. Although Lumumba was not "tribal," as were Tshombe and Kassavubu, he was clearly the dominant symbol of the national culture that was undermined by the West. See 098.

074 Linden, Ian. "The Roman Catholic Church in Social Crisis: The Case of Rwanda." In *Christianity in Independent Africa*, ed. by Edward Fasholé-Luke, Richard Gray, Adrian Hastings and Godwin Tasie, 242-254. Bloomington: Indiana University Press, 1978.

Linden examines the racist enmity between the Bantu Hutu and the "Hamitic" Tutsi——who were like feudal lords to the Hutu——and reveals the complicity of the Roman Catholic Church in the savage, civil war that undermined the country. (Linden also notes the shameful conflicts of race and class in Burundi——a context very much like Belgian Rwanda. Burundi bears the heroic legacy of Michel Kayoya. See 375-376.) In regard to that complicity, Linden refers to the perspective of Alexis Kagame, a Rwandian who has made a contribution to African theology. See 187, 369. Kagame has criticized the church for supporting Tutsi hegemony by way of *politicisme*. According to Kagame *politicisme* is a system that seeks to cloak its real intentions to enforce injustice——i.e., *veut en réalité asseoir des bases solides à l'emprise dominatrice d'un corps culturel sur l'esprit des autochtonnes* (p. 252). Part of this hegemonic, cultural domination has been carried out by the church; indeed, the africanization of the church has been a means of indirect rule. For Linden——and the new guard undoubtedly agrees with him——Rwanda is a paradigm of the decay of the continent since "independence."

075 Lodge, Tom. *Black Politics in South Africa Since 1945*. New York: 1984.

A useful text, which like Gerhart's——see 039——focuses on black resistance and offers insight into the political sensibilities of black South African theologians. Particularly edifying are Lodge's analyses of the role of the gangs and women in black politics.

076 Long, Norman. "Religion and Socio-Economic Action among the Serenje-Lala of Zambia." In *Christianity in Tropical Africa: Studies Presented and Discussed at the Seventh International African Seminar, University of Ghana, April, 1965*, ed. by C.G. Baëta, 396-416. London: Oxford University Press, 1968.

Long examines the phenomenon of African Christianity in Zambia, with a focus on the Watch Tower movement (Jehovah Witnesses). See 027. Long argues that the Watch Tower movement, given its apocalyptic focus, has socioeconomic ramifications. Indeed, church doctrine, argues Long, is always inextricable from social realities and constitutes, therefore, a religious ethic. For Long, "the ethic of a particular religion or domination may vary according to the economic circumstances of the group, though the doctrine remains essentially the same" (p. 409). His essay exemplifies the implications of social analysis since he indicates ways in which theology is modified by and modifies social realities.

077 Lonsdale, John, with Stanley Booth-Clibborn and Andrew Hake. "The Emerging pattern of Church and State co-operation in Kenya." In *Christianity in Independent Africa*, ed. by Edward Fasholé-Luke, Richard Gray, Adrian Hastings and Godwin Tasie, 267-284. Bloomington: Indiana University Press, 1978.

Lonsdale analyzes the role denominationalism plays in ideological conflict in Kenya. See 061. He writes that Protestants have been either conservative evangelicals or modernists (liberals). Theologically, the two differed in christology. The former held to a view of the incarnation in which the divinity of the God-man is accentuated. The latter (the modernists), tended to be more adoptionist in orientation. Whereas the evangelicals tended to emphasize faith and individual piety, the liberals tended to emphasize the ethical implications of a social gospel (crypto-Pelagianism). Lonsdale critiques the view that the liberals were more amenable to Kenyan nationalism. Both "Christianities" tended to legitimate colonial rule. In that regard, it was the conservative evangelicals who sharpened the contradictions that led to nationalism. Whereas, he argues, the liberals tended to champion inculturation——based on the view that Eurocentric Christianity and the political structure that had erected it would uproot traditional religion——the conservatives were intolerant of traditional religion and thus the policy of indirect rule that manipulated and maintained traditional structures. According to Lonsdale, African resistance to the conservatives gave rise to the great Revival, *Bankole*, and thus the independent churches——phenomena related to the masses who constituted the force of Mau-Mau and other modes of resistance. The liberals, on the other hand, patronized, with some exceptions, the westernized, educated elite. See 034-035. Lonsdale, reveals, moreover, that a hot-bed of progressive political thought, in the post-independence period, was St. Paul's United Theological College at Lamer, which he places in the evangelical camp. Lonsdale also reveals that neocolonialism is maintained through the National Christian Council of Kenya (NCCK). Liberal in orientation, it had been a factor in Kenyan nationalism. Now, though, it is a potent power in the maintenance of neocolonial relations.

078 *Lumumba.* London: Panaf, 1978.

The anonymous author (Nkrumah?), weaves an engrossing tale in which bourgeois capital emerges victorious to the detriment of the peasants and lumpenized proletariat. The tragic tale of Patrice Lumumba, the celebrated Congolese revolutionary, is (as a metonym) the horrifying record of the masses, who are being consumed by the politics of greed and corruption. See 107, 437. Removed from power and assassinated by draconian forces, his name, like Nkrumah's, Cabral's and Biko's, is synonymous with progressive political thought on the Continent. See 096-101; 023-025; 013-015. Lumumba, *mutandis mutatis*, exemplifies Cabral's definition of a petty bourgeois politician who commits "class suicide." See 025, 035. Indeed, no one concerned about the underdevelopment of Africa can afford to ignore the legacy of Lumumba and the matrix of intrigue forming the Congo crisis of 1960-61. What is more, the Belgian Congo (now Zaire) is a critical context for understanding issues related to liberation and africanization. See 302, 367-368; 387. The Congo has produced theologians such as Vincent Mulago who was influenced by Placid Tempels. See 415-421, 261-262.

079 Lumumba, Patrice. *Congo, My Country.* Translated by Colin Legum. New York: Praeger, 1962.

Here Lumumba reveals his early role as a reformer and loyal devotee of Belgium. As one source explains, Lumumba wrote this text "in 1965-57, while in Stanleyville, and in it one can see the same kind of thinking as that of the...liberal bourgeoisie nurtured by the colonial power and operating within the ranks of Congolese nationalist." Here, then, one may examine a genre not unlike that of the old guard. Pertinent to the new guard, however, is Lumumba's very progressive analysis of women's oppression. See 452-459.

080 Lumumba, Patrice. "A Rejection of European Rule with a Demand for Independence." In *The Africa Reader: Independent Africa*, ed. by Wilfred Cartey and Martin Kilson, 87-89. New York: Vintage Books, 1970.

This brief essay, from *La pensée politique de Patrice Lumumba*, indicates the Pan-African and anti-imperial trajectory of Lumumba's thought. Fundamental to the piece is

Lumumba's rhetorical reliance on the notion of African personality——a notion found in the work of African theologians. See 007.

081 Lynch. Hollis. *Edward Wilmot Blyden. Pan-Negro Patriot*. New York: Oxford University Press, 1970.
This is perhaps the definitive biography of Edward Blyden, whose ideas anticipated much of what is involved in African theology. See 016-018.

082 Lynch, Hollis. *Black Spokesman: Selected Published Writings of Edward Wilmot Blyden*. London: Frank Cass and Company, 1971.
A compilation of many of Blyden's seminal writings. See 081.

083 Magubane, Bernard. *The Political Economy of Race and Class in South Africa*. New York: Monthly Review Press, 1979.
Magubane's work is a historical analysis of South Africa from a Marxist perspective. He discusses the roles of the African National Congress, the Pan-Africanist Congress and the South African Communist party in a way that facilitates an understanding of the radical values of many black theologians today, such as Jerry Mosala. See 572-578.

084 Magubane, Bernard. "Imperialism and the Making of the South African Working Class." *Contemporary Marxism* 6 (Spring 1984): 19-56.
According to Magubane: "A materialist theory of history teaches that only during a period of impending revolution does the class struggle follow the lines dictated by the relations of production" (p. 53). His analysis complements the theology of Jerry Mosala, who focuses on the contradictions of labor relations and the role of the workers in forwarding the revolution in South Africa. See 572-578.

085 Mandela, Nelson. *The Struggle is My Life*. New York: Pathfinder Press, 1986.
Providing an overview of the developments of the African National Congress from the 1940s to the 1980s, this volume contains the political thought of Nelson Mandela, the celebrated hero of the black struggle for liberation in South Africa. See 012. Because Mandela remains a leading theoretician of the struggle against racial and economic injustices, and has influenced the character of social analysis in black South African theology, *The Struggle is My Life* helps set the socioeconomic context for the study of black theology.

086 Mandela, Winnie. *Part of My Soul Went with Him*. New York: Norton, 1985.
Here Winnie Mandela, the wife of Nelson Mandela, narrates her story——the recollections of one once married to the black nation's foremost freedom fighter. See 012, 085. Particularly useful is Mrs. Mandela's report of the brutality she suffered while detained in South Africa. One gets from her accounts insight into the heinousness of apartheid——insights that help one appreciate the revolutionary values of black South African theologians. See 565-568. Also quite useful is the appendix; it contains the Preamble of the *Freedom Charter*——the document of the ANC, and other non-racial organizations——which is emblematic of the vision of a non-racial South Africa. Indeed, certain black theologians, like Alan Boesak, uphold the Freedom Charter. See 517-520.

087 Markwell, Mateiv. "Harry Sawyerr's Patron (Bishop T.S. Johnson)." In *New Testament Christianity for Africa and the World: Essays in Honor of Harry Sawyerr*, ed. by Mark Glasswell and Edward W. Fasholé-Luke, 179-197. London: SPCK, 1974.
Markwell reveals that the late Harry Sawyerr was a grandson of Bishop T.S. Johnson (1873-1955), a contemporary of Crowther and Holy Johnson. (On Sawyerr, see

241-243; 474-478; on Crowther and Johnson, see 007, 109.) Like Crowther, Johnson's grandparent was a recaptive who associated christianization with liberation. See 051. Johnson believed that Africans could amplify the universality of the gospel by way of values gleaned from African culture.

088 Martin, David, and Phyllis Johnson. *The Struggle for Zimbabwe*. Foreword by Robert Mugabe. New York: Monthly Review Press, 1981.

The Struggle for Zimbabwe provides insight into the study of African theology within the matrix of Southern Africa. The text not only puts the African theology of that region into recent historical perspective, but also defines issues pertinent to the study of the emergent liberation theology of Zimbabwe. See 295, 430, 583. The book is an account of the revolutionary situation of the Second War, i.e., the second *Chimurenga*, 1972-1980. *A fortiori*, *The Struggle for Zimbabwe* indicates that a liberating theology——free to tackle the problems of inculturation *and* economic development——is facilitated by armed struggle. See 070, 089.

089 Masanja, Patrick. "Neocolonialism and Revolution in Africa." In *The Emergent Gospel: Theology from the Developing World. Papers from the Ecumenical Dialogue of Third World Theologians, Dar es Salaam, August 5-12, 1976*, ed. by Sergio Torres and Virginia Fabella, 9-20. London: Geoffrey Chapman, 1978.

Masanja argues that "imperialism has discarded the outmoded formula of 'direct occupation and colonization'" in favor of neocolonialism. Independence is only ostensible as the economic and social structures of expropriation, manned by the West, continue to consume African resources. See 004. With reference to the thought of Cabral——see 023-025——Masanja argues that, whereas most of Black Africa has entered the neocolonial era relatively peacefully (by way of devolution rather than revolution), Zimbabwe and Guinea-Bissau have had to employ armed struggle to oust the Portuguese and the whites of Southern Rhodesia. (On devolution, see 124.) The struggle continues within the context of the settler regime of South Africa. Masanja, in addition, provides insight into the relation of social and religio-cultural analyses. He argues that the ruling class tends to legitimate itself culturally through propaganda and the agglutination of capital. When the oppressed contradict those self-serving values, they do so through the celebration of their own culture. For Masanja, the critical question——that African theologians must answer——is whether theology reveals an option for the poor or an alliance with the bourgeoisie. His question illumines the distinction between the old and new guards.

090 Mathabane, Mark. *Kaffir Boy*. New York: Plume, 1986.

It is difficult to appreciate the tremendous injustice of apartheid without an immersion in the South African context. Graphic, brutally revelatory——heart-breaking——Mathabane's book is one of the best substitutes for a "real-life" immersion experience. Mathabane's autobiography is a searing and gripping account of the immense suffering and pain common to the majority of "Bantu" youth who grow up black and poor in the squalor and deprivation produced by the apartheid regime. See 128. This *Kaffir Boy* illumines the contemporary South African situation, including edifying accounts of the Soweto rebellions of 1976 and the subsequent murder of Steve Biko. See 013-015. What is more, the book provides indispensable insight into Takatso Mofokeng's re-definition of the meaning of the Cross in South African theology. See 565.

091 Mazrui, Ali. *The Africans: A Triple Heritage*. Boston: Little, Brown and Company, 1986.

Mazrui offers an analysis of postcolonial Africa from an Afrocentric perspective. Throughout the text, Mazrui reveals the interrelation and the tensions among the Western, traditional and Islamic dimensions of contemporary Africa. So the text is useful for getting a picture of the present affairs of Africa and is to that extent useful for study of African theology. Indeed, Mazrui discusses the liberation theology found in South Africa. He asserts that liberation theology may help Africa find its way despite the obstacles hurled in its path by the hostile West.

092 M'buyinga, Elena. *Pan-Africanism or Neocolonialism: The Bankruptcy of the OAU.* London: Zed Press, 1982.

African theology is a Pan-African discourse and often signifies the alleged fact that Africa has been liberated from colonialism. As M'buyinga shows, however, Pan-African rhetoric may dissimulate dependence upon the West. According to M'buyinga, Nkrumah's theory that the Organization of African Unity (OAU) would be a fortress against the "balkanization" of the African people was only a dream. See 096. Indeed, the OAU——tragically——has been the instrument of what M'buyinga calls "neocolonialist imperialism." See 437. Counter-revolutionary forces have successfully prevented the alliance of *African* socialist forces captive to neither the West nor the now defunct Soviets. *Pan-Africanism or Neocolonialism* deepens an understanding of the internal and external contradictions which influence the orientation of African theologians. See 072, 437.

093 Morel, E.D. *Red Rubber.* New York: Negro Universities Press, 1969.

Red Rubber provides a disturbingly graphic narration of the horrors of olden colonialism. Its relevance to African theology is heightened by the fact that the text sets the prehistory——so to speak——of Zaire, a context indispensable for an understanding of the political and religio-cultural issues explored in the work of the new guard. See 061, 073, 078-080; 098, 107, 302, 313, 367-368. Specifically, Morel exposes the cruelty of King Leopold of Belgium. He asks: "Did King Leopold know that the concomitants to the enormous revenues he [drew] from the labour of the Congo races were the misery, degradation, enslavement and partial extermination of those people?" (See p. 157.) For Morel, the answer is——yes. What is more, Morel provides the reader with photographs of Congolese whose limbs had been amputated for not producing their quota of rubber.

094 Moses, Wilson. *Alexander Crummell: A Study of Civilization and Discontent.* New York: Oxford University Press, 1989.

Moses offers a penetrating study of Alexander Crummell——a tragic, supercilious figure integral to the history of Christianity in Africa. See 028-029; 063.

095 Neuberger, Benjamin. "A Comparative Analysis of Pan-Africanism." In *African Philosophy: An Introduction*, ed. by Richard A. Davis, 245-263. Lanham: University Press of America, 1984.

Neuberger examines the Pan-African ideology of Nkrumah. See 096-101. Although Nkrumah's vision of a United States of Africa exists in thought only, the theory itself, *mutandis mutatis*, would prevent the spread of neocolonialism. See 092. Neuberger's analysis deepens insight into the ideology of African theologians whose Pan-Africanism is similar to Nkrumah's. See 334-341; 432-440.

096 Nkrumah, Kwame. *Africa Must Unite.* New York: International Publishers, 1963.

Nkrumah's views are inextricable from the political and socioeconomic issues relevant to the study of African theology, particularly in terms of the difference between the old guard and the new guard. In *Africa Must Unite*, an important text——however utopian it may be——Nkrumah defines his vision of a United States of Africa, a vision relevant to African theologians with a radical, Pan-African consciousness. See 092, 095.

097 Nkrumah, Kwame. *Neo-Colonialism*. New York: International Publishers, 1965.

Nkrumah's book reveals African consciousness of the problem of neocolonialism——the continual Western export of capital and ideology to Africa. African theologians are very much concerned with the problem of neocolonialism, a problem that reveals the continuation of the praxis of imperialism. See 003, 096.

098 Nkrumah, Kwame. *The Challenge of the Congo*. New York: International Publishers, 1967.

Nkrumah narrates his account of the Congo crisis that led to the assassination of Lumumba and the Western support of Mobutu. See 078-080, 107. The book provides more insight into Lumumba's legacy and the ways in which the Congo crisis foreshadowed the intrigue characteristic of neocolonialism. See 092.

099 Nkrumah, Kwame. *Consciencism: Philosophy and Ideology for Decolonization*. New York: Monthly Review Press, 1970.

Considered to be an important paradigm of African philosophy——see 005, 140, 155, 171, 176, 187——*Consciencism* is also relevant to African theology because it explores the issue of africanization, i.e., inculturation and acculturation. See 061. Unlike *Class Struggle in Africa*, however, *Consciencism* succumbs to the myth of African socialism, which is related to *négritude*. See 102-106; 114. Specifically, *Consciencism* presents a theoretical base for the notion of African personality. See 007. For Nkrumah, African personality would "enable African society to digest the Western...and the Euro-Christian elements in Africa and develop them in such a way that they fit into the African personality" (p. 79). According to Nkrumah, the African personality "is itself defined by the cluster of humanist principles which underlie the traditional African society."

100 Nkrumah, Kwame. *Class Struggle in Africa*. New York: International Publishers, 1970.

Class Struggle in Africa is valuable in that it exemplifies the social analysis which informs the work of African *liberation* theologians. See 288, 334-341; 432-440; 452-459. This little book marks Nkrumah's turn from the notion of African socialism to the more orthodox trajectory of Marxist-Leninism. See 108. Whereas Nkrumah, like Nyerere——see 103-107——had claimed that Africa was free of societal contradiction prior to colonialism, he now claims that Africa suffered from those contradictions, contradictions defined by Marx and Engels. Theologians such as Éla and Mosala make a similar point. See 336; 573.

101 Nkrumah, Kwame. *Revolutionary Path*. New York: International Publishers, 1980.

A compilation of Nkrumah's writings which reveals the trajectory of his revolutionary consciousness, a consciousness that corresponds to the writings of new guard theologians. See 095, 099.

102 Nyerere, Julius. "The Church and Society." In *Man and Development (Binadamu na Maendeleo)*, 82-101. New York: Oxford University Press, 1974.

Nyerere, former President of Tanzania, is the architect of *ujamaa*——the Tanzanian variety of African socialism——and indicates here the relevancy of social analysis to African theology. A devout Catholic, Nyerere addresses Maryknoll Sisters' conference in October 1970. Consistent with the social analysis within the context of the Ecumenical Association of Third World Theologians, (EATWOT) Nyerere defines the problem of humankind as the "division...into rich and poor, North and South." On EATWOT, see, 137, 301, 352.

103 Nyerere, Julius. "Ujamaa: The Basis of African Socialism." Chap. 1 in *Ujamaa: Essays on Socialism*, 1-12. New York: Oxford University Press, 1981.

Nyerere defines *ujamaa* as the return to the values of traditional Africa. He argues that "the 'rich' and the 'poor' individual were completely secure in African [traditional] society....Nobody starved, either of food or of human dignity, because he lacked personal wealth; he could depend on the wealth possessed by the community of which he was a member. That was socialism. That *is* socialism" (p. 3-4). According to Nyerere, Africans need not read Marx or Lenin and plot thereby a socialist course based essentially on European realities. Rather, Africans need only to "draw from [their] traditional heritage the recognition of 'society' as an extension of the basic family unit" (p. 12). As scholars have shown, however, Nyerere's definition of African socialism is ahistorical. Traditional Africa reveals material contradictions seen in the precolonial history of the African poor. See 052.

104 Nyerere, Julius. "The Arusha Declaration." Chap. 2 in *Ujamaa: Essays on Socialism*, 13-39. New York: Oxford University Press, 1981.

The document——that Nyerere helped formulate and which represents his national policy——reveals the socialist path of Tanzania as defined by TANU, the one party of the country. See 103.

105 Nyerere, Julius. "The Varied Paths to Socialism." Chap. 5 in *Ujamaa: Essays on Socialism*, 76-90. New York: Oxford University Press, 1981.

Nyerere, in an address to students of Cairo University in 1967, confesses his Christianity, which he relates to his socialism. For Nyerere, Christianity, insofar as it reveals the Word of God, is infallible; but socialism, created essentially by human beings, is fallible. Socialists, then, he argues, should be open to other views, eschewing self-righteous dogmatism in favor of genuine dialogue. See 315. Having explored what may be called the distinction between faith and religion, Nyerere offers his definition of socialism: "the basic purpose is the well-being of the people, and the basic assumption is an acceptance of human equality" (p. 78).

106 Nyerere, Julius. "After the Arusha Declaration." Chap. 8 in *Ujamaa: Essays on Socialism*, 145-177. New York: Oxford University Press, 1981.

Nyerere assesses the significance of the Arusha Declaration in the light of Tanzania's struggles. He concludes that Tanzania has not yet actualized its socialist vision. Still, Nyerere shares his hope regarding the *ujamaa* villages. According to Nyerere, these villages would use "local resources and traditional knowledge." See 104.

107 Nzongola-Ntalaja. "Class Struggle and National Liberation in Zaire." *Contemporary Marxism* 6 (Spring 1983): 57-94.

Nzongola-Ntalaja provides insight into the Zairian context, thereby heightening one's appreciation of the social analysis valorized by the new guard. See 078-080, 093, 098. He asserts that the anticolonial struggle in the Belgian Congo was not unlike "the 1848 national revolutions in Europe." Here, radical intellectuals attempted to heighten the contradictions that give impetus to revolutionary movement, only to be stifled by forces inimical to revolutionary change. "Lacking 'organic intellectuals'," writes Nzongola-Ntalaja, "the African masses of the Congo and other colonial territories were incapable of accomplishing their own revolution" (p. 87). See 072. The paucity of freedom fighters such as Lumumba, then, led to the rise of pseudo-bourgeois forces in collusion with the West. In short, Nzongola-Ntalaja "attempts to show how easily the people's representative turned into the people's oppressor, with all the consequences this entails for the quality of life of the African masses" (p. 87). See 011. Nzongola substantiates Austin's claim that the colonial state has remained. See 004. He also provides additional insight into the disingenuousness of the old guard's position that "independence" precludes the relevance of liberation theology for Africa. See 406.

108 Ottaway, David and Marina. *Afrocommunism*. New York: Holmes & Meier, 1981.

The Ottaways deepen an appreciation of a social analysis that investigates levels of contradictions: capitalist West vs. Soviet bloc; the relation of peasants to workers; the romantic notion of African socialism vs. the more scientific paradigms of Marxist thought, etc. See 072, 099. Not unlike Éla and Adoukonou, moreover, the Ottaways indicate that Africans may well modify Marxist thought in a way uniquely suited to African realities. See 288, 338

109 Page, Jesse. *The Black Bishop: Samuel Adjai Crowther*. New York: Fleming H. Revell, 1908.

Page's biography of a great ancestor of African theology also provides insight into Protestant mission in the nineteenth century. See 057-058. The biography chronicles Crowther's life from slavery to his ascendancy to the episcopacy of West Africa. Page also discusses the unscrupulous way Crowther's episcopacy was undermined in the latter years of the nineteenth century. See 112.

110 Rodney, Walter. *How Europe Underdeveloped Africa*. Washington, D.C.: Howard University Press, 1982.

According to Rodney, Africa, at the advent of olden colonialism, had not reached the stage of "class-ridden feudalism." "When Europe and Africa established close relations through trade, there was already a slight edge in Europe's favor——an edge representing the difference between a fledgling capitalist society and one that was still emerging from communalism" (p. 70). The new guard theologian, Barthélemy Adoukonou, makes a similar point. See 288. In short, Rodney's guiding hypothesis is that Europe's developmental edge over Africa explains African underdevelopment. Africa's subjugation by the West is not the result of the alleged inferiority of blacks, but is an accident of history, which reveals the depth of human cruelty. See 288.

111 Roth, Donald. "The 'Black Man's Burden': The Racial Background of Afro-American Missionaries." In *Black Americans and the Missionary Movement in Africa*, ed. by Sylvia Jacobs, 31-40. Westport: Greenwood Press, 1982.

Another essay——see 054——exploring the role of African people in the planting of Christianity in Africa: Roth brings out nuances of African-American ambivalence toward Africa. Whereas one is likely to say that black missionaries identified Christianity with European civilization, Roth indicates that such missionaries were aware of the limitations of that civilization. He also gives an example of a specific way in which black North American missionaries were beset by white paternalism. Roth narrates the story of William Sheppard——see 126-127——upon whom white supervision was thrust with the rationale that Sheppard would be saddled with lust at the "the sight of half-naked African women." Roth records that Sheppard, despite white "supervision," became a distinguished missionary. Sheppard, moreover, took it upon himself to expose the heinous crimes King Leopold perpetrated on the Congolese people. See 093. He also taught African-Americans that African culture had integrity, bringing "impressive examples of African artwork" back to the States. Indeed, W.E.B. Du Bois, a seminal figure in the history of Pan-Africanism——noted for his suspicion of Christian missionaries——invited Sheppard to deliver a major address at the "1919 National Association of Colored People...symposium on Africa" (p. 37).

112 Sanneh, Lamin. *West African Christianity: The Religious Impact.* Maryknoll, N.Y.: Orbis Books, 1983.

A short history of West African Christianity, which covers ground similar to that in Groves (see 042), Ayandele (see 006-007) and Clarke (see 026). According to Sanneh, African traditional religions "have penetrated both Christianity and Islam and endowed them with a tolerant, absorptive capacity....In this sense traditional religions have performed a universal mission towards Christianity and Islam" (p. 87).

113 Sanneh, Lamin.   "Reciprocal Influences: African Traditional Religions and Christianity." In *Third World Liberation Theologies: A Reader*, ed. by Deane William Ferm, 232-239. Maryknoll, N.Y.: Orbis Books, 1986.

An excerpt from *West African Christianity: The Religious Impact.* See 112. Here Sanneh argues that African traditional religion opens one's understanding to the distinct ways in which African people read the Bible. According to Sanneh, African traditional religionists are far more tolerant of pluralism than Western Christians. Thus, argues Sanneh, Africans are more biblical than the totalitarian "form of European Christianity" (p. 233). For Sanneh, the good news of redemption and salvation is but a crystallization of salutary values found in African traditional religion. In this regard he is like Gray. See 041. For Sanneh, then, the acculturative process indicates the broadness of God's historical presence, while the inculturative process specifies the redemptive message peculiar to Christianity——a message of liberation from all forces that would truncate health and well-being.

114 Senghor, Léopold Sédar. *On African Socialism.* Translated and with an Introduction by Mercer Cook. New York: Frederick A. Praeger, 1964.

Senghor, first president of Senegal and leading exponent of *négritude*, discusses his socialist vision. For Senghor, African socialism is an eclectic blend of communalism, French socialism, Marxist-Leninism, and the theosophy of Pierre Teilhard de Chardin. Its epistemological base, however, is what he calls "Negro-African knowledge." According to Senghor:

> In contrast to the classic European, the Negro African does not draw a line
> between himself and the object; he does not hold it at a distance, nor does
> he merely look at it and analyze it. After holding it at a distance [sic], after
> scanning it without analyzing it, he takes it vibrant in his hands, careful not
> to kill or fix it. He touches it, feels it, *smells* it. The Negro African is like
> one of those Third Day worms, a pure field of sensations (p. 72).

This quote helps to explain why Adoukonou——see 288——appeals to Stanislas Adotévi, who wrote the seminal *Négritude et négrologues.* (Adotévi, whom Adoukonou quotes, writes, in rejection of Senghor's views, *Le Nègre doit devenir dangereux!*) For many, then, Senghor's *négritude* is a reification of African realities——which brings to mind the insights of Fanon, especially those regarding "centrifugal tendencies" of the masses. See 034. What is more, Senghor's African socialism, an expression of his *négritude*, is part of what African philosopher Hountondji calls an alienated discourse. See 176. Senghor's views have also been challenged by other scholars, such as Tshiamalenga Ntumba, who, like Adotévi, alleges that Senghor, in the final analysis, surrenders *négritude* to Eurocentrism. See 209.

115 Senghor, Léopold Sédar. "Negritude: A Humanism of the Twentieth Century." In *The Africa Reader: Independent Africa* ed. by Wilfred Cartey and Martin Kilson, 179-194. New York: Vintage Books, 1970.

Here, Senghor defines *négritude* as a universal humanism that eschews racialism, though it represents the subjectivity of the African personality. See 007. *Négritude*, for

Senghor, is the ethos of Africa and Diaspora——what he calls "a certain active presence in the world, or better, the universe." Pride of place here is given to communal values; these make *négritude* a humanism, post-modern and vital——the counterpart of "the modern humanism that European philosophers have been preparing since the end of the nineteenth century, and as Teilhard de Chardin and the writers and artists of the twentieth century present it" (p. 184). This humanism, moreover, is derived from Africans' essential concern to promote forces that expand fullness of life. For Senghor, *négritude* reflects the opposition and complementarity of essential poles: man and woman; sky and earth——"a call of harmony to the harmony of union that enriches *Being*" (p. 191). African art, argues Senghor——bringing to mind Engelbert Mveng, see 432, 434——best objectivizes *négritude* since it depicts the events whereby the African, as the center of the cosmos, becomes one with nature. For Senghor, the essence of *négritude*, is rhythm——the fleeting, yet sustained, constellation of myriad patterns that communicate the totality of Africanity. Felicitously, Senghor put it this way: "Rhythm is simply the movement of attraction or repulsion that expresses the life of the cosmic forces; symmetry and asymmetry, repetition or opposition: in short, lines of force that link the meaningful signs that shapes and colors, timbre and tones, are" (p. 192).

116 Sklar, Richard. "The Colonial Imprint on African Political Thought." In *African Independence: The First Twenty-Five Years*, ed. by Gwendolen Carter and Patrick O'Meara, 1-30. Bloomington: Indiana University Press 1985.

Sklar, a professor at the University of California, looks at Blyden, a significant ancestor of African theology. See 016-018; 081-082. According to Sklar, Blyden's thought "anticipated the comprehensive impact of cultural domination and charted a course of resistance to cultural imperialism together with a tentative program for principled interaction with colonial institutions" (p. 22). Sklar presents colonialism as if it were a neutral thing that can be manipulated from an Afrocentric perspective. Colonialism, however, both old and new, can only be manipulated by the Western powers. Indeed, Sklar's analysis of Blyden is far too pro-Western for African theologians who realize that neutral acceptance of colonialism enhances precisely the underdevelopment that exacerbates the misery of the African poor.

117 Small, Adam. "Blackness Versus Nihilism: Black Racism Rejected." In *The Challenge of Black Theology in South Africa*, ed. by Basil Moore, 11-17. Atlanta, Georgia: John Knox Press, 1973.

A historic essay on black theology's relation to Black Consciousness: see 015. Small argues that South African blacks who accept white values as normative too often reject themselves as a result. Rejection here is tantamount to self-hatred, which is the retrogressive element in the liberation struggle and its most pernicious contradiction. Black Consciousness, however, nurtures blacks in a way that celebrates, rather than denigrates, blackness. See 036, 039. For Small, Black Consciousness is the *a priori* of a praxis that rejects apartheid, but not for the sake of integration. In sum, nihilism, for Small, is tantamount to white supremacy——a self-destructive misanthropy that breeds violence in blatant defiance of peace and justice.

118 Southall, Roger. *South Africa's Transkei: The Political Economy of an "Independent" Bantustan*. New York: Monthly Review Press, 1983.

Southall helps one appreciate the structure of apartheid in terms of the Homeland Policy. He explains that the homelands are a peculiar form of neocolonialism and the "logical" outcome of apartheid. Homelands were set up to divest "Bantu" people of any legal claim to South African citizenship. The goal of the Pretoria regime——before events that led to the release of Nelson Mandela——was to "devolve" independence on homelands, such as has been done in Transkei, in order to preclude black peoples' first-class citizenship in South Africa proper. (On devolution, see 124.) What is more, the Homeland Policy seeks to divide and conquer "Bantu" people in order to deepen the alienation that slows down the liberation struggle. Africans are assigned to homelands according to their ethnicity. Transkei, as well as Ciskei, are !Xhosa nations, for instance. Zulus go to Kwazulu; Vendas, Vendaland, and so forth. The Homeland Policy had also been integral to "influx control"——blacks without "passes" attesting to their employment were not permitted in South Africa proper. Those without passes, then, had no legal right to live in the townships inside South Africa, which have been the contexts housing the most accessible labor pool. The homelands also constitute a labor pool: the people are quick to leave the homelands because they are barren tracts in which indigence abounds. See 128.

119 Tasie, Godwin, and Richard Gray. "Introduction". In *Christianity in Independent Africa*, ed. by Edward Fasholé-Luke, Richard Gray, Adrian Hastings and Godwin Tasie, 3-15. Bloomington: Indiana University Press, 1978.

In introducing this significant volume on the proceedings of an ecumenical conference held at the Jos Campus of the University of Ibadan, Nigeria, in 1975, Gray and Tasie examine the tension between the goals of nationalism and the mission establishment. The authors point out that there would not have been an africanization of the historic churches had the nationalist not pressed the issue of "independence." Still, the mission churches remain under the specter of imperialism. A ramification of this is that the church is in Africa, not of Africa: africanization is only ostensible. This contradiction is curious. Although the historic churches claim a moratorium on mission would be harmful, only the thorough "decolonization" of the mission church facilitates its africanization. Tasie and Gray note the way in which women have been the backbone of the African church——their observation augers well for the development of feminist theology in Africa.

120 Temu, A., and B. Swai. *Historians and Africanist History: A Critique*. London: Zed Press, 1981.

This volume, dedicated to Walter Rodney——see 110——is a fine example of the relation of historiography to social analysis. The authors assert that European historians have tended to argue that colonialism has positively shaped African development. See 116. Nationalist historians, assert Temu and Swai, have attempted to correct that view. Their vindicationist position, however, renders them poorly equipped to investigate the current hardships of the African people. See 008, 034, 063. This is because vindicationists' essentially bourgeois scholarship is a continuum of the path of their First World counterparts. See 055. Swai and Temu write that the vindicationist break with

colonial historiography is mythical, but it is a myth which has been useful
in creating the illusion of independence with which the African petty
bourgeoisie have liked to associate themselves. The current African
endeavor to make a fetish of formal independence in the present epoch of
imperialism is not restricted to the discipline of history (p. 98-99).

Indeed, the crisis in postcolonial historiography is similar to that in African theology. The new guard would agree with Temu and Swai that the intellectual's ideas are never separate from the political economy that shapes them with specific ideological nuance. One might say, then, that the old guard has produced a vindicationist scholarship that reproduces colonial contradictions. The paradigms for their work have been essentially European. (See Chapter 2 of this bibliography.) Like the new guard, Swai and Temu represent a new critical school of organic intellectuals allied with the African poor. Here activists seek to forge a hegemony that strikes against that of the pseudo-bourgeois elite, who legitimize "the present arrangements of everyday life...by creating false connections between the history of the oppressed classes and their oppressors" (p. 52). An essential premise of this new and re-Africanized school is put in the form of a question: "Isn't Africa, if one were to be allowed to speculate, one of the weakest links in the imperialist chain? Is it any wonder then that the crude violence meted out to African producers should be coupled with an equally violent intellectual assault?" Indeed, *mutandis mutatis,* their question and orientation are that of new guard theologians such as Jean-Marc Éla and Barthélemy Adoukonou. See 288, 334-341.

121 Thebehali, David. "Has Christianity Any Relevance and Any Future?" In *A New Look at Christianity in Africa,* 40-45. Geneva: WSCF Books, 1972.

Like Zulu's essay below——see 130——Thebehali critically examines the close relationship between British aggression and Christianity. Thebehali notes that few 19th century, white missionaries were able to extricate their theology from the expropriating mores of the civilization that produced them. Reminiscent of Eboussi Boulaga and R. Bureau——see 020, 307——Thebehali notes that Europeans in Africa greatly impeded inculturation because of their hostility to African culture. Thebehali, moreover, reveals the values that bore fruit in the Black Consciousness Movement——the African field in which black South African theology took root. See 015, 036, 039.

122 Turner, Henry M. *Respect Black: The Writings of Henry McNeal Turner.* Edited by Edwin Redkey. New York: Arno Press, 1971.

Respect Black: a volume on a celebrated African-American. Bishop Turner's heroic legacy of black nationalism and Pan-Africanism is recorded here in his speeches, sermons, and letters. Particularly pertinent are his essays that focus on African-American emigration and reveal his role in establishing independent black churches in Southern Africa. See 027, 028-029; 054, 111, 126-127, 518.

123 Twaddle, Michael. "Was the Democratic Party of Uganda a Purely Confessional Party?" In *Christianity in Independent Africa,* ed. by Edward Fasholé-Luke, Richard Gray; Adrian Hastings and Godwin Tasie, 255-266. Bloomington: Indiana University Press, 1978.

Uganda, due to the horrific legacy of Idi Amin, is a context in which the relevance of the theme of liberation is glaringly apparent. See 053, 071, 335. Twaddle's essay deepens an understanding of that context as he links ecclesial tensions among missionaries to the political conflicts that produced the rise of Amin. It had been alleged that Roman Catholicism, rather than Protestantism, was able to forge a truly national, democratic party, thus overcoming micro-nationalism (so-called tribalism) and other factors inimical to the forging of a national culture in Uganda. According to Twaddle, however, Catholicism was used as a foil in micro-nationalistic strife, particularly in regard to the Catholic schools which dominated the area of education. Twaddle reveals that distinct factions sought to weaken or to use these schools to their advantage regardless of whether they were Roman Catholic. Roman Catholicism, then, neither overcame tribalism nor other obstacles to national culture, but was a vehicle of partisan interest.

124 Wallerstein, Immanuel. *Africa: The Politics of Independence.* New York: Vintage Books, 1961.

Wallerstein, a leading historian of African politics, examines issues pertinent to the period between olden colonialism and "independence." Particularly useful is Wallerstein's definition of "devolution." As opposed to revolution, devolution signifies the gradual granting of power to the African petty bourgeoisie. This process sets the stage for a more pernicious form of indirect rule——neocolonialism. Wallerstein also offers a definition of African theology. According to Wallerstein, African theology is the "review [of] Christian rituals and their relation to African rituals...that would allow the universal principals of Christianity to take on specifically African form" (p. 131). Wallerstein notes the disingenuousness of that project in terms of the notion of *négritude*. See 114. Here he notes an inner contradiction within the *négritude* movement——namely that it obfuscates the feudal contradictions of traditional society. (The bell Wallerstein rings here is also rung by Éla. See 336.) An outcome of such contradictions was slavery——a form of exploitation that the pre-colonial elite facilitated.

125 Wallerstein, Immanuel. "The Integration of the National Liberation Movement in the Field of International Liberation." In *Contemporary Marxism* 6 (Spring 1983): 166-171.
Here Wallerstein focuses on the legacy of Cabral. See 023-025. Like Cabral, Wallerstein asserts that Africa's greatest question is whether the African bourgeoisie will identify with the workers and the peasants. According to Wallerstein, organic intellectuals——exemplified by certain new guard theologians——"need to reflect on whether...present strategy, mode of organization, and categories of thought serve...this period of crisis, of intensified class struggle, and above all of clever adjustment by the world's bourgeoisie who are seeking to survive as privileged strata under entirely new guises."

126 Williams, Walter L. "The Missionary: Introduction." In *Black Americans and the Evangelization of Africa 1877-1900*, ed. by Sylvia Jacobs, 131-134. Westport: Greenwood Press, 1982.
Williams further evinces the fact that African people played an indispensable role in the planting of Christianity in Africa. See 027, 028-029; 054, 111, 122, 127. Particularly relevant here are William's discussions of Blyden and Crummell. See 016-018; 028-029. He also discusses the missiology of other African-Americans, such as the Reverend William H. Sheppard. See 111, 127. He notes that blacks, during the 19th century, had outnumbered whites in missionary work in Africa. With medical advances, however, Africa was no longer "the white man's grave"; thus white missionaries began to outnumber the black ones in the late 19th century. His discussion of clergy, such as Alexander Crummell——see 028-029; 094——reveals that African people helped export Eurocentric ideology to Africa.

127 Williams, Walter L. "William Henry Sheppard, Afro-American Missionary in the Congo, 1890-1910." In *Black Americans and the Missionary Movement in Africa*, ed. by Sylvia Jacobs, 135-154. Westport: Greenwood Press, 1982.
Like Edward Blyden——see 016-018——Sheppard was an African-American Presbyterian who made a contribution to the planting of Christianity in Africa. See 111. Williams provides biographical information on Sheppard, indicating his virtues as a missionary and Pan-Africanist. Williams reveals that Sheppard was influenced by Blyden, who spoke, in 1883, at Hampton Institute—— Sheppard's *alma mater*. Fluent in Congo languages, particularly Bakuba, Sheppard was thought by a Bakuba king to be a reincarnated ancestor. Like Crowther, however——see 109——Sheppard had little tolerance for traditional religion, though he appreciated the virtues of certain traditional values. At any rate, Sheppard, by 1900, "had a total of three hundred and fifty converts" (p. 145).

128 Wilson, Francis, and Mamphele Ramphele. *Uprooting Poverty: The South African Challenge*. New York: W.W. Norton & Company, 1989.
This text lays bare the obscene contradictions which oppress the poor in South Africa. The authors' conclusion provide a sense of the power of the text:

Frantz Fanon [see 034-035], one of the most perceptive observers of the Algerian revolution, expressed the matter succinctly when he wrote: "...What counts today, the question which is looming on the horizon, is the need for redistribution of wealth. Humanity must reply to this question, or be shaken to pieces by it." That is surely the fundamental question facing South Africa today. Have we courage to face and answer it? (See p. 357.) Surely black theologians, such Mofokeng (see 564-567), Mosala (see 572- 578), and Boesak (see 517-522) do.

129 Wood, Donald. *Biko*. New York: Paddington Press, 1978.

Wood's controversial——because allegedly paternalistic——narration of his friendship with Biko provides information on the contradictions of the Republic of South Africa, contradictions addressed by the Black Consciousness Movement and black theology. See 013-015. The best part of the book is the transcript of Biko's trial, in which Biko displays his formidable intellect. See 015. The text also brings out the obscenity of Biko's murder and the suspicion cast on the South African Security Police in the wake of his death.

130 Zulu, Lawrence. "A Black Assessment of Nineteenth-Century Missionaries." In *A New Look at Christianity in Africa*, 35-39. Geneva: WSCF Books, 1972.

A discussion of the contradictions of European missionaries in South Africa, the most glaring of which is the antithesis between Christianity and racism. Zulu notes, however, that missionaries made contributions to African education and health care. Still, he asks South African theologians not to reproduce the bigotries of yesterday. His essays facilitates social analysis, with a focus on Eurocentric missiology.

7

African Traditional Religion and Religio-Cultural Analysis

131 Abraham, W.E. *The Mind of Africa*. Chicago: University of Chicago Press, 1962.
Abraham asserts that traditional African values form a Pan-African culture that can lift Africa from servility to the West. Abraham examines traditional values in terms of the Akan, who, he claims, constitute a generic, traditional, Pan-African consciousness. See 139, 153, 155, 163, 171, 206. According to Abraham, Western ideology has been exported to Africa, and is but the apotheosis of Western consciousness. Indeed, this consciousness, when it is internalized by Africans, is the structure of alienation in Africa. The remedy for this self-estrangement, argues Abraham, is found in the return to Akan-like values. Unlike idolatrous Westerners, argues Abraham, Africans (Akans) have recognized that God is greater than what humans fashion. For Abraham, the Akan worldview is liberating since it returns the African to a more wholesome orientation and allows him/her to appreciate the salvific import of Christian monotheism. Indeed, Abraham valorizes the monotheistic dimension of Akan religion to such an extent that he calls the veneration of the lesser gods, *abascom*, superstition. Although one suspects that Abraham's view of the *abascom* is apologetic in the face of Western values, his analysis provides excellent insight into Akan culture. Abraham also anticipates the issues of acculturation and inculturation that are so integral to African theology. He notes that Christianity will thrive in Africa to the extent it "can overcome or accommodate elements in the society into which it has been introduced" (p. 137). On inculturation see: 154, 253. On acculturation see: 160, 169, 180.

132 Achebe, Chinua. *Things Fall Apart*. New York: Fawcett Crest, 1984.
Things Fall Apart is a classic African novel that provides an inside view of traditional religion and the way in which it was disrupted by a pervasive Christianity that blessed the sword of olden colonialism. Indeed, African Christians, such as Ogbu Kalu, have cited Achebe's work as indispensable for those who would gain insight into the encounter between African traditional culture (Igbo) and Christianity. See 063, 328. Achebe introduces us to characters as diverse as Okonkwo——a warrior and the protagonist of the novel——and his less than virile son, Nwoye, who, like Okonwo's father, is an offense to Okonkwo. The conflict between father and son is exacerbated as Nwoye becomes a Christian——the intrusion of the whites into Igbo culture strikes too close to the home of its most powerful son. Okonkwo, an powerful symbol of Igbo culture, is undermined by his very own. "Living fire begets cold, impotent ash." Okonkwo defends his culture by beheading a messenger of the British government——symbolized by the commissioner——who wished to disrupt a traditional palaver. Rather than be executed according to British law, Okonkwo hangs himself. He commits an abomination; Achebe

explains: "It [suicide] is an offense against the earth, and a man who commits it will not be buried by his clansmen. His body is evil, and only strangers may touch it" (p. 190). So Okonkwo's people ask the soldiers to take him down. The commissioner, in the process of writing a book on his African experience, knows that the story of Okonkwo's suicide will be quite marketable. He decides to name the text *The Pacification of the Primitive Tribes of the Lower Niger*. Indeed, Achebe's work provides insight to a powerful point made by the black priests, Dosseh and Sastre, who question themselves about the meaning of *Propagande Missionaire et Veritè*. See 329.

133 Achebe, Chinua. *Arrow of God*. With an Introduction by K.W. J. Post. Garden City: Anchor Books, 1969.
    "When suffering knocks at our door and you say there is no seat left for him, he tells you not to worry because he has brought his own stool." The aphorism, taken from Chapter 8 of the novel, is a fitting way to begin an annotation of Achebe's *Arrow of God*——a tragedy not unlike *Things Fall Apart*. Achebe probes deeper into the sacred cosmos of the Igbo by way of another strong elder of Igbo culture——Ezeulu, Chief Priest of Ulu. The novel richly details nuances of Igbo culture. Readers are drawn into the life of the village (culture), and the spirit world of the deep forest (nature). On the Igbo see: 144, 162, 180, 181, 182, 183, 213, 226. Ulu, a divinity, is the guardian of the village, Umuaro, and the overseer of each new year. Each new year demands an essential ritual——the harvesting of new yams. Ezeulu, the wealthy, proud, even supercilious, priest, presides over the harvesting of the new yams; he is the Arrow of Ulu. "One half of him was man," writes Achebe, "and the other half *mmo*——the half that was painted over with the white chalk at important religious moments. And half of the things he ever did were done by this spirit side" (p. 220). Like *Things Fall Apart*, *Arrow of God* provides insight into the chaos Christianity——always buttressed by the "indirect rule" of Great Britain——caused among Igbo people. And again, the tragedy of colonialism is made painfully clear in the conflict between father, Ezeulu, and son, Oduche. The latter is a Christian so westernized that he nearly kills a sacred python out of contempt for Ulu. Ezeulu had thought Oduche would spy out and report the machinations of the white world, personified by the church. His plan bore no fruit——"He who will swallow *udala* seeds must consider the size of his anus." Like Okonkwo, Ezeulu, though virtuous, truthful and brave, was inflexible. Valorization of tradition produces great tragedy. Ezeulu's stubbornness and ambition cost him another scion, his beautiful, but rancorous, son. Obika——a paragon of traditional skill and virility——dies in exerting himself in a funeral ritual, which he would not have done if his father had not been so self-righteously fastidious in regard to the Festival of the New Yams. In the end, the Arrow of God boomerangs, destroying not only the priest of Ulu, but Ulu itself, cleaving a path for the church and the commissioner. *Arrow of God* heightens one's awareness of the violence done to African culture by whites, a theme accentuated in the works of theologians such as Oduyoye, and Éla. See 334-341; 452-459. The novel also provides insight into the humanity of African people.

134 Achebe, Chinua. *Anthills of the Savannah*. New York: Anchor Books, 1988.
    Here, we leave olden colonialism and cross the threshold into neocolonialism. One observes the obscenity of an "independent" Africa where the masses are oppressed by blacks. Achebe's *Anthills of the Savanna* points to the scorched ruins of "independence," of which new guard theologians——such as Jean-Marc Éla (see 334-341); Eboussi Boulaga (see 305-307); and Engelbert Mveng (see 432-440)——write prophetically. Achebe eloquently weaves together the narratives of three of the intelligentsia, Chris Oriko, Ikem Osodi, and Beatrice Okoh. Very high-up in the government, highly sophisticated and urbane, the three are deeply offended by the waxing corruption and contempt of the poor.

Their values are strengthened by the majesty of African culture, of which Achebe writes very powerfully:

> Man's best artifice to snare and hold the grandeur of divinity always crumbles in his hands, and the more ardently he strives the more paltry and incongruous the result. So it were better he did not try all; far better to ritualize that incongruity and by invoking the mystery of metaphor to hint at the most unattainable glory by its very opposite, the most mundane starkness——a mere stream, a tree, a stone, a mound of earth, a little clay bowl containing fingers of chalk (p. 94).

None of the three can stand the hubris of the elite, who have little integrity, and are too estranged from the poetics of the culture Achebe defines so exquisitely. Chris and Ikem, though finally killed for their integrity and love for the masses, are indeed the hope of a new Africa, as is Beatrice, who outlives them both. This new Africa will be a creative humanity, and wise enough not to turn its back on the legacies of the ancestors. Indeed,

> the arrogant fool who sits astride the story as though it were a bowl of foo-foo set before him by his wife understands little about the world. The story will roll him into a ball, dip him in the soup and swallow him first. I tell you he is like the puppy who swings himself around and farts into a blazing fire with the aim to put it out. Can he? No, the story is everlasting.... Like fire, when it is not blazing it is smoldering under its own ashes or sleeping and resting inside its flint house (p. 114).

Anthills of the Savannah helps the student of African theology appreciate the power of Africa's own, native values——values that are the acculturative force of African theology.

135   Adegbola, E.A. Adeolu. "A Historical Study of Yoruba Religion." In *Traditional Religion in West Africa*, ed. by E.A. Ade Adegbola, 408-418. Accra: Asempa Publishers, 1983.

Adegbola examines historical issues pertinent to an appreciation of the diversity of Yoruba religion.   On the Yoruba, see, 140, 145, 146, 151, 164, 177.   According to Adegbola, the history of migrations; the diversity of great cultural heros; the variety of Yoruba kingdoms——all account for the nuances of Yoruba beliefs and rituals. Adegbola concludes that it is better to examine the sacred artifacts of Yoruba religion in terms of "the social history of the people rather than to regard the whole as one intellectually logical complex in which the 'gods and goddesses' became the ministers of the Supreme God, *Olodumare*, or evolutionary emanations of divinity belonging to a hierarchical order populated with a high-god, nature divinities, ancestral ghosts and charms and amulets in a descending order" (p. 418). Adegbola's method implies the critique levied against the old guard, who tended to reify traditional religion in ignoring the nuances of culture, which resist definition in terms of the survey approach to African traditional religion. See 008, 136, 239.

136   Ajayi, J.F.A., and E.A. Ayandele. "Emerging Themes of West African Religious History." In *Traditional Religion in West Africa*, ed. by E.A. Ade Adegbola, 446-457. Accra: Asempa Publishers, 1983.

Ajayi and Ayandele discuss issues pertinent to the old guard, whose prolegomena to African theology consisted of studies that failed to consider the dynamism of African traditional religion. The authors divide the history of African traditional religion into four groups. The first is that of the 19th century missionaries, who distorted the religion in terms of their Christian commitments and enlisted colonial violence to accomplish their christianizing goals. These missionaries were offset by the second group, represented by James Johnson (see 007, 087). The works of the second group "are by no means purged of prejudices. By and large, these writers see in African Traditional Religion a valid system of beliefs, valid for pre-revelation and pre-Christian Africa" (p. 448). The third group is made of anthropologists, whose work was less skewed than that of missionaries by virtue of a more "objective"——that is less Christian——approach. The fourth group is made up of "professional social anthropologists and specialists in African Traditional Religion" (p. 449). According to Ayandele and Ajayi, none of these groups has studied African traditional religion adequately. African religions have yet to be studied autochthonously as dynamic and living cultural forces. All the groups mentioned above tend to reify African traditional religions, treating them as static, waning entities.

137 Appiah-Kubi, Kofi. "Indigenous African Christian Churches: Signs of Authenticity." In *African Theology en Route*, ed. by Kofi Appiah-Kubi and Sergio Torres, 117-125. Maryknoll, N.Y.: Orbis Books, 1979.

Appiah-Kubi's essay was delivered at the historic Pan-African gathering in Accra, Ghana in 1977. See 003. He holds that the independent African churches, because of their acculturative power, provide the most fertile ground for African theology. See 008, 046. He examines these churches with a focus on the praying (Aladura) churches of Ghana. See 063. Appiah-Kubi prefers to call these churches indigenous African churches. "Independent," he asserts, "suggests that there is some more important reference point outside of these churches" (p. 117). According to Appiah-Kubi, indigenous churches do not spring from socioeconomic contradictions, but from "spiritual hunger." He argues that they are a continuum of traditional practices such as "healing, prophesying and visioning." The traditional concern for healing is particularly central to the life of these churches. Appiah-Kubi's sense that the independent churches have little political meaning is to be seen in relation to new guard theologians who claim that these churches *are* to be understood in political terms. See 340, 458.

138 Appiah-Kubi, Kofi. "Indigenous African Christian Churches: Signs of Authenticity." In *Third World Liberation Theologies: A Reader*, ed. by Deane William Ferm, 222-230. Maryknoll, N.Y.: Orbis Books, 1986.

See 137.

139 Appiah-Kubi, Kofi. "The Akan Concept of Human Personality." In *Traditional Religion in West Africa*, ed. by E.A. Ade Adegbola, 259-264. Accra: Asempa Publishers, 1983.

Appiah-Kubi's essay provides insight into the acculturative issues theologians such as Mercy Oduyoye (see 452-459), John Pobee (see 468-469), and Kwesi Dickson (see 322-327) are exploring. He shows that the Akan anthropology is to be appreciated in relation to a person's souls derived from his/her mother and father——and from God. On the Akan, see 131. On the African sense of multiple souls, see 231, 384. Like J.B. Danquah——see 155——and John Pobee, Appiah-Kubi discusses the souls in terms of *moya*, *sunsum*, and *okra*. His discussion helps one appreciate Ghanaian theologians' attempts to forge a Christian anthropology in traditional Akan terms. See 468.

140 Ayoade, John. "Time in Yoruba Thought." In *African Philosophy: An Introduction*, ed. by Richard A. Davis, 93-112. Lanham: University Press of America, 1984.

Although Ayoade's essay is part of a volume on African philosophy, the epistemological issues he raises are pertinent to African theology. Indeed, both African theology and philosophy are fields of enquiry in which one tries to determine the relation of a certain *Western logos* to African traditional religion. Ayoade's essay is particularly pertinent to African theology as Yoruba religion figures intimately into the work of theologians such as Idowu. See 051, 177-179, 356-357. Ayoade also critiques Mbiti's well-noted notion of *Zamani*. See 200, 396-397. According to Ayoade, Yoruba conceptions of time have more nuances than Mbiti appears to realize. Whereas Mbiti holds that Africans have a truncated sense of the future and thus over-emphasize the past, Ayoade argues that the Yoruba have a well-developed sense of the future.

141 Barrett, D.B. "Church Growth and Independency as Organic Phenomena: An Analysis of Two Hundred African Tribes." In *Christianity in Tropical Africa: Studies Presented and Discussed at the Seventh International African Seminar, University of Ghana, April, 1965*, ed. by C.G. Baëta, 269-288. London: Oxford University Press, 1968.

An essay that provides insight into the claim that the independent churches model what African theology should be. See 137. Barrett argues that the African independent churches constitute an organic whole, rather than "multiform manifestations." This organism, he argues, is anchored in traditional religion, especially the belief in ancestors and the sacredness of the earth. On the ancestors see: 285, 291, 308, 412. According to Barrett, independency——i.e., the independent churches as an organic whole——is a defense against the missionary attempt to alienate the people from the ancestors and the land. The dynamics of this defense varies from people to people; and the translation of Scripture into the vernacular gave impetus to African convictions that christianization was not identical with de-africanization.

142 Barrett, D.B. *Schism and Renewal in Africa: An Analysis of Six Thousand Contemporary African Movements*. Nairobi: Oxford University Press, 1968.

A seminal text that explores the proliferation of the African independent churches: Barrett chronicles the astounding proliferation of these churches and defines them as a "massive and largely unconscious attempt to synthesize the apostolic *kerygma* with authentic African insight, based on biblical criteria from vernacular translations of the scriptures" (p. 278). For Barrett, the independent churches, their heterodoxy notwithstanding, evince African ingenuity——the dogged commitment to repel cultural imperialism. Indeed, Barrett's observation of the heterodoxy of African Christianity is a theme integral Mercy Oduyoye's *Hearing and Knowing*. See 458.

143 Barrett, Leonard. "African Religion in the Americas: The 'Islands in Between'." In *African Religions: A Symposium*, ed. by Newell Booth, 183-216. New York: NOK Publishers, 1977.

Barrett's essay is one of several delivered at a Colloquium on African Religion at Western College in Oxford, Ohio during 1969-1970. See 149, 150, 152, 185, 194, 263. Barrett's discussion of African-American religions reveals a special nuance of the Pan-African implications of African theology (a nuance that may facilitate the forging of closer ties between black and African theologies). See 152, 606-609. Barrett reveals that Africans enslaved in the New World doggedly held on to memories of the ways of their ancestors. He thus provides insight into transmogrified African structures that help one understand African Christianity. As a result of his work, one wonders the extent to which there are structural similarities between the African independent churches and the so-called syncretisms found in Haiti and Brazil. See 464.

144 Barrington-Ward, Simon. "'The Centre Cannot Hold...'Spirit Possession as Redefinition." In *Christianity in Independent Africa*, ed. by Edward Fasholé-Luke, Richard Gray, Adrian Hastings and Godwin Tasie, 455-470. Bloomington: Indiana University Press, 1978.

An examination of Isoko, Urhobo, Itsekiri and Igbo peoples of Nigeria. Barrington-Ward discusses how communications between the invisible and visible——spirits and human beings——were made through ritual disassociation (possession trance). The spirits became part of the one they possessed——such that the possessed became part human and part spirit. See 133. Colonialism set off spirits, which, having been dormant, erupted, "invariably directed towards healing, cleansing away evil and either killing or purifying witches" (p. 459) According to Barrington-Ward, "Christianity first entered the area in a similar guise" (p. 461). Here, Barrington-Ward refers to Robin Horton's argument that "Christianity was a catalyst," the effects of which must be understood within the matrix of traditional religion, and with a focus on the independent churches. See 174. According to Barrington-Ward, however, we do not find a monotheistic development in this dynamic. Rather, one observes a bevy of spirit bands that vie for ascendancy "in the sudden offer of a new *'theoria,'* a new 'rough beast slouching off towards Bethlehem to be born'" (p. 469).

145 Bascom, William. *The Yoruba of South Western Nigeria.* Prospect Heights, Illinois: Waveland Press, 1984.

Bascom's discussion of the Yoruba is very concise, but comprehensive. Bascom identifies Samuel Crowther as one of the recaptives——see 051——who had been enslaved due to the Yoruba civil wars of the 19th Century. See 109. Especially valuable is Bascom's discussion of Yoruba religion and the aesthetic values emblematic of it. *The Yoruba of South Western Nigeria* is an excellent companion volume to Idowu's *Olodumare.* See 177.

146 Bascom, William. *Ifa Divination: Communication between Gods and Men in West Africa.* Bloomington: Indiana University Press, 1969.

Like his *The Yoruba of South Western Nigeria,* Bascom's *Ifa Divination* complements Idowu's work on Yoruba religion, especially in offering detailed research on divination and the role of the priest diviner. See 177. The text is composed primarily of *odu*——the corpus of verses that religious specialists memorize and apply to the various patterns obtained in the practice of divination from palm nuts and other sacred insignia. Bascom's work reveals the sophistication of Yoruba culture, and deepens one's insight into the acculturative power of African traditional religion. See 135.

147 Beetham, T.A. *Christianity and the New Africa.* London: Pall Mall Press, 1967.

Beetham asks whether Christianity in Black Africa is firmly rooted in African soil. He attempts to answer the question by investigating the history of Christianity in Africa and the weaknesses and strengths of the church during the demise of olden colonialism. The primary weakness, he argues, has been the Eurocentric paradigms that have governed the "African" church. On the basis of a christology that accentuates the human diversity implicit in a certain understanding of the incarnation, Beetham asserts the "need for an African liturgy and an African theology." Beetham also examines the role of African Christians in war torn areas of "independent" Africa, such as Burundi. See 074. He points out that the internecine conflicts that have claimed the lives of committed Christians, such as Michel Kayoya——see 375-376——is yet another obstacle for inculturation. Still, Beetham is certain that Christ will triumph over all obstacles. Christianity will be essentially African for the Africans.

148 Blakeley, Thomas. "The Categories of Mtu and the Categories of Aristotle." In *African Philosophy: An Introduction,* ed. by Richard A. Davis, 163-170. Lanham: University Press of America, 1984.

Blakeley's essay may be read in relation to Alexis Kagame, who attempted to articulate a Bantu philosophy in terms of Aristotle. Kagame is a significant figure in the history of African theology, particularly given his attempt to critique the Bantu philosophy of Placide Tempels. See 187, 369. According to Blakeley, Aristotle's work is the foundation of the Kantian and Hegelian philosophies, and is thus basic to Western philosophy. He asks whether Bantu thought corresponds to the Aristotelian categories seminal to Western thought——i.e., quantity, quality, relation, place, time, position, state, activity, passivity. According to Blakeley, more research is needed to determine whether that is so. He suggests that the first step would be to see whether there are correspondences in the area of the "pre-categorical"——the *a priori* of the categories themselves. Blakeley's work raises issues similar to those discussed by Tshiamalenga Ntumba. See 209, 444.

149   Booth, Newell. "An Approach to African Religion." In *African Religions: A Symposium*, ed. by Newell Booth, 1-12. New York: NOK Publishers, 1977.

Booth's essay is useful for the study of African theology in that he recognizes the acculturative power of African traditional religion. He argues that African Christianity is an African religion precisely because it has been "understood in terms of the basic underlying concepts of African religion" (p. 9). Booth explains that the "monographic approach," integral to *African Religions: A Symposium*, eschews study of African traditional religions in terms of high gods and the ancestors. Rather one discusses African traditional religions in terms of more general——and perhaps reified——themes such as "life-power." Indeed, "life-power" is suspect since it is reminiscent of Tempels's problematic notion of *force-vitale*. See 261-262. Booth's view that African traditional religions must be studied in terms of an essential humanism and the quest for wholeness is more satisfactory than his views regarding "life-power." Indeed, humankind is the focus of African traditional religion, as is the quest to maintain equilibrium between the visible and invisible paths of the cosmos.

150   Booth, Newell. "The View from Kasongo Niembo." In *African Religions: A Symposium*, ed. by Newell Booth, 31-68. New York: NOK Publishers, 1977.

Booth examines the Baluba, a Bantu people who were the object of Placide Tempels's *Bantu Philosophy*——see 261——and who are not unlike the BaKongo whom I discuss below. See 185, 198, 199, 238, 263. Booth focuses on Kasongo Niembo, a traditional kingdom that provides clues to the proto-Bantu culture whose diaspora extends into Southern Africa. Booth discusses the mythic structure of the Baluba memory of great ancestors, who are emblematic of a tradition based on kingship. Also essential to Baluba tradition are the centrality of healing and the complementarity of the visible and the invisible. The themes of this structure are fecundity and fertility, which are basic to rituals of marriage, birth and death. The latter two rituals signify the liminal tension between the ancestors and the unborn. All must cross the threshold between the two if they are to maintain *communitas*. On liminality, see 247, 272, 273, 274.

151   Booth, Newell. "God and the Gods in West Africa." In *African Religions: A Symposium*, ed. by Newell Booth, 159-182. New York: NOK Publishers, 1977.

Booth explores traditional Yoruba and Fon religions. See 135, 231, 288. He argues that the religions are neither polytheistic nor monotheistic. In part, asserts Booth, the argument that traditional Fon and Yoruba religions are monotheistic is contradicted by the host of divinities (orishas and vodu). Conversely, that the religions are essentially polytheistic is contradicted by the fact that the divinities signify a diffusion of the Supreme Being. This *ambi*valence provides insight into the claim that Yoruba and Fon people tolerate a mixture of Christian, Muslim and traditional values. See 112, 113, 195. Indeed, as Yoruba and Fon religions cannot be pigeonholed as either polytheistic or monotheistic, they purvey concepts of God that——though having no real counterpart in Christianity——are not hostile to Christianity.

152 Brown, Charles, and Yvonne Chappelle. "African Religions and the Quest for Afro-American Heritage." In *African Religions: A Symposium*, ed. by Newell Booth, 241-255. New York: NOK Publishers, 1977

　　　Brown and Chappelle argue that African traditional religion provides critical insight into the meanings of African-American culture. See 143. An African spirituality, they argue, is discovered in African-American memory. That is, Africa is "*subliminally* present in [African-American] feelings, perceptions, and attitudes" (p. 242). The discontinuity between Africans and African-Americans, however, makes the issue of Africanity——and by implication "soft culture"——in North America problematic. The writers explain that this fact does not weaken black Americans' essential Africanity. Nor should this fact weaken African-American interest in Africa. Brown and Chappelle are "convinced that the commitment implied in the interest described above makes it no less credible——or more suspect——than any other 'interest' in the investigation of African culture" (p. 243). The essay is relevant to the study of African theology in that it provides a Pan-African perspective integral to questions regarding the relations between African-American and African theologies. See 606-609.   The essay is also relevant for the study of African theology because of the authors' provocative claim that biblical religion may have "closer affinities with the African tradition than with the classical tradition of the West" (p. 253). See 294.

153 Busia, K.A. "The African World-view." In *African Heritage*, ed. by Jacob Drachler, 146-150. London: Collier Books, 1970.

　　　Busia, rival of Nkrumah——see 096-101——addresses a conference on the Christian faith and African culture, which was held in 1955. Busia aptly points out——as does Kato see 374——that African concepts of God, such as Akan concepts, differ significantly from Christian concepts.   The latter, he argues, transcend evil and hold that God is quintessentially Good, having no role in the genesis of evil; the former, he asserts, are content to "coexist" with myriad, diabolic spirits and necromancers. Despite disparity between the two religions, Christianity, argues Busia, must draw from the matter of African culture if it is to flower in Africa. He thus recognizes the tension between acculturation and inculturation. See 131. Regarding acculturation, he asserts that a formidable barrier to Christian development in Africa is the failure of missionaries to appreciate the richness of African culture, which must be the ground that nurtures an African Christianity. Busia defines the problem of inculturation as follows: "Can the African be Christian only by giving up his culture or is there a way by which Christianity can ennoble it? Something...must die, but only in order that it may bear fruit. To [Africans] is entrusted the husbandry" (p. 151).

154 Busia, K.A. "The Ashanti of the Gold Coast." In *African Worlds: Studies in the Cosmological Ideas and Social Values of African Peoples*, ed. by Daryll Forde, 190-209. New York: Oxford University Press, 1976.

　　　Busia——see 021-022——provides an informative essay on the Ashanti of Ghana, the legendary nation of the Akan who migrated to the forest-belt of the region in the 17th century. (On the Akan/Ashanti see, 131.) Busia notes that Ashanti religion resiliently absorbs dimensions of other religions without losing its identity. In that regard, Busia's essay complements the view of Sanneh. See 112-113. Busia's description of Ashanti religion is similar to Parrinder's and Mbiti's in that he begins with a discussion of a supreme being, and moves "downward" to a discussion of divinities, spirits, ancestors and religious paraphernalia. See 200, 229-231. See also 239. Busia, however, discusses the sociological and political organization of the Ashanti. See 131, 155, 468. As Akan culture continues to play an important role in African theology——see 453, 458, 468,

477——Busia's essay deepens one's understanding of the contextuality of religio-cultural issues.

155 Danquah, J.B. *The Akan Doctrine of God*. London: Frank Cass, 1966.

Danquah's text is the forerunner of studies on African traditional religion produced by the old guard. Danquah——compatriot of Busia and later nemesis of Nkrumah (see 153)——attempts to explain Akan concepts, i.e., *esu, sunsum, kra, honhom,* in terms of Aristotelian categories. See 154. The text is relevant for the study of African theology insofar as it argues for the integrity of African conceptions of God. Indeed, Danquah was one of the first to challenge the European view that the God of traditional African religion is a *deus otiose*. See 156, 173, 177, 178, 179, 203, 384. Like the African theologians who came after him, Danquah argues that the African God is not a remote high God. According to Danquah, the notion of a sky God truncates the traditional Akan view of the tension between the immanence and transcendence of God. Notable is Danquah's definition of the way in which the Akan God——*Nyame Nyankopon Odomonkama*——is of the same blood as the Akan "race." See 242. As the source of Being, the Akan God, argues Danquah, is the quintessential Ancestor, diffused in the essential spirit——*kra*——of the Akan people.

156 Davidson, J. "The Doctrine of God in the Life of the Ngombe, Belgian Congo." In *African Ideas of God: A Symposium*, ed. by E.W.E. Smith, 162-179. London: Edinburgh House Press, 1950.

Davidson notes that the forest explains why Ngombe images of God are related to the skill of hunting. Unfortunately, he equates the ostensible lack of a "well-formulated doctrine of God" to the Ngombe's alleged lack of sophistication. He also posits that the Ngombe have no "purely spiritual faith"——whatever that would be. Like several scholars of the old guard, in addition, Davidson notes that the Ngombe God, *Akongo,* is not a remote *deus otiose*. See 155. Davidson notes that "the ancestors"——central to Ngombe religion——"are not worshipped but taken for granted" (p. 164). See 161, 178, 188, 308, 479, 485. He notes, however, that infractions against the community are offensive first and foremost to the ancestors, who enforce——we are to understand——traditional ethics. See 141.

157 de Heusch, Luc. *The Drunken King, or, the Origin of the State*. Translated by Roy Willis. Bloomington: Indiana University Press, 1982.

As with *Sacrifice in Africa*, this text facilitates a critique of the christianization of African traditional religion——a fundamental epistemological problem in African theology. (See Chapter 2 of this bibliography.) The *Drunken King* also provides insight into the ways in which the study of African traditional religion entails an appreciation of the social and political matrix often overlooked by the old guard. In *The Drunken King, or, The Origin of the State* de Heusch analyzes Bantu myths in terms of the structuralist paradigms of Lévi-Strauss. Again, de Heusch focuses on the King as the symbolic key that opens up the meaning and intention of the mythological consciousness and magico-religious practices of traditional African people.

158 de Heusch, Luc. *Sacrifice in Africa: A Structuralist Approach*. Translated by Linda O'Brien and Alice Morton. Bloomington: Indiana University Press, 1985.

De Heusch finds that the structuralist method, of which the work of Claude Lévi-Strauss is the definitive paradigm, provides the best grammar for the study and interpretation of African traditional religion. Fundamental to this method is the identification of paired polarities integral to a localized cosmos——its taxonomy, topology, and the mythical archetypes and ritual symbols that give space and things religious meaning. For de Heusch, moreover, the archaic memory of kingship is the structure of immolation. See 241, 501. According to de Heusch, "human sacrifice is most often only a means of deferring the sacrifice of the king" (pp. 215-216). Here sacrifice, practiced to promote the prolongation of the visible ethnic group, involves a *quid pro quo*. The symbolic sacrifice of the King——the posterity of the ancestral community——to the invisible facilitates the survival of the group since the victim is potent enough to stay the forces of barrenness and death. The value of the text for the study of African theology is the methodological principles it represents as a corrective to the anthropology of Christian missionaries. See 162, 239, 279. Allegedly, the structuralist approach to African traditional religion is more "value-free" than approaches that construe traditional phenomena in terms of Christian symbols. To this extent de Heusch implicitly critiques the old guard as he reveals the methodological errors in Evans-Pritchard's classic study *Nuer Religion*. See 164. According to de Heusch, Evans-Pritchard understood Nuer sacrifice in terms of sin, but the "Western concept of sin is inapplicable to Nuer thought" (p. 8).

159 de Rosny, Eric. *Healers in the Night*. Translated by Robert R. Barr. Maryknoll, N.Y.: Orbis Books, 1985.

Here a Roman Catholic priest recounts his initiation into the "shades" of the Duala people of Cameroon. His guide, Din, is a necromancer or priest-diviner. Din is a high priest of the sacred forces that promote healing, overcome malevolent necromancers and sustain fecundity. A traditional intellectual, Din explains the nuances of traditional religion in terms of the delicate balance between human beings and their numinous counterparts. de Rosny's experiences have strengthened his appreciation of the difficulty of inculturation; he concludes that the *tabula rasa* approach was truly an abomination born from Eurocentric hubris.

160 Douglas, Mary. "The Lele of Kasai." In *African Worlds: Studies in the Cosmological Ideas and Social Values of African Peoples*, ed. by Daryll Forde, 1-26. New York: Oxford University Press, 1976.

"The Lele of Kasai" helps one appreciate the importance of looking at the issue of acculturation in terms of the consciousness of a traditional people. See 061. Douglas asserts that one should study Lele religion in terms of the ritual categories set by the Lele themselves. According to Douglas, Lele religion reveals a structure in which opposites indicate the tension between myth and ritual, the invisible and visible. See 157, 277. Integral to this structure are the tensions among the village, the forest, and male and female. The thresholds between these entities define the principles of congruity and liminality in Lele religion. On liminality see 247, 272, 273, 274. It is in relation to this well-defined matrix of opposites that Douglas discusses Lele theism and Lele respect of numinous beings of the sacred forest.

161 Dymond, G.W. "The Idea of God in Ovamboland South-West Africa." In *African Ideas of God: A Symposium*, ed. by E.W.E. Smith, 135-155. London: Edinburgh House Press, 1950.

Dymond discusses the "theism" of the Ambo within the context of the history their system of kingship. He makes the reductionistic, "Durkheimian," claim that traditional Ambo religion is but the sacralization of social relations among the Ambo. Dymond also claims that the ancestors are more critical than the worship of God. See 156. It is likely, however, that the traditional Ambo do not worship the ancestors, but see them as the extension of human life. See 308. The ancestors, then, are not barriers to an appreciation of God. God is experienced through the ancestors. In short, Dymond assumes——as did the old guard——that traditional religion, i.e., Ambo religion, constitutes a privation.

Western Christianity serves to fill the void and thus serves as an *a priori* that vitiates his study of African traditional religion.

162 Ejizu, Chris Ifeanyi. *Ofo: Igbo Ritual Symbol*. Enugu: Fourth Dimension Publishing, 1986.

The text is introduced by Professor O.U Kalu——see 060-063——who makes the point that though the old guard made important advances in the study of African traditional religion, their efforts were "tainted with Christian bias" (p. xi). See 008, 239. Ejizu's work, however, is free from such bias as it interprets Igbo religion within its own ambit, and by way of an epistemology related to the work of Victor Turner. See 268-277. In assimilating Turner's work on the meaning of religious symbolism, Ejizu focuses on the Ofo stick——a modality of Igbo religion that links the Igbo to their ancestors and thus valorizes Igbo identity. According to Ejizu, Ofo is a polyvalent, or multivocal, symbol and signifies "the dynamics of Igbo social and cultural life" (p. xv). *Ofo: Igbo Ritual Symbol* is useful for the study of African theology insofar as it valorizes the acculturative force of African traditional religion, which is the critical impetus for the africanization of Christianity. Ejizu shows clearly that African traditional religion will continue to define an African orientation toward the sacred. See 008, 112-113.

163 Evans, H. St. John. "The Akan Doctrine of God." In *African Ideas of God: A Symposium*, ed. by E.W.E. Smith, 241-259. London: Edinburgh House Press, 1950.

Evans's essay should be read in the light of the pioneering volume by Danquah. See 155. Like Danquah, Evans focuses on the Ashanti, one of the dominant people of the Twi speaking Akan. See 131. Evans reveals a Eurocentric bias; he claims Ashanti posses a primitive logic——as if he were establishing his claim by way of pure reason. Evans's work is also saddled by a very general taxonomy——the survey approach——found in the works of John Mbiti. See 162, 200, 201, 202, 239, 279. Evans, in addition, discusses an issue with which the old guard were concerned——whether the ancestors are worshipped. See 156. Evans concludes that the ancestors are not worshipped, but are venerated much in the same way a community esteems their elderly. Nonetheless, one gets the impression that Evans subscribes to the theory of Father Schmidt, which holds that African traditional religion is but the memory of a pristine monotheism now vitiated by an animistic polytheism. See 179, 221, 244. Evans ends his essay with the outrageous opinion that the "best hope of preserving all that is of value in Akan [religion] is undoubtedly to Christianize it" (p. 259). His remark indicates the Eurocentric structure of many theologies of inculturation. That is, one gets the impression that christianization and europeanization are identical for Evans.

164 Evans-Pritchard, E.E. *The Nuer*. New York: Oxford University Press, 1974.

The Nuer, like *Witchcraft Oracles and Magic among the Azande*, is often referred to by the old guard. Idowu——see 177-178——has gleaned from the book a notion of a diffused monotheism, which, he claims, defines Yoruba religion. Evans-Pritchard's view that sacrifice among the Nuer is related to their sense of sin has been criticized. See 158.

165 Evans-Pritchard, E.E. *Witchcraft Oracles and Magic among the Azande*. Abridged with an Introduction by Eva Gillies. Oxford: Clarendon Press, 1983.

Evans-Pritchard's work on witchcraft is considered a classic in the literature on African traditional religion. African theologians frequently refer to it when discussing the problem that traditional witchcraft posed for Christian missionaries. See 178. Indeed, Evans-Pritchard's text clearly defines the cosmological values and the socio-political matrix that a christological orientation would abolish or modify.

166 Fernandez, James W. *Bwiti: An Ethnology of the Religious Imagination in Africa.*
Princeton: Princeton University Press, 1982.

Fernandez's *Bwiti* is rich in detail on the Fang people of Gabon. His method
appears to be primarily that of the structuralists. See 157-158. (Indeed, Fernandez
acknowledges his debt to Claude Lévi-Strauss.) Fernandez discusses Fang traditional
religion in terms of the juxtaposition of polarities. See 160. For instance, a Fang sense
of the Supreme Being and lesser gods directs one toward the sky——a vertical, spatial
dimension. The earth is the horizontal plane of both the ancestors and their living
progeny. These vertical and the horizontal vectors, with their attendant meanings,
intersect, constituting the crossroads of Fang ritual. More horizontal than vertical, another
set of correspondences is embodied by the tensions between the village and the
forest——doorways to the thresholds where sacred spaces and times also unfold.
Regardless of the specificity of various rituals, each entails the interplay of the totality of
Fang religion, which resists systemization——reification and commodification. For
Fernandez, an exegesis of Bwiti——a "Christian" cult——requires this grounding in Fang
traditional religion, the acculturative force of Fang Christianity, circa the 1950s. To call
Bwiti Christian, however, is not to "label latter-day Bwiti theology as Christocentric and
to type Bwiti as a separatist or independent form of Christianity" (p. 341). Rather, one
should interpret Bwiti in terms of *Fang* modes, which *are* dynamic rather than static.
According to Fernandez, then, Bwiti, consistent with Fang values, has a

> plenipotentiary quality that engages the member's attention, that satisfies his
> need to escape the one dimensional condition of colonial domination and
> administration, and that pleases by appearing to reconcile those many
> aspects of his life which have fallen apart: the dead reconciled with the
> living, man reconciled with woman, children with parents, the old ways of
> life with new ways of life, the past with the present, the corporeal self with
> the social self, the villagers with the forest, the infant with the adult (p.
> 564).

A Fascinating and moving *tour de force.*

167 Fortes, Meyers. *Oedipus and Job in African Traditional Religion.* With an Essay by
Robin Horton. New York: Cambridge University Press, 1983.

This edition is a reissued version of the earlier work published in 1959, but without
the essay by Horton. *Oedipus and Job in African Traditional Religion* focuses on how the
ancestors shape one's understanding of African traditional religion, particularly that of the
Tallensi. The book is referred to often by the old guard and explores the relation of
African traditional religion to Judaism. See 294. Indeed, it is primarily because Fortes
assumes there are similarities between African traditional religion and Judaic values that
the text held a certain fascination for theologians. Furthermore, Horton's essay is helpful
for the study of African theology as he seeks to evaluate African traditional religion on its
own terms rather than from the assumption that the religion must of necessity dissolve in
the presence of Christianity. That is, Horton insists on the integrity of African traditional
religion and makes the point that it must be evaluated "as serious intellectual constructions
on the same level as" western systems. See 174-175.

168 Glaze, Anita. *Art and Death in a Senufo Village.* Bloomington: Indiana University
Press, 1981.

The text is another expression of the vitality of African traditional religion as it
exemplifies the acculturative force that de-europeanizes Christianity. Glaze looks at the
Senufo of Burkina Faso and the Ivory Coast, and interprets Senufo traditional
religion——the topologies, taxonomies, and the socio-political contexts——through their
poetic imagination. Glaze claims that the mythical genealogy of death among the Senufo

valorizes the production of art which Senufo enjoy; thus death reproduces the artifacts pleasing to the Senufo and provides insight into Boulaga's claim that African traditional religion feeds on death. See 307. See also 243. Neither his statement nor Glaze's work should be misconstrued as a form of necrophilia. Funeral rituals provide insight into the link between the visible and the invisible, the living and the dead. Death in this sense is but a transition, which entails both "ancestorhood" and reincarnation. Death, then, is a threshold of renewal. Senufu art in this regard is not a creepy fascination with the dead; rather it is a metaphor for the dogged commitment to fertility and fecundity——i.e., life itself.

169 Greenberg, Joseph. "African Languages." In *Peoples and Cultures of Africa*, ed. by Elliot P. Skinner, 71-80. New York: The Doubleday/Natural History Press, 1973.

      Greenberg is a leading authority on the classification of African languages. Here, he discusses the great variety of African languages and African dialects. See 220. The multiplicity of both indicates the awesome diversity of African cultures and the nuances of African traditional religion——a *mélange* and subtlety too often ignored in the work of the old guard. His essay augments one's understanding of the people African theologians study in attempting to define the relation of inculturation to acculturation. See 061.

170 Guillebaud, Rosemary. "The Doctrine Of God In Ruanda-Urundi." In *African Ideas of God: A Symposium*, ed. by E.W.E. Smith, 180-200. London: Edinburgh House Press, 1950.

      Guilleband distinguishes the language groups of Rwanda-Urundi from one another and interprets traditional theism there in terms of the hierarchical structure of the people. The Supreme Being, *Imana,* is sovereign over lesser beings much in the same way that the Tutsi are sovereign over the Hutu. See 074, 369, 375, 376. This taxonomy has been characteristic of studies on African traditional religion, and can be seen in the work of old guard theologians, such as John Mbiti. See 200, 239. Guilleband claims that traditional ideas of God signify a general revelation, which buttresses the alleged ultimacy of Christian monotheism.

171 Gyekye, Kwame. "The Akan Concept of a Person." In *African Philosophy: An Introduction*, ed. by Richard A. Davis, 199-212. Lanham: University Press of America, 1984.

      Gyekye explores the Akan, a people who hold a certain fascination for certain African theologians. Here Gyekye explores the anthropology discussed by Danquah, Busia, and others. See 131, 153, 155. He concludes that the category *sunsum* should be reevaluated, as it signifies spirit more than matter.

172 Harris, W.T. "The Idea of God among the Mende." In *African Ideas of God: A Symposium*, ed. by E.W.E. Smith, 277-297. London: Edinburgh House Press, 1950.

      Harris's essay may prove useful as part of a study focused on the significance of the late Harry Sawyer, whose work on the Mende people of Sierra Leone had been integral to his vocation as an African theologian. This is particularly the case as one of Sawyerr's early works deals, in part, with whether the Mende God, *Ngewo,* is——in the orthodox, Western sense——the Supreme Being or an apotheosized ancestor. Like Sawyerr, Harris concludes Mende traditional religion *must* give way to Christianity or Islam. On Sawyerr, see 241-243, 476-480.

173 Hopgood, Cecil. "Conceptions of God amongst the Tonga of Northern Rhodesia." In *African Ideas of God: A Symposium*, ed. by E.W.E. Smith, 61-74. London: Edinburgh House Press, 1950.

The essay is another example of the way in which the scholarship of white missionaries served as important paradigms for the old guard. Hopgood notes how the arid land of the Tonga influences their conception of God. He also notes the centrality of the ancestors, which he mistakenly attributes to animism——an inept and derogatory classification. Contrary to the general claim that the African God is remote——*deus otiose*——Hopgood maintains that the Tonga God, Leza, is constantly acknowledged by the Tonga. Hopgood also discusses the possibility that the relation of Leza to the ancestral spirits may be explained by the sociological structure of the Tonga, in which lesser regents are subordinate to the Paramount. According to Hopgood, in addition, Tonga sociology indicates that the ancestors and God are "essentially akin in their nature" (p. 70). See 242. Hopgood concludes that Leza is analogous to Yahweh of the Old Testament, though he reserves judgment as to whether Leza is as moral as the Judeo-Christian God. He further concludes that belief in the ancestors——*mizimu*——must be purged in order to make room for the christianization of Leza.

174 Horton, Robin. "African Conversion." *Africa* 41,2 (April 1971): 85-108.

Horton argues that African traditional religion should be respected in terms of its own structure——a structure that explains the intention of African conversion to missionary religions. According to Horton, the structure of conversion is imminently rational and owes its genius to the spontaneity and innovation of African religion more than to the *logos* of a Christian-eschatology. According to Horton, African religionists had already moved in directions of the missionaries, as they too had sought to modify traditional beliefs.

175 Horton, Robin. "African Traditional Thought and Western Science. Part I." *Africa* 37,1 (1975): 50-71.

Here Horton examines traditional religion in terms of its relationship to Western science. He examines the usefulness of the theoretical model——integral to such science——as an intellectual tool and finds it applicable to both traditional African thought and Western thought. The differences between the employment of such thought has little to do with the loaded distinction between "the primitive and the progressive," and more to do with linguistic and cultural distinctions between the West and traditional Africa. Hence the African model is to be appreciated within its own ambit, and in terms of its essential integrity. So Horton casts "doubt on most of the well-worn dichotomies used to conceptualize the difference between scientific and traditional religious thought. Intellectual versus emotional; rational versus mystical...: all of these are shown to more or less inappropriate" (p. 69).

176 Hountondji, Paulin. *African Philosophy: Myth and Reality*. Translated by Henri Evans with the collaboration of Jonathan Ree. Introduction by Abiola Irele. Bloomington: Indiana University Press, 1983.

Hountondji critiques the works of scholars seminal for an understanding of African theology——i.e., Placide Tempels (see 261-262), Alex Kagame (see 187, 369-370) and John Mbiti (see 200-204; 396-410). According to Hountondji, their works are not philosophies, but reproductions of Eurocentric notions of the noble savage. What is more, Hountondji calls Mbiti, Kagame and Tempels "church ethnophilosophers." According to Hountondji, these men sought

> to find a psychological and cultural basis for rooting the Christian message
> in the African's mind without betraying either; of course this is an
> eminently legitimate concern up to a certain point. But it means that these
> authors are compelled to conceive of philosophy on the model of religion,
> as a permanent, stable system of beliefs, unaffected by evolution,
> impervious to time and to history, ever identical with itself (p. 59).

While Hountondji's view of religion is static, his point is that an *African* discourse does not have to be derived from traditional religion. An African discourse simply signifies the "geographical origin of the authors."

177   Idowu, Bolaji. *Olodumare: God in Yoruba Belief.* London: Longmans, 1962.

Idowu's work is recommended for those who wish to increase their understanding of Yoruba culture; and it also exemplifies the old guard's approach to African traditional religion. See 135. He assumes that Yoruba religion, despite its hundreds of orishas (divinities) is essentially monotheistic. Thus he claims that Yoruba religion is a diffused monotheism, which prepares the Yoruba for christianization. See 164. According to Idowu, "Christianity, by its unique and universal message, stands the best chance of fulfilling that which is implied in the Yoruba concept of God" (p. 215).

178   Idowu, Bolaji. *African Traditional Religion: A Definition.* Maryknoll, N.Y.: Orbis Books, 1973.

Idowu looks at African traditional religion in terms of the discipline of history of religion, and in order to uncover the essence of African religiosity. Idowu rightly notes that the study of African traditional religion should involve what Africans actually believe, and not the assumption that their beliefs are so moribund that they have no dynamism from one generation to the next.   Idowu examines several paradigms——e.g., Freud, Durkheim——only to adopt a notion of revelation in terms of Rudolf Otto, Emil Brunner, and Harold DeWolf. Consistent with his interest in the christianization of African concepts of God, Idowu assumes that African tradition religion is essentially monotheistic. "Religion in its essence," he writes, "is the means by which God as Spirit and man's essential self communicate" (p. 75). Idowu's definition appears to be far more Western than African. He notes, however, that it is incorrect to assume that Africans have *worshipped* their ancestors. See 156. He thus takes a position considered by some to be highly problematic. See 485. In concluding, Idowu suggests that the essential dynamism of African religion accounts for the fact that the majority of Africans subscribe to it. For Idowu, African traditional religion will continue to be a powerful worldview expressing the continent's sense of the meaning of the sacred.

179   Idowu, Bolaji. "God." In *Biblical Revelation and African Belief*, ed. by Kwesi Dickson and Paul Ellingworth, 17-29. Maryknoll, N.Y.: Orbis Books, 1969.

Biblical Revelation and African Belief is a landmark text that marks the development of African theology in the wake of independence. See 241, 343, 396, 493. Idowu argues that traditional African people have been recipients of a general revelation that allowed them to know of God long before the arrival of European missionaries. In that regard, he shows the influence Wilhelm Schmidt has had on him. See 221, 244. With Schmidt as the authority for his position, Idowu asserts: "The Supreme Being of the primitive culture is a genuinely monotheistic Deity, described as Father, Creator, eternal, completely beneficent, ethically holy, and creatively omnipotent" (p. 18).

180   Ilogu, Edmund. "Transition——Igbo Burial Customs." In *Traditional Religion in West Africa*, ed. by E.A. Ade Adegbola, 109-111. Accra: Asempa Publishers, 1983.

Dr. Ilogu, an Anglican priest, discusses the meaning of death among the Igbo. He reveals that death is the threshold one crosses en route to the realm of the ancestors——the living-dead who comprise part of the invisible dimension of the human community. The significance of his essay for African theology is gauged by the questions he appends to this essay: "Is the statement of Jesus: 'let the dead bury the dead' tenable"; "What does Jesus's observation that 'God is the God of the living and not of the dead say about West African funeral customs?" His questions reveal his on-going interest in acculturation.

181 Ilogu, Edmund. "Iro Mmuo and Ikpu Ala." In *Traditional Religion in West Africa*, ed. by E.A. Ade Adegbola, 138-140. Accra: Asempa Publishers, 1983.

Ilogu examines dimensions of Igbo religion and highlights their social significance. See 132, 133. In that way, he wishes to substantiate his point that Igbo religion——a folk religion——is "community oriented, as opposed to the Christian Reformed emphasis on religion which is principally the affair of the individual and his God" (p. 138). *Iro Mmuo*, explains Ilogu, is a ritual coincident with the harvest and valorizes communal values that emphasize fertility and fecundity. *Ikpu Àla* signifies a ritual integral to traditional atonement. Given the traditional quest to maintain harmony among elemental forces, we are to understand that the misdeeds of an individual can foster chaos. *Ikpu Ala* involves the sacrifice of a goat, which removes an abomination from the face of the land. Ilogu points out that historical change has made the meaning of pollution highly ambiguous among the Igbo. He wonders whether Christianity can bring a measure of stability to the disorder wrought by colonialism.

182 Ilogu, Edmund. *Igbo Life and Thought*. Nigeria: University Publishing Company, 1985.

Ilogu discusses dimensions of traditional Igbo religion——such as conceptions of God, and ethics——and compares and contrasts them with Christian beliefs. He indicates the dynamics of cultural change, which he understands in terms of acculturation. Here, both traditional Igbo religion and Eurocentric Christianity are modified in their encounter with each other. Christianity, however, though somewhat africanized, continues to come into conflict with Igbo mores that resist christianization. For Ilogu, the challenge of African theology is to find a threshold that dissolves the conflict between African and Christian mores. Such solutions, writes Ilogu, will "save the Igbo Christian and all people's of African countries in his kind of situation from the unnecessary either/or of choosing between the traditional way of life and culture and the Christian way of life, [creative solutions will]...give to them the better stance which is a combination of both the traditional and the Christian" (p. 37).

183 Ilogu, Edmund. "Christ and Crisis in Africa: Acculturation." *Chicago Studies* 29,2 (August 1990): 197-204.

Ilogu examines how the African independent churches edify the study of the problem of acculturation in Africa. While these churches remain ambivalent to traditional Igbo religion, and while there is a need for more theological sophistication among them, they evince, for Ilogu, an *African* Christianity. These Aladura churches reveal: the traditional quest for equilibrium; the practice of divination and polygamy; and the use of traditional paraphernalia. Ilogu suggests that the more "orthodox" churches would do well do study these "heterodox" churches, for they are responsive to the needs of the people.

184 Jacobs, Donald. "African Culture and African Church." In *A New Look at Christianity in Africa*, 3-8. Geneva: WSCF Books, 1972.

For Jacobs, the gospel——by virtue of God's sovereign power——plants itself automatically in different cultures, becoming incarnate while maintaining its transhistorical origin and transcultural meaning. Despite this assertion, however, Jacobs finds little edifying in the independent churches. See 183. He believes they constitute a return to paganism. See 227. According to Jacobs, the tensions between African traditional religions and Christian faith constitute a dangerous contradiction that threatens to weaken African Christianity.

185 Janzen, John. "The Tradition of Renewal in Kongo Religion." In *African Religions: A Symposium*, ed. by Newell Booth, 69-116. New York: NOK Publishers, 1977.

According to Janzen, BaKongo religion, far from being an old relic, is resilient and able to renew itself. (On the BaKongo, see 150.) Renewal is effected, in part, by the prophet (*ngunza*), who brings about change by standing on the periphery (*mpeve*) of the circle of culture. For Janzen, the independent churches, i.e., messianism, qua Kimbanguism, exemplify a renewal based on outside authority (mpeve). Janzen also examines traditional BaKongo paraphernalia in relation to a theory of ritual symbols. According to Janzen, the significance of paraphernalia (*sacra*) wax and wane according to the intensity of the historic events to which the BaKongo have responded. What remains relatively constant is the structure of the traditional religion. Thus the relative disuse of *minkisi*——traditional artifacts which have been metaphors and metonyms of the ancestors——is not a sign of the decline of ancestral values. Rather their disuse is to be attributed to the ingenious response of BaKongo——such as Simon Kimbangu and Dona Béatrice——to olden colonialism, a response that must be understood in terms of traditional BaKongo structure. (On Béatrice and Kimbangu, see Chapter 1 of this bibliography.) Thus crises produced by colonialism are mitigated by an impetus toward renewal endemic to BaKongo religion. Janzen defines this autochthonous process as inversion: phenomena become their opposites——a women past menopause may be the mother of chiefs; *Christianity becomes African traditional religion.* In sum, Janzen gives little weight to inculturation; rather, focus is on the acculturative "process of incorporation by [way of] ritual inversion [which strengthens] the flexibility of the incorporating tradition" (p. 92).

186 Jassey, Marie-France Perrin. *Basic Community in the African Churches.* Translated by Sister Jeanne Marie Lyons. Maryknoll, N.Y.: Orbis Books, 1973.

Jassey, a cultural anthropologist, examines independent churches among the Luo. She argues that the Luo break off from the historic churches in "economic and social frustration," and in a profound religious dissatisfaction with the Eurocentric mores of the missionaries. In overcoming such alienation, the Luo resort to traditional religion, though Christianity has modified traditional beliefs remarkably. *Basic Community in the African Churches* is an early exploration of the tensions between acculturation and inculturation.

187 Kagame, Alexis. *La philosophie bantou-rwandaise de l'être.* Brussels: Académie Royale des Sciences Coloniales, 1956.

Kagame, a Rwandais priest (see 074, 370) sought to deepen the work of Placide Tempels——see 261-262——by articulating Bantu thought through the categories of Aristotle. He sought to display the distinction between "African" and "European" philosophies. Focusing on the grammar of the Kinyarwanda, he argues that the Bantu are essentially theists, though human beings are the focus of religion. Human beings are muntu——a highly influential Bantu idiom in the study of African traditional religion. His work marks the period in which *négritude* was in vogue and indicates the relation of religio-cultural analysis to bourgeois nationalism.

188 Kenyatta, Jomo. *Facing Mt. Kenya.* Introduction by B. Malinowski. New York: Vintage Books, 1965.

Apologetic in tenor, the text establishes the integrity of traditional Kikuyu values and is a fine monograph of traditional Kikuyu religion. Its value for the study of African theology is not only its insight into African traditional religion, but its capturing of the nationalist fervor which gave impetus to the emergence of African theology. Kenyatta——the first president of Kenya——and erroneously associated with *Mau-Mau*——wrote the book during the Kenyan struggle for independence. The book is thus emblematic of a nationalist consciousness, primarily Kikuyu, which focused on the traditional meaning and importance of traditional clitoridectomies. See 064. *Facing Mt. Kenya* has also made its way into the bibliographies and writings of the old guard. Idowu refers to it in his discussion on whether the ancestors in traditional religion are *worshipped* (see 178).

189 Kenyatta, Jomo. "The Kikuyu System of Government." In *The Africa Reader: Independent Africa*, ed. by Wilfred Cartey and Martin Kilson, 19-28. New York: Vintage Books, 1970.

An excerpt from *Facing Mt Kenya*: here Kenyatta argues for the integrity of the socioeconomic values of the Kikuyu. He writes: "The Kikuyu system of government prior to the advent of the Europeans was based on true democratic principles." Kenyatta makes a point not unlike that made by the African socialists. See. 102-106, 114. Particularly edifying here is Kenyatta's implication that religio-cultural and social analysis go together. Indeed, Amilcar Cabral has shown the relation of the two in his explanation of the land's relation to national culture. See 023-025. Kenyatta also evinces the relation of culture to political struggle in his assertion that the land is sacred. That is, the British of colonial Kenya usurped the land from the Kenyan people and thus alienated them from their religion as well as their socioeconomic structure——thereby giving impetus to the anti-colonial movement. *A fortiori*, the essay indicates that study of African traditional religion has political implications that the old guard tended to ignore.

190 Kenyatta, Jomo. "Marriage System." In *Peoples and Cultures of Africa*, ed. by Elliot P. Skinner, 250-279. New York: The Doubleday/Natural History Press, 1973.

The eighth chapter of *Facing Mt. Kenya* in which Kenyatta describes the socio-religious meaning of marriage——an essential *rite de passage* that valorizes the sacred relationship among the ancestors, the unborn and the living.

191 Kaunda, Kenneth. "Humanism and Community in Africa." In *African Christian Spirituality*, ed. by Aylward Shorter, 135-140. Maryknoll, N.Y.: Orbis Books, 1980.

In this excerpt from *A Humanist in Africa*, Kaunda defines humanism in terms of African traditional culture. See 066-070. He asserts that traditional African society was essentially egalitarian, and that one gauges Africa's traditional benevolence by the ways in which the elderly are cared for. In truth, though, the elderly swelled the ranks of Africa's pre-colonial poor. (Indeed, Iliff has shown that Kaunda's view is a romanticization of a more bitter reality——see 052.)

192 King, Noel. *African Cosmos: An Introduction to Religion in Africa*. Belmont: Wadsworth Publishing Company, 1986.

King's text, like Mitchell's——see 207——is a good introduction to African traditional religion. Unlike Mitchell, however, King notes that African traditional religion——far from being a waning relic——lives "to contribute to world religion and civilization" (p.112). Insofar as he looks fairly substantially at specific religions——Yoruba, Asante, Luo——King's work does not fit the survey genre, but rather reflects the importance of studying African traditional religion in terms of distinct ethnic groups. Part of the text considers African traditional religion in terms of themes such as sacrifice, possession trance, drumming and dancing. As it valorizes the integrity of African traditional religion, which is critical for the study of African theology, *African Cosmos* provides an instructive introduction to religio-cultural issues related to the planting of Christianity in Africa. Particularly edifying is King's discussion of African independent churches. See 046, 141. Indeed, as King points out, African traditional religion survives not only in its own right, *but through independent churches and African theologies*. *African Cosmos* also provides a very helpful biographical essay on African traditional religions as well a glossary of idioms intrinsic to their appreciation.

193 Kirwen, Michael. *The Missionary and the Diviner*. Maryknoll, N.Y.: Orbis Books, 1988.
  The text is organized around dialogues between Kirwen, the American missionary, and Riana, the Luo diviner. See 275. The dialogues reveal: the African commitment to the ancestors; the traditional reciprocity between the living and the dead; and the sacredness of the unborn, who integrate the living and the dead. In an edifying style, Kirwen elucidates the differences between Christianity and African traditional religion——differences that disable attempts to interpret one religion in terms of the other.

194 Koech, Kipng'eno. "African Mythology: A Key to Understanding African Religion." In *African Religions: A Symposium*, ed. by Newell Booth, 117-140. New York: NOK Publishers, 1977.
  Koech argues that African mythology expresses the continent's archaic sense of ultimate truth. An essential dimension of truth here is the link between the living and the dead, which valorizes the perpetuity of life on earth in terms of reincarnation. Often, myths define the leitmotifs of traditional religion: initiation; the priest-diviner; sacrifice; the union of the living and the dead.

195 Laitin, David. *Hegemony and Culture: Politics and Religious Change among the Yoruba*. Chicago: University of Chicago Press, 1986.
  According to Laitin, traditional Yoruba values tend to prevent the political dominance of either Christianity or Islam. See 135. Thus, traditional Yoruba values——specifically those that emphasize the common genealogy of Yoruba people——constitute the hegemonic force in which Christianity and Islam acquiesce. Laitin's text is helpful for the study of African theology as it gives substance to the new guard's realization of the vitality of traditional religion. The text is also useful as it reveals the political meaning of traditional religion——a meaning nearly ignored by the old guard. Indeed, his work facilitates critique of Idowu's analysis of the meaning of Yoruba culture. See 177.

196 Laye, Camara. *The Dark Child: The Autobiography of an African Boy*. Introduction by Philippe Thoby-Marcellin. New York: Farrar, Straus and Giroux, 1978.
  Laye's autobiographical novel is a well-noted story of an African boy, who remembers the poetry and magic of traditional life in Upper Guinea. Although Jean-Marc Éla lumps the text with the romanticizing genre of *négritude*——see 340——*The Dark Child* has been referred to more positively by theologians such as Idowu and Sawyerr. They note Laye's narrative of the blood shed during circumcision:
> ...the hemorrhage that follows the operation is abundant, very long and disturbing. All that blood lost! I watched my blood flowing away, and my heart contracted. I thought: "Is my body going to be entirely emptied?" And I raised imploring eyes to our healer, the *séma*. "The blood must flow," said the *séma*. "If it did not flow...."

Idowu and Sawyerr speculate that the *séma* is telling the initiate that the flow onto the earth is a libation to the Malinké ancestors, thus nourishing——with life's very essence——the continuity of the living and the dead. In that sense, the earth, as well as the blood are metonyms of ancestral continuity. *The Dark Child* reveals how Africans, whether christianized, or islamicized, do not forsake the ways of their ancestors. The dark child's parents were Muslims, but they continued to venerate the ancestor, such as a specific snake——"the guiding spirit" of the Malinké. His father continued the sacred craft of smelting gold and his mother——perfectly at home among her cousins, the crocodiles——was gifted with the abilities of healing, divination, and the identification of witches.

197 Little, Kenneth. "The Mende in Sierra Leone." In *African Worlds: Studies in the Cosmological Ideas and Social Values of African Peoples*, ed. by Daryll Forde, 111-137. New York: Oxford University Press, 1976.

Little explores the Mende, on whom Harry Sawyerr tended to focus. See 241-243. According to Little, the Mende have little interest in the esoteric implications of their religion. Imminently practical, Mende attitudes toward religion, claims Little, are "quite empirical." Pride of place in Little's essay is given to the ancestors. The ancestors, he argues, are the Mende's link to God. His view is not unlike Sawyerr's. See 242.

198 MacGaffey, Wyatt. *Religion and Society in Central Africa*. Chicago: University Press of Chicago, 1986.

In the tradition of Karl E. Laman, MacGaffey is a specialist on traditional BaKongo religion. Influenced by Durkheim, he looks at BaKongo religion in terms of the social values it articulates and the political structure it valorizes. MacGaffey argues that BaKongo traditional values have been shaped by a socio-political matrix that requires one to distinguish African codes from European codes. That is, BaKongo "developed various forms of what missiologists call syncretism as they attempted to accommodate in their individual lives, in Christian practice, and in 'traditional' religious practice, the values appropriate to the two opposed worlds in which they participated" (p. 18). See 185. MacGaffey's interpretation of BaKongo religion helps one explain how BaKongo sought to make sense of the contradictions of colonial experience. In revealing the richness of the metaphoric and metonymic dimensions that structure BaKongo religion, MacGaffey makes a point not unlike that made by Adrian Hastings. See 046. That is, the key to understanding African independent churches rests not so much in a Western, dogmatic discipline, but in an Africanity that makes the study of African traditional religions indispensable.

199   MacGaffey, Wyatt. *Modern Kongo Prophets: Religion in a Plural Society*. Bloomington: Indiana University Press, 1983.

Here MacGaffey——who BaKongo believed was an ancestor returned from the New World——analyzes independent churches that reveal the memory of traditional BaKongo religion. In appreciating the critical *difference* between the cosmologies of European and African civilizations, MacGaffey, unlike the old guard, recognizes the distortion that results in interpreting one cosmology in terms of the other. While recognizing the westernizing influence of colonialism, he values the essential Africanity of the independent churches. Here, Africanity may be appreciated in terms of the prophet who, symbolizing the BaKongo memory of the priest-diviner, facilitates the inculturation of an imported Christianity. See 185. The prophet, then, represents the acculturative force of ancestral values——the "organizing principles" that structure "new rituals."

200 Mbiti, John. *African Religions and Philosophy*. New York: Anchor Books, 1970.

An excellent example of the way in which the study and interpretation of African traditional religion was integral to the methodology of the old guard. *African Religions and Philosophy* is a survey of African traditional societies and is constructed on a model forged by European missionaries, such as Geoffrey Parrinder. See 229-231. Mbiti examines African traditional religion under headings such as God, spiritual beings and *rites de passage*. Fundamental to Mbiti's survey is his claim that African traditional religion can be understood in terms of a "philosophy," of which the dominant category is time. According to Mbiti, African religion is determined by an orientation to the past (*Zamani*), which truncates the present (*sasa*) and virtually aborts the future. According to certain scholars, the notion of *Zamani*——necrophilic in implication——is a reification of African consciousness. See 176, 223. Other Africanists claim that Mbiti's methodology is flawed by Christian bias. See 233, 239, 279.

201 Mbiti, John. *Introduction to African Religion*. New York: Praeger Publishers, 1975.
This book is similar in method and intent to *African Religions and Philosophy*. According to Mbiti, "the book is an introduction to [African traditional religion] and is therefore written in a fairly simple style" (p. v).

202 Mbiti, John. *The Prayers of African People*. Maryknoll, N.Y.: Orbis Books, 1975.
Here Mbiti catalogues traditional prayers with the intention of substantiating his claim that African traditional religion has been essentially monotheistic.

203 Mbiti, John. *Concepts of God in Africa*. London: SPCK, 1979.
Like *African Religions and Philosophy*, this text is an excellent example of the way in which African theologians studied African traditional religion——in Christian terms. In *African Concepts of God*, Mbiti discusses the alleged monotheism of African people in terms derived from systematic theology. Thus Mbiti, in a survey of hundreds of ethnic groups, discussed African conceptions under the headings: "the intrinsic attributes of God"; "the eternal attributes of God"; "the providence and sustenance of God"; and so forth. By imposing a Christian conception of God on autochthonous conceptions, Mbiti attempts to advance the problematic claim that the African and Western conceptions of God are basically identical, though the Christian concept is definitive. In short, he claims that Africans have always known——however dimly——the Triune God.

204 Mbiti, John. "God, Sin, and Salvation in African Religion." *The A.M.E. Quarterly Review* 99,4 (January, 1989): 2-8.
According to Mbiti, one should view traditional religion "as if [it] had prepared the spiritual ground for the planting of Christianity" (p. 2). Thus Mbiti looks at the religion in terms of God, sin, and salvation. He argues that an indigenous soteriology——itself a problematic assumption——is completed and sanctified in "the ultimate salvation brought about through Jesus Christ" (p. 7).

205 Menkiti, Ifeanyi. "Person and Community in African Traditional Thought." In *African Philosophy: An Introduction*, ed. by Richard A. Davis, 171-182. Lanham: University Press of America, 1984.
Menkiti refers to Mbiti and Tempels as authorities for the study of African traditional thought. Mbiti is cited in confirmation of Menkiti's view that traditional religion is supremely ethical because it is essentially communal. See 200-204. Focusing on the meaning of rites of initiation and other *rites de passage*, Menkiti argues that the individual in traditional African is sublated to the community, whereas the opposite is the case in the West.

206 Minkus, Helaine. "Causal Theory in Akwapim Akan Philosophy." In *African Philosophy: An Introduction*, ed. by Richard A. Davis, 113-148. Lanham: University Press of America, 1984.
Yet another source that adds depth to the religio-cultural context of Ghanian theologians. See 139. According to Minkus, the Akwapim merit study because they, though highly westernized, reveal the basic worldview of the Akan. See 131. Minkus defines this worldview in terms of the causal theory: events, whether propitious or pernicious, are effected by spiritual forces. Fundamental to an understanding of this theory, claims Minkus, is *sunsum*——the essential spiritual "stuff" that pervades all things with a potency relative to their level within the localized cosmos. See 155, 477. Minkus's

observation of the persistent belief in witchcraft provides insight into the preoccupation of the independent churches with healing and wholeness. Independent churches often focus on the eradication of witchcraft. See 224.

207   Mitchell, Robert Cameron. *African Primal Religions*. Illinois: Argus Communications, 1977.

Mitchell assumes that African traditional religion will give way to either Christianity or Islam because it cannot withstand the modernity they embody. Mitchell's perspective is thus quite different from the perspective of African scholars, such as Lamin Sanneh. See 112-113. Nonetheless Mitchell reveals that Africa contains more devotees to primal religion than any other place in the world. The book is particularly relevant to the study of African theology as it discusses the independent churches under the heading "Prophet-Healing Religion." See 208. Mitchell suggests that the key to understanding these churches is African traditional religion. Mitchell also notes that African theology will reflect "some of the religious insights of the primal world view and put them into a Christian context" (p. 91). Indeed, given the work of the new guard, one sees that the African independent churches facilitate the production of truly African theologies. See 340, 452-459.

208   Ndiokwere, Nathaniel. *Prophecy and Revolution: The Role of Prophets in the Independent African Churches and in Biblical Tradition*. London: SPCK, 1981.

Ndiokwere examines the implications of the African independent churches, with a focus on prophets such as Simon Kimbangu, Isaiah Sheınbe and William Wade Harris. See 047. Ndiokwere argues that the independent churches reveal, in part, an African opposition to colonialism. Africans, in addition, have interpreted the Old Testament through hermeneutics derived from similarities between traditional African culture and the Hebrew culture depicted in the Bible. See 294. The influence of the Old Testament on these churches can been seen in the importance attached to "Zion-Jerusalem, 'City of David', 'the dwelling-place of Yahweh'." Ndiokwere, however, has not "equated the African prophetic movements to those of Israel, as bearing the same weight, importance, or significance. [He stresses the] uniqueness and originality of Israelite prophetism" (p. 268).

209   Ntumba, Tshiamalenga.   "La philosophie dans la situation actuelle de l'Afrique." In *Combats pour un christianisme africain: Mélanges en l'honneur du Professeur V. Mulago*, ed. by A. Ngindu Mushete, 171-188. Kinshasa: Faculté de Théologie Catholique, 1981.

According to Tshiamalenga Ntumba, the first draft of African philosophy was produced by African-Americans, such as Edward Blyden, who influenced Africans wrestling with the implications of Africanity. See 016-018. Blyden, he shows, was perhaps the first to talk in terms of African personality——*une sorte d'ethos nègre intégral*. Senghor——see 114-115——developed Blyden's position further in terms of *négritude*, a form of cultural nationalism. Senghor, however, in the final analysis, sublates blacks to whites. Tshiamalenga Ntumba writes: *Senghor comprend sa 'négritude'/('être-nègre'; 'sensibilité', état') de façon biologico-statique, son Nègre en vient à être, pour toujours, inférieur à l'Européen en toute dépendance vis-vis la francité et du 'cartésianisme'* (p. 174-175). Tshiamalenga Ntumba also critiques the philosophies of Nkrumah and Mobutu. According to Tshiamalenga Ntumba, moreover, the "Placide Tempels school" of African philosophy is *une construction ontologisante*. Tempels' work, for Tshiamalenga Ntumba, reified Baluba thought, presenting a Bantu philosophy that had little to do with the Baluba. The *"Tempelsiens,"* argues Tshiamalenga Ntumba, have reproduced that error in trying to ontologize traditional thought, thereby *succombant...à simple projection 'eurocentriste'*. For Tshiamalenga Ntumba, the Tempelsiens include Kagame and Mulago. See 187, 370;

415-421. Africans, asserts Tshiamalenga Ntumba, must eschew the alien epistemologies that have made the enterprise of creative black thought somewhat abortive. Africans must develop philosophies emergent from their own realities——what Adoukonou calls an *Africanisme du dedans*, see 288——thereby overcoming the reductionistic, Eurocentric projection that has vitiated African thought.

210 Oduyoye, Modupe. *"Àdàmú Orìsà."* In *Traditional Religion in West Africa*, ed. by E.A. Ade Adegbola, 112-116. Accra: Asempa Publishers, 1983.
Modupe Oduyoye, Literature Secretary of the Christian Council of Nigeria, explores, through the science of linguistics, correspondences between traditional religion and the Bible. According to Oduyoye, Àdàmú Orìsà is a ritual through which deified ancestors, eminent members of a Yoruba community, manifest themselves and are celebrated. These ancestors, revelations of primordial beings, are not unlike the biblical Adam, whose Hebrew name is cognate with the Yoruba, Àdàmú. For Oduyoye, then, there is a relation between ancestor veneration and Old Testament religion. See 156, 294. He posits that one can attain insight into the ambiguity of the ancestors——qua the living-dead——"by studying the Hebrew words *met* 'to be dead' and *mat* 'human being, living soul'. They are not merely homonymous: for when a man dies he becomes totally spirit. And spirit is deathless: He becomes spirit, unencumbered by flesh (the element susceptible to death and putrefaction)" (p. 115-116). Oduyoye provides an example of how comparative exegeses of African traditional religion and the Bible can serve African theology.

211 Oduyoye, Modupe. "Agbara: God's Powerful Agents." In *Traditional Religion in West Africa*, ed. by E.A. Ade Adegbola, 396-407. Accra: Asempa Publishers, 1983.
An exploration of the diffusion of God's sovereignty in supernatural beings: Oduyoye explores the correspondence between angels, depicted in the Old Testament, and the orishas, depicted in the Yoruba pantheon. Specifically, he examines the parity between the trickster Esù Elégbara and the angel Gabriel. Both represent the freedom of God as they are entirely unpredictable——able to overcome the best laid plans of "gods and men." According to Oduyoye, the "Yoruba propitiated Esù Elégbara so that he might come to them as Gabriel and not as Michael" (p. 399).

212 Oduyoye, Modupe. "Festivals: The Cultivation of Nature and the Celebration of History." In *Traditional Religion in West Africa*, ed. by E.A. Ade Adegbola, 150-169. Accra: Asempa Publishers, 1983.
Again, Oduyoye explores the correspondences among biblical and African traditional religions through cognate studies. He first examines festivals of the Ewe and Akan of Ghana, as well as those of the Yoruba of Nigeria. He reveals that festivals are large rituals that celebrate a people's ties to their land and their ancestors. Festivals constitute liminal events that valorize human community in the recreation of sacred time.
Second, Oduyoye examines the relation of festivals among Hebrew, Canaanite and African cultures. According to Oduyoye, the symbolic dimensions of food and family are present in all the rituals.

213 Oduyoye, Modupe. "Man's Self and its Spiritual Double." In *Traditional Religion in West Africa*, ed. by E.A. Ade Adegbola, 273-288. Accra: Asempa Publishers, 1983.
Oduyoye explores the relation between African and Hebrew anthropology in terms of the cognate relations of their conceptions of souls. Both the Africans and the biblical Hebrews think human beings have at least two essential souls, one of which has theological significance. Africans——such as the Yoruba and the Igbo——highly regard a soul derived from God (i.e., *ori, chi*, which are not unlike the Hebrew word for spirit, *rwh*).

According to Oduyoye, the terms, *ori,* and *rwh,* have bearing in determining the meaning of sin.

214   Oduyoye, Modupe.   "The Medicine-Man, the Magician and the Wise Man."   In *Traditional Religion in West Africa,* ed. by E.A. Ade Adegbola, 55-72. Accra: Asempa Publishers, 1983.
        Here, Oduyoye examines the religious specialist as a type cast in African traditional religions, Judaism, Christianity, and Islam. He concludes that the cognate relations among these religions make it imperative that Africans adopt a certain orthodox perspective. That is, the normative paradigm for what is proper to the priest-diviner is found in the so-called world religions. For instance, though the biblical Jesus may appear to resemble an African priest-diviner, Jesus must not be thought to be a magician.

215   Oduyoye, Modupe.   "Patrilineal Spirits."   In *Traditional Religion in West Africa,* ed. by E.A. Ade Adegbola, 289-296. Accra: Asempa Publishers, 1983.   Here   Oduyoye examines an Akan anthropology for the most part. See 206. Again, he examines the analogies among African words, such as *ntoro* and mogya, and cognate Hebrew words, such as 'ebu'' s and *beyt 'ab.* He thus deepens one's appreciation of the analogies between African traditional religion and the Old Testament.

216   Oduyoye, Modupe.   "Polytheism and Monotheism——Conceptual Difference."   In *Traditional Religion in West Africa,* ed. by E.A. Ade Adegbola, 244-258. Accra: Asempa Publishers, 1983.
        Oduyoye examines the Arabic *mil-lah,* which is analogous to the Yoruba *orò-orò* ilé. Both words mean religion, or "family ritual"——that is, "the religion...a man and his ancestors...defend in the face of new creeds" (p. 244). The Muslims, implies Oduyoye, have realized that "family ritual" was not something to be abolished. They thus set a precedent for inculturation that should edify Christians, particularly as Muslims were favorable to the *mil-lah* of Abraham, the great ancestor of faith, according to Christians. According to Oduyoye, the Western tendency to extirpate so-called primitive religion is a continuum of a hubris to which the Israelites succumbed in colonizing Canaan. Here, polytheism was ascribed to the Canaanite as a derogatory characteristic——which was in fact a misunderstanding of Canaanite religion. Religion, concludes Oduyoye, is neither good nor bad; rather religion constitutes indices through which one comes to understand the evolution of human experience. Religion is not, therefore, inimical to faith; religion is the field in which faith takes root. Christians, for instance, call Christ "the Rock of ages." For Oduyoye, one should research the religious background of Christianity in order to understand the significance of "rock" as metaphor. Part of this significance has to do with polytheism. According to Oduyoye, polytheism is a religious expression through which human beings express the diffusion of the Supreme Being. "In fact," he writes, "one of the methods by which monotheism reduced the many deities of polytheistic religions to only one [was] by converting the *names* of the many nature divinities of polytheism into *many titles* for the one God of monotheism" (p. 252).

217   Oduyoye, Modupe.   "Potent Speech."   In *Traditional Religion in West Africa,* ed. by E.A. Ade Adegbola, 203-204. Accra: Asempa Publishers, 1983.
        Oduyoye examines the significance of ritual symbolism, such as that purveyed by the Ofo stick of the Igbo. See 162, 180-183. According to Oduyoye, "Ofo symbolizes the truthfulness and righteousness expected to proceed out of the mouths of judges, priests, and kings" (p. 203). The Ofo rod is cognate with the Hebrew *mat-teh 'oz* found in Ezekiel. Oduyoye also reveals other Hebrew words that, analogous to Igbo and Yoruba idioms, signify traditional authority.   Thus he provides other examples of the

correspondences between African traditional religion and the Old Testament——a correspondence that serves as an epistemological foundation of inculturation.

218 Oduyoye, Modupe. "The Sky: Lightning and Thunder." In *Traditional Religion in West Africa*, ed. by E.A. Ade Adegbola, 389-395. Accra: Asempa Publishers, 1983.

Here Oduyoye examines the relation between nature divinities, such as the Yoruba thunder god, Sàngó, and Hebrew words which signify that nature is the voice of God. He thus explores his contention that polytheism can be translated into an essentially monotheistic structure. See 216.

219 Oduyoye, Modupe. "The Spider, the Chameleon and the Creation of the Earth." In *Traditional Religion in West Africa*, ed. by E.A. Ade Adegbola, 374-388. Accra: Asempa Publishers, 1983.

Through an examination of cognitive similarities, Oduyoye discusses the analogies between biblical and African myths pertaining to creation. See 220, 453, 456. Specifically, he looks at similarities between the Yoruba's myths, regarding the creative meaning of the spider, and Hebrew creation myths. Thus he provides yet another example of how the correspondence between African traditional religion and the Old Testament might facilitate inculturation.

220 Oduyoye, Modupe. *Sons of God and the Daughters of Men: An Afro-Asiatic Interpretation of Genesis 1-11*. Maryknoll, N.Y.: Orbis Books, 1984.

An exploration of mythic structures related to African traditional religions and the Old Testament, with a focus on Genesis. Oduyoye seeks to "expose the 'extremely remote relationship between the Niger-Congo and Hamitic families as a whole' which J.H. Greenberg [see 169] admitted" (p. 34). Through the Hamitic connection, Oduyoye seeks to show the philological affinity between African languages and Semitic ones.

221 Ogot, Bethwell A. "On the Making of a Sanctuary: Some Thoughts on the History of Religion in Padhola." In *The Historical Study of African Religion*, ed. by T.O. Ranger and I.N. Kimambo, 122-136. Berkeley and Los Angeles: University of California Press, 1976.

Ogot argues that the Padhola, a so-called Nilotic speaking people of Eastern Uganda——see 169——were essentially a monotheistic people independent of Christianity and Islam. According to Ogot: "The monotheism introduced by the latter-day higher religions such as Christianity and Islam in the area represented neither a revival, nor an innovation, but an attempted merger of the differently derived concepts of God" (p. 122). Ogot observes that Padhola, in encountering Christianity, retained their traditional religion as an Old Testament and only appeared to convert.

222 Oguah, Benjamin. "African and Western Philosophy: A Comparative Study." In *African Philosophy: An Introduction*, ed. by Richard A. Davis, 213-226. Lanham: University Press of America, 1984.

Oguah discusses the Akan, with a focus on the Fanti. See 131. According to Oguah, Fanti religion is a philosophical theology. The Fanti, he argues, possess ontological, cosmological, and teleological arguments regarding God, and also address the problem of evil. Attributing the doctrine of free will to Augustine, Oguah makes the claim that "the Western doctrine of the will is also a Fanti doctrine." Indeed, throughout his essay, he correlates Western doctrine with Fanti tradition, as if they were identical. Oguah, then, is far more uncritical than theologians such as Mbiti and Sawyerr, who gave more discussion than Oguah to the problem of discontinuity.

223   Okere, Theophilus. *African Philosophy: A Historico-Hermeneutical Investigation of the Conditions of its Possibility*. Lanham: University Press of America, 1983.

Okere critiques Tempels, Kagame and Mbiti——all of whom figure intimately into the study of African theology. See 187, 200, 261-262. According to Okere, "Tempels has tried to found a Bantu philosophy from a general consideration of the culture, Kagame, from an analysis of the language [and] Mbiti endeavored to found an African philosophy from the consideration of time" (p. 9). Indeed, Okere critiques Mbiti's work on African traditional religion and his principal theological work, *New Testament Eschatology in An African Background*. See 397. According to Okere, Mbiti "seems more than slightly confused in his own conceptions of time and does not seem to appreciate the difference in the use of the concept in different contexts——psychological, social, mythologico-theological, scientific, and philosophical" (p. 10). In sum, the works of Mbiti, Kagame, and Tempels——and by implication the totality of the old guard——are based upon assumptions that, for Okere, cannot render the integrity of traditional religion or be called philosophical.

224   Omoyajowo, Akin. "What is Witchcraft?" In *Traditional Religion in West Africa*, ed. by E.A. Ade Adegbola, 317-337. Accra: Asempa Publishers, 1983.

Witchcraft has been significant for African theologians in that it has been integral to the discussion of both African traditional religion and the African independent churches. Omoyajowo, an African theologian, asserts: "The Bible recognizes witchcraft and I have often heard people quote the Bible to support their own belief in witchcraft" (p. 319). Omoyajowo, however, holds that witchcraft is an archaic religious form, the problem of evil notwithstanding. He suggests that witchcraft is a product of mass paranoia, rather than the numinous. African Christians, he asserts, are best equipped to divest their compatriots of the *belief* in witches by virtue of their *faith* in Jesus Christ——*Christus Victor*.

225   Omoyajowo, Akin. "The Aladura Churches in Nigeria since Independence." In *Christianity in Independent Africa*, ed. by Edward Fasholé-Luke, Richard Gray, Adrian Hastings and Godwin Tasie, 96-110. Bloomington: Indiana University Press, 1978.

Omoyajowo discusses the Aladura, or praying churches, of Nigeria. See 063, 137, 183, 234. He asserts that the Aladura filled a void created by the historic churches hostile to African traditional religion. For the Africans, the historic churches are arms of imperialism. See 046-047. The Aladura churches, asserts Omoyajowo, overcome the alienation planted by the historic churches and are the "true African expression of the Christian religion" (p. 110). His view is thus not unlike that of the new guard, who also valorize the independent churches. See 306-307; 334-341; 452-459.

226   Onwuanibe, Richard. "The Human Person and Immortality in Ibo (African) Metaphysics." In *African Philosophy: An Introduction*, ed. by Richard A. Davis, 183-198. Lanham: University Press of America, 1984.

Onwuanibe focuses on the Igbo conception of the person in terms of both the transcendental element of the soul, *mkpuru obi*, and the profound social value of the human presence. See 133. He writes: "A metaphysical analysis of the presence of the human person shows the distinction of the human person as subject and not as object" (p. 187). In arguing for the integrity of Igbo metaphysics in this way, Onwuanibe discusses the philosophies of Kant, Buber, and Husserl, comparing and contrasting their anthropologies with that of the Igbo. He argues that Igbo thought bears an affinity to Buber's thought. Onwuanibe also discusses the Igbo conception of God. According to Onwuanibe: "A major reason for the establishment and growth of Christianity among the Ibos is the fertile soil of the Ibo metaphysics of the human person which includes orientation to God, or connatural knowledge of God" (p. 193).

227 Oosthuizen, G.C. *Post-Christianity in Africa: A Theological and Anthropological Study*. Grand Rapids: William B. Eerdmans, 1968.

According to Oosthuizen, the African independent churches, such as the Aladura, are not really "churches." See 225. They are much too akin to so-called tribal religions. So independent churches only understand the gospel in a

syncretistic way...which means *freedom to self-expression*, and more vital force to attain one's own ends and the ends of one's community. Here is no idea of losing oneself for Christ's sake. It is in a sense a selfish morality, and a type of expectation which is non-Christian (p. 103).

For Oosthuizen, then, the independent "churches" constitute a mixture of a vitiated Christian faith and an unadulterated pagan religion. To that extent independentism——the phenomenon of the independent churches——is to be seen as a post-Christianity that can only be redeemed through a theological education commensurate with the alleged travesty of a certain neo-paganism. He writes that if "independentism is an indication that [theological education in Africa is inept], then the Church in Africa must seriously reconsider its very nature, especially when, as a result of its foreignness and aloofness from the African approach, it is itself co-responsible for the development of post-Christianity" (p. 263).

228 Oshun, C.O. "Aladura Revivals in a Colonial Situation: A Conflict Model in Mission." In *African Church Historiography: An Ecumenical Perspective*, ed. by Ogbu Kalu, 197-220. Bern: Evangelische Arbeitsstelle Oekumene Schweiz, 1988.

According to Oshun, the Aladura churches——see 225——emerged due to the failure of the historic churches to appreciate African values and the necessity of African leadership. Led by the prophet Babalola, and constituted by assemblies such as the Faith Tabernacle, the Aladura churches have an essentially religious significance for Oshun. He thus minimizes the claim that the independent churches constitute rebellion against colonial rule.

229 Parrinder, Geoffrey. "Theistic Beliefs of the Yoruba and Ewe Peoples of West Africa." In *African Ideas of God: A Symposium*, ed. by E.W.E. Smith, 224-240. London: Edinburgh House Press, 1950.

According to Parrinder, the two people are closely related, in part because they are linked to the Fon of Dahomey. See 288. Parrinder argues that the Fon, Ewe, and Yoruba divinities represent apotheoses of phenomena such as thunder, smallpox, war, and iron. See 218. What is more, the Yoruba and Ewe pantheons are presided over by a Supreme Being, who is not an apotheosized ancestor, as is the Yoruba thunder god, Sango. See 145. Both people highly prize a trickster god, who is the link between the visible and invisible *and* the amoral catalyst who affects human destiny. Parrinder concludes his essay with a discussion of Christianity and traditional religion. He makes the interesting observation that only the less westernized Ewe and Yoruba are equipped to distinguish primal ideas of God from those influenced by Christianity. Unlike his essays discussed below, Parrinder criticizes assertions regarding the exclusivity of Christianity. He writes: "The chief scandal of Christianity lies in its absolute claims. How far these are exclusive still needs to be carefully thought out" (p. 239).

230 Parrinder, Geoffrey. *African Traditional Religion*. New York: Harper & Row, 1976.

Parrinder is a European whose method was assimilated by the old guard, particularly Mbiti. See 200-204; 396-410. Here, Parrinder discusses the religions of many black African people, with the assumption that the religions are similar enough to talk in the singular about them——i.e., African traditional *religion*. Although Parrinder's work is useful, it is generally held today that it is better to stress the distinctiveness of African traditional religions, the fact that these religions reveal similar structures notwithstanding. See 239, 279. As with the work of other committed Christians, Parrinder's text is vitiated by his Christian bias——a bias which raises epistemological problems similar to the ones encountered when working through the studies of the old guard. Indeed, Parrinder concludes his work with the words of Placide Tempels (who is criticized for his paternalistic attitude toward Africans): "African paganism, the ancient African wisdom, aspires from the root of its soul toward the very soul of Christian spirituality" (p. 147). See 261-262. As Lamin Sanneh (see 112-113); Michael Kirwen (see 193); and Ogot p'Biteck (see 233) all reveal, nothing could be farther from the truth. African traditional religion must be studied in distinction from Christianity. Whatever similarities are found between the two is no support for the notion of "preparation for the gospel." Rather, as Gray argues (see 041), all religions reveal common themes.

231 Parrinder, Geoffrey. *West African Psychology: A Comparative Study of Psychological and Religious Thought*. New York: Ams Press, 1976.
        Equipped with a survey methodology similar to that in *African Traditional Religion*, Parrinder explores dimensions of traditional African anthropology. His insights are helpful as they evince the way in which the African concept of "person" includes the view that each individual constitutes a multiplicity of souls which signify the nuances of the cosmos. See 213, 384. According to Parrinder, untutored Africans are unable to define their values clearly. It is, he claims, for the European to tell the Africans "what is their intimate conception of things" (p. 2). Nonetheless, the last chapter of the book, "The Development of Religion," offers a very fine discussion of the differences between Christianity and African traditional religion. While the discussion provides insight into the distinct structures of both religions, his proselytizing agenda is too transparent as he valorizes the notion of the ultimacy of Christianity. Indeed, Parrinder ends *West African Psychology* as he does *African Traditional Religion*——with Placide Tempels's quote indicating the absoluteness of Christianity. See 230. Parrinder, however, discusses the genealogy of West African religion in relation to ancient Egypt——a topic quite relevant to Pan-Africanists and black nationalists of the United States who also study African theology. Particularly fascinating in that regard is Parrinder's claim that "The religious beliefs of the pre-dynastic Egyptians provided the foundation for the later Egyptian religion, which was based upon the indigenous African rather than upon Asiatic religion" (p. 230).

232 Parsons, Robert. "The Idea of God among the Kono of Sierra Leone." In *African Ideas of God: A Symposium*, ed. by E.W.E. Smith, 260-276. London: Edinburgh House Press, 1950.
        Parsons discusses Kono religion in terms of three categories: theism, spiritism, and dynamism. In regard to theism, Parsons notes that the proper name for the Kono's Supreme Being is *Yataa*, who is evoked in ritual. Essentially, though, *Yataa* is remote. Parsons concludes that the remoteness of *Yataa* indicates that theism is subordinate to spiritism and dynamism. Spiritism signifies propitiation of ancestors and, by implication, lesser gods such as the hypostatized Earth. Dynamism signifies a ubiquitous, amoral energy that is manipulated by the living and the dead.

233 p'Biteck, Ogot. *African Religions in Western Scholarship*. Nairobi: East African Publishing House, 1970.
        P'Biteck, an atheist, argues that African traditional religion should be examined on its own terms. P'Biteck, also an African nationalist, holds that the biased works of Christian theologians, such as John Mbiti, serve the export of crippling, racist ideology to Africa. According to p'Biteck, nationalists such as, Danquah (see 155); Senghor (see 114); Busia (see 021); and Mbiti (see 200)

protest vigorously against any Western scholar who describes African culture in disparaging terms. Their works are mainly addressed to the *unbelieving* Europeans, and they attempt to show that the African peoples were as civilized as the Western peoples. They dress up African deities with Hellenic robes and parade them before the Western world (p. 41).

African theology must be de-hellenized, if the African masses are to recognize the values that are allegedly African. What is more: "The aim of the study of African religions should be to understand the religious beliefs and practices of African peoples, rather than to discover the Christian God in Africa" (p. 111).

234 Peel, J.D.Y. *Aladura: A Religious Movement among the Yoruba*. London: Oxford University Press, 1968.

Peel's work on the Aladura is a seminal volume on the African independent churches. He argues that the Yoruba, Aladura churches owe their origins to the flexibility of traditional Yoruba civilization. See 195. Yoruba conversion to Christianity, Peel explains, "follows from the fact that Yoruba religion was this-worldly and loosely organized." Imminently practical, Yoruba religion sought to increase favor from the ancestors and divinities so that the living might enjoy fertility, fecundity, health, prosperity. Christianity was tolerated as it, too, could be construed as a means to material well-being. While the Aladura bear some affinity to what Peel calls "John Calvin's predestinarian theology," they reveal essentially a Yoruba religiosity. Peel defines this phenomenon in terms of Weber's notion of *rationalization*——the reordering of a religion coincident with an independent insight. Preoccupied with healing——a practical goal consistent with the this-worldly focus of Yoruba religion——Yoruba Christians "never came to assert that one must forsake all material means and rely solely on God for healing" (p. 296).

235 Peel, J.D.Y. "The Christianization of African Society: Some Possible Models." In *Christianity in Independent Africa*, ed. by Edward Fasholé-Luke, Richard Gray, Adrian Hastings and Godwin Tasie, 443-454. Bloomington: Indiana University Press, 1978.

Peel argues that the christianization of Africa is part of a larger phenomena: "The gradual supplanting of local and ethnic religious identities by the world religions" (p. 443). Not unlike Horton——see 174-175——Peel defines this process as *primary conversion*, a process followed by "the further development of Christianity, in more heterogeneous areas, such as the nation, the city, and multi-ethnic contexts" (p. 445). Peel argues that primary conversion should be appreciated in terms of the dynamism of traditional religion, such as that of the Yoruba. While the Christianity produced——such as that of the Aladura churches——is distinctly African, it is, explains Peel, no less Christian. See 234. "Here," he asserts, "syncretism tends to muddy the waters, as if there were no syncretism involved in European Christianities."

236 Radin, Paul. *Primitive Man as Philosopher*. New York: Dover Publications, 1957.

Primitive Man as Philosopher involves discussion of the works of Danquah (see 155), and Tempels (see 261-262). Radin is very critical of Tempels's work as it impugns the cognitive abilities of traditional people. According to Radin, so-called primitive people have "the same distribution of temperament and ability as among [Westerners]" (p. 5). Not unlike Robin Horton——see 174-175——Radin challenges the crypto-Hegelian view that traditional societies lack epistemological sophistication since they do not (allegedly) distinguish between subject and object.

237   Ranger, Terence. "Missionary Adaptation of African Religious Institutions: The Masasi Case." In *The Historical Study of African Religion*, ed. by T.O. Ranger and I.N. Kimambo, 221-251. Berkeley and Los Angeles: University of California Press, 1976.

Terence Ranger reveals how inculturation was attempted among the Masasi of southern Tanzania. Due to the efforts of Vincent Lucas and several African Christians, an attempt was made to christianize men's rites of initiation. According to Ranger, "the Christianisation of the initiation rites has helped to preserve the idea of their importance and necessity at a time when the general crisis of initiation might have resulted in the dwindling away of initiation into the mere act of infant circumcision" (p. 247). Ranger's remark here provides another way of looking at Sanneh's argument that Christianity tended to accentuate African traditional religion. See 112-113.

238   Ranger, Terence. "The Churches, the Nationalist State and African Religion." In *Christianity in Independent Africa*, ed. by Edward Fasholé-Luke, Richard Gray, Adrian Hastings and Godwin Tasie, 479-502. Bloomington: Indiana University Press, 1978.

According to Ranger, Christianity and traditional religion do not differ substantially; and traditional religion is not inimical to national development. See 041. Traditional religious values can be quite progressive; they adapt impressively to development projects and historic change. Indeed, the word "traditional" is misleading; it does no justice to the creativity of African religion. Words like "survival," "continuity," "revival," moreover, rarely convey the dynamism of African religion. "The point is," he explains, "that the religious formations at every point in the spectrum have been developing their ideas, symbols and rituals during the twentieth century" (p. 498). For Ranger, the BaKongo of Zaire are fine examples of the dynamism of popular religion. See 185, 198, 199. "For the BaKongo," explains Ranger, "it is almost impossible to think of society either repudiating Christianity in the name of traditionalism or repudiating traditionalism in the name of Christianity" (p. 489). Ranger also critiques the praxis of inculturation. He explains that inculturation involves the christianization of defunct practices. (Here Ranger calls to mind the insights of Fanon——"culture has never the translucidity of custom." See 034.)

239   Ray, Benjamin. *African Religions: Symbol, Ritual, and Community*. Englewood Cliffs, N.J.: Prentice-Hall, 1976.

Ray's work is useful for the study of African theology in part because he critiques the old guard's survey approach to African traditional religion. According to Ray, the survey approach obfuscates the specific taxonomies and topologies of distinct ethnic groups. Here Ray refers to Mbiti, who, following in the tradition of Parrinder (see 230), concentrates

> upon "beliefs" without giving the recognition to the sociocultural and ritual fabric within which they are imbedded. Thus [he reduces] African religions to a set of "doctrines" analogous in structure to Western faiths: God, at the top, followed by a graded order of divinities, then the ancestor spirits, and lastly, the forest spirits and magical objects (p. 14).

Ray also critiques the old guard's tendency to interpret African traditional religion as a *praeparatio evangelica* (preparation for the gospel). Here, Ray makes specific references to Danquah and Idowu as well as Mbiti. Ray discusses African traditional religions in terms of specific ethnic groups that provide distinct insights into archetypical symbols and rituals——i.e., mythological structure and its liminal expression in space. Especially valuable is Ray's discussion of the African independent churches. He writes that the "prophet-healing churches have transformed Christianity according to preexisting symbols, rituals, and types of community....The examination of African Independent Christianity has brought us back to the enuring themes of African traditional religions" (p. 215). See 142, 225, 234.

240   Rieber, Calvin.   "Traditional Christianity as an African Religion." In *African religions: A Symposium*, ed. by Newell Booth, 255-274. New York: NOK Publishers, 1977.

Rieber makes the intriguing claim that Christianity is an African religion because it predates Islam in Africa and spread in Black Africa in large measure due to African missionaries. According to Rieber, African Christianity "has manifested a distinctive African character even in the mission-related churches that constitute "traditional Christianity in Africa" (p. 272). Rieber also discusses the origins of the African independent churches that, he argues, emerged from the missionary institutions.

241 Sawyerr, Harry. "Sacrifice." In *Biblical Revelation and African Belief*, ed. by Kwesi Dickson and Paul Ellingworth, 57-82. Maryknoll, N.Y.: Orbis Books, 1969.

Sawyerr focuses on the Mende, Yoruba, Ashanti and Kikuyu. With reference to the work of Tempels——see 261-262——Sawyerr claims that too little attention has been given to traditional modes of sacrifice. See 158. For Sawyerr, an understanding of these modes is the key to inculturation since African Christians continue to practice sacrifice in accordance with their traditional values. He argues that the persistence of traditional immolation is the continuum of the ancestral quest to maintain harmonious relationships among elements of the localized cosmos. Fundamental to his argument is Tempels' problematic notion, *force vitale*. See 261-262. Sacrifice, as a mode of expiation and propitiation, appeases and accommodates forces that had withheld their vital force, but are now obligated to release life-sustaining "energy." Sawyerr calls the sacrifice "the gift factor." For Sawyerr, the correspondence between traditional sacrifice and Christianity is based on the tension between placation, removal of a stain, and the amelioration of alienation. "*The* gift factor," however, is to be seen as the one perfect and sufficient sacrifice of the incarnate Christian God, the Son.

242 Sawyerr, Harry. *God: Ancestor or Creator?* London: Longman Group, 1970.

The late Sawyerr's book raises issues not unlike those found in Danquah (see 155). Sawyerr examines three traditional people: the Akan (Ghana); the Mende (Sierra Leone); and the Yoruba (Nigeria). He concludes that these traditional people see God as the fount of ultimacy who makes creation possible; yet he examines a way in which God, as the quintessential ancestor, is inextricable from a "racial" consciousness. Sawyerr's work, like Mbiti's (see 200-204) and Idowu's (see 177-179), reveals a way in which studies of African traditional religion were prolegomena to African theologies.

243 Sawyerr, Harry. "The African Concept of Death." In *A New Look at Christianity in Africa*, 22-34. Geneva: WSCF Books, 1972.

Sawyerr's essay indicates the way in which the study of African traditional religion was integral to the African theology of the old guard. With reference to the works of Danquah, Kenyatta, and Tempels, Sawyerr examines the African concept of death, which he links to birth. See 155, 188-190, 261-262. According to Sawyerr, *rites de passage* signify the reincarnation of the ancestors in the living. Sawyerr's discussion of reincarnation focuses on the Yoruba, the Mende, and the Akan. See 135, 139, 172, 197. In sum, reincarnation, among these people, indicates the *ambi*valence of existence——death involves the passing away and the return of life much in the same way that winter involves spring.

244   Schmidt, Wilhelm. *The Origin and Growth of Religion: Facts and Theories.* Translated by H.J. Rose. London: Methuen & Company, 1931.
Father Schmidt explores his theory of primitive monotheism. See 177-179.

245 Schoffeleers, Matthew and Ian Linden. "The Resistance of the Nyau Societies to the Roman Catholic Missions in Colonial Malawi." In *The Historical Study of African Religion*, ed. by T.O. Ranger and I.N. Kimambo, 252-276. Berkeley and Los Angeles: University of California Press, 1976.
The traditional religion of the Chewu-speaking people, of which the Nyau *cult* was a central institution, was the structure that resisted British hegemony in colonial Malawi. See 371. In focusing on autochthonous values of the Chewa, Schoffeleers, and Linden indicate that *European* Christianity gains inculturative force through the military might that represses indigenous spontaneity. Here, then, inculturation has little to do with the pneumatic power of Christianity. Indeed, the Africans recognize that Christianity is used by colonial powers as a foil to advance colonialism. Their discovery, then, of the "centrifugal force" (Fanon) of autochthonous culture flows logically from their refusal to be totalized by strangers.

246 Shorter, Aylward. *African Culture and the Christian Church.* Maryknoll, N.Y.: Orbis Books, 1974.
Shorter, a missionary, has written extensively on African theology and African traditional religion. See 490-491. Shorter defines his work as "pastoral anthropology"——an orientation in which Christian ministry profits from the structuralist's (see 157-158, 166) approach to the study of culture. More specifically, pastoral anthropology is, according to Shorter, "the application of anthropology to pastoral needs and programmes." In addition to discussing ideologies such as *ujamaa* and *négritude*, Shorter examines African traditional religion in order to create a catechesis that would make Christianity plain to Africans. He notes that the independent churches provide clues as to the distinctiveness of an African church. See 137, 208, 234. Unfortunately, that important observation is tainted with a certain paternalism. While Shorter notes that these churches "offer a more through-going African adaptation," he *asserts* that "their lack of sophistication does not augur well for their survival in their present form. The chances are that their development will be towards more orthodox forms of Christianity" (p. 24). See 227. For Shorter, the privation of the independent churches is due in large measure to the shortcomings of African traditional religion. He asserts that traditional religion "is ill-adapted to help the African find meaning in his life, and to integrate him with his [urbanized] society" (p. 22). Shorter thus displays a Western arrogance: "The best hope for religious development in Africa lies with the established forms of Christianity which possesses powers of expansion, penetration, and creativity" (p. 24). See 267. When——one wonders——has "established" Christianity made inroads among Third World people without an antichristian violence? And, since when——or rather according to *whom*——is it the case that creativity and imperialism are identical? What is more, where is the ultimate, value-free point that allows one to determine whether a people's religion is sophisticated? Shorter's "pastoral anthropology" is crippled by a troubling contradiction——he would serve the African church by attempting, however benignly, to make it a *carbon* copy of the West.

247 Shorter, Aylward. "Symbolism, Ritual and History: An Examination of the work of Victor Turner." In *The Historical Study of African Religion*, ed. by T.O. Ranger and I.N. Kimambo, 139-150. Berkeley and Los Angeles: University of California Press, 1976.
Shorter discusses the work of Victor Turner, a pioneer in the study of African traditional religion whose structuralist's approach is considered an advance beyond the

survey approach of scholars such as Mbiti and Parrinder. See 162, 268-277. Indeed——Shorter's Christian triumphalism notwithstanding——Turner's work is an alternative to scholarship that would examine African traditional religion in terms of the absoluteness of Christianity. Shorter focuses on the significance of Turner's definition of *communitas*——a liminal event that precludes hierarchy and division. The liminal event, explains Shorter, is

> a period of instability between two fixed terms, a period of ambiguity, uniformity, passivity, lack of structure and lack of status. It is characterized by the unstructured sense of comity which goes to the root of the individual's being and which gives him a profound sense of oneness with humanity. This is what Turner calls "communitas." Communitas is antistructure in its very essence, and yet paradoxically it serves to emphasize the need for structure. Liminal ritual gives structural inferiors structural superiority, and structural superiors aspire to the rediscovery of their humanity through the experience of communitas. This is why people don masks and join secret societies (p. 143)

Whereas Victor Turner asserts that liminality is essentially conservative, Aylward Shorter argues that "liminal ritual can build a bridge between the ritual symbolism of the old order and the ideologies, political and religious, of the new" (p. 147).

248 Shorter, Aylward. "Recent Developments in African Christian Spirituality." In *Christianity in Independent Africa*, ed. by Edward Fasholé-Luke, Richard Gray, Adrian Hastings and Godwin Tasie, 531-544. Bloomington: Indiana University Press, 1978.

According to Shorter, a study of African spirituality involves an examination of tensions between Christianity and African traditional religions. Shorter reveals that a leading theme of Christian spirituality entailed the duty to extirpate "paganism." African and Christian spiritualities naturally clashed, as one was perceived as the antithesis of the other. Shorter discusses how African theologians have attempted to reconcile the two in positing that traditional religion constitutes a *praeparatio evangelica*. For Shorter, the independent churches also exemplify the rapprochement between Christianity and traditional values. Other examples include Tempels's defunct *jamaa* movement; Kaunda's humanism (see 066-070); Senghor's *négritude* (see 114-115); and Nyerere's *ujamaa* (see 102-106).

249 Shorter, Aylward. "Spiritual Writing in Contemporary Africa." In *African Christian Spirituality*, ed. by Aylward Shorter, 3-8. Maryknoll, N.Y.: Orbis Books, 1980.

Shorter notes that African intellectuals seek a *tertium quid*——one beyond African traditionalism and Eurocentrism, and yet itself a product of the encounter between African and Western cultures. He describes their quest as the pursuit of a "neo-African culture." Noting contributions made by Kaunda, Nyerere, Senghor, and Kayoya——see 375-377——toward that end, Shorter also notes the positive impact of Teilhard de Chardin on African consciousness. Shorter notes as well that African-Americans have influenced black South Africans.

250 Shorter, Aylward. "A World of the Spirit." In *African Christian Spirituality*, ed. by Aylward Shorter, 9-14. Maryknoll, N.Y.: Orbis Books, 1980.

According to Shorter, Victor Turner's re-definition of liminality——see 251, 247——and Joseph Goetz's concept of cosmobiology have greatly influenced Africans in their efforts to produce a neo-African discourse. Specifically, Shorter notes the work of Alexis Kagame, who, influenced by Tempels, considered African traditional religion to be a source for African theology. See 074, 370. According to Shorter, cosmobiology has it that humankind is organically related to the rhythm of nature. He writes, moreover, that it is likely that de Chardin appeals to intellectuals such as Kaunda and Senghor because he [microbiologically] "draws a continuum between humanity and the material world" (p. 10). According to Shorter, then, the African believes she is essentially related to the earth's processes——its waxing and waning, its flow and ebb. Indeed, perceptions of the earth's processes are fundamental to an African spirituality that appropriates the cosmos in terms of empirical forces that dissimulate——to the uninitiated——the attendant realm of the spirit.

251 Shorter, Aylward. "African Religions." In *A Handbook of Living Religions*, ed. by John Hinnells, 425-438. New York: Penguin Books, 1985.

For Shorter, the study of African traditional religion is indispensable for an understanding of African theology, particularly in terms of the related idioms, acculturation/africanization, and christianization/inculturation. In "African Religions," Shorter briefly discusses African traditional religion. Shorter's succinct, clear definition of "liminal" is particularly valuable. See 247, 272, 273, 274. According to Shorter, the liminal "is an experience of temporary loss of status and social distinctions in which the deep springs of human relatedness are rediscovered" (p. 434). Here Shorter goes to the heart of the traditional religion——the crossroads where the ancestral community and its posterity merge, crossing the thresholds of their boundaries in the equitable valorization of one another. Yet another of Shorter's edifying observations here is his discussion of independency. Like Hastings and MacGaffey——see 046, 198-199——Shorter notes that the essential grammar of African traditional religion is present in the African independent churches.

252 Shorter, Aylward. *Jesus and the Witchdoctor: An Approach to Healing and Wholeness*. Maryknoll, N.Y.: Orbis Books, 1985.

Shorter's work here is similar to Kirwen's. See 193. Unlike Kirwen, however, Shorter displays an intransigent impulse toward christianization. Shorter argues that Jesus is, as it were, *the* priest-diviner, and attention to that fact should facilitate the inculturation of Christianity. Shorter, however, diminishes the role of acculturation, for essential authority is given to a christology that, after all, is mediated through European consciousness.

253 Shorter, Aylward. *Toward a Theology of Inculturation*. Maryknoll, N.Y.: Orbis Books, 1988.

Toward a Theology of Inculturation may be described as a continuation of *African Culture and the African Church*. See 246. Both contain important insights regarding the problems African culture poses for Western Christians. *Toward a Theology of Inculturation*, however, has less of the paternalism found in *African Culture*——an indulgence disagreeable to Africans and African-Americans alike. Here, Shorter's definitions of inculturation are edifying. He notes that inculturation "is all about a symbiosis of different symbol-systems" (p. 35). That is, inculturation involves acculturation. In fact, he asserts that "acculturation...is a necessary condition for inculturation" (p. 43). Acculturation has to do with africanization; inculturation, with the transcultural significance of the gospel. Through acculturation, the gospel is africanized——as in a "Yoruba-inculturated Christianity"——but remains no less the gospel. According to Shorter, inculturation pertains to the incarnation: God——through anhypostasis/enhypostasis——becomes man. "The Incarnation," argues Shorter, possesses a logic of its own. Once the mystery of the Word made flesh is grasped, the implications are seemingly endless. Every cultural reality is graced and transformed" (p. 81). Also edifying is Shorter's discussion of new guard theologian, Jean-Marc Éla, for whom inculturation is a mode of liberation. See 334-341. While Shorter agrees with Éla, he has problems with Éla's radical critique of the Western church. According to Shorter, Éla tends "to calumniate Western Christianity as a decadent and decomposing church....The argument for African inculturation is not strengthened by denigrating the parent church of Europe" (p. 247).

254 Smith, E.W. "The Whole Subject in Perspective: An Introductory Perspective." In *African Ideas of God: A Symposium*, ed. by E.W.E. Smith, 1-35. London: Edinburgh House Press, 1950.

Smith argues for a method whereby the interpreter brackets his/her biases in order to render the integrity of African traditional realities. He defines traditional religion in terms of its mythic structure and he goes on to say that "myths of God's departure from earth and of the coming of death represent what may be called the African's doctrine of the Fall of man" (p. 8). Here Smith reveals the great limitation of the "objective method." Smith also discusses other salient features of traditional religion, such as the propitiation of ancestors and the magico-religious management of the localized cosmos. The essay exemplifies the scholarship upon which the old guard tended to rely.

255 Smith, E.W. "The Idea of God among South African Tribes". In *African Ideas of God: A Symposium*, ed. by E.W.E. Smith, 78-134. London: Edinburgh House Press, 1950.

Here Smith examines ideas of God among language groups as different as the aboriginal !Khoisan and the Nguni settlers. As in the essay by Hopgood——see 173——Smith notes that the environment conditions traditional conceptions of God. He notes as well how socioeconomic and political values influence traditional religion. For Smith, in addition, the traditional attempt to master the localized cosmos is to be appreciated in terms of the dominance of "pervasive powers...manifest in" sacred paraphernalia (p. 83). According to Smith, these pervasive powers are centered in the ancestors: the horizons of the visible and the invisible meet in the propitiation of the ancestors. See 156. According to Smith, such propitiation——the hub of magico-religious praxis——defines the context of traditional "theism" in Southern Africa.

256 Stevenson, R.C. "The Doctrine of God in the Nuba Mountains." In *African Ideas of God: A Symposium*, ed. by E.W.E. Smith, 208-224. London: Edinburgh House Press, 1950.

Stevenson notes that the belief in a so-called high God is a central, if esoteric, dimension of traditional religion. According to Stevenson, belief in poltergeists and other numinous beings are far more fundamental to Nuba religion than is theism. The taxonomy Stevenson employs in discussing Nuba religion is not unlike that which one finds in Mbiti's work. See 200-204, 239.

257 Strum, Fred Gillette. "Afro-Brazilian Cults." In *African Religions: A Symposium*, ed. by Newell Booth, 217-240. New York: NOK Publishers, 1977.

This essay broadens one's perspective of African theology as it includes the Americas in the discussion of African religions. Strum reveals the way in which African-American religions, consistent with ancestral prototypes, tolerate and absorb diverse religious traditions. See 112-113, 195. Fundamental to this structure, according to Strum, is the crossing, through ritual, of the thresholds between the living and their spirit world. Such rituals promote healing and prosperity. The dominant idioms used in ritual are Yoruba, according to Strum. See 135.

258 Sundkler, Bengt. *Bantu Prophets*. 2nd ed. Oxford: Oxford University Press, 1976.

A landmark work on the African independent churches. See 235. Sundkler classifies the independent churches in South Africa in terms of the Ethiopian and Zionist churches, both of which bear the legacies of denominationalism. The Ethiopian type reveals more continuity with the historic churches than the Zionist type that tends to be "syncretistic." At any rate both churches constitute African resistance to "the colour-bar of White South Africa." Such resistance, warns Sundkler, should not be construed as well-defined, political opposition——though these churches tend to nationalistic. Here nationalism might be understood as micro-nationalism——so-called tribalism. According to Sundkler, then: "The phenomenon of the tribal church is...a symptom of awakening Bantu race-consciousness and nationalism, the African's reply to the colour bar of the Whites" (p. 297). Thus, the African values that define the "theologies" of the independent churches——particularly the Zionists——are to be appreciated in terms of the distinct language groups of the Bantu native to South Africa. Like the independent churches in other parts of Africa, these churches reveal a preoccupation with healing and the eradication of malignant forces, such as witchcraft. See 165, 224. To explain this phenomenon, Sundkler refers to the principle, *interpretatio Africana*, which he employs in analyzing Zulu churches such as those led by the prophet Isaiah Shembe. Here, Christian commitment is expressed through a ritualistic ardor grounded in traditional religion.   Indeed, Sundkler argues that "the independent church, tribal and nationalistic...isolated from effective Christian teaching, is in the long run defenseless against the forces of the old African heritage" (p. 298). See 227. This conclusion is little different from his earlier view that the Zionist churches constitute a "syncretistic sect"——"a bridge over which Africans are brought back to heathenism" (p. 297).

259 Sundkler, B. "Worship and Spirituality," In *Christianity in Independent Africa*, ed. by Edward Fasholé-Luke, Richard Gray, Adrian Hastings and Godwin Tasie, 545-553. Bloomington: Indiana University Press, 1978.

According to Sundkler, African spirituality, in its Christian mode, is essentially communal and best observed within the independent churches. Here, argues Sundkler, one finds a Christianity with "roots both in genuine African experience and in an archetypal inspiration of Biblical teaching" (p. 545).   According to Sundkler, the independent churches tend to focus on baptism and confession and emphasize dreams as a means of God's communication to the faithful——a communication often mediated by the ancestors.

260 Taylor, J.V. *The Primal Vision*. London: SCM Press, 1963.

According to Taylor, millions of Africans are "neither Muslim nor Christian. That...should be reason enough for taking their traditional religion seriously" (p. 28). What is more, Taylor asserts that African traditional religion is a "world class" religion. Referring to the seminal *Des prêtres noirs s'interrogent*——see 294, 303, 329, 353, 370, 415, 416, 464, 475, 500, 511——Taylor reveals that even "Lucian Lévy-Brühl, who in the early years of this century classified this [traditional consciousness] as 'pre-logical, renounced the term towards the end of his life on the sounder grounds that 'the logical structure of the human mind is the same in all men'" (p. 30). See 294. Despite the power of African traditional religion, Taylor asserts that Africans should realize that Christianity is the ultimate religion. "It meets the ultimate point of need in the African world-view by bringing together two factors which African thought has never considered in the same frame of reference, namely God and the destructive antagonism of sin" (p. 194). Taylor goes on to define the significance of the incarnation and atonement. "At the heart of the totality stands the Cross, cosmic because it is the Creator who hangs upon it" (p. 195). Unlike Gray——see 041——Taylor did not recognize that inculturation is bound to occur in Africa because Christianity and African traditional religion are not as different as one would assume.

261 Tempels, Placide. *Bantu Philosophy*. Paris: Presence Africaine, 1959.

A seminal work in the study of African theology: according to Tempels the leitmotif of Bantu culture——i.e., Baluba religion, see 150, 209——is "life, force, to live strongly, or vital force" (p. 30). For the Bantu, according to Tempels,

all beings in the universe possess vital force of their own: human, animal, or inanimate. Each being has been endowed by God with a certain force, capable of strengthening the vital energy of the strongest being of all creation: man. (p. 32.)

Tempels holds that the christianization of the Bantu would be facilitated as missionaries become aware of the African valorization of "force" and use it to convince the Bantu of the superiority of Christianity. He writes:

Our system of education, our civilizing power, should learn to adapt themselves to this idea of vital force and fullness of life. So that it can at once burst into flower and purify itself, we must devote ourselves to the service of the life which is already theirs....If we do not go this way to work, there remains no other way but to extirpate completely the whole Bantu philosophy. Now, who could do that? (See p. 117.)

Progressive African theologians have moved far beyond Tempels in their position that Christianity will be enriched and transformed by African traditional values. See 288, 335. Africans, such as Tshiamalenga Ntumba, moreover, find Tempels far too paternalistic and epistemologically unsound to be of any value to the process of re-Africanization. See 209, 024.

262 Tempels, Placide. "Concepts of Wickedness in Bantu Philosophy." In *African Heritage*, ed. by Jacob Drachler, 258-266. London: Collier Books, 1970.

In this excerpt from *Bantu Philosophy*, Tempels explores *Baluba* conceptions of evil, an infectious force which is life-diminishing——what Temples called "anti-ontological." Thus much of Bantu religion, according to Tempels, constitutes the African's (muntu's) attempt to oppose evil through the potent and benevolent exercise of vital force.

263 Thomas, George. "Kimbanguism: Authentically African, Authentically Christian." In *African Religions: A Symposium*, ed. by Newell Booth, 275-296. New York: NOK Publishers, 1977.

Thomas explores Kimbanguism as a seminal paradigm of an African Christianity true to both the religion of the BaKongo ancestors and the faith of the early church. See 185, 192, 199, 208, 330. Thomas notes that the name of the prophet, Kimbangu, is an idiom relevant to both Christian and BaKongo values. "The name Kimbangu", writes Thomas, "was an invocation of [a] traditional...consciousness: he who reveals is he who is hidden" (p. 276). According to Thomas, moreover, Kimbanguism is not only a definitive model of inculturation; it is also an indication of a grassroots phenomena relevant to the praxis of liberation theology in Africa. See 330.

264 Thomas, H.B. "The Doctrine of God in Uganda." In *African Ideas of God: A Symposium*, ed. by E.W.E. Smith, 201-207. London: Edinburgh House Press, 1950.

Thomas begins by noting the distinction among Ugandan people. The Bantu are dominant. See 148, 150, 157, 187, 209, 258, 261, 262, 274. He then examines the history of migrations to Uganda and how they have affected religion. Thomas speculates that theism in Uganda is traceable to the "Hamites," who, migrating from Ethiopia perhaps, have been influenced by a monophysite christology. See 043. Similarly, Thomas thinks it possible that the theism of the Luo people——see 186, 192, 193——is traceable to both the enigmatic Christianity of ancient Nubia and Sudanese Islam. The essay is useful for the study of African theology insofar as it notes the early sources of African

Christianity, which for Thomas indicate the feasibility of "the existence of a primitive monotheism in this remote region" (p. 207). See 244.

265 Turner, H.W. *History of an African Independent Church.* 2 vols. Oxford: Clarendon Press, 1967.
    Turner explores the Aladura churches of West Africa. See 137, 183, 225, 227, 234, 267. According to Turner, West Africa had no "land problem[s], little race conflict, and a relatively trouble-free and rapid advance to political independence" (p. I, xiv). On this problematic premise, he claims that the independent churches constitute a pure "type, in which [a] basic religious nature is readily discernable." Turner, then, gives little attention to the alienation caused by colonialism and asserts that the Aladura movement essentially emerged from the need for spiritual self-expression.

266 Turner, H.W. "The Contribution of Studies on Religion in Africa to Western Religious Studies." In *New Testament Christianity for Africa and the World: Essays in Honor of Harry Sawyerr*, ed. by Mark Glasswell and Edward W. Fasholé-Luke, 169-178. London: SPCK, 1974.
    In this collection of essays dedicated to the work of the late Harry Sawyerr——see 241-243, 476-480——Turner argues that the African independent churches provide the best contexts for the study of African Christianity. See 046. What is more, he argues that "Western studies of Christianity remain distorted since they take little account of Christian forms in non-Western cultures and of local and contemporary forms in all cultures" (p. 170). For Turner, then, Western Christians have only a partial understanding of Christianity and interpret the Bible very narrowly. Westerners, for instance, virtually ignore biblical passages in which dreams are modes of revelation. In the independent churches, however, dreams are central to an understanding of the Bible (and inextricable from traditional religion). Turner also posits that the independent churches offer insights into the history of the early church. For Turner, moreover, the independent churches offer new vistas to missiology since they offer a field upon which perplexing questions of Christian identity may be worked out. To that end, the independent churches, writes Turner, are valuable models for systematic theology. Here, asserts Turner, contributions may be made to ecclesiology, soteriology, ethics and polemics. As a postscript, Turner notes that the independent churches also have much to offer the fields of phenomenology and history of religions. According to Turner, these churches reveal the dynamism of traditional religion and offer news ways to study categories such as sacred space and time, symbolism, liminality, religious structure and orientation, ritual, *sacra*, and so forth.

267 Turner, H.W. "The Relationship between Development and New Religious Movements in the Tribal Societies of the Third World." In *God and Global Justice: Religion and Poverty in an Unequal World*, ed. by Frederick Ferré and Rita Mataragon, 84-110. New York: Paragon House, 1985.
    According to Turner, the export of Christianity overcomes traditional religions allegedly incapable of progressive innovations. Examples of such Christianity are found in the independent churches. Reminiscent of Mbiti——see 396——Turner writes: "Eschatology in primal religions is characteristically either absent, underdeveloped, or clearly conservative, with paradise understood as restoration of something lost in the past, as following the models of culture heroes, and maintaining reciprocity with the ancestors" (p. 96). A Christian eschatology, however, opens one to the future. According to Turner, one can see this new dynamism in the Aladura churches, "whose leader travels in a Mercedes-Benz, and whose leading layman is a millionaire" (p. 97-98). Indeed, Turner reveals that eschatologies are never value-free.

268 Turner, Victor. "New Religious Movements in Primal Societies." In *A Handbook of Living Religions*, ed. by John Hinnells, 439-449. New York: Penguin Books, 1985.

Although Turner's essay does not focus exclusively on the African matrix, his essay provides a good discussion of the "type" of neo-traditional religion at work in the African independent churches. See 141-142. According to Victor Turner, devotees of independent churches are "less likely to articulate...the form of theology, doctrine, or creed in a Western Christian manner" (p. 444). He thus offers insight into Zuesse's conclusion that ritualistic modes——at work in the independent churches——are more meaningful to Africans than the theologies produced by westernized Africans. See 283. Consistent with the legacies of their ancestors, Africans of the independent churches "do" their religion——they dance, sing, and succumb to possession trance (ritual disassociation). Finally, Turner provides insight into the new guard's struggle to produce theologies in touch with the substratum of national cultures. Indeed, if African spirituality favors experience over discourse, how does one produce African theologies true to ancestral values? See 288.

269 Turner, Victor. "Symbols in Ndembu Ritual." Chap. 1 in *The Forest of Symbols: Aspects of Ndembu Ritual*, 19-47. Ithaca: Cornell University Press, 1989.

This collection of his essays is helpful as a prolegomena to African theology, but not in the way of the old guard. In fact, Turner indicates that study of African traditional religion requires that one bracket his/her religious orientation in order to appreciate what is extended in space. His essay here heightens one's awareness of the rich, symbolic cosmos of the people who truly africanize Christianity in the independent churches.

According to Turner, ritual constitutes formalized behavior of devotees of a specific religion. Symbols are the essential units "of specific structure in a ritual context" (p. 19). Ndembu rituals are occasioned by either "life-crisis" (*rites de passage*) or rituals of affliction (rites related to societal misfortune and thus the activities of the numinous dead or malevolent necromancers). Ndembu symbols include insignia, paraphernalia, relationships, episodes, gestures, spatial elements, and fauna and flora. The milktree, for instance, symbolizes: ancestral tradition; matricentricity, the transition to womanhood; the opposition of female to male; and subterranean, interpersonal enmity. The symbol, then, is both conjunctive and disjunctive.

270 Turner, Victor. "Ritual Symbolism, Morality, and Social Structure among the Ndembu." Chap. 2 in *The Forest of Symbols: Aspects of Ndembu Ritual*, 48-58. Ithaca: Cornell University Press, 1989.

"Ritual Symbolism, Morality, and Social Structure among the Ndembu" is another example of Turner's knowledge of the richness of traditional religion. And again, his work facilitates a critique of the work of theologians whose analysis of traditional religion is truncated by the facile correlation of African traditional religion and European Christianity. Here Turner explores how symbols connote movement across the threshold between the empirical world and its numinous "shade"——the threshold between the visible and invisible, the living and the dead, the earth and the sky. Symbols are cryptograms that signify inevitable transitions between life and death, and the sacredness of the social and numinous order. Essentially, for Turner, symbols signify the fact that mundane entities give way to their deeper meanings. Thus symbols in Ndembu religion work at different levels——the ostensible (gross) level and the cosmological level that is the structure of the symbol itself. The color "white"——*mpemba*——for instance, ordinary in itself, is multivocal, inclusive of both the living and the dead.

271 Turner, Victor. "Color Classification in Ndembu Ritual: A Problem in Primitive Classification." Chap. 3 in *The Forest of Symbols: Aspects of Ndembu Ritual*, 59-92. Ithaca: Cornell University Press, 1989.

Whereas certain African theologians have tended to think that much of traditional ritual is expendable——see 374——Turner indicates the precious legacy these rituals bequeath to posterity. Whereas African theologians have tended to see elements of African traditional religion as a preparation for the gospel——see 396-410; 476-480——Turner indicates that the religion contributes to the richness of global pluralism. According to Turner, traditional religion has its own *logos*. Colors, for instance——especially red, white and black——signify a matrix which is no less sophisticated than that found in other religions. Colors yield a code (cryptogram) related to the continuity and ambiguity of life. In addition to discussing the significance of colors, Turner turns Durkheim on his head. Whereas Durkheim held that social relations define religious structure and thus the individual, Turner holds that the individual defines religious structure and thus social relations. That is, "the human organism and its crucial experience are the *fons et origio* of all classifications. Human biology demands certain intense experiences of relationship" (p. 90). African symbols——black, red, white——edify an understanding of the (human) genus as they signify an individual's carnal processes.   One wonders whether the crucifixion (the mortification of the body of Christ) suggests the correctness of Turner's claim. The immolation and resurrection of *the* human body is indeed the soteriological basis for the church. In sum, Turner indicates that study of African traditional religion (acculturation) may edify Christianity (inculturation).

272 Turner, Victor. "'Betwixt and Between': The Liminal Period in Rites de Passage." Chap. 4 in *The Forest of Symbols: Aspects of Ndembu Ritual*, 93-111. Ithaca: Cornell University Press, 1989.

During much of the first twenty-five years of African theology——despite the first-rate scholarship of Mbiti, Sawyerr, Dickson, and Mulago——the difference between christianization and africanization was dissimulated in a Christian triumphalism. Indeed, the old guard's obfuscation of this problem makes it imperative to read Turner. He reveals the integrity of African traditional religion to the uninitiated, a revelation that must truly enter into the discussion of Christianity in Africa. Only such discussion allows one to develop insight into the problematic of African theology——the tension between acculturation and inculturation. Indeed, deliberation on the tension between the two enables one to distinguish them in the contexts of the independent churches. "'Betwixt and Between': The Liminal Period in Rites de Passage"——one of Turner's seminal essays——sets forth a critical reality in the interpretation of acculturation: the study of African ritual in terms of liminality. See 247, 250. "Liminality", explains Turner, "is the realm of primitive hypothesis, where there is a certain freedom to juggle with the factors of existence." The liminal is that plane——neither in space nor in time——on which the initiate, poised at the crossroads of stateless being (neither boy nor man) is transformed. He leaves the stateless void between boyhood and manhood and crosses over to the latter. Fundamental to these *rites de passage* are *sacra*: sacred paraphernalia, movements and speech——all of which are pregnant with symbolic meaning and constitute a microcosm of the local cosmos. See 269-270.

273 Turner, Victor. "Liminality and Communitas." Chap. 3 in *The Ritual Process: Structure and Anti-Structure*, 94-130. Ithaca, New York: Cornell University Press, 1989.

Turner deepens his definition of liminality in terms of antistructure. He thus explores the implications of his major thesis in *The Ritual Process*: focus on structure alone truncates human experience. One must also be conscious of antistructure——the moments of human experience that require a suspension of the prevailing grammar, thereby allowing one to better appreciate the richness of human experience in terms of other (more universal?) planes of existence. Turner explains that liminality, that is antistructure, is akin to passing, gestation, invisibility, darkness, androgyny and so forth. What is more, the

attributes of liminality or of liminal *personae* ("threshold people") are necessarily ambiguous, since this condition and these persons elude or slip through the network of classifications that normally locate states and positions in cultural space. Liminal entities are neither here nor there; they are betwixt and between [see 272] the positions assigned and arrayed by law, custom, convention, and ceremonial. As such, their ambiguous and indeterminate attributes are expressed by a rich variety of symbols in the many societies that ritualize social and cultural transitions (p. 95).

As liminality dissolves social distinctions, it heightens interpersonal equity. It is *communitas*. See 247. Turner prefers this Latin term to community because *communitas* has nothing to do with space. *Communitas* is a sacred time, and thus it transcends temporality. It is antistructure——homogeneity rather than heterogeneity, totality rather than partiality, humility rather than "just pride of position." Could not one say that Christianity——with its values related to kenosis, incarnation, crucifixion——is itself based on liminality and *communitas*?

274 Turner, Victor. "Humility and Hierarchy: The Liminality of Status Elevation and Reversal." Chap. 5 in *The Ritual Process: Structure and Anti-Structure*, 166-203. Ithaca, New York: Cornell University Press, 1989.

Here Turner discusses liminality and *communitas* generically, showing how they apply to diverse human situations. His discussion of the independent churches of South Africa is particularly pertinent. See 546, 554, 555, 581, 585, 590, 592, 599. He examines Sundkler's discussion——see 258——of the Zionists' rejection of apartheid in terms of "status reversal." That is, the oppressed Bantu achieve, through what Sundkler calls *interpretatio Africana*, a foretaste of a heaven. In heaven, blacks will rule whites. See 258-259. Turner points out that, strictly speaking, such reversal does not constitute *communitas*. See 247, 273. Rather, the churches suggest "that religions that stress hierarchy, whether direct or inverted, as a general attribute of religious life, are generated from the midst of the structurally inferior in a socio-political system that rests as much upon force as on consensus" (p. 190). (One wonders whether consensus in regard to the South African context is a euphemism for white supremacy.)

275 Turner, Victor. "Muchona the Hornet, Interpreter of Religion." Chap. 6 in *The Forest of Symbols: Aspects of Ndembu Ritual*, 131-150. Ithaca: Cornell University Press, 1989.

The problem of inculturation has been explored in terms of the dialogue between traditional priest-diviners and Christian missionaries. See 193, 252. In this essay, first published in 1959, one gains more insight into the priest-diviner. Turner records all that he learned about Ndembu ritual from Muchona, a diviner. Although he is marginalized and nomadic due to his low social status——derived from being the progeny of slaves——Muchona possesses sharp insight into Ndembu religion. Indeed, Turner argues that Muchona is an intellectual, not a "witch doctor." See 236. Muchona's marginality facilitates his role as a traditional healer, diviner, and exorcist. As a master of traditional symbols and interpreter of the tensions between the visible and invisible, Muchona is a purveyor of healing and wholeness——liminal values that transcend social status and are uniformly esteemed. "Muchona the Hornet, Interpreter of Religion," exemplifies how disingenuous an African theology must seem to traditional intellectuals. See 193. The lack of candor comes from the facile correlation African theologians have made between

Christian symbols and traditional ritual. See 200-204. "Muchona The Hornet," in addition, has heuristic value as it indicates the correspondence between the *prophet* of the independent churches and the priest-diviner. Indeed, Turner notes the similarity between "Old Testament...and Ndembu observances."

276 Turner, Victor. "Witchcraft and Sorcery." Chap. 5 in *The Forest of Symbols: Aspects of Ndembu Ritual*, 112-127. Ithaca: Cornell University Press, 1989.

According to Turner, the distinction between witchcraft and sorcery is often false. That is, "a holistic or 'labeling' approach to the definitional problems [concerning necromancy] is likely to sidetrack investigation from the study of actual behavior in a social field context to an obsession with the proper pigeonholing of beliefs and practices as either 'witchcraft' or 'sorcery.'" It is likely that such pigeonholing was at work in the accomplishments of African theologians, who have focused on the problem of witchcraft and sorcery in traditional society. Here, Turner corrects their tendency to reify witchcraft, since he argues that witchcraft does not present itself according to the formulas of scholars of African traditional religion. See 165, 224.

277 Turner, Victor. "Planes of Classification." Chap. 1 in *The Ritual Process: Structure and Anti-Structure*, 1-43. Ithaca, New York: Cornell University Press, 1989.

In "Planes of Classification," Turner examines Ndembu rituals designed to overcome infertility in women. As in most of these rituals, correction of the problem involves religious specialists (see 275), who must prescribe and conduct the proper ritual. Here, the organization of such ritual involves certain "fields"——the village, the stream and the forest——and the tunnels of a burrowing animal. The animal and its hole represent the problem of infertility, which must be opened or cleared in order for conception to occur. Thus, ritual space involves the correspondence among the burrows, the afflicted woman, her spouse, and points between the village and the forest. Fundamental here——as in many traditional religions studied *à l'anthropologie lévi-straussienne*——is the juxtaposition of spatial and binary opposites:

left	right
woman	man
death	life
nature	culture

According to Turner, the tendency has been to assume that man is always to life as woman is to death. That is not the case, however; one must understand binary opposition within the confines of a given ritual.

278 Welbourn, F.B. *East African Rebels: A Study of some Independent Churches*. London: SCM Press, 1961.

A provocative and informative text on the independent churches. See 046, 234, 265. "If," Welbourn writes, "the independent churches are an offense to the growing consciousness of the need for one Church, they reveal——by their very existence——some of the failure of the Church as it is. They need be not an offence only but might be a stimulus to radical reform" (p. 12). Thus Welbourn evinces a creative and imaginative approach to African Christianity; he eschews the hubristic approach of certain interpreters of the phenomenon. See 227.

279 Westerlund, David. *African Religion in African Scholarship: A Preliminary Study of the Religious and Political Background*. Stockholm: Almqvist & Wiksell International, 1985.

This text is quite valuable in the study of African theology, particularly that of the old guard. Westerlund provides insight into why Africans such as Idowu and Mbiti——see

356-357; 396-410——reproduced the methodologies of Europeans such as Geoffrey Parrinder and J.V. Taylor. See 229-231, 260. Westerlund compares Parrinder's work——with whom Idowu studied——with that of anthropologists influenced by Marx and Durkheim. Whereas the scholars influenced by Marx and Durkheim tended to view African traditional religion sociologically, the scholars influenced by a Christian exclusivism tended to dissimulate social contradictions. For Westerlund, their Christian bias distorted the presentation of African religion. Westerlund also notes the influence of nationalism on the formulations of the old guard——a nationalism in which petty bourgeois politics censured the theme of liberation. He also argues that nationalism has tended to lead to the glorification of traditional religion in the works of Idowu and p'Biteck. See 233.

280 Wiredu, K. "How Not to Compare African Thought with Western Thought." In *African Philosophy: An Introduction*, ed. by Richard A. Davis, 149-162. Lanham: University Press of America, 1984.

Wiredu focuses on an Akan anthropology and thus deepens study of the Ghanaian context of African theology. See 139. He assumes that Christianity, like Akan religion, "teaches of a whole hierarchy of spirits," which extends from the Trinity to deceased mortals. Indeed, Wiredu correctly notes that Christianity has not replaced African traditional religion; rather, the two have merged. For Wiredu, however, religious belief of any sort is baseless. He argues that African traditional religion, in particular, is an archaism that facilitated and maintained colonialism and thus must be overcome. For Wiredu, traditional religion is superstition in that it is, allegedly, "a rationally unsupported belief in entities of any sort." Although Wiredu acknowledges that Western philosophy is oppressively Eurocentric, and that African philosophers must incorporate ancestral values in order to overcome Eurocentrism, he seems too captive to European assumptions regarding the value of African traditional religion. In addition, Wiredu does not consider that African traditional religion has been fundamental to African resistance to colonialism.

281 Young, T. Cullen. "The Idea of God in Northern Nysaland." In *African Ideas of God: A Symposium*, ed. by E.W.E. Smith, 36-57. London: Edinburgh House Press, 1950.

Young——who lived in the region for at least 27 seven years——looks at Nyasaland (Malawi) theism "through the thought-area occupied by the ancestors" (p. 38). See 156. Young claims to be "moving within a sphere where reference to God is simply not required" (p. 38). He thus establishes the primacy of the ancestors, who are the chief means of contacting the invisible realm, and through whom one may ambush a people's conception of God.

282 Zahan, Dominique. *The Religion, Spirituality and Thought of Traditional Africa.* Translated by Kate Ezra Martin and Lawrence M. Martin. Chicago: University Press of Chicago, 1979.

The Religion, Spirituality and Thought of Traditional Africa is one of the finest, general introductions to African traditional religion. Zahan, an authority on the Bambara of Mali, clearly appreciates traditional African values; and his work belongs to a genre that valorizes the contribution African traditional religion may make to world culture. His work thus heightens one's awareness of the acculturative force of African traditional religion in the context of African Christianity. Although Zahan discusses African traditional religion thematically——in a way not unlike Parrinder and Mbiti——he is able to communicate the integrity of traditional values far more effectively than the other two writers. See 200-204, 229-231. Zahan has come to understand and appreciate much of the inner meaning and intention of mythic consciousness and ritual action. His central thesis is that the moral and mystical life is the focus of African spirituality. The African attempts to master his/her environment by way of a moral discipline that radically submits the physical to the spiritual, the visible to the invisible. See 298. Africans thus endure hardship and pain in the quest to actualize themselves as spirit. Whatever dichotomy or dualism appears to derive from that sublation is only ostensible. As Zahan reveals, traditional religion seeks to overcome dualism in the liminal experiences that draw opposites together and valorize the sacredness of the human being and the earth that sustains her. Especially edifying in this regard is chapter eight, "Ethics and Spiritual Life," in which his knowledge of the Bambara comes to the fore.

283   Zuesse, Evan. *Ritual Cosmos: The Sanctification of Life in African Religions.* Athens: Ohio University Press, 1979.

Zuesse focuses on: the Mbuti Pygmies; the Lele; the Lega; and the Ila peoples——all of central Africa. Like Zahan, Zuesse argues that African traditional religion has much to offer world culture, and particularly the Christianity to which it has been close. Particularly edifying in this regard is the distinction he makes between religions of salvation (Christianity) and religions of structure (African traditional religion). The former, he argues, devalues the concrete world in favor of an imaginative, eschatological vision of the transhistorical Kingdom of God——which is the Christian's goal. The latter celebrates the processes and nuances of this world. Here, reincarnation is the goal. According to Zuesse, African traditional religion, "rejoices in the sanctification of everyday life, and finds eternity in the midst of change" (p. 7). Essential to this valorization of the earth are organic processes, related to time, and topological juxtapositions, related to space. *A fortiori*, Zuesse suggests that the structure of traditional religion runs so deep in the souls of Africans that it would be exceeding difficult for a *theology* to respond to the existential and cosmological values of peasant culture. See 268.

8

African Theology: Old and New Guards

284   Abega, P. "Liturgical Adaptation." In *Christianity in Independent Africa*, ed. by Edward Fasholé-Luke, Richard Gray, Adrian Hastings and Godwin Tasie, 597-605. Bloomington: Indiana University Press, 1978.

Abega examines the problem of inculturation in the context of the Cameroon, and ties it to "the mystery of the Incarnation" (p. 599). For Abega, the reality of the incarnation is discovered in the Eucharist. Abega examines the principle——integral to the performance of the sacrament——"This is my body, this is my blood." He argues that the principle is to be contextualized——i.e., acculturated: made African, so that the catholicity it signifies and imparts is a living reality. Abega thus makes an argument for Christian diversity, which is the *a priori* of inculturation. See 299.

285   Abogunrin, S.O. "The Search for the Historical Jesus in Relation to Christianity in Africa." *Africa Theological Journal* 9,2 (November 1980): 18-29.

Abogunrin discusses the quests for the historical Jesus with a focus on Albert Schweitzer, Rudolf Bultmann, and certain "post-Bultmannians." He argues that the quest itself is irrelevant to African Christians, for whom the problem of faith versus reason is a *non sequitur*. According to Abogunrin, a demythologized Christ would be divested of religious significance. The gospel takes root so spontaneously in the context of the independent churches precisely because the sacred cosmos of the Bible is like the sacred cosmos of the ancestors. A Jesus who did not truly manipulate the visible and invisible realms of that Cosmos could not——we are to understand——be Lord. While Abogunrin does not eschew the critical orientation of higher criticism, he notes that an African exegesis should develop from autochthonous rather than exported hermeneutics.

286   Adegbola, E.A. Adeolu. "The Theological Basis of Ethics." In *Biblical Revelation and African Belief*, ed. by Kwesi Dickson and Paul Ellingworth, 116-136. Maryknoll, N.Y.: Orbis Books, 1969.

Adegbola's essay is an indication of how African theologians have been influenced by the work of Placide Tempels (see 261-262); Geoffrey Parrinder (see 229-231); and Edwin Smith (see 254-255). In determining whether there is a correspondence between Christian definitions of sin and traditional Yoruba morality——see 135——Adegbola relies heavily on the work of those missionaries. For Adegbola, Yoruba conceptions of evil are analogous to Christian conceptions of evil because both are thought to constitute an estrangement from God. With respect to inculturation, he argues that the proclamation of the cross will release the Yoruba from the neurosis of their "demons."

287 Adelowo, Dada E. "Islamic Monotheism and the Christian Traditional African Concepts of the Godhead." *Africa Theological Journal* 9,2 (July 1980): 62-76.

Adelowo discusses the concept of the Godhead in Islam, Christianity, and African traditional religions. See 017, 365. Despite the fact that traditional religions, such as the Yoruba, embody hundreds of divinities, Adelowo asserts that they are essentially monotheistic. Here Adelowo employs Idowu's notion of diffused monotheism——see 177——and implies that African traditional religion is not unlike Christianity in that God, in both cases, signifies a certain plurality of being as well as an ineffable aseity. Not unlike Lamin Sanneh——see 112-113——Adelowo concludes his essay with the assertion that Africans tend to tolerate, indeed thrive on, religious pluralism. See 195. This tolerance creates the conditions whereby Christianity is africanized, without losing its identity.

288 Adoukonou, Barthélemy. *Jalons pour une théologie africaine: Essai d'une herméneutique chrétienne du Vodun dahoméen. Tome I: Critique théologique.* Paris: Éditions Lethielleux, 1980.

Adoukonou lays the foundation for an African theology grounded in pneumatology and the traditional religion of Dahomey. By way of Vodun, the African attains *une compréhension chrétienne des événements de la mort-résurrection de Jésus* (p. 306). The African theology he envisions is derived from a hermeneutic suspicion based on the distinction between *l'Africanisme du dedans* and *l'Africanisme du dehors*. The inside Africanity is emergent from African realities, but the outside Africanity is *la projection de tous les phantasmes de l'Occident blanc* (p. 29). It is only by way of the inside track that the African names himself. Only through *l'Africanisme du dedans* do Africans overcome the Eurocentric significations akin to *négritude*. That is, Vodun and Christian faith only make sense to Africans today if both religious modes attain relevance in accordance with the historical and cultural realities of black experience. One of these realities involves an African re-interpretation of the slave trade. The slave trade, he argues, led *en vérité à la plus terrible histoire des temps modernes et à côte de laquelle la bagatelle du nazisme ne sera qu'un jeu d'enfant* (p. 40). The death of six million Jews *livrés au four crématoire*, pales beside the *100 millions d'esclaves déportes en Amérique par le même hybris de l'homme*. According to Adoukonou, three quarters of those Africans perished in the underside of those schooners. While such perversion, like a boomerang, reveals that the West woefully lacks humanity (*le retour du boomerang a réveillé l'Occident épouvanté*), few have considered the theological implications of its ugly hubris (p.40). For Adoukonou, this issue is critical; and "thingified" Africans must investigate why their oppression has not taken center stage in investigations regarding providence and theodicy. According to Adoukonou, Africans, themselves, must *reposer la question de l'altérité d'une maniéré nouvelle*. Indeed, the question implies a determination of what heresy is (*le véritable fil d'Ariane de notre questionnement théologique*). *Jalons pour une théologie africaine: Essai d'une herméneutique chrétienne du Vodun dahoméen* is one of the strongest African theologies published to date.

289 All Africa Council of Churches. "The Confession of Alexandria." In *Mission Trends No. 3: Third World Theologies. Asian, African and Latin American Contributions to a Radical, Theological Realignment in the Church,* ed. by Gerald Anderson and Thomas Stransky, 132-134. New York: Paulist Press; Grand Rapids: Wm. B. Eerdmans, 1976.

This document is the confession adopted by the AACC at the conference held in 1976 in Alexandria, Egypt. In addition to highlighting commitments to economic justice, peace and the liberation of persons, the AACC affirms its continuity with the African church of the Patristic period.

290   Amoah, Elizabeth, and Mercy Amba Oduyoye.   "The Christ for African Women."
In *With Passion and Compassion: Third World Women Doing Theology*, ed. by V[irginia]
Fabella and M[ercy] Oduyoye, 47-59. Maryknoll, N.Y.: Orbis Books, 1989.

In exploring African women's christology, Oduyoye——see 452-459——and Amoah
first examine African men's christologies which, despite their sexism, have recognized that
Western paradigms are too otherworldly for Africans whose traditional memory has been
shaped by values that emphasize health and wholeness now.   The authors reveal that
Western christology has been especially challenged by the independent churches that
indicate the correctness of African theologians' position that Jesus should be understood
as *Christus Victor*. See 400.   For Oduyoye and Amoah, this view of the atonement may
be appreciated in terms of a realized eschatology——see 397——which empowers the
African poor to struggle against the forces inimical to health and wholeness, an
empowering consistent with the indelible structures of their primal religions.   See 338.
While the pioneering enquiries of African men are appreciated by African women, the need
for an African women's christology is critical because women's consciousness is peripheral
to men's work.

291   Anyanwu, Onyema H.   "Why the Igbos Abandoned their God." *Africa Theological
Journal* 14,2 (1985): 91-99.

According to Anyanwu, the traditional Igbo have revered a Supreme Being, creator
of the universe. See 133.   For the Igbos, in addition, the cosmos is nuanced by three
essential spaces: (1) the sky, where God (Chukwe) dwells with primordial spirits; (2) the
earth——the goddess——with her taxonomy, the apex of which is humankind with whom
dwells a myriad of spirits between the forest and the village; and (3) the world below in
which the ancestors and guardian spirits dwell.   Harmony is achieved in the culture
through the mediation and propitiation of numinous beings, such as the ancestors and Ala,
the Earth goddess.   They can be punitive if religious principles are not fastidiously
observed.   Anyanwu, moreover, asserts what Achebe portrays vividly in several of his
novels: missionaries came to Igboland in bogus ignorance of the depth and integrity of
traditional religion. See 132-133.   Igbos often converted because they saw social and
economic advantage in joining the church, backed as it was by the firepower of British
rule.   The church offered the lower classes of society——the *osu*——status, a new form
of security and a respectable identity, all of which traditional society did not allow.   For
Anyanwu, then, the christianization of the Igbo had to do with both the contradictions of
traditional Igboland and the imperialistic designs of the Western church.

292   Arazu, Raymond.   "A Cultural Model for Christian Prayer." In *African Christian
Spirituality*, ed. by Aylward Shorter, 112-116. Maryknoll, N.Y.: Orbis Books, 1980.

Arazu, an Igbo and a Roman Catholic priest, distinguishes theology from idolatry
at the outset of this essay.   Idolatry signifies the apotheosis of the human mind as found,
for instance, in Feuerbach's *The Essence of Christianity*.   Less grievous, but no less
hubristic, than the anti-theologians, writes Arazu, are theologians who are quasi-atheistic
in their reduction of God to an abstraction.   For Arazu, God is the One who became man
in the incarnation.   In the incarnation God and the image of God join in a perfect, true
union. See 284.   According to Arazu, Igbo rites of initiation, particularly in regard to the
Ozo title——see 360——"captured this truth [of incarnation] long before Christian
messages came to modern Africa" (p. 114).   Here, the *Ozo* chief undergoes a liminality
in an initiation where he "becomes man and no longer man."   See 133.   In the trials that
test the initiate, the chief is leveled and transformed as he straddles the threshold of God
and man——an experience *"betwixt and between"* God and God's image. See 272.   The
significance of this liminality is recounted in a myth that Arazu recounts.   *Chukwu* (God)
looked at its newly created world and ordered: "Let goodness exist——*Mma-du!*" *Mma-*

du, reveals Arazu, is the Igbo word for man. Thus, in a way not unlike a Christian way, he argues, God's Being and Act are identical and *Mma-du* corresponds to this unity. Another correspondence between Christian and Igbo religions is found in their sense of human alienation from God. In both cases, alienation, or sin, is rooted in a primordial turn from God to man (*incurvatus in se*)——a deformed orientation; "let badness exist." The Ozo chief, however, a chief priest, is the living memory of the first ancestor, a hierophany of *Mma-du*. In sum, Arazu africanizes——i.e., "Igbonizes"——aspects of Christian thought and practice.

293 Bacon, G. "Music in Theology." In *Relevant Theology for Africa*, ed. by Hans-Jurgen Becken, 155-157. Durban: Lutheran Publishing House, 1973.

Bacon examines the reluctance with which traditional music was made a part of worship in the South African churches. The reluctance was due, in part, to the feeling that European music alone is sublime enough to complement Christian piety. African music, which entails a sophisticated polyrhythmic and polyphonic sensibility, with nuances beyond the laws of European harmony, had been precluded as a medium of Christian piety. Yet, argues Bacon, African-Americans, through the rhythmic sophistication and the plaintiveness (blueness) of their spirituals——themselves progeny of Africa——show clearly that an African music can greatly enrich Christian self-understanding. See 353. Thus he asserts that African music should be respected and properly employed as a medium of Christian worship. By properly, one means that the tone, timbre, and accents of traditional music should africanize various hymns and serve as the basis for new compositions reflecting the particularity of Bantu Christians.

294 Bajeux, J. C. "Mentalité noire et mentalité biblique." In *Des prêtres noirs s'interrogent*, ed. by A. Abble, et al., 57-82. Paris: Les Éditions du Cerf, 1956.

According to Bajeux, Africa's gift to the world is a humanism that extends to the Diaspora. See 068-070, 114-115. In order to appreciate this humanism, argues Bajeux, one must divest himself of the notion that blacks have a *"mentalité prélogique"* qui ferait du *"Noir"* un être fermé aux principes premiers de la raison. According to Bajeux, *Lévy-Brühl lui-même a abandonné comme l'attestent ses carnets posthumes*. See 260. Bajeux suggests that an understanding of African humanism is facilitated when one contrasts and compares it to the Bible and to Western culture. On that basis, Bajeux argues blacks are much nearer to the Bible than to the theology of Aquinas or the philosophy of Aristotle. For Bajeux, the Bible presents a cosmos not unlike the Africans'. See 179, 241, 286, 343, 357, 381, 419, 493. Greek philosophy, however, accords with neither the biblical ethos nor the African one. This does not mean Africans have no aptitude for science. Neither the scientific nor numinous realms appear strange or contradictory to the Africans; *c'est là un des traits de leur mentalité* (p. 63). Like the biblical chosen people, Africans, while admitting other possibilities, attribute all real change to God. One might say, then, that African people——as personified in *le paysan haïtien*——are as religious as were the Old Testament Hebrews. Westerners, however, are less spiritual than the Haitian or the Hebrew. In short, Bajeux reads scripture through the lenses of *négritude*——see 114-115——a reading he substantiates with references to Placide Tempels. See 261-262.

295 Banana, Canaan. *The Lord's Prayer according to the Ghetto*. Harare: Mambo Press, 1990.

Dr. Banana, former president of Zimbabwe, freedom-fighter and wise revolutionary, contextualizes the Lord's Prayer and thus indicates a liturgical and theological dimension of liberation theology in Southern Africa.

Our Father who art in the ghetto,
degraded is thy name, thy servitude abounds,

thy will is mocked,
as pie in the sky.

Teach us to demand
our share of gold,
forgive us our docility,
as we demand our share of justice.

Lead us not into complicity,
deliver us from our fears.

For ours is thy sovereignty,
the power and the liberation,
for ever and ever. Amen.

Should one subscribe to Kato's *Theological Pitfalls in Africa*——see 374——he or she would think President Banana's profound and powerful adaptation is a trap to be avoided. As it is, however, *The Lord's Prayer according to the Ghetto*, replete with courageous and prudent theological insight, reflects the prophetic power of theology in Southern Africa.

296 Batlle, Rosario and Augustin. "An African Case Study." In *Theology by the People: Reflections on doing Theology in Community*, ed. by John Pobee, 84-90. Geneva: World Council of Churches, 1986.

The Batlles, a couple from Chile, who live and work among the people of Kenya, direct the Theological Education Programme by Extension Training for the African Independent Churches. They report that such churches are built on a traditional structure characterized by the quest for harmony between the visible and invisible dimensions of the cosmos. See 046. Primal here is the complementarity between opposites, which effects healing and wholeness, fecundity and harmony. See 166, 185, 270, 277. Although these churches have developed into institutions——as exemplified by the Organization of Independent Churches (OAIC) founded in Cairo in 1978——the churches remain true to their roots in the masses. According to the Batlles, the independent churches embody a theology that expresses the *African* piety of the people rather than the erudition of highly trained theologians. The Batlles' observation is consistent with the perspective of new guard theologians such Oduyoye and Éla. See 452-459, 334-341.

297 Benson, Stanley. "The Conquering Sacrament: Baptism and Demon Possession among the Maasai of Tanzania." *Africa Theological Journal* 9,2 (July 1980): 53-61.

Benson discusses demon possession among the Maasai. Women, according to Benson, are the primary victims of this catharsis, which he attributes to psychic stress. Stress here is related to what Turner calls a liminal period in history——the interval between the rapid passage from the traditional order to the neocolonial one. See 247. Maasai have tended to resist the new order that continues to impinge upon their "domain." Maasai view Christianity as an intrusion. According to Benson, demon possession has irrupted during baptismal services. The possessed convulse, make guttural sounds, or go into a catatonic state. That such occurrences signify liminality is suggested by Benson's claim that many enter into a state of "non-person." See 272. Resorting to "antistructure"——see 273——the Maasai employ autochthonous methods. Priest-diviners, in attempts to cure the possessed, use dancing, chanting, and traditional medicine, such as "blood letting." Their efforts do not prevent the recurrence of possession. It is likely that both possession and the traditional attempts to cure it sustain one another as a way of resisting westernization. Making an effort at inculturation, the church has attempted to supplant the priest-diviner by making faith alone the cure. It was found, for instance, that the possessed respond when Christians pray aloud and sing hymns. What is more, asserts Benson, individuals who had been instructed in the faith and then baptized did not have reoccurring episodes of demon possession. Those who were baptized without catechesis succumbed to traditional ritual disassociation. In conclusion, Benson valorizes a biblical and pneumatological perspective in which the power of the Holy Spirit overcomes demon possession; the church, he argues, when inculturated, will defeat the rulers of darkness in the sacrament of baptism.

298 Bimwenyi-Kweshi, O. "Avènement dans l'événement. Trébuchement du muntu vers l'improbable." *Bulletin de théologie africaine* 1,1 (janvier-juin 1979): 105-122.

According to Bimwenyi-Kweshi, self-exploration always involves "the recognition of the other." *Ainsi apparaît la constitution du muntu comme un être-tourné-vers, sans cesse en-chemin-vers-lui-même autant que vers-l'autre* (p. 105). This self-examination——one might call it "eschatological"——which is simultaneously an openness to the other entails the *ambiguïté de la rencontre de l'autre, de l'étranger qui-vient-d'ailleurs* (p. 105). In opening himself to the stranger, muntu is susceptible to great risks. The stranger could be an adversary. Still, the risk is indispensable for it promises an encounter through which the other facilitates the upward path of the self. One must remember that openness to the other is only truly beneficial when both parties are free to chose and assimilate what appears to be conducive to fecundity. (Fecundity is a celebrated goal of traditional life and thought. See 432.) This freedom to chose, however, demands self-mastery; self-mastery diminishes the risk to the other. Self-control heightens the likelihood that one will act with integrity toward the other. See 282. For it is more difficult to know oneself than to *faire le tour du monde*. And it bears reiteration that self-mastery is contingent upon recognition of the other. *Par là*, he writes, *me faire advenir, me créer[,] me promouvoir. Avènement dans l'événement* (p. 107).

299 Bimwenyi-Kweshi, O. "Inculturation en Afrique et attitude des agents de l'évangélisme." *Bulletin de théologie africaine* 3,5 (janvier-juin 1981): 5-18.

Here Bimwenyi-Kweshi argues that inculturation signifies the negation of a missiology that cut the African off from herself. *Aggiornamento*——the Vatican II idiom——and inculturation, moreover, are not identical. The former pertains to a European context where the church has sought to revitalize the gospel in a "world grown of age" (Bonhoeffer). In *aggiornamento* one assumes a homogeneous cultural matrix in which there is a continuity between the past and the present. In Africa, one cannot suppose such continuity. In general, missionaries sought to alienate Africans from their past in order to make them carbon copies of Europeans. But: *Le hier chrétien de l'occident ne peut pas être revendiqué par l'Afrique comme son véritable hier* (p. 6). That this essential fact was ignored has produced an alienated liturgy, an alienated Christian ethics, and an alienated theology in Africa. Inculturation, however, signifies a new orientation that, in making use of traditional values, explores the possibilities of an African Christianity unfettered by the yesterday of European domination. Inculturation involves the chance that Christianity and African culture will enrich each other by way of the edification that comes from the revelation of Christ in both.

300 Bimwenyi-Kweshi, O. "L'Afrique au synode. Problèmes de la famille." *Bulletin de théologie africaine* 4,7 (janvier-juin 1982): 55-74.

Bimwenyi-Kweshi recounts the events of the Fifth General Assembly of the Synod of Bishops held in Rome in 1980. He focuses on the implications of the Synod for Africa. In concert with other Third Word theologians, he asserts that the struggle for a New International Economic Order must set the terms for a theological discussion on the family. According to Bimwenyi-Kweshi: *Les pays en voie de développement sont exploités par une*

*structure injuste du commerce mondial et de ce qui est appelé 'l'aide au développement',
dont les mailles sont bien nouées; et ces pays sont également exploités par une élite locale*
(pp. 59-60). That structure of violence must be addressed prophetically, if family life is
to improve among the poor of the Third World. Bimwenyi-Kweshi exemplifies the
relationship between social analysis and inculturation. Without an appreciation of the
decimation wrought by neo-colonialism, there is no impetus to safe-guard the human
family——the only proper field of inculturation. The struggle for liberation, then, makes
inculturation possible and is a prerequisite for a consideration of *mariage africain comme
acte personnel et communautaire, réalisé selon un processus dynamique, ouvert à la
fécondité, connaissant aussi la polygamie et le divorce* (p. 62). See 310, 320.

301 Bimwenyi-Kweshi, O. "Dieu dans la théologie africaine." *Bulletin de théologie
africaine* 5,9 (janvier-juin 1983): 85-92.

Here Bimwenyi-Kweshi, a Zairian, and member of the Ecumenical Association of
African Theologians, responds to the deliberations of the fifth meeting of the Ecumenical
Association of Third World Theologians. See 002-003. He notes that the irruption of the
Third World——the theme of that meeting——is perceived as *un défi à la théologie
chrétienne*. This challenge is critical, not only because it takes Eurocentric theology to
task, but also because Third World theology is *en même temps, 'irruption des religions non
chrétiennes'*. The challenge, observes Bimwenyi-Kweshi, is more pressing in Latin
America and Africa than in Asia. Asia *has scarcely been Christianized*. The three
continents together, observes Kweshi, constitute a huge body of non-Christians, which
outweighs the Christian body, globally considered. Fundamental to Bimwenyi-Kweshi's
valorization of non-Christian religions is a notion of general revelation. For Bimwenyi-
Kweshi, traditional perceptions of God constitute preparations for the gospel. It is entirely
possible, then, that God has been present to Third World people long before their
christianization. For Bimwenyi-Kweshi, resistance to this possibility indicates a certain
Christian hubris (*Arrogance et démesure des chrétiens*). In fact, argues the author, respect
of a peoples' autochthonous religiosity is the *a priori* of inculturation. Although one
should not assume that Christianity and African traditional religion are identical, attempts
to weed the former from the bed of the latter would cripple African Christianity.

302 Bimwenyi-Kweshi, O. "Quelques options de la Conférence Episcopale du Zaïre."
Bulletin de théologie africaine 5,10 (juillet-décembre 1983): 317-321.

Bimwenyi-Kweshi addresses a meeting of the *Secrétaires des Conférences
Episcopales du Rwanda, du Burundi et Zaïre*. He notes that the African church must
define, by way of an African Council——see 505——the theanthropological (*théandrique*)
realities of Africa. Bimwenyi-Kweshi graciously notes that alien (i.e., white) missionaries
may play a role in that quest for the humanity of God; but they must, as a first step, be
edified by indigenous pastors (i.e., *pasteurs zaïrois*). For Bimwenyi-Kweshi, the role of
autochthonous pastors is critical as they symbolize the conviction that the church is
particular and universal. That is: *L'adhésion à la foi des apôtres et des martyrs par des
fidèles africains n'est pas remise en question, mais son expression culturelle grecque,
germanique, latine, hindoue ou bantou ne peut être considérée comme étant de droit divin
et donc, à ce titre, 'universelle'* (p. 318). The fact remains, though, that African churches
must become self-sufficient in several respects in order to realize its own peculiar
contribution to the universal church. Toward that end, African theology must be promoted
in order to overcome the alienation of a colonial history, the theological consequences of
which has been that Christ himself has been presented *comme la réponse aux questions que
se posent les occidentaux et comme solution à leurs aspirations* (p. 321). Africans must
address *their* questions; Afrocentric issues cannot be answered Eurocentrically.

303 Bissainthe, Gérard. "Catholicisme et indigénisme religieux." In *Des prêtres noirs s'interrogent*, ed. by A. Abble, et al., 111-136. Paris: Les Éditions du Cerf, 1956.

Bissainthe prefers the word indigenization (*indigénisme*) to nationalism. Nationalism, he claims, brings to mind a certain xenophobia, a certain collective egotism. Indigenization is truer, he claims, to the essential meaning of religion. And by religion, Bissainthe means *the universal, the catholic—choses essentiellement ouvertes*—as opposed to things xenophobic (p. 111). Thus, according to Bissainthe, African Christianity must be true to itself, without depreciating or deprecating its European counterpart. For too long, though, Eurocentric Christianity has been perceived as *the* Christianity. But, asks Bissainthe, *cet émerveillement ne risque-t-il pas de n'être et de ne demeurer jamais que de l'émerveillement, une sorte d'émotion esthétique qui ne pénètre pas le sujet jusque dans son être intime?* (See p. 114.) For Bissainthe, then, Africa must go beyond the superficiality of being awestruck by Europe. According to Bissainthe, such superficiality in the presentation of Christianity accounts for blacks' return to the satisfactions derived from African religion. Here Bissainthe cites Haitian Vodun as an example. Many Haitians are only ostensibly Roman Catholic. Fundamentally, they are devoted to the African (American) divinities—the loas—rather than Jesus Christ. Indeed, Haiti is a paradigm of a fairly pervasive phenomenon: Africans' deep-rooted dissatisfaction with Eurocentric Christianity. According to Bissainthe, a certain parity between Christianity and black consciousness is achieved through *négritude*. See 114-115. *Négritude*, claims Bissainthe, when compared to Western civilization, is quite basic, *sans embellissement*. Négritude, for him, indicates African values that are life-sustaining rather than life-threatening, and these values should be appreciated in light of Western attempts to destroy Black Africa's right to wholeness and health. Such destruction, argues Bissainthe, was attempted under the pretext that Africa has no true human value and requires Eurocentric Christian tutelage if it were not to wallow in sinful benightedness. Bissainthe challenges that view—that one must *abandon la culture africaine, toute païenne, et adopter la civilisation occidentale toute chrétienne* (p. 120). Africans must africanize Christianity unapologetically. In order to illustrate how africanization works, Bissainthe focuses on the themes of creation and baptism. The result would be an authentic Christian creation—not unlike that of Augustine, for whom neoplatonism was a fitting vehicle for the expression of Christian faith.

304 Bosch, David. "God through African Eyes." In *Relevant Theology for Africa*, ed. by Hans-Jurgen Becken, 68-78. Durban: Lutheran Publishing House, 1973.

Bosch, a white South African missiologist, considers the issue of God in African theology. He argues that theologians, such as Idowu—see 051, 177-179, 356-357—have cast aspersions on whites who deign to try to make a contribution to African theology. According to Bosh, the ferment in European theologies over the meaning of God makes it imperative that Europeans engage Africans in dialogue for the sake of the church. Bosch claims that white theologians have too often ignored the biblical God in a crypto-Greek natural theology, in which culture is given pride of place over God's self-disclosure. The continuum of that acculturation, according to Bosch, is seen in Nazi Germany. According to Bosch, the Nazis reveal "bizarre attempts to revive the ancient Germanic pagan religion." (One wonders why he chose not to focus on apartheid.) For Bosch, African theology may also be reproducing the turn from God to *man* in seeking to "paganize" the biblical God, who is not made with human hands. Indeed, argues Bosch, theologians such as Mbiti (see 396-410); Danquah (see 155); Idowu; and Sawyerr (see 241-243, 476-480) all assert that the African, traditional God is not, by the very nature of the case itself, the biblical God of *salvation history*. Indeed, according to Bosch, Mbiti asserts that the African God is a *Deus ex machina*—"'He is brought into the picture primarily as an attempt to explain what is otherwise difficult [for] the human mind.'" See 203.

According to Bosch, the African God, "stays apart. He won't harm anybody. He does not make a nuisance of himself. In fact, he shows startling similarities with El of Ugarit" (p. 74). For Bosch, one must sublate the African god to the biblical God. This sublation involves the distinction between syncretism and indigenization. Indigenization for Bosch means that the biblical God becomes inculturated in an African context. Syncretism means that the African god receives a veneer of Christian meaning. For Bosch, then, the Zulu God, *Nkulunkulu,* is the threshold between the biblical God and the Zulu. (Nkulunkulu is really the primordial ancestor rather than the Supreme Being,*who is Unvelinquangi.)* For Bosch, one must cross over the Zulu god, and embrace the Triune God of all creation, who became incarnate for the redemption of humankind.

305 Boulaga, Eboussi. "Le Bantou problématique." *Présence Africaine* 66 (1968): 4-40.
  Boulaga critiques Tempels' *Bantu Philosophy.* See 209, 261-262. He argues that Tempels caricatures the Bantu——they spew forth profound prose without recognizing its philosophical import. Hence the white man is indispensable in revealing to the Bantu the richness of their own thought. And the Bantu are to be eternally grateful to the great White Father for such benevolence. For Boulaga, Africans profit from such Bantuism when they recognize that it is a form of alienation to be overcome. For Boulaga, then, Bantuism is to be discarded with the rest of what Adoukonou calls the Friday syndrome——the Eurocentric, paternalistic naming of blacks, which constitutes *l' Africanisme du dehors.* See 288. Boulaga, however, does not completely reject "ethnological philosophy." The traditional values of Africa are not to be overlooked or scornfully rejected out of hand.

306 Boulaga, Eboussi. "The African Christian in Search of Identity?" *Concilium* (June 1977): 26-35.
  Africans, argues Boulaga, in all their diversity, must overcome narrow-minded, racist discourse. Indeed, Africans must overcome all forms of over-generalization, asserts Boulaga. "The African," he explains, "has no actual content; he exists with a specific location only if he adopts his physical, biological, cultural and historical conditioning factors." Those factors, however, are to be overcome. Boulaga calls for a certain demythologization born from profound respect of the creativity——dynamic and unpredictable——of self-definition. See 298. Demythologization entails redefinitions of Christianity; Christianity is relative, argues Boulaga; no one expression is normative. What is more, "The internal criterion for the legitimation of a specific Christianity is [a] standing-down in order to receive oneself from others, while becoming the food of life for others" (p. 33). African Christian identity therefore should be in flux——it must be if the faithful are to escape the worship of fetishes. According to Boulaga: "We have to be willing to die in order to be reborn somewhere else, somewhere far away" (p. 34). An eschatological vision?

307 Boulaga, Eboussi. *Christianity without Fetishes.* Maryknoll, N.Y.: Orbis Books, 1984.
  A powerful critique of Eurocentric Christianity, graced by prose that reads like poetry: Boulaga exposes the hubris of a missiology that is essentially an extension of imperialism. For him such idolatry is incalculably wicked; the tragedy of its perniciousness is seen in the fact that Africans have internalized white values, as if *those values* constituted Christian faith. "The neophyte," he writes, "all uprooted, is rendered incapable of the act of assuming his or her worldly being——of perhaps recognizing the 'gift of God' (John 4:10) there" (p. 26). The Africans, asserts Boulaga, taking their cue from the independent churches and other modes of *l'Africanisme du dedans*——see

288——must forge a Christianity independent of the West. Boulaga's views in this regard are based on the premise that idolatry is guarded against only if Africans are

> given over to [themselves] in order to be and to do what [they] can and do 'by [themselves]', alone, without vicarious substitution, to be given over to themselves as the means of nothing, *ad instar ipsius Dei,* on the model of God himself....The glory of God, that is, the splendor of his brilliance, is human beings, coming to be, producing themselves, together with others, these free spontaneities that are the means of nothing and recognized by word, respect, and the reciprocity of gratuity (p. 192-193).

For Boulaga, such graciousness requires one to *"admit* the metaphorical character of the notion or expression of 'revelation' or 'Word *of* God'" (p. 11). When metaphor gives way to dogma, itself made authoritative by technological might, faith is but a fetish——which is no faith at all.

308 Bujo, Bénézet. "Pour une éthique africano-christocentrique." In *Combats pour un christianisme africain: Mélanges en l'honneur du Professeur V. Mulago,* ed. by A. Ngindu Mushete, 21-31. Kinshasa: Faculté de Théologie Catholique, 1981.

According to Bujo, the enquiry into Christian ethics is *celle de savoir ce qui fait le proprium christianum en tant que tel*" (p. 17). For Bujo, the problem must be tackled with attention to the historical Jesus revealed in the legacy of the apostles. That legacy, he argues, retains the marks of its cultural specificity. Given the post-modern context, that legacy must be reinterpreted, or it will become an old relic. So theologians should rediscover the true humanity of Jesus——such that his message is not reified (*ne s'évapore pas dans l'abstrait*) but addresses modern dilemmas. This issue of relevancy is exacerbated in Africa by the fact that African Christianity is still in the shell of a Euro-American sensibility. In an effort to de-europeanize the gospel, Bujo focuses on the ancestors, who are the foundations of traditional societies. Insignia and mnemonics related to their legacy, asserts Bujo, constitute the grammar of traditional society and the soil of inculturation. According to Bujo, the memory of the ancestors constitutes a *sorte de sotériologie commémorativo-narrative* that has been destined to comfort the ultimate community——*au-delà de la tombe, avec tous les ancêtres bons et bienfaisants* (p. 24). Because of the legacies of the ancestors, the ground is fertile for an African understanding of Christ as the Ancestor, the first Ancestor (from all eternity?). See 156, 334. The mystery of the incarnation; the notion of kenosis; the titles "Word" and "Lord"——all are surpassed and made clear in the assertion that Christ is the *proto-ancêtre*. The title, Ancestor, will surely signify more for Africans than the titles Logos and Lord. Those titles will not be forsaken, but Africans must adopt other titles that have meaning for them. For Bujo, then, Christian ethics involves an africanization that allows blacks to live in accordance with the very best of ancestral traditions.

309 Bujo, Bénézet. "Pour une éthique africano-christocentrique." *Bulletin de théologie africaine* 3,5 (janvier-juin 1981): 41-52.
     See 308.

310 Bujo, Bénézet. "Notes complémentaires à la contribution de R. Haes sur le mariage africain et chrétien." In *Combats pour un Christianisme africain: Mélanges en l'honneur du Professeur V. Mulago,* ed. by A. Ngindu Mushete, 41-49. Kinshasa: Faculté de Théologie Catholique, 1981.

Bujo examines De Haes's perspective concerning marriage by steps. See 320. According to Bujo, De Haes deals with this issue too Eurocentrically. For Bujo, it not *always* necessary to have recourse to European paradigms, *pour résoudre 'per similitudinem' les problèmes africains* (p. 46). Rather, problems must be worked out in accordance with African realities. Certain African people, for instance, have customs which, like the Christian ideal, forbid cohabitation until *l'engagement définitif.* In that case, the return to tradition is not a step backward, but a stepping stone to an African Christianity. Bujo argues, moreover, that the issue of cohabitation *prématrimoniale* has rarely, if ever, considered women's perspectives. Indeed, Bujo asks whether cohabitation *prématrimoniale,* itself designed to determine if the woman is fertile, can be construed in a way favorable to women. Indeed, asserts Bujo, infertility is not a criterion for judging whether Christians are to be wed. According to Bujo, Vincent Mulago's——see 415-421——sense of marriage by steps is more edifying than De Haes's. For Mulago, the idiom purveys a communal, dynamic, incremental process that is sacred and religious in character. Here, nuptial consent is truly mutual, since it occurs before the community and before God, and celebrates the gifts of the betrothed, one to the other. According to Bujo, Mulago——*malgré la place de la fécondité soulignée dans la description*——neither endorses cohabitation nor isolation of the couple as they move toward Christian marriage, *le degré suprême du mariage.* Still, asserts Bujo, the theological problems regarding the problem of Christian marriage in Africa are as yet unsolved.

311 Bujo, Bénézet. "Qu'est-ce que l'apostolat?" *Bulletin de théologie africaine* 3,5 (janvier-juin 1981): 121-127.

Bujo addresses an assembly on the occasion of the 25th anniversary *de l'ordination sacerdotale du premier prêtre du diocèse de Bunia* (p. 121). He notes the distinction the majority of clergy——especially the foreign missionaries——have made between intellectual formation and the call to ministry. For many, intellectual work is tantamount to leisure, but the parish ministry is hard work. Although many who assume such a distinction are committed to ecclesial service, with all its vicissitudes, they have, asserts Bujo, a truncated view of the apostolate. According to Bujo: *N'est-il pas trop étroit de réduire tout l'apostolat à ces formes propres au ministère paroissial?* (See p. 122.) What is more, is it not the case that parish ministers may be critically edified by clergy who are scholars in service to the church? Indeed: *Chacun profite du travail et vice versa* (p. 122). An uneducated clergy, argues Bujo, cannot attend to the pressing problems of inculturation. Given the outdated scholarship on African peoples, the africanization of Christianity requires rigorous study. For Bujo, moreover, *les missionnaires étrangers doivent être ouverts au dialogue et compléter leurs lacunes en matière culturelle, pastorale et doctrinale propre à l'Afrique par les critiques de leurs confrères autochtones* (p. 123). Such edification is only possible if the church encourages African intellectuals to work diligently on religio-cultural problems related to African theology.

312 Bujo, Bénézet. "Déchristianiser en christianisant?" *Bulletin de théologie africaine* 4,7 (janvier-juin 1982): 229-242.

The orientation of bishops affects African theology, explains Bujo. Should they be progressive, so much the better; if they are reactionary, African theologians must press on with the production of relevant theologies for Africa nonetheless. More precisely, if the church hierarchy is inattentive to the problems of the highest priority, the theologian must still press on in his *responsabilité 'prophétique' pour le plus grand bien du peuple de Dieu* (p. 229). Above this issue of accountability to the African people looms Rome. According to Bujo, the specter of neocolonialism is blessed by the Vatican. Here, an unjust International Economic Order has its counterpart in a Eurocentric theological bloc that deigns to assess African realities ex cathedra. See 340, 474. For Bujo, however, ignorance is bliss: Eurocentric Christians plop themselves down into the African context only because they are sure, hubristically sure, of triumph in an milieu of the poor, that is, *au milieu des sous-développés.* These "pariahs" keep quiet regarding such hubris *pour des motifs qu'un peut deviner sans grande imagination* (p. 231). For Bujo, dechristianization requires one to eschew and confront this travesty——triumphant imperialism——in light of the promise of a truer Christianity. Thus Bujo calls for a restructuring of the Catholic Church in Africa, a restructuring dependent upon priests and religious committed to a certain dechristianization, i.e., those against *les évêques 'parachutistes' au Zaïre*.

313 Bujo, Bénézet. "Tendances actuelles en éthique théologique catholique." *Bulletin de théologie africaine* 5,9 (janvier-juin 1983): 147-157.

Bujo focuses on the ferment in ethics, with attention to German perspectives on: morality (*l'autonomie de la morale*); deontological and teleological arguments; and *le modèle de l'éthique narrative*. He traces the quest for moral norms to the Greeks and Kant's categorical imperative. According to Bujo, however, there is no *signification constante du mot 'autonomie,' mais, il faut chaque fois voir le contexte dans lequel les auteurs en parlent* (p. 148). Still, Bujo holds that the structure of correct ethics——despite its "variety"——is derived from "*les 'promessesparachèvements' en Dieu. Norme*, construed theologically, is thus the anchor from which a variety of ethics surfaces in line with God's ultimate plan. To that eschatological perspective, Bujo adds *l'éthique fidéiste*. The valorization of faith, however, often appears uncritical and reactionary to those who wish to be ethical without surrendering the autonomy of critical thought. The deontological approach to ethics, writes Bujo, *désigne la théorie suivant laquelle, en morale, on ne peut pas juger les actes à partir de leurs conséquences bonnes ou mauvaises* (p. 153). God, however, has so designed nature that all good ethics necessarily participate in an ultimate goodness. From this perspective, the deontological is the ontological, even when christology is not at the center of the discourse. This basic "truth," asserts Bujo, is, in its pristine form, found in a narrative mode traceable to Jesus and the earliest Christian community. The latter lost its simplicity over time as Christianity became discursive, *sans jamais provoquer un choc qui ferait de l'homme un 'faiseur' de la Parole* (p. 154). Among Germans, J.B. Metz recognizes the apostasy of a post-narrative christology more concerned with intellection than action——i.e., the ethical praxis of Jesus. For Metz, writes Bujo, theology cannot simply tell the story; theology must have a socioeconomic character and convey the promise of liberation. Social analysis is thus the basis of a hermeneutic of suspicion based on the dangerous memory of the crucifixion and the resurrection. In sum, the gospel, for Bujo, is the ethical plumbline, against which much philosophical discussion comes up short. Indeed, this narrative form strikes a responsive chord in Africans whose pedagogues have valorized proverbs and especially dramatic depictions of ethical values (*qui mettaient en scène les figures modèles dont la conduite était louable ou blâmable).* (p. 157.) Finally: African theologians must assimilate the narrative forms of the gospel, so that a Afro-Christian ethics can be born.

314 Bukasa, K. "Les sciences sociales dans la théologies de libération." *Bulletin de théologie africaine* 5,10 (juillet-juin 1983): 269-292.

The Latin Americans, asserts Bukasa, are pioneers in the use of a critical social analysis that helps clarify the meaning of the gospel. They have discovered the indispensability of praxis: *L'acte politique lui-même est transformé en une application technique de la solution scientifique* (p. 270). Pride of place here is given to Marxism as a heuristic tool——the theoretical and practical implications of which allow one to see that alienation and its antithesis are politically produced. Bukasa reviews critiques of Latin American theology——such as those of Lopez Trujillo——which argue that liberation theology is atheistic Marxism in disguise. Bukasa concludes that Marxism is indeed different from the gospel, but facilitates critique of bourgeois sociologies and theologies that valorize the status quo. Taking his cue from Marx's *German Ideology*, Bukasa rejects theologies that dissimulate how the center is parasitic on its periphery, and how the supra and pseudo bourgeoisie prey on the masses. See 040, 072.

315 Bukasa, K. "Les sciences sociales dans la théologies de la libération (suite et fin)."
Bulletin de théologie africaine 6,11 (janvier-juin 1984): 77-93.

Bukasa distinguishes reformist theologies from those committed to radical, structural change. Reformists, under the guise of "the social doctrine of the churches," differ from theologians such as Gustavo Gutiérrez. See 352. According to Bukasa, the Jesuit sociologist, Paolo Tufari, points out that the reformist faction seeks to gain control of the oppressed for the sake of the status quo. Here, he explains, *on serait en présence d'un simple changement de symboles par une institution forte, afin de les adapter aux circonstances changées et ainsi maintenir son pouvoir d'autrefois* (p. 78). Liberation theologians, by contrast, are engaged in radical praxis——*c'est un processus de libération avec la participation active des opprimés eux-mêmes* (p. 79). Here the oppressed adopt revolutionary practice as a strategy epiphenomenal to the gospel itself. Such a position——which makes theology the second step, but faith the essential *a priori*——is the precondition of opposition to the positions of Cardinal Trujillo and Pope John Paul II. In Africa, writes Bukasa, switching gears, the cultural dimension of liberation is more developed than in Latin America because culture and religion——the objects of Western contempt——are most constitutive of Africans' vision of liberation. Nonetheless, argues Bukasa, social analysis is indispensable for Africa. There is no question here of succumbing to the Eurocentrism endemic to Marxist thought, which limits the relevance of marxism for African people. For Bukasa, Marxism is only a metaphor that must be contextualized. For Bukasa, then, social analysis must bend to African realities, not vice-versa. See 072, 120.

316 Carr, Burgess. "The Engagement of Lusaka." In *The Struggle Continues: Lusaka 1974*, 73-81. Nairobi: All Africa Conference of Churches, 1975.

Canon Carr notes the alienation that the Partition has wrought in Africa——"the rapid disintegration of the tribal framework of social norms and values by which [the] ancestors had ordered their lives; the 'bursting up of their faith', the plunder and exploitation of [African] natural resources; the murder of [African] peoples" (p. 73). Carr asserts that such alienation is the result of capitalist greed, and that African Christians must devote their energies to remedying the pathetic situation. The struggle, as he sees it, is one in which Africans must strive to recover the "stolen dignity of...black personhood" (p. 74). Black personhood is defined in terms of the African values whites attempted to extirpate or perniciously manipulate. According to Carr, the African independent churches signify the spontaneous assertion of black dignity, which should edify African theologians. See 046, 141, 235. These churches give impetus, he asserts, to the movement calling for a moratorium on mission. See 119, 371. Black personhood is also attained, for Carr, through uncompromising opposition to neocolonial contradictions that thrive in contexts of civil war. The essential contradiction here, according to Carr, is that between the masses and the elites. See 339-341. He explains that "the deep antagonisms that have erupted in Nigeria, Burundi, Uganda" are not really due to tribalism. For Carr, "there are only two tribes in Africa: the *elites* and the *masses*! As such what is usually described as *tribalism* in Africa is essentially a class struggle" (p. 77). See 001, 120, 338, 340. For Carr, true ecumenicity in Africa necessitates that the church be critical of its "identification with the elites," who struggle among themselves "for the limited opportunities, privileges and power available in our dependent societies. The masses get caught in the cross-fire and become victims" (p. 77). See 011, 040, 044, 072. The example of the independent churches and an analysis of neocolonial contradictions, asserts Carr, should push African theologians to adopt liberation as the essence of their vocation. See 314-315. As if he had anticipated the new guard, Carr asserts that African theology must "advance beyond academic phenomenological analysis to a deeper appropriation of the ethical sanctions inherent in [African] traditional religious experience" (p. 78).

317 Carr, Burgess. "The Relation of Union to Mission." In *Mission Trends No.3: Third World Theologies. Asian, African and Latin American Contributions to a Radical, Theological Realignment in the Church,* ed. by Gerald Anderson and Thomas Stransky, 158-168. New York: Paulist Press; Grand Rapids: Wm. B. Eerdmans, 1976.

Canon Carr, former head of the AACC——see 002, 066——examines the relation of ecumenicity to African theology. He notes that ecumenism is tied to mission since European denominations sought to attain unanimity in Africa in order to strengthen the planting of Christianity there. See 061. Most missionaries, however, never considered the contradiction between ecumenicity and their mistreatment of the Africans. For Carr, true ecumenicity, true union, involves the "traditional [African] trinity of *corporateness, community,* and *celebration.*" True ecumenicity, asserts Carr, also involves appreciation of other Pan-African values, such as those envisioned in the notion of African personality. (For a discussion of African personality, see Chapter 2 of this bibliography.) Carr notes that nationalism proved to be the catalyst that put Africa on the road to its own, truer, ecumenicity. Part of this entails the emergence of African theology and the independent churches. See 046.

318 Carvalho, Emilio J.M. "Who Is Jesus Christ for Africa Today?" *Africa Theological Journal* 10,1 (1981): 27-36.

Carvalho valorizes African traditional religion as a critical source of African theology. Similar to African theologians such as Idowu and Mbiti——see 356-357, 396-410——Carvalho questions the European assessment that the Africans' traditional God was a *deus otiose.* See 384. For Carvalho, as for Idowu, traditional religion was essentially, and richly, monotheistic. Despite his sensitivity to African traditional religion, Carvalho makes the problematic claim that the Christian God, revealed in Jesus Christ, is the God of traditional Africa. (If African traditional religion has its own integrity, then why should one assume that the Triune, "perichoretic," Christian God is the same God of traditional religion.)

319 Chipenda, José B. "Theological Options in Africa Today". In *African Theology en Route,* ed. by Kofi Appiah-Kubi and Sergio Torres, 66-72. Maryknoll, N.Y.: Orbis Books, 1979.

Chipenda, whose context is defined by the revolutionary and internecine conflicts of Angola, notes that liberation and africanization must converge in African theology. Asserting the relevance of the praxis of liberation——see 314-315——he provides insights into the correctness of Cabral's and Fanon's assertion that revolution (i.e., liberation) is never present in the absence of cultural innovation. See 023-025, 034-035. For Chipenda, such praxis is quickened through socialist analysis, which is efficacious to the extent that it illuminates the path of struggle. For Chipenda, African theology must: (1) understand God through the particularity of African history; (2) recognize the critical importance of a general revelation; (3) "spring from the people and go to the people" (hence the relevance of Cabral); (4) "realize that faith does not come from doctrine to life," but rather from life to doctrine.

320 De Haes, René. "Recherches africaines sur le mariage Chrétien." In *Combats pour un christianisme africain. Mélanges en l'honneur du Professeur V. Mulago,* ed. by A. Ngindu Mushete, 33-41. Kinshasa: Faculté de Théologie Catholique, 1981.

Marriage, for De Haes, is a mandate of God. See 312. Each culture, he argues, stamps the institution with its particularity. Among African people, the marriage contract is symbolic, emblematic of the life traceable to *l'ancêtre fondateur,* a life which continues and is strengthened through the new bond between two families. This alliance is sealed by the dowry, *symbole et instrument juridique et social de l'union* (p. 34). According to

De Haes, Mulago is a pioneer regarding the inculturation of Christian marriage within African contexts. See 415-421. Mulago, reveals De Haes, has examined Bantu people and shown the correspondence between their conceptions of marriage and Christian conceptions. The Roman Catholic Church, claims De Haes, upholds Mulago's position. The critical question here, though, is: *tout mariage entre chrétiens est-il sacrement* (p. 37). In several contexts, asserts De Haes, marriage is valid outside of the church. What is more, he asserts that the history of marriage in the West attests to the fact that *le mariage traditionnel, coutumier,* is a valid one and to be maintained alongside *du mariage religieux qui vient après 'confirmer' le mariage coutumier* (p. 37). For De Haes, in addition, failures to respect the validity of traditional marriages as *une forme publique* would impose a Eurocentric orientation on a context that, at bottom, has little to do with Europe. Even in Europe, *la forme canonique du mariage* is optional. De Haes's argument is that it should be as optional in Africa as it is in Europe. For De Haes, the African church should consider reappropriating that practice and allow Africans to be married in the customary ways. Inculturation would involve Africans' approach to the sacrament in steps. This incremental approach is necessary given crises that have beset the institution of marriage in Africa. De Haes shows that the crises are in large measure products of the upheaval and chaos of the period of "independence." De Haes claims, moreover, that it is a pastoral duty to raise the consciousness of Africans——such that they would reverently desire the sacrament of marriage. At that point, polygamy would be excluded.

321 De Haes, René. "La prolifération des sectes en Afrique." *Bulletin de théologie africaine* 3,6 (juillet-décembre 1981): 281-291.

The proliferation of sects in Africa today, writes De Haes, is part of a far-reaching phenomenon emergent from the human longing for religious meaning (*la soif religieuse de l'humanité*). In Africa, such longing manifests itself in the rapid growth of the independent churches, the distinguishing characteristics of which are preoccupations with prayer and healing. See 046, 137, 225. As these churches have proliferated in Central Africa, De Haes focuses on the context of Zaire. According to De Haes, a sect (that is, an independent "church") constitutes a covenant (*un groupement contractuel)* of like-mined persons who have similar religious experiences. A church differs from a sect insofar as it is confessional and should eschew the xenophobia common to a sect. Sects tend to proliferate in contexts troubled by socioeconomic tensions the church fails to address. What is more, the sects embody an edifying laboratory that facilitates study of the tension between africanization and christianization. According to De Haes, sects evince there is a *religiosité vivante dont l'expression se situe entre les religions traditionnelles et les religions à caractère universaliste* (p. 285). What is more, sects constitute a rejection of Eurocentric secularism that——having made its way into the historic churches——threaten traditional religious values. Despite what is edifying regarding the sects, they often encourage an immaturity on the part of its members. That is they *désirent trouver de façon immédiate la solution à leurs problèmes en croyant pouvoir échapper à la dure réalité de la vie où l'homme doit acquérir de haute lutte sa liberté et sa libération* (p. 289). Finally, if the *dévotes* of sects remain exceedingly narrow in their spiritual vision, they cut themselves off from the expansion of God's Word within the historic churches. In part such an abridgement of God's Word has resulted from the bigotry of Eurocentric missionaries unequipped to recognize God's incarnation in African contexts. See 284.

322 Dickson, Kwesi. "Towards a Theologia Africana." In *New Testament Christianity for Africa and the World: Essays in Honor of Harry Sawyerr,* ed. by Mark Glasswell and Edward W. Fasholé-Luke, 198-208. London: SPCK, 1974.

According to Dickson, Christianity is growing in Africa. This growth explains the current quest for African theology. For Dickson, African theology must be appreciated in relation to the historic mis-identification of Christianity with Europe and North America. He thus distinguishes Eurocentric religion from Christian faith. Apart, however, from its historic relation to imperialism, argues Dickson, Eurocentrism is not necessarily bad. Indeed, the fact that whites have interpreted the gospel by way of their own cultures indicates that Africans should feel free, given the problem of colonialism, to interpret Christianity in terms of their own cultures. Indeed, Dickson notes the growing discourse on the relation of the faith to African traditional religion——a discourse which he argues must be more intentionally biblical.

323　Dickson, Kwesi. "African Theology: Origin, Methodology and Content." *Journal of Religious Thought* 32 (Fall-Winter 1975): 34-45.
　　　Dickson explores issues pertinent to African theology. See 324-325.

324　Dickson, Kwesi. "The African Theological Task." In *The Emergent Gospel*, ed. by Sergio Torres and Virginia Fabella, 46-49. London: Geoffrey Chapman, 1978.
　　　Dickson argues that theology is never value-free since it is expressed through the cultural modes of the theologian. Thus, he argues, African theology must be understood in terms of the distinctiveness of African contexts. For Dickson, this means that black South African theology and African theology are different. He asserts that "South African black theology...is closer to the U.S. black theology than to what is likely to issue from the West African situation" (p. 48). (We have seen, though, that the new guard, many of them West Africans, are very similar to black South African theologians.) According to Dickson, African theologians should be concerned with three areas: (1) the Bible; (2) liturgy; and (3) "the restatement of Christian belief." Each area is to be defined, he posits, through hermeneutics true to the Christian tradition and the African matrix. For Dickson, biblical study is critical, as it is the foundation of Christian identity. Biblical study, he asserts, is especially needed within the context of the African independent churches. According to Dickson, these churches tend to misunderstand the "nature and meaning" of the Bible. See 227. Having established the biblical foundation of African theology, Dickson then discusses its format. Here he elaborates on the third area of African theology——restatement of Christian belief——in terms of systematic theology. He argues that systematic theology entails the arrangement of Christian doctrine——such that their interrelation is made clear. He also notes that part of the systematic theologian's task often includes a focus on a particular dimension of Christian doctrine. For instance, a christology might accentuate the soteriological and eschatological connotations of the resurrection. The African's understanding of resurrection, however, might differ from that of the European. The European, he posits, may define salvation in a way that highlights the crucifixion. Here the Cross is understood exclusively in terms of sin (hamartiology), which determines the meaning of the resurrection (soteriology). Dickson argues that the Africans view of death is less somber. Traditionally, he claims, "death is not conceived as putting an end to natural-self expression" (p. 49). Death is the threshold to the land of the ancestors, which bonds the human community, both visible and invisible. For Dickson, then, an African understanding of death would be truer to biblical implications of the resurrection. Dickson's point is that Africans, "wanting to restate Christian teaching for themselves[,] should not work from the assumption that the traditional categories of doctrinal statement are immutable" (p. 49).

325　Dickson, Kwesi. "Continuity and Discontinuity between the Old Testament and African Life and Thought." In *African Theology en Route*, ed. by Kofi Appiah-Kubi and Sergio Torres, 95-109. Maryknoll, N.Y.: Orbis Books, 1979.
　　　Dickson discusses the relation of the Old Testament to Christianity. See 294. He examines, for instance, the dichotomy posited by Marcion and later reinterpreted by

Friedreich Schleiermacher and Adolf Von Harnack. (The latter two are Germans whose work is seminal to historical theology in the West.) Dickson then examines the work of the Asian, G.E. Phillips, who asserts that Hinduism, itself bequeathing sacred Scripture to posterity, should replace the Old Testament within the context of Asian theology. According to Dickson, Phillip's view "is of a piece with the neo-Marcionism espoused by Schleiermacher and Harnack, for it assumes that the Old Testament is not essential to the story of God in human history" (p. 97). This pitfall is to be avoided as Africans——notably within the independent churches——display a "predilection for the Old Testament." He attributes that predilection to several factors: missionaries tendencies to sublate grace to law; the correspondence between African and Old Testament rituals; the appeal of the Old Testament to the down-trodden who associate themselves with the liberation themes of the Exodus; the similarity between the sacred cosmos of the Old Testament Hebrew and the traditional African. Dickson, furthermore, proposes three levels of continuity between African culture and the Old Testament: (1) theological: the Old Testament "contains the seeds of universality." Yahweh is thus God "of the whole earth and is concerned with Israel *and* the *goyim*." (2) Religio-cultural: there may have been contact between black Africans and Jews, which explains the affinity of the two cultures. What is more, "various elements in the African religio-cultural ethos recall ancient Israelite beliefs and practices." See 210-220. Fundamental here is the sacredness of existence——tress and rocks constitute *sacra*——*actual entities*——and thus indicate a "theology of nature." (3) Hermeneutical: the diversity of biblical interpretations is owed to the diversity of human cultures. Thus African hermeneutics will be conducted through the currents of traditional religion. This would be impossible were the two——hermeneutics and traditional religion——in disagreement with the gospel.

326   Dickson, Kwesi. "The Methodist Witness and the African Situation." In *Sanctification and Liberation*, ed. by Theodore Runyon, 193-208. Nashville, Tennessee: Abingdon, 1981.

Dickson begins his essay with social analysis. Although he states that "Africa is running its own affairs"——a view many would dispute——he notes "there is a general feeling that things have not gone as well as they might." Dickson recognizes that the internal problems of corruption and the dictates of the world market exacerbate the misery of the African poor. See 134. Dickson also notes that much of Africa's deterioration is due to the conflicting praxes of the superpowers, which scramble——still!——for strategic advantage and Africa's resources. Having set the matrix, Dickson notes the proliferation of the African independent churches. See 046, 234, 265. He writes that these churches' attitudes "toward traditional beliefs...[enable] their leadership to accept the fears of the worshippers with respect to witchcraft and the influence of malevolent spirits" (p. 195). The spontaneity of the independent churches challenges the missiology of Methodists who, proselytizing among Ghanaian people during the epoch of olden colonialism, confused Christianity with Eurocentricity and, evangelism with capitalism. Dickson also distinguishes African theology from both black and Latin American theologies in this essay. Black theology, he argues, is emergent from the problem of white supremacy; Latin American theology, from a continent in which social analysis defines much of the discourse to the exclusion of religio-cultural analysis. African theology, on the other hand, asserts Dickson, is "somewhat ill-defined." This problem is related to a superficial africanization, which indicates a methodological quandary. Dickson's way out is to configure an African theology from the tension between African Christianity and the living dynamism of African traditional religion. Dickson establishes the integrity of this view in alluding to a notion of general revelation as found in Danquah. See 155.

327 Dickson, Kwesi. *Theology in Africa*. Maryknoll, N.Y.: Orbis Books, 1984.

Here Dickson explores, in greater depth, the issues he has discussed in his many essays.

328 Dinwiddy, Hugh. "Missions and Missionaries as Portrayed by English-Speaking Writers of Contemporary African Literature." In *Christianity in Independent Africa*, ed. by Edward Fasholé-Luke, Richard Gray, Adrian Hastings and Godwin Tasie, 426-442. Bloomington: Indiana University Press, 1978.

Dinwiddy argues that writers such as Chinua Achebe——see 132-134——provide insight into the experience of Bishop Crowther. See 109. Crowther, asserts Dinwiddy, underlines "a dilemma presented in the work of many subsequent African poets and novelists" (p. 427). How can one be Christian *and* African? See 494. Dinwiddy also notes the work of Edward Blyden, who also recognized this problem, a problem related to the intransigence and integrity of traditional religion. See 016-018. According to Dinwiddy, writers such as Achebe are the progeny of Blyden, and as such they are radically critical of any Christian expression that caricatures the integrity of African traditional religion. (Indeed, Dinwiddy refers to Achebe's *Arrow of God* as an example of African thinking on colonialism. See 133.)

329 Dosseh, R., and R. Sastre. "Propagande et vérité." In *Des prêtres noirs s'interrogent*, ed. by A. Abble, et al., 137-152. Paris: Les Éditions du Cerf, 1956.

Dosseh and Sastre claim the Apostle Paul has established that a "living" missiology participates in Truth if it is grounded in love. The authors, however, wonder whether Paul's injunction has been followed by those who have written about Black Africa. They argue that the history of slavery and colonialism, and the complicity of the church in its maintenance, reveal that too many European missionaries did not, in their writings and lectures, spread love, but brutal domination. *L'esclavage——on oublie souvent de signaler que c'est sous ce signe que s'est faite d'abord la rencontre de l'Europe et du monde noir,——l'esclavage avait mis les consciences nègres à l'encan, on allait les 'civiliser' par la colonisation* (p. 138). In their role as "civilizers," argue the authors, Europeans have lied about an entire continent in a discourse that reveals their hubris. Indeed, quip the authors, one who *voudrait écrire des chroniques 'martiennes'* has only to consult the tales on *'le nègre unijambiste'* (p. 139). See 599. Dosseh and Sastre note that not all missionaries are guilty of propagating white supremacy and fantastic stories of "exotic Africa." Certain missionaries have been true to the Pauline sense of mission. What is more, the authors assert that certain missionaries have demonstrated a love which has revealed true Africanity to the African. Still, contend Dosseh and Sastre, the public does not listen to those writers. *On l'a habitué à l'exotisme, il y a pris goût.* The public at large, the authors contend, enjoy reading missionaries who are androids of Western civilization. The authors contend, however, that the black world is united in exploding the myth of the Negro past, and they conclude with three suggestions for those who would do mission work in Africa. (1) One must abandon all bigotry toward blacks. (2) One must leave the interpretation of Africa to the Africans themselves and forego the irresponsible writers who cater to sensationalism and know nothing of African life and cultures. (3) One must love one's neighbor as herself and thus speak only the truth, prudently and in the spirit of justice.

330 Dubois, Jules. "Les kimbanguistes vus par eux-mêmes." In *Combats pour un christianisme africain. Mélanges en l'honneur du Professeur V. Mulago*, ed. by A. Ngindu Mushete, 127-135. Kinshasa: Faculté de Théologie Catholique, 1981.

Dubois notes the interest Kimbanguism has engendered across the world. See 185, 192, 199, 208, 263. According to Dubois, Kimbanguism is now an organized church and has attracted historians and foreign politicians, especially the radicals (*'les gens de gauche'*). For them, Kimbangu is a hero in the struggle for independence rather than a prophet with a religious message. Today, however, scholars are interested essentially in the faith of Kimbangu. Still, argues Dubois, the Kimbanguists have yet to express themselves. Thus Dubois seeks to allow them to do so. Kimbangu's genius was that he was able to use things African in propagating Christianity in the Congo. The gospel, explains Dubois, was propagated in a vacuum, as if Africans had no living historical and cultural memory. But, continues Dubois, the *théologie Kimbanguiste* has been in solidarity with the struggles of these oppressed and alienated people. He notes how Kimbanguism is built on the theism of BaKongo traditional religion. Not unlike Mbiti and others, Dubois holds that BaKongo religion was in fact a preparation for the gospel. In regard to inculturation, Dubois explains that the Kimbanguist Church, while truly African, is Christian——taking its authority from the Council of Nicaea. The church, reveals Dubois, practices four sacraments: baptism, communion, marriage, and ordination. Baptism is without water and takes place with prayer and the laying on of hands. One observes acculturation in the way in which Kimbanguists celebrate the Eucharist. He writes:

--*Pour le sang du Christ, c'est le miel dilué qu'il faudra utiliser. Jean-Baptiste s'en nourrissait bien;*
--*quant* au corps *du Christ, il faut employer un gâteau à base de pommes de terre, d'oeufs, de farine de mais et de bananes vertes* (p. 131).

Here, Dubois calls to mind Éla's and Sanon's positions against use of imported materials in the celebration of Communion. See 340, 474. In regard to social analysis, Dubois asserts that the Kimbanguist Church must not be indifferent to the flagrant violations of human rights, which occur in Zaire.

331 Dussel, Enrique. *Philosophy of Liberation*. Maryknoll, N.Y.: Orbis Books, 1985.

Ostensibly, Dussel's work is more germane to Latin American theology than to African theology. In *Philosophy of Liberation*, however, he offers an epistemology that covers much of the Third World. That is, *Philosophy of Liberation* is a generic text with references to the contributions African theologians are making to Third World theology. Dussel rejects the praxis of domination, i.e., imperialism and neo-imperialism. He argues that the oppressed must assert their alterity——*their* "politico-cultural" sense of self, which enables them to resist imperialism with revolutionary intention. The essential mode of alterity, for Dussel, is popular culture. According to Dussel, popular culture "preserves the best of the Third World and is the one whence new alternatives will emerge for future world culture, which will not be a mere replication of cultures of the center" (p. 90). A word Dussel uses to signify alterity is exteriority——a useful term in regard to the religio-cultural analysis of the new guard. The Eurocentric bloc, explains Dussel, has attempted, violently, to totalize exteriority. He writes: "The other, who is not different (as totality asserts) but distinct (always other), who has a history, a culture, an exteriority, has not always been respected; the center has not let the other *be* other" (p. 53). The "exteriority of popular culture is *the best guarantee and the least contaminated nucleus of the new humankind*. Its values, scorned today and not even recognized by the people itself, must be studied carefully; they must be augmented within a new pedagogy of the oppressed [emphasis added]" (p. 90).

332 Edet, Rosemary, and Bette Ekeya. "Church Women of Africa: A Theological Community." In *Passion and Compassion: Third World Women Doing Theology*, ed. by V. Fabella and M. Oduyoye, 3-13. Maryknoll, N.Y.: Orbis Books, 1989.

According to Edet and Ekeya, sexism contradicts a seminal biblical theme: women and men form a unity that may be called the primordial androgyny. "In both chapters 1 and 2 of Genesis," they write, "there is unity and diversity in the human image and likeness of God, but neither domination nor subordination" (Edet and Ekeya 4). See 290.

Unfortunately, the oppression of women contradicts that insight. African women's theology must raise this issue in a way that reveals that misogynism is not biblical and intrinsic to the structure of oppression. Edet and Ekeya reveal that African women are probing traditional culture, affirming what is liberating and advocating a purging of what is oppressive. They write: "African women theologically have the task of reclaiming the theological heritage stored in the participation of African women in traditional religion: the grassroots theology of Christian women and the theology that undergirds the spirituality of Christian women in Africa, especially those in the African Independent Churches" (pp. 11-12).

333 Ekechkwu, A. "The Problem of Suffering in Igbo Traditional Religion." *Bulletin of African Theology* 5,9 (January-June 1983): 51-64.

According to Ekechkwu, Eurocentric Christianity has upset and displaced the traditional Igbo approach to "sin," sickness and health. What is more, Western medicine, championed by the missionaries, was poorly suited to provide holistic care to Africans, for whom health involves much more than care of somatic distress. Essential to African well-being is the sense that all is correct in the invisible and the visible realms. To disrupt Igbo culture is to provoke forces inimical to health. See 133. The independent churches, as they draw from Christian and traditional modes, focus on healing in a way that relieves the anxiety of Africans. See 141-143, 234. Moreover, the independent churches——which Ekechkwu calls "The Healing Churches or Religions of the Oppressed"——enable a true inculturation. For Ekechkwu, inculturation——as the independent churches show——has little to do with the superficial translation of liturgy into Igbo idiom. Rather, inculturation has to do with acculturation (in this case "Igbonization"). Here African ritual would transform Christian liturgy, replacing the staid aesthetics of the missionaries with the lively poetics of Igbo ritual. One must recognize, moreover, "that ritual has a therapeutic power to heal states of depression" (p. 64).

334 Éla, Jean-Marc. "Ancestors and Christian Faith: An African problem." *Concilium* 2 (1977): 34-50.

"Can the Church in Black Africa," asks Éla, "become the possible location of communication with the ancestors?" See 341. The question is critical as it defines whether one respects the humanity of African people. For Éla, the ancestors symbolize Africans' most hallowed values. They signify Africans' profound connections with the realm of the invisible and with their origins. The invisible, often associated with the sky, connotes the extension of the realm of the earth, the realm of the living and its flora and fauna——that is, the realm of the visible. The invisible is a "spiritual" realm, a place inhabited by ancestors (the living-dead) and other numinous beings who vibrate in the matrix of the localized cosmos. The invisible and the visible signify the matrix in which the living have relations with the Supreme Being. Such relations are usually indirect, diffused through the agents of the invisible, principally, the ancestors. In revering their ancestors, Africans indicate their sense of sacred time and give religious significance to kinship and social responsibility. Sacred time is a ritualistic and liminal mode in which Africans revel in their ancestral connection to God; kinship thus has a theological implication. In respecting one's ancestors, he/she valorizes both patterns of kinship established by them and the human community established by God. Failure to propitiate the ancestors invites disaster and chaos——the antithesis of fecundity and wholeness, both of which define an African sense of community and connection to God. For Éla, then, a Christianity that would forsake the ancestors is devoid of a meaningful anthropology. Salvation would be truncated and Christianity meaningless if the African sense of humanity were diminished by the exclusion of the ancestors. According to Éla, the notion that the communion of saints can replace the ancestors is a symptom of the will to truncate African

Christianity. Should that occur, he argues, there would be extirpation rather than inculturation. Inculturation——and the acculturation it implies——would take place if the Communion of Saints were to include the ancestors. For Éla, then, the African church can become the location for communion with the ancestors. The scope of salvation, he asserts, is exceeding broad. He writes: "To live in the African way the mystery of communion in the Christ who recapitulated the visible and the invisible...is to assume a dimension of our total faith" (p. 49).

335 Éla, Jean-Marc. "Ecclesial Ministry and the Problems of the Young Churches." *Concilium* (June 1977): 45-53.

Ecclesiology, asserts Éla, concerns "the ministry of Christ in the Spirit," whose work is not confined to the ordained. Baptism itself——through the Spirit——bestows upon the laity the authority to minister. Éla argues, moreover, that the laity constitutes the africanizing force of the younger churches. He writes: "To manage with no priests, or very few, is a purifying ordeal, forcing the churches to make the most of the creative resources made available to them by the Spirit, in that margin for interrogation opened to the faith, so as to achieve a total interpretation of the gospel for our time" (p. 52).

336 Éla, Jean-Marc. *L'Afrique des villages*. Paris: Éditions Karthala, 1982.

Here Éla evinces the substantial way in which the new guard is committed to social analysis. He lays bare how anthropologists examine African culture without attention to the deep socioeconomic and political alienation of the rural people. He notes the quaintness of a *négritude* discourse, in which idyllic representations of the *"authentic,"* non-westernized African is but a dissimulation of the dire straits of the peasants. Éla then examines neocolonial problems such as improper health care, infant mortality and illiteracy. See 338. These problems, for Éla, are the result of a colonial violence that gives priority to the cities because the elite live there. According to Éla, the rural masses must organize themselves and oppose this violent structure that "thingifies" them. He writes:

> If the peasants take courage, they are going to take their lives in their own hands and become noble together. For the peasants who speak and stand up can change the political, economic and social landscape of a region. Today, only the groups conscious of their rights can seize the power of speech and denounce the encroachment on their rights. *L'Afrique des villages* needs these groups if it is to no longer be a land of pariahs [my translation]. (See p. 228.)

According to Éla, freedom-loving Africans——especially those living in the city——must join the peasants of the bush in political struggle.

337 Éla, Jean-Marc. *La ville en Afrique noire*. Paris: Éditions Karthala, 1983.

Again Éla demonstrates the critical function of social analysis, with a focus on the urban areas. He notes that cities are not a European creation in Africa, but have a long pre-colonial history. The cities today, however, bear the mark of colonialism. That is, they signify an urbanization without industrialization, despite the huge ports or mining centers. According to Éla, this sad situation has prevailed throughout Africa and must be understood in terms of *d'une économie de traite dont le moteur n'est pas le développement mais l'exploitation des ressources naturelles pour le grand profit de l'Europe industrielle* (p. 14). Now, in the era of neocolonialism, the African poor are gripped in a vise of exploitation operated by the elite. The ranks of the urban poor are swelling with migrating peasants, who come to the city to escape the festering poverty of *l'arrière-pays*. In the cities, the poor are assaulted by a barrage of socioeconomic contradictions: the conflict between traditional values and the urban ethos (*implantations urbaines et mentalité ethnique*); conflicts between *les ruraux et les citadins*, and so forth. A major contradiction is that between the elites and the masses. *Les éléments de modernisme sont réservés, dans les quartiers résidentiels, à la classes dirigeante tandis que les populations de bas étage s'entassent dans les bas-quartiers et les bidonvilles où il n'y a pas d'urbanisme* (p. 79). See 338. These contradictions tend to keep the poor in a horrible state of inertia, itself maintained by the myth of independence. According to Éla, this myth, which involves the sacralization of the capitals, must be exploded by a concentration on the rural areas——that is, a re-Africanization must take place. Here, he refers to Cabral. See 023-025. *Rêverie d'utopiste? En tout cas, prise de conscience lucide des tentations qui menacent de l'intérieur les Etats africains atteints par la maladie des capitales* (p. 219).

338 Éla, Jean-Marc. "Luttes pour la santé de l'homme et Royaume de Dieu dans l'Afrique d'aujourd'hui." *Bulletin de théologie africaine* 5,9 (janvier-juin 1983): 65-84.

Éla examines how health care, and the European church, which has blessed and kept it, is yet vitiated by values carried over from olden colonialism. This is best observed in *un texte savoureux de l'époque coloniale*——namely *un manuel de conseils d'hygiène aux écoliers dahoméens*. Whites, the manual reveals, needed palm oil that they could not attain at home since palm trees are not found in Europe; whites needed cotton, maize, etc. Who would provide the necessary (cheap) labor but the blacks? If they die, who will climb the trees, *qui fera l'huile, qui le portera les factoreries?* What is more: *L'administration a besoin d'impôt; si tes enfants ne vivent pas, qui le payera?* (See p. 65.) According to Éla, the totality of the health care system is part of a global system of domination. Within this system, the French real-bourgeoisie and the African pseudo-bourgeoisie have waxed as the African peasants have waned. See 011, 035. There is thus a huge gap between the privileged minority, *aisée et nantie[,] et celui de la majorité déshéritée* (p. 68). Despite rural development, infants starve to death in Africa. According to Éla, then, there is today, as there was yesterday, no true *santé*. See 341. Une famille kirdi [a traditional people of Cameroon] *est réduite à faire de la viande ou du poisson un simple condiment* (p. 68). How, he cries, can a people be healthy when *only* the elite are well-fed, well-heeled, and well-protected from the diseases of the bush? These——endemic parasites——prey upon the masses; *l'eau potable est un véritable luxe des quartiers résidentiels réservés à la caste privilégiée* (p. 69). The Bible, for Éla, reveals that justice, mercy, and love——Christian virtues——are inextricable from health. He writes: *le message fondamental de l'évangile, c'est la rédemption de notre corps* (p. 75). Ultimate salvation is, providentially, part of penultimate well-being. The few, asserts Éla, who enjoy health and prosperity at the expense of the many are woefully sinful. And Africa, he argues, is *the* context which exemplifies the ostensible triumph of sin. Africa——where babies die, more often than anywhere else on the planet, from diarrhea and measles——is the context where one sees both the antithesis and the symbol of God's Kingdom. Éla writes: *Il y a là précisément, le visage noir du 'péché du monde,' que porte et enlève l'Agneau de Dieu* (p. 78). By implication, only those in solidarity with the crucified masses are citizens of God's Kingdom and faithful to Christ, the lamb of God. For Éla, the essential question is whether Christians are ready to take up the cross for the sake of the *santé de l'homme*, and create praxes of liberation. By that Éla means praxes capable of rendering to the poor their dignity in the actual situation of Black Africa.

339 Éla, Jean-Marc. "Le rôle des Eglises dans la libération du continent africain." *Bulletin de théologie africaine* 6,12 (juillet-décembre 1984): 281-302.

Éla addresses the assembly of the Yaounde Colloquium on The Churches and Black Theology. See 439. He notes the horrible suffering of the African people and asserts that the criteria for inculturation is implied in the question: *les Eglises d'Afrique peuvent-elles se libérer elle-mêmes sans participer aux combats des Africains contre les forces d'exploitation et d'oppression* (p. 238). See 253. For Éla, the church itself must be a battleground, which, in heightening the contradictions between the oppressors and the oppressed, readies the ground for inculturation. See 572-578. Church folk who recognize that inculturation is impossible without struggle against oppression eschew the notion of *négritude*. See 336, 340. These radicals, asserts Éla, favor an analysis of *la condition des paysans et des néo-ruraux qui s'agglutinent dans les bidonvilles connaissent des changements profonds* (p. 285). For Éla, the real Africa——the real Pan-Africa——is that of the shanty town poor, not that of the *négritude*, bourgeois intellectuals who have reified and romanticized Africa. Indeed: *Dépouillée de folklore la réalité apparaît, brutale et sombre* (p. 288). Part of the brutal and somber reality is that the elite are in cahoots with the West and partly responsible for the pauperization of the African poor——*de l'Afrique 'd'en-bas'*. The liberating and inculturating church, however, is in solidarity with this underside, argues Éla——the popular base of true liberation. Indeed, for Éla: *La remise en question doit être radicale pour délivrer le message chrétien de la captivité où l'a enfermé l'embourgeoisement de l'Evangile par les classes dominantes d'occident* (p. 298).

340 Éla, Jean-Marc. *African Cry*. Maryknoll, N.Y.: Orbis Books, 1986.

African Cry, in the English speaking world, is considered to be a milestone in African theology because it shows clearly that African theologians are in fact liberation theologians. Éla begins his powerful book with a description of the Kirdi peasants of Cameroon, who are so alienated from the land that sustains them that they, under the command of the state, grow cotton instead of the life-giving millet. Éla points out that this alienation is a result of a form of neocolonialism purveyed in part by the Roman Catholic Church. See 004, 044, 092, 097. According to Éla, the church exacerbates peasant alienation through its imperial requirement that only ordained priests administer the Eucharist. This requirement, he argues, is cruel because the shortage of priests deprives the peasants of the sustenance of Holy Communion. What is more, the peasants are made to import the costly wine and wafers that, always in short supply, have no meaning for the Kirdi who grow neither. It would be far more meaningful if the peasants used millet——itself pregnant with meaning——and nut beer, which they grow. See 474. The present symbols of the Eucharist, and the economic and cultural imperialism they prolong, are but examples of the ambiguities of mission. Éla argues that the African peasants must depart from such ecclesial imperialism on the basis of the Exodus. Here he employs a hermeneutic in which the Exodus is reread in light of African experience and the faith that liberation is the essence of the promise and hope of the gospel. For Éla, evangelical hope, and the liberation it bestows, is inextricable from ancestral values. One observes this fact in the independent churches. See 330. For Éla, such churches, by virtue of their Africanity, seek, "that dynamism of revelation that colonialism has prevented Christianity in Africa from expressing and assimilating" (p. 48). These churches, in addition, despite their excesses, reveal the disingenuousness of *négritude* theories. See 114-115. Out of touch with the revolutionary values of the peasants——who embody the exteriority of popular culture (see 331)——such theories have no revolutionary power. He argues that they turn "out to be the theoretical and ideological language of a local bourgeoisie seeking to dissimulate the alienation of the masses in order to profit from the meager resources of the neocolonial apparatus" (p. 129). In discussing the revolutionary values of the peasants, Éla leans heavily upon Fanon's *The Wretched of the Earth*. See 034. From Fanon, Éla has learned one "has to die to the state of having become bourgeois in order to find yourself a person with the soul of a revolutionary, poor among the poor, shoulder to shoulder with the poor along the pathways of struggle that lead to final victory" (p. 58).

341 Éla, Jean-Marc. *My Faith as an African*. Maryknoll, N.Y.: Orbis Books, 1988.

Éla argues that one's appreciation of the ancestors will condition his/her understanding of the ways in which the African worldview is rich with symbolism. See 308, 334. In Africa, relationships among human beings, and between human beings and nature, are understood in terms of the invisible——the veiled matrix where all reality acquires meaning. The truly real is invisible and the visible is only appearance; all visible existence is a symbol, a metonym or a metaphor, of an invisible value. Inculturation is facilitated when one is initiated into the invisible——acquires insight into the indices of the forest and the village——and recognizes the hidden presence of the ancestors and other spiritual beings. For Éla, moreover, those religio-cultural issues attain clarity only in relation to social analyses that unmask the victimization of the African poor. In *My Faith as an African*, social analysis exposes the travesty of *santé* in Africa. See 338. He also examines the crises of the rural and urban areas. See 336-337. Éla concludes that Christ today must be understood in terms of the poor of the Third World, whose ranks are swelled by the indigent of Africa. "If we view the cross of Jesus Christ as the cross of the Third World," he writes, "the very existence of the Third World shows us what sin is and how it is structured in history. The Third World carries within itself the hidden Christ. It is the historic body of Christ today" (p. 99).

342 Etuk, Udo. "New Trends in Traditional Divination." *Africa Theological Journal* 13,2 (1984): 83-91.

Etuk examines the way in which Annang-Ibibio priest-diviners of the Cross River state of eastern Nigeria have healed in the name of Jesus. Bringing to mind the views of Sanneh——see 112-113——Etuk holds that Jesus here has little, if anything, to do with Christianity. Etuk suggests that priest-diviners may use the name of Jesus for two reasons: (1) recognition and acknowledgement of the power of Jesus; and (2) recognition of the intermediary role of Jesus. See 234. According to Etuk, the diviner may be familiar with the New Testament depiction of Jesus as a powerful priest with phenomenal strength in the areas of healing and the manipulation of nature. To call his name is to pad one's hand in the battle with spirits, known and unknown. The diviner, explicitly or tacitly, uses Jesus' name to legitimate his work, thus attracting church-going clients. Furthermore, argues Etuk, the name of Jesus has connotations that can accommodate new religions or divinities without conflict of interests or ambivalence. See 195. What, asks Etuk, are the implications of this for African theology? For Etuk, the resurgence of divination attests to the vitality of traditional culture. Can the church, he wonders, be edified by this phenomenon? Can the African churches accept polytheism or, rather, henotheism. Etuk is doubtful, given the difference between African tradition, with its dense numinous field, and Christianity's monotheistic tradition.

343 Ezeanya, Stephen. "God Spirits and the Spirit World." In *Biblical Revelation and African Belief*, ed. by Kwesi Dickson and Paul Ellingworth, 30-46. Maryknoll, N.Y.: Orbis Books, 1969.

Ezeanya focuses on the continuities between traditional Igbo religion and Christianity. See 180-183. For him, the two are brought together under the principle of *adaptation* (a word related to inculturation). According to Ezeanya *adaptation* involves a two-fold process: the evangelist must study the traditional values of the people in order to "graft the good scion of the gospel message upon the stock of the traditional heritage in order that it may bear a crop of more delicious fruit." Intrinsic to his definition here is a notion of accommodation——the truth of the Gospel must not be abridged, yet it must be fed to the people coincident with their understanding at the moment. Evangelism is thus facilitated by the study of the Igbo religion.

344 Fabella, Virginia, and Mercy Amba Oduyoye. "Introduction." In *Passion and Compassion: Third World Women Doing Theology*, ed. by V. Fabella and M. Oduyoye, ix-xv. Maryknoll, N.Y.: Orbis Books, 1989.

The authors introduce the essays published from the historic conference of the EATWOT women, held in Oaxtepec, Mexico, 1986. See 290, 332. They note the women's commitment to social and religio-cultural analyses——prerequisites for hermeneutics of suspicion as defined within the broader context of EATWOT.

345 Fasholé-Luke, Edward. "Ancestor Veneration and the Communion of Saints." In *New Testament Christianity for Africa and the World: Essays in Honor of Harry Sawyerr*, ed. by Mark Glasswell and Edward W. Fasholé-Luke, 209-220. London: SPCK, 1974.

For Fasholé-Luke, the prevailing assumption that one can erase the memory and practice of African religion heightens the necessity today for a revisionist approach to African missiology. The fact is that traditional values cannot be purged. One of the heartiest of those values is veneration of the ancestors. See 161, 178, 479, 485. According to Fasholé-Luke, it is imperative to plant Christian doctrine in the soil of the ancestors. See 308. Thus, the church must "develop a theology of the Communion of Saints that will satisfy the passionate desire of Africans, Christians and non-Christians alike, to be linked with their dead ancestors" (p. 210). See 334. According to Fasholé-Luke——and here he takes issue with Harry Sawyerr——Africans make qualitative distinctions between the ancestors and the Supreme Being: the ancestors are not worshipped. See 242. Fasholé-Luke notes that J.V. Taylor (see 260) has helped to clarify this, as has Jomo Kenyatta (see 188-190). With them, Fasholé-Luke concludes that Africans *venerate* their ancestors. Fasholé-Luke reveals that Meyer Fortes's *Oedipus and Job in West African Religion* has also helped clarify this matter. See 167. Fortes's work on the Tallensi shows that "veneration," rather than "worship," captures the esteem in which ancestors are held. There is no way one can confuse veneration with worship, argues Fasholé-Luke. The light is green, then, for seeking correspondences between veneration of the ancestors and the Communion of Saints.

346 Fasholé-Luke, Edward. "The Quest for African Theologies." In *Mission Trends No.3: Third World Theologies. Asian, African and Latin American Contributions to a Radical, Theological Realignment in the Church*, ed. by Gerald H. Anderson and Thomas F. Stransky, 135-150. New York: Paulist Press; Grand Rapids: Wm. B. Eerdmans, 1976.

Fasholé-Luke begins by noting that what is meant by African theology is not clear. He notes the historicity of the quest for African theologies, however, in terms of the legacies of historic African Christians——i.e., Crowther, Johnson, and Blyden. See 109, 007, 016-018. Fasholé-Luke asserts that African theology at present suffers from a lack of focus, which he attributes to: the paucity of autochthonous theologians; the alienation which drives certain Africans to African traditional religion; the parroting of Eurocentric thought; white Christians' aversion to African cultures. Despite those problems, Fasholé-Luke claims that the sources of African theology are: (1) the Bible; (2) the living Christ; (3) pneumatological revelation; (4) African traditional religion; (5) theological foundations of European churches; and (6) the African independent churches.

347 Fasholé-Luke, E.W. "Introduction." In *Christianity in Independent Africa*, ed. by Edward Fasholé-Luke, Richard Gray, Adrian Hastings and Godwin Tasie, 357-363. Bloomington: Indiana University Press, 1978.

Fasholé-Luke introduces Part Two of *Christianity in Independent Africa*, entitled "Traditional Religion and Christianity: Continuities and Conflicts." He notes that, despite significant differences, African theologies are significantly similar. He attributes their similarity to common colonial experiences under missionaries. While noting their positive contributions, he also notes the estrangement missionaries effected between Africans and their traditional culture. What is more, the missionary attempt to alienate Africans from their culture, asserts Fasholé-Luke, was legitimated by Western imperialism. Fasholé-Luke also reveals how colonialism continues today——such that African Christianity is still culturally and financially dependent upon the metropolitan church. According to Fasholé-Luke, neocolonialism, and black complicity in its maintenance, make the praxis of liberation relevant across the continent. See 004, 097, 314-315.

348 Fasholé-Luke, Edward. "Footpaths and Signposts to African Christian Theology." *Bulletin of African Theology* 3,5 (January-June 1981): 19-40.

Fasholé-Luke examines the astonishing proliferation of African Christianity——astonishing given the poor prognosis, proffered by Western Christians and cynical African nationalists, regarding the survival of African Christianity. The rapid growth of African Christianity, for Fasholé-Luke, makes the quest for African theologies all the more urgent. His call for theological independence is sharpened in a critique of Mbiti (see 396-410), Oosthuizen (see 227), and Hastings (see 045-047). He accuses them of a certain narrowness in their assessment of African theology. Fasholé-Luke also points to the illegitimacy of white books on African theology, lamenting the fact that Aylward Shorter's *African Christian Theology* has been more widely distributed than Charles Nyamiti's *African Theology: Its Nature, Problems and Methods*. See 490, 445. After reviewing significant events in the history of African theology, Fasholé-Luke concludes "that only Africans, even detribalised Africans, descendants of slaves, can say what the shape, content and future of African Christian theologies should be" (p. 40).

349 Gaba, Christian R. "Man's Salvation: Its Nature and Meaning in African Traditional Religion." In *Christianity in Independent Africa*, ed. by Edward Fasholé-Luke, Richard Gray, Adrian Hastings and Godwin Tasie, 389-401. Bloomington: Indiana University Press, 1978.

Gaba argues that the meaning of African Christianity is entangled in the structure of traditional religion. Precision in defining African Christianity, moreover, is attained through a focus on *an* ethnic group. Here, Gaba focuses on the Anlo Awe people of West Africa and their pre-Christian understanding of salvation. According to Gaba, salvation, *i.e., Dagbe*, is best understood as abundant life, not eternal life. To that extent *Dagbe* is closer to *shalom* than salvation. *Dagbe,* asserts Gaba, for the Anlo people, comes from God, to whom they have access through ancestors, and other numinous beings, who enforce the morality of God. God is propitiated through ritual immolation offered to the ancestors. Thus, vicarious sacrifice takes away the impropriety and evil which threatens *Dagbe,* asserts Gaba. See 158. In sum, Gaba argues that inculturation is impossible unless Anlo "soteriology" is rooted in the structure of *Dagbe*.

350 Gantin, B. "Théologie africaine et catholicité." *Bulletin de théologie africaine* 4,7 (janvier-juin 1982): 165-172.

Gantin, a European cardinal, delivers an address to the international symposium of the theological schools of Kinshasa and St. Augustine. He argues that acculturation is an encounter between cultures, in which there is no synthesis. Inculturation, however, signifies a quintessential synthesis because it corresponds to the incarnation. Whereas acculturation signifies an encounter in which one entity is not integrated into the other, inculturation signifies true integration——not unlike hypostatic union; anhypostasis/enhypostasis. In inculturation then: *Le message Evangélique serait en rapport avec notre culture de même que la divinité est en rapport avec l'humanité* (p. 166). According to Gantin, in addition, there is an integration between *l'altérité constitutive de toute culture* and the *catholicité* of the cross. Inculturation, for Gantin, therefore, has to do with *la théologie de la différence*.   See 288, 331.   That is, inculturation effects a *new* expression of the ubiquity of the incarnation.   For Gantin, *La théologie en Afrique sera africaine ou elle ne sera pas*.   But, cautions Gantin, African theology will not be if it is not as catholic as it is African.

351   Glasswell, Mark.   "The Beginning of the Gospel: A Study of St. Mark Gospel with Regard to its First Verse." In *New Testament Christianity for Africa and the World: Essays in Honor of Harry Sawyerr*, ed. by Mark Glasswell and Edward W. Fasholé-Luke, 36-43. London: SPCK, 1974.

Glasswell's exegesis of Mark focuses on the view that one should read the gospel backward rather than forward——such that the resurrection is seen as the structure of the text.   What precedes the resurrection——and here one prescinds of thought of the incarnation——is epiphenomenal to the resurrection itself.   What precedes the resurrection is but the human narrative of the revelation of God-in-Christ.   Apart from the gospel, the good news of the resurrection, the narrative of Jesus's baptism, ministry, and passion have no essential connection to God.   But insofar as the resurrection is the basis of the narrative, the narrative itself has its ultimate origin in God.   According to Glasswell, the gospel of Mark provides insight into "Harry Sawyerr's christocentric approach in *Creative Evangelism*" (p. 41).   See 476.   Glasswell's essay, then, gives one an appreciation of the biblical theology that tended to govern Sawyerr's work.

352   Gutiérrez, Gustavo.   "Two Theological Perspectives: Liberation Theology and Progressivist Theology." In *The Emergent Gospel*, ed. by Sergio Torres and Virginia Fabella, 227-258. London: Geoffrey Chapman, 1978.

Gutiérrez is a Latin American theologian whose work on liberation is authoritative for other liberation theologians of the South.   His essay here, delivered at the historic EATWOT conference in Dar es Salaam in 1976, is seminal because it defines the ideological suspicion integral to the epistemological break of the South from the North. See 483.   According to Gutiérrez, liberation theology is emergent from the underside of history.   That is, liberation theology is focused on the "non-person"——the oppressed of the Third World, who have been rendered nearly invisible in the post-modern discourse of the First World.   First World theologians, in distinction from Third World theologians, focus on the problem of the "non-believer."   Critical for them is the disjunction between faith and reason——the problematic of the Enlightenment.   Little attention is given to the ways in which the Enlightenment gave impetus to chattel slavery and colonialism——the problems of the non-person.   In short, "Two Theological Perspectives: Liberation Theology and Progressivist Theology," provides a pioneering paradigm of social analysis that contains important idioms of liberation theology.

353   Hebga, Meinrad.   "Christianisme et négritude." In *Des prêtres noirs s'interrogent*, ed. by A. Abble, et al., 189-204. Paris: Les Éditions du Cerf, 1956.

According to Hebga, many African nationalists argue that Christianity is *un produit d'exportation, un agent d'impérialisme*.   Indeed, he notes, imperialism is responsible for the irruption of violence that stems in part from a *paganisme inhibé*.   Imperialism accounts for the rise and ostensible success of messianic movements, such as the one in East Africa that claimed to be able to save Africans through a black messiah.   For Hebga, however, the nationalists, in pointing to the proliferation of anti-colonial cults and movements, are cleverly obfuscating the meaning of Christianity.   According to Hebga, nationalists' diatribes must not detour the African priest from investigating Christianity's relation to *négritude*.   He himself wonders, then, whether the two are *compossible*.   He asserts that they are: *négritude* can be assumed by Christianity without losing its essential African soul.   Christ, he argues, is the savior of all "races."   The blacks, then, may bring their particularity to the rest of the *goyim*, who are compelled to join the rag-tag army of Christian faith. Indeed, négritude, according to Hebga, makes blacks predisposed to accept Christianity. The African knows that there has been a tragic fall; *la négritude est l'intuition chronique* of a universal frustration; it is the insight that something essential is lacking in human existence. Nostalgically, *négritude* craves a return to paradise lost. Given the African's longing for an atonement of cosmic proportion, *adaptation* is possible, he argues, provided one adopts an *anti-impérialisme culturel* (p. 200). He explains his aversion to cultural imperialism in relation to music. Hebga acknowledges that European musicians, such as Bach and Wagner, have made an indelible contribution to worship. But, he asks, *savez-vous rien de plus pénitent, de plus poignant, que les blues négro-américains? N'avez-vous jamais été saisis d'une sainte frayeur à l'éclatement soudain d'un* negro spiritual: <u>Steal away to Jesus</u>, *ou* <u>My Lord what a Morning</u>? (See p. 201.) Thus, for Hebga, *négritude*, as embodied in the uncanny spirituality of African-American music, can edify Christian piety. For Hebga, blacks can be loyal and obedient to the church without losing their African souls.

354 Hebga, Meinrad. *"Universality in Theology and Inculturation." Bulletin of African Theology* 5,10 (July-December 1983): 179-192.
Exploring the tension between the universality of the gospel and the specificity of its inculturations, Hebga asserts that Christianity must be plural, "so it can reach all the nations in their manifold diversities" (p. 180). For Hebga, one discovers, through the juxtaposition of Christianity and African traditional religion, "a healthy pluralism," which is emblematic of the union between particularity and universality.

355 Hillman, Eugene. "Polygamy Reconsidered." In *Third World Liberation Theologies*, ed. by Deane William Ferm, 248-255. Maryknoll, N.Y.: Orbis Books, 1986.
Hillman ponders the contradiction between Christians' exclusion of polygamists and the church's assertion that marriage is indissoluble. He wonders whether the church's stand against polygamy sublates the gospel to the law, the spirit to the letter. He writes that external conformity to monogamy is a "legal prescription [that] has become so overwhelmingly important and finally decisive in practice that it seems almost to have become a substitute for the real conversion of faith, which alone leads to the newness of Christian faith" (p. 249). For Hillman, then, dogmatic insistence on monogamy may be tantamount to "sowing seeds on rock." One must respect polygamy on Africans' own terms if he/she is to plant Christianity in Africa.

356 Idowu, E. Bolaji. *Towards an Indigenous Church*. London: Oxford University Press, 1965.
Towards an Indigenous Church is a pioneering work on indigenization in Nigeria. After establishing Bishop Crowther——see 109——as a seminal ancestor of indigenization, Idowu defines indigenization as follows.

> By indigenization in this context, we mean that the Church in Nigeria should be the Church which affords Nigerians the means of worshipping God as Nigerians; that is, in a way which is compatible with their own spiritual temperament, of singing to the glory of God in their own way, of praying to God and hearing His holy Word in idiom which is clearly intelligible to them (p. 11).

He asserts that the independent churches are in the vanguard of attempts to africanize Christianity. That is, they are paradigms of what an indigenous church looks like, though one must be wary of their syncretism and emotionalism. Idowu also notes that it "is certainly impossible for the Church in Nigeria to develop its own character unless European and American vested interests release their stranglehold upon her" (p. 54).

357 Idowu, E. Bolaji. "Introduction." In *Biblical Revelation and African Beliefs*, ed. by Kwesi Dickson and Paul Ellingworth, 9-16. Maryknoll, N.Y.: Orbis Books, 1969.

Idowu criticizes the missiology of the Europeans who, in general, entertained very derogatory opinions about African people. See 329. For Idowu, their racist imagination is idolatrous; it truncates the fullness of God's revelation to the African in deifying European civilization. Quoting Bishop Crowther, Idowu notes the indispensable role that doctrines of general revelation play in African theology. Thus he argues that God was known generally to the Africans before the inculturation of the specific revelation of the gospel. According to Idowu, however, African values are dying; hence African theologies must move quickly in establishing the continuities between failing traditions and Christianity. His essay takes no account, though, of the dynamism of traditional values, which were truly africanizing Christianity in the independent churches——a point he brings out in his seminal *Towards an Indigenous Church*.

358 Ikenga-Metuh, Emefie. "Towards An African Theology of Man." *African Theological Journal* 11,2 (1982): 141-150.

Ikenga-Metuh compares and contrasts the anthropologies of African traditional religion and African Christian theology. He surveys the anthropologies of the Ashanti, Igbo and the Yoruba. See 131, 139, 133, 135. Human beings in the African religions, claims Ikenga-Metuh, are essentially creatures of God and inextricable from their environment. For Ikenga-Metuh, however, the traditional anthropologies would remain somewhat truncated without a Christian anthropology. Here *anthropos* is defined as a sinner who is acceptable to God only because of the atoning sacrifice of Christ. For Ikenga-Metuh, then, the traditional, general understanding of God awaits fruition in special revelation, who is Christ. In sum, Ikenga-Metuh holds that the inculturative power of the doctrine of the *imago Dei*——the meaning of which is made clear in Christ——would free Africans from the cul-de sac of sinful nature.

359 Ikenga-Metuh, Emefie. "The Theological Study of African Traditional Religion: Case Study of Igbo Theodicy." *Africa Theological Journal* 14,1 (1985): 55-65.

Here Ikenga-Metuh discusses traditional Igbo concepts of God, with a focus on the problem of theodicy. See 333. According to Ikenga-Metuh, Igbo use three personal names for God: *Chukwu*; the Great *Chi*; *Chineke*; and *Osebuluwa*. *Chi* is often used as a prefix to *Chukwu* and *Chineke*; *Ukwu* and *Eke* are suffixes and signify attributes of *Chi*. Ikenga-Mutuh reveals that *Chi* has three interrelated meanings: (1) God; (2) one's Caretaker Spirit, itself bestowed by God; and (3) individual fate, also obtained from God. The precise nuance of *Chi* is reckoned according to the way in which it is signified in ritual or less sacred circumstances. In short, traditional Igbo concepts of God are ambiguous. Nonetheless, Ikenga-Metuh is clear that "creator, protector, and giver of destiny" are fundamental to a understanding of *Chukwu*. What is more, Ikenga-Metuh asserts that Creator and Master of Providence, are prominent functions of God. The essential benevolence of God, moreover, is such that a myriad of misfortune can hardly be attributed to "him."

360 Ilogu, Edmund. *Christianity and Igbo Culture: A Study of the Interaction of Christianity and Igbo Culture*. New York: Nok Publishers, 1974.

Ilogu's pioneering monograph on elements of Igbo culture is a fine example of early efforts at religio-cultural analysis in African theology. Specifically, Ilogu examines the correspondence between "Christian ethics and Ibo traditional morality" (p. 9). His method is primarily sociological; he focuses on values and convictions essential to the matrix of relationships constituted by Igbo culture. Ilogu surveys Igbo religion and society in terms of the "the impersonality of *Chukwu*, the Igbo's God, whose deity is extended through lesser gods, ancestors and elements of the natural milieu. See 359. He discusses Igbo society in terms of the *Ozo* title, of which the *Ofo* stick is emblematic. See 162. Ilogu argues that religion and society form a unity. The *Ozo* title, then——see 292——is at once a religious and a socio-political institution, and is emblematic of all the Igbo prize as supremely ethical. White missionaries were ignorant of the sophistication of Igbo religion and the integrity of Igbo society. African missionaries such as Crowther, however,——see 109, 356-357——were more respectful, though not unlike their white colleagues in the assumption that Igbo religion had to be eventually uprooted. Another factor in the christianization of the Igbo, reveals Ilogu, has been the independent churches that reveal continuity with the *code ésotérique* of the traditional Igbo. Whether Igbos adhere to the historical or charismatic churches, inculturation is evident in the fact that certain traditional practices——such as the murder of twins, human sacrifice, and the burying of slaves with the deceased of the highest caste——have been eliminated. While most would agree those changes were humane and necessary, not all the effects of inculturation have been positive. The *Ozo* title, for instance, was opposed by missionaries, though it has proved irrepressible. In short, though the church has made significant contributions to the quality of human life in Igboland, it viciously sought to destroy the center of Igbo culture, abetting the shameful falling apart of things. See 132. Ilogu, though, makes a distinction between the church as a sociological (Eurocentric) institution, and the values of Christianity, which transcend bigotry and complement nuances of Igbo morality. For example: "The Ibo's emphasis on *ndu*, justice, co-operation, when enhanced by the believers' fruit of the Spirit in love, joy and peace...creates new cultural dimensions out of these values, and would make possible new social and integrative forces, around which the Ibo can regroup for a new lease of community as well as individual life" (p. 231).

361 Ilunga, Bakole Wa. *Paths of Liberation: A Third World Spirituality*. Maryknoll, N.Y.: Orbis Books, 1984.

An exploration of an African spirituality that is christocentric and less politically polemic than the works of theologians like Éla: Ilunga holds that the "attainment of authentic liberation" is dependent upon learning "how patiently to discover the true face of God" (p. 4).

362 Ilunga, Bakole Wa. "Signification et pratique chrétiennes des droits de l'homme." *Bulletin de théologie africaine* 6,11 (janvier-juin 1984): 29-38.

Ilunga considers the relationship between the church and the transnational corporations. For Ilunga, the two go together since the spiritual and the temporal go together, as do the world and Christian faith. What is more, the juxtaposition of world and faith suggests that Christians are to be fully (i.e., prophetically) engaged in world affairs——*à la manière d'une 'avant-garde' du Règne de Dieu, pour le salut de ce monde, dans toute sa complexité* (p. 29). From that perspective, a Christian is duty-bound to prophesy regarding human rights. Moreover, human rights, Ilunga asserts, have a christological structure. It is only in Christ, for Ilunga, that one truly discovers that human rights are the rights of God. Implying here the definition of Chalcedon, 451, Ilunga holds that human rights are really a gift. His meaning is made clear in his quotation of Romans 5,8: *'Mais la preuve que Dieu nous aime, c'est que le Christ, alors que nous étions encore pécheurs, est mort pour nous.'*

363 Ilunga, Kabongo. "Comment étudier les églises dites: syncrétiques: Un point de vue d'un politicologue." In *Combats pour un christianisme africain. Mélanges en l'honneur du Professeur V. Mulago*, ed. by A. Ngindu Mushete, 81-88. Kinshasa: Faculté de Théologie Catholique, 1981.

Ilunga argues that a Hegelian analysis is fundamental to a rigorous analysis of the independent churches. That is, analysis of these churches involves a thesis and an antithesis which lead to a synthesis that gives rise to yet another thesis and antithesis. According to Ilunga, the phenomenon, *syncrétisme,* is a synthesis of a world religion and its opposite——in this case, *la tradition animiste common to the majority of the people of Zaire.* Each religion's grammar defines the orientation of its devotee. One's orientation, argues Ilunga, is not always determined by the world religion. Indeed, African religions tend to overpower the world religion. To explain why this is so——why the independent churches wax as the official church wanes——he draws on Weber's typology: *Le prophète, le prêtre et le sorcier,* which illustrates his valorization of a Hegelian dialectic. Religious bodies, for Ilunga, are founded by a charismatic figure (thesis); later such bodies become routinized in the development of a priesthood. *Et,* asserts Ilunga, *c'est la décadence* (antithesis): the sorcerer appears, who is really a charlatan, whom God opposes. The independent churches, must be seen as a prophetic movement emergent from the routinization of the official church and fear of the traditional necromancer (thesis as well as synthesis). Ilunga, as an outsider to African theology, argues that the independent churches tend to be: (1) too otherworldly (2) in need of *une Bible authentique, d'une Bible noire*; and (3) too dependent upon orality (p. 88).

364 Imasogie, Osadolor. *Guidelines For Christian Theology in Africa.* Achimota: Africa Christian Press, 1983.

According to Imasogie, Christianity becomes a living faith to the extent that it is contextualized. See 513. Contexualization here refers to an africanization that overcomes the popular reversion to traditional religions. Contextualization, for Imasogie, also entails an openness to new theological possibilities. New possibilities entail enquiries into: (1) the tension between post-modernity and Christian faith; and (2) the problem of bourgeois control of post-modern theology. For Imasgogie, both poles revolve around "the quasi-scientific world-view," represented by David Tracy and Juan L. Segundo (see 483). According to Imasogie, the quasi-scientific worldview differs from orthodox science in that the latter prescinds of thought of a spiritual realm. Both worldviews are foreign to African soil that yields another cosmology. The African's worldview involves, *inter alia,* an orientation to the numinous forces of the earth and sky, to whom humankind are bound. The African worldview involves rituals that, organized around specific taxonomies and topologies, disclose rich metaphoric and metonymic dimensions, of which most missionaries were ignorant and contemptuous. Drawing on Segundo's reinterpretation of the hermeneutic circle——see 483——Imasgogie argues that Africans must be suspicious of alienating ways of reading scripture and tradition in order to overcome the "quasi-scientific world view."

365 Jomier, Jacques. "Christianisme et Islam dans l'Afrique d'aujourd'hui." In *Combats pour un christianisme africain. Mélanges en l'honneur du Professeur V. Mulago,* ed. by A. Ngindu Mushete, 63-80. Kinshasa: Faculté de Théologie Catholique, 1981.

Jomier notes that Christianity rooted itself first in Africa; Islam came second and advanced from North Africa. Islam, reveals Jomier, was a critical unifying factor of the great Western Sudanese Kingdoms and became further entrenched in Black Africa during the Sokoto jihads. The impact of Islam in East Africa, writes Jomier, can be seen in the prevalence of the language, Swahili. *Le mot même de Swahili est un mot arabe, au pluriel* Sawahel *signifiant les côtes, les régions situées le long de la mer* (p. 67). Islam, he argues, gave Africans respite from colonialism and has greatly reduced the number of African traditional religionists. The esteem in which Africans hold both religions——Islam and Christianity——argues Jomier, should serve to diminish tensions between the two. Indeed, argues Jomier, study of Edward Blyden facilitates such an irenic orientation. See

016-018. Still, theological differences make dialogue between the two exceeding problematic. Christian theology tends to be defined in a christology Muslims cannot accept. Jomier concludes with the hope that present efforts to root Christianity deeply in African soil will also seek to edify Africans as to the profound values of Islam.

366 Kabasele, F. "Du canon romain au rite zaïrois." *Bulletin de théologie africaine* 4,7 (janvier-juin 1982): 213-228.

Pope Paul II's refusal to participate in an African liturgy, during his visit to Kinshasa in 1980, has led Kabasele to ask: *Du canon romain au rite zaïrois de la messe, y-a-t-il de la marge?* He asserts that the African rite is not so odd and estranged from "orthodox" liturgy if one appreciates how eucharistic prayer abolishes the religious fastidiousness of the Pope's rejection of an africanized liturgy. Kabasela explanation of the *rite zaïrois,* in addition, is reminiscent of Cabral's definition of re-Africanization. See 024. The most alienated recognize they must return to the bush (*se remettre à l'école de leurs traditions*) and be edified by the peasants. He thus argues that de-europeanization is indispensable for African inculturation. Critical here are the ancestors. See 308. Without the ancestors, African Christianity is not African. See 308, 334, 345. Kabasele argues that the Vatican should recognize that an African Christianity must be rooted in the ancestors. *Car un peuple sans mémoire, est un peuple sans avenir.*

367 Kabasele, F. "A travers des rites nouveaux, un christianisme africain." *Bulletin de théologie africaine* 5,10 (juillet-décembre 1983): 223-238.

Kabasele examines the tension between acculturation and inculturation as seen, for instance, in *l'invocation des Ancêtres dans le rite Zaïrois*. See 366. Here, faith and Africanity signify a hendiadys in which Africanity, at one moment, is a stepping stone to faith while faith, in the next moment, edifies Africanity. That *binôme* sparks Kabasele to ask: *Pourquoi un peuple en Afrique, ayant reçu la foi des successeurs des Apôtres qui sont venus de Rome, n'aurait pas le droit d'avoir un rite qui serait dénommé Zaïrois, Béninois, etc?* (See p. 227.) For Kabasele, Africans are free to "play their own game," to make sense of their faith according to the insights of their ancestors. See 307. It is thus appropriate to summon the ancestors in the *rites eucharistiques*. What is more, Kabasele calls for the utilization of ancestral initiation symbols in the ordination of priest.

368 Kabesa, A. "Salut, libération, promotion humain." *Bulletin de théologie africaine* 3,5 (janvier-juin 1981): 127-131.

Kabesa's remarks were given in the context of the centennial of the church of Zaire. He defines the Eucharist as the sacrament through which humankind and the universe are deified. The essential ground for this ontological promotion is the incarnation. In the Eucharist, one participates in God's hypostatic union with humanity. Humans are thus Christified. *Ils sont Christifiés.* Christified persons act ethically for the liberation of others. Such ethics demand prophetic encounter with the dehumanizing forces of neocolonialism. Indeed, the incarnation negates all bigotry (i.e., *les théories de racisme et d'apartheid).* Kabesa concludes that human history is now the venue of the Word, from whom proceeds new possibilities for liberation (i.e., *le salut déjà acquis dans le Christ sur le plan ontologique radical).* For Kabesa, the fullness of the promise of salvation is anticipated in all attempts——everywhere begun——to promote liberation.

369 Kagame, Alexis. "La littérature orale au Ruanda." In *Des prêtres noirs s'interrogent,* ed. by A. Abble, et al., 205-212. Paris: Les Éditions du Cerf, 1956.

Kagame notes that the people of Rwanda have a mnemonic rather than a chirographic culture. He focuses on their praise songs. According to Kagame, three basic elements define nuances of praise-songs and signify the leitmotifs of orality in

Rwanda: (1) the king——see 157-158——who symbolizes the well-being of the people; (2) the warrior, the right arm of the king; and (3) the cow——the means and symbol of the king's power, which links diverse members of the hierarchy of the country. Thus, Rwanda has three essential poetic genres: the dynastic that exalts the king; the warrior that sings of heroes and their valor; and *le pastoral*, that exalts the cow. According to Kagame, praise-poems, as a genre, particularly those of the Tutsi——the subjects of *poèmes dynastique*——are similar to biblical psalms (*psautier hébraïque*).

370 Kagame, Alexis. "Ode à la Vierge Immaculée." In *Des prêtres noirs s'interrogent*, ed. by A. Abble, et al., 261-264. Paris: Les Éditions du Cerf, 1956.
    Kagame's poem indicates his Roman Catholic piety, i.e, his sense of mariology:
    Il [God] orna sa beauté d'intacte perfection,
    Epancha sur son sein la blancheur éclatante;
Indeed, Mary, for Kagame, is *Blanc-Joyau-de-Sion*. One wonders how "Ode à la Vierge Immaculée" is related to *African* theology.

371 Kalilombe, Patrick A. "Self-Reliance of the African Church: A Catholic Perspective." In *African Theology en Route*, ed. by Kofi Appiah-Kubi and Sergio Torres, 36-58. Maryknoll, N.Y.: Orbis Books, 1979.
    Kalilombe, of Malawi, examines the issue of the moratorium on mission explored at the Third Assembly of the AACC in Zambia, 1974. For Kalilombe, the issue is whether the African church can become independent of the metropole churches, specifically Roman Catholic churches. According to Kalilombe, the African contingent of the Roman Catholic Church has been concerned with the moratorium as early as 1956, coincident with the publication of *Des prêtres noirs s'interrogent*. See 329, 353, 370. Kalilombe reveals that African priests, including Vincent Mulago——see 415——pondered the issue before, and in a way consistent with, Vatican II. Their call for *adaptation* (i.e. inculturation) was resisted, claims Kalilombe, by Eurocentric clergy and educated African laity. If missionaries were once critical of inculturation, reveals Kalilombe, they now zealously support it. He suspects this "new" development is little more than covert paternalism, which is also found, asserts Kalilombe, in the quest for indigenous priests, the shibboleth of which is "vocations in the church." For Kalilombe, the call for such vocations is part of an effort to increase African dependency on outside support. Compounding the problem is the fact that both *adaptation* and "vocations" are in theory and practice alienated from the masses, who comprise the laity and define African realities. See 335. These realities often take the shape of independent churches. See 046, 225, 234, 330. Kalilombe concludes by asserting that cooperation among churches of the North and South is critical if there is to be ecumenicity. Cooperation and manipulation, though, are not identical. The latter is a product of neocolonialism, the former, a product of liberation.

372 Kalilombe, Patrick A. "An Outline of Chewa Traditional Religion." *Africa Theological Journal* 9,2 (July 1980): 39-51.
    Kalilombe discusses nuances of Chewa traditional religion in terms of its rain shrines and cults. See 245. These religious institutions best express Chewa beliefs about the Supreme Being——variously called, Chiuta, Leza, Mphambe, or *Mulungu*. Essentially, the Chewa's God establishes cosmic order and harmony, is the protector of the people, and is only consulted in times of catastrophe. Women, Kalilombe reveals, are, in a sense, more central to Chewa religion than the Supreme Being, though they are in no sense deified. They are essential to rituals related to the rain shrines. Here women serve as God's consort and imply the metonymic relationship between rain and fertility, both of which are indispensable for the survival of the species. Thus woman is the link between God and the society. Far more fundamental to religion than women and *Chiuta* are the

ancestors. They are the mediators between God and the Chewa. The ancestors receive sacrifices and prayers and direct the rituals and customs of the people in the cycle of life and death.

373 Kange, F. "Alioune Diop à travers son commentaire de l'Encyclique Progressio Populorum." *Bulletin de théologie africaine* 4,7 (janvier-juin 1982): 75 -86.
    Kange reflects on the renowned intellectual's visit to Rome. Diop, the founder of *Présence Africaine,* visited Rome to address Pope Paul's seminal *Progressio Populorum.* Kange reports that Diop was particularly interested in issues regarding *les peuples de la faim et les peuples de l'opulence.* Diop, writes Kange, asserted that the contradiction between the two alienated people——the hungry and the full——can be seen in light of the enmity between blacks and whites. Another way to see this hostility is in terms of *la fragilité du monde noir en face de la puissance explosive de l' occident* (p. 77). Kange holds that Diop's edifying sense of the divided world in which we live comes from the insight that blackness affords one. No other colored "race" has been as humiliated as blacks have in the Third World's encounter with the West. See 288. That fact, however, does not obscure the good things wrought in Africa by the West, asserts Diop (as recorded by Kange). The upshot of Diop's address was a call for reconciliation between whites and blacks. Kange was embarrassed, however, by Diop's claim to have abandoned ideological commitment in the quest for reconciliation. Here, argues Kange, Diop, a preeminent writer, is at odds with the tendency of African writers to be engaged in the esthetics of their writing. See 132-134. Still, writes Kange, Diop made important suggestions regarding health care and the employment of Africans people. Despite, then, Diop's strange appeal to ideological neutrality, Kange applauds him as a great scholar and human being——one on par with Helder Camara and Martin Luther King, Jr.

374 Kato, Byang. *Theological Pitfalls in Africa.* Kisumu: Evangel Publishing House, 1973.
    The late Byang Kato, whose work was endorsed by the American evangelist, Billy Graham, rejects much of the theology of the old guard and, by implication, the new guard. First and foremost he warns against the pitfall, "universalism," indicating that John Mbiti (see 396-410), and Bolaji Idowu (see 356-357), come perilously close to being in the tradition of Origen.   (Origen was a seminal African theologian of the patristic period——later ruled a heretic——whose universalism, i.e., *apocatastasis,* posited that even Satan would "go to heaven.") According to Kato, it is essentially this universalism that is responsible for the preoccupation with African traditional religion. For Kato, however, most of African traditional religion——specifically that of his own people, the Jaba of Nigeria——is like so much chaff, to be burned in the course of the apocalypse. Integral to Kato's perspective is a biblical fundamentalism that rejects much of African theology as a syncretism that is unsupported biblically. Nevertheless, his position that African traditional and Christian conceptions of God are radically different has merit. Indeed, his view is very much like that of scholars who also take the old guard to task for attempting to force African traditional religion into a Christian structure. See 239, 279. Here, Kato is particularly critical of Mbiti. According to Kato, Mbiti's seminal *Concepts of God in Africa* "may rightly be called *A Systematic Theology of African Traditional Religion.*" See 203.   Specifically, Kato alleges that Mbiti virtually ignores Scripture, as if African understandings of God were "complete" and in no need of "any further light from elsewhere" (p. 69). He claims, in addition, that Mbiti's examination of the relation of New Testament eschatology to Akamba eschatology is sated with "abiblicism." See 396, 397, 408. For Kato, Mbiti operates with a flawed hermeneutic that is only equipped to make the case for an unholy syncretism. Kato concludes his study with a ten-point proposal for "safeguarding Biblical Christianity in Africa." According to Kato, the biblical

answer to the question of the salvation of unchristianized Africans is straightforward. "The Biblical answer to the question concerning those who died before hearing the gospel seems to be that they go to hell. There is no clear basis for optimism in this case" (p. 181). His position is rejected by theologians such as Mercy Oduyoye. See 458.

375 Kayoya, Michel. *My Father's Footprints*. Translated by Aylward Shorter and Marie-Agnes Baldwin. Nairobi: East African Publishing House, 1973.
     My Father's Footprints is a classic text that foreshadows the new guard's concern for the neocolonial problems of the continent: Kayoya was a Hutu Christian priest who criticized the oppression and corruption within "independent" Burundi. For that, he was arrested and executed without a trial. Although he was buried in a mass grave with thousands of other victims, he is far from anonymous. Courageous theologians everywhere remember him with admiration and respect. See 376-377.

376 Kayoya, Michel. "Rediscovery." In *African Christian Spirituality*, ed. by Aylward Shorter, 43-44. Maryknoll, N.Y.: Orbis Books, 1978.
     This excerpt, from the martyred Hutu priest's *My Father's Footprints*, extols African values. Kayoya focuses on death as the great liminality——especially when *communitas* is appreciated christologically:
     Do you understand that, my good man?
     What are you doing with your
     awakening and your
     noble death?
     Since the coming of Jesus Christ
     it is no longer difficult to
     die nobly
     Jesus Christ!
     Do you know him?
(On liminality and *communitas*, see 247, 272.)

377 Kayoya, Michel. "A Struggle that is Human." In *African Christian Spirituality*, ed. by Aylward Shorter, 89-91. Maryknoll, N.Y.: Orbis Books, 1978.
     Father Kayoya's elegant prose-poem on the obscenity of internecine violence could well be one of the most poignant expressions of the black fratricide desiccating Africa below the Sahara.
     After one colonization,
     were we going to be subjected to
     another?
     Another more terrible
     colonization?....
     The struggle for liberation
     becomes a struggle between
     brothers tearing each other apart.
Kayoya, himself butchered during the civil war, laments the fact that Africans engaged in civil war——i.e., the racist enmity between Tutsi and Hutu——have become alienated from the best of their ancestral legacies. See 074.

378 Kibicho, Samuel G. "African Traditional Religion and Christianity." In *A New Look at Christianity in Africa*, 14-21. Geneva: WSCF Books, 1972.
     According to Kibicho, the problem of African theology involves the tension between africanization (acculturation) and christianization (inculturation). Whereas certain African theologians hold that African values must be christianized, Kibicho notes how Christianity

is enriched by African traditional religion. His focus, then, is on africanization. In his discussion of African traditional religion, Kibicho, a Kikuyu——see 188-190——begins with a discussion of God and moves downward to the ancestral spirits and then to humankind. Like Mbiti——see 396-410——and others of the old guard, he also stresses the "communalism" of African traditional religion. Communalism, asserts Kibicho, is redemptive and counters the Eurocentric religion that is too individualistic.

379   Kibicho, Samuel G.   "The Continuity of the African Conception of God into and through Christianity: A Kikuyu Case-Study." In *Christianity in Independent Africa*, ed. by Edward Fasholé-Luke, Richard Gray, Adrian Hastings and Godwin Tasie, 370-388. Bloomington: Indiana University Press, 1978.

   Kibicho explores the relation between the Kikuyu God (*Nsai*) and the Christian God. See 378. According to Kibicho, the Kikuyu conception of God is very much alive in Kikuyu Christianity. In Kikuyu minds, *Nsai* is *God*; and this indicates the process of acculturation insofar as *Nsai* was "used" in Kenyan expressions of God. Inculturation was also a factor——Kikuyu culture was modified by Christianity.   For many, who would focus more on inculturation than acculturation, the continuity between *Nsai* and the Christian God supports the view that African traditional religion is a *preparation for the gospel*.   From this perspective, Christianity would increase as traditional religion decreases.   According to Kibicho, though, that "attitude towards African traditional religion...is a relic of the old prejudiced, evolutionary view of African religion" (p. 380). For Kibicho, true africanization would require a reformulation of "major Christian doctrines" in terms of an epistemology that is truly African.

380   Kibicho, Samuel G.   "Revelation in African Religion." *Africa Theological Journal* 12,3 (1983): 166-177.

   In contrast to much Eurocentric scholarship, Kibicho asserts that African traditional religions are neither primitive nor animistic. Kibicho thus rejects Karl Barth's views on religions. (Barth is perhaps the most well-noted and highly esteemed theologian of the twentieth century, though his work is undoubtedly limited by the cultural parameters of the Swiss, German and European-American contexts.) Kibicho also rejects Karl Rahner's notion of "anonymous Christians." (Rahner is a highly regarded Roman Catholic theologian.) According to Kibicho, Rahner's view is paternalistic and smacks of a certain Christian triumphalism.   Kibicho also discusses the concept of general and special revelation.   He concludes that the distinction is specious because the notion of general revelation undermines the integrity of Africans' traditional sense of salvation.   For Kibicho, the notion of the exclusivity of Christ——special revelation——is far too provincial and must not totalize other concepts of salvation.   He argues that African, traditional, religious specialists are as significant in the healing process as Christ is within the ambit of Christianity.   According to Kibicho, then, revelation in African traditional religion is as full and salutary as revelation in Christianity.

381   Kibongi, R. Buana.   "Priesthood." In *Biblical Revelation and African Beliefs*, ed by Kwesi Dickson and Paul Ellingworth, 47-56. Maryknoll, N.Y.: Orbis Books, 1969.

   Kibongi focuses on a Bantu-speaking people in terms of *nganga*, i.e., priest-diviners. According to Kibongi, the *nganga* receive power from the invisible, especially ancestors and spirits. A significant function of *nganga* is the prescription of sacrifices that appease the numinous world. The missionaries, claimed Kibongi, were understood by the Bantu as *nganga*. What is more, Kibongi argues that there is a correspondence between the traditional *nganga* and Christ, who fulfills the role of the *nganga*. Kibongi understands this correspondence pneumatologically.   "The elements to be used or condemned, therefore," he writes, "depend on the sovereign liberty of the Holy Spirit, and on the Church's obedience to the Spirit of Christ" (p. 55).

382 Kijanga, Peter. "Old and New African Society in Relation to the Gospel." *Africa Theological Journal* 13,3 (1984): 186-198.

Kijanga addresses the historic role of Christian missions in Africa and the imperialist agenda that became an intricate part of the process. To become Christian, Kijanga argues, was often to acquiesce in colonialism and reject——on the surface——African values. Identified as pagans, Africans were thought to require true religion, itself inextricable, in Eurocentric minds, from Western civilization. Yet, contends Kijanga, traditional African values proved intransigent and will shape an African theology destined to make a contribution to the universal church. According to Kijanga, African theology is becoming an incarnational theology replete with hermeneutics forged from African contexts. Incarnational theology is produced, moreover, in a praxis that reclaims indigenous tradition and proclaims the liberation of the oppressed.

383 Kunambi, Bernadette. "The Place of Women in the Christian Community." In *African Christian Spirituality*, ed. by Aylward Shorter, 151-154. Maryknoll, N.Y.: Orbis Books, 1978.

Ms. Kunambi, a member of the Tanzanian Parliament, argues that Western civilization, imported to Africa, has elevated the status of women and exacerbated their traditional mistreatment. "Liberated" women are ostracized by traditional society and are thus alienated from their children. Motherhood, she argues, is the essence of woman; and women, she argues, should not seek other avenues of fulfillment before they have achieved motherhood. She then critiques the church for giving only lip service to the equal rights of women. See 452-459.

384 Lalèyé, Issiaka-Prosper. "La personnalité africaine: Pierres d'attente pour une société globale." In Combats *pour un christianisme africain: Mélanges en l'honneur du Professeur V. Mulago, ed.* by A. Ngindu Mushete, 137-147. Kinshasa: Faculté de Théologie Catholique, 1981.

In the tradition of Blyden——see 016-018——and other vindicationists, Lalèyé argues that Africa, by virtue of its dynamic, traditional understandings of human personality, may make a profound contribution to the world. Africans, asserts Lalèyé, have——we are to understand——multiple human souls. See 231. One might understand such souls as spiritual entities that signify the presence of the ancestors, divinities, or even the Supreme Being himself. Unlike African theologians such as Mbiti (see 395-410) and Idowu (see 356-357), Lalèyé agrees with anthropologists who claim that the African traditional God is a *deus otiose*, even if a better expression remains to be found. For Lalèyé, God's distance allows humans to act freely and ethically. One who acts contrary to what promotes unity, complementarity, and harmony acts, by implication, against God. God's distance, construed as an eschatology, in addition, allows the African true novelty and creativity: he or she can "play" with the ambiguities of existence. Order and disorder, the positive and the negative, good and evil, are not, in African religion, Manichean polarities. These are mobile entities; though polar, they complement one another——and they mutate rapidly in a holistic matrix in which humankind is given pride of place as essential catalysts of change. For Lalèyé, then, the African eschatology is a dynamic process in which opposites——fluid moments emblematic of the essential and salvific movement of the cosmos——produce ever-changing possibilities. Lalèyé concludes that the African eschatology can advance the cause of global peace. The fact that humankind has not yet reached "Beloved Community" does not, claims Lalèyé, discourage the African. *C'est que dire cet inachèvement n'est nullement synonyme d'imperfection; il apparaît...comme fondement de dynamisme...d'action créatrice* (p. 145). Lalêyé goes so far as to assert that Africans would be willing to sacrifice themselves for the sake of a new humanity.

385 Lalêyé, Issiaka-Prosper. "Penser et pouvoir. Essai sur les limites du pouvoir de penser dans la société africaine contemporaine." *Bulletin de théologie africaine* 4,7 (janvier-juin 1982): 301-316.

For Lalêyé, thought is vital to the extent that it responds to *le réel* in all its ambiguity (*altérité*). One thinks, he asserts, in a milieu that one codes, but always in tension with its otherness. According to Lalêyé, the thinking person comes to grips with this otherness in order to overcome what limits human growth and development. That is, the thoughtful person seeks the power to overcome things, especially things that truncate human possibility. According to Lalêyé, African history and contemporary experience enable one to see intrinsic relations between thought and power (particularly as Africa is *the* matrix in which powerlessness truncates thought). Africa today, he argues, has not power enough to realize its *possibilities*. Adequate health care, for instance, is virtually absent due to the presence of Western imperialists——both European and Euro-American. See 338. Yet, the prohibitive cost of Western medicine——and the alienation it brings——heightens the contradictions between such medicine and traditional medicine. Here, then, thought develops in valorization of traditional medicine, which is at least accessible. According to Lalêyé, the issue in this regard is not africanization; africanization often masks the powerlessness of Africans. The issue is sustained reflection on thought and power: *expérimenter la nécessité pour [penser] de se prolonger par une action, autrement dit de se muer ou se transformer en pouvoir sur les hommes et sur les chose* (p. 311).

386 Lefebvre, P. "Les communautés ecclésiales de base à Kinshasa. Elément d'analyse critique." *Bulletin de théologie africaine* 6,11 (janvier-juin 1984): 5-16.

Lefebvre stresses at the up-shot that one must understand the Zairian struggle for Basic Christian Communities (CEB) in strict appreciation of the context of the Zairian church. The church has been erected in social inequity that renders the laity dependent on alien ecclesial authority. This vertical arrangement is but a mirror of colonial contradictions. See 340. Emboldened, however, by Vatican II, i.e., *Lumen Gentium*, a movement to *remet en question le vieux schéma pyramidal* got underway. This movement essentially involves an impetus to grass-roots organization, particularly in regard to the popular understanding of *authenticité*——a movement initiated by President Mobutu, which seeks to valorize African values. (*Authenticité*, however, is exceeding problematic given the tremendous corruption of Mobutu and his regime. See 061, 071, 098.) According to Lefebvre, *authenticité*, seen in relation to the Basic Christian Communities, has to do with the people's will, especially in urban areas such as Kinshasa, to return to and participate in spontaneous self-expression (*d'expression spontanée de soi*). Here authenticity must produce: (1) a revalorization of African communalism (see 103, 114); (2) the invention of new styles of authority and the exercise of power; (3) the invention of new Christian liturgies and theologies ; (4) the commitment to a liberating struggle for the restoration of human dignity; (5) the emergence of competent leaders.

387 Lupwishi, Mbuyama. "Traditions musicales du Zaïre." *Bulletin de théologie africaine* 5,10 (juillet-décembre 1983): 330-336.

Classic music, argues Lupwishi, is sacred if it transcends itself: *un lien, un moyen et non une fin*. It is a means through which God makes divine insights known. Given racist enmity toward African people, however, African classical music is not really accessible in music scholarship. In order to attain knowledge of African music, one must adopt the best method. Lupwishi valorizes that of Norma McLeud: "'The key to ethnomusicological investigation is field work in living societies'" (p. 331). After discussing the earliest expressions of African music in Central Africa (*des Pygmées de l'Ituri*) and other examples of traditional music, Lupwishi notes that missionaries studied traditional music in order to expose the soul of the African to the gospel. They did not seek to be edified by an autochthonous understanding of the music. Thus, while certain missionaries adopted the proper method, their intentions were skewed by a too Eurocentric approach to mission. African music, however, must be appreciated on its own terms. The richness of African music entails the rites which ground the music's meaning in a given context. He writes: *Alors que dans la vie courante et récréative, la musique accompagne l'activité, ici c'est le rite qui dépend de la musique et est la musique* (p. 336). The rite is the rhythm (the drum), and remains, as the essential measure, what Mveng calls the logos of African culture. See 433. A Christianity not in "hypostatic union" with this logos is only ostensible.

388 Lwasa, Damian. "Traditional and Christian Community in Africa." In *African Christian Spirituality*, ed. by Aylward Shorter, 141-150. Maryknoll, N.Y.: Orbis Books, 1980.

Lwasa, an Ugandan, argues that the centrality of a single ancestor to an African community is not unlike the centrality of Christ to his body——the church. See 308, 334, 415-416. Similarly, the blood of Christ, understood here in terms of Holy Communion, is not unlike the African understanding of blood's symbolic power. For the traditional Buganda, for instance, blood "symbolizes life itself"; for the Christian, Christ's blood, symbolized by the wine, is a means of eternal life.

389 Lyimo, Camillus. "An Ujamaa Theology." In *African Christian Spirituality*, ed. by Aylward Shorter, 126-129. Maryknoll, N.Y.: Orbis Books, 1980.

Lyimo, a Tanzanian, explores the theological implications of *ujamaa*. See 103-106. He defines *ujamaa* theology as a liberation theology, and thus a prophetic theology. It is interdisciplinary, requiring cooperation among African theologians and the masses they are to serve. According to Lyimo, the perfect *ujamaa* is the Trinity, since there is in God an economic and essential sharing among persons who are one.

390 Magesa, Laurenti. "Towards a Theology of Liberation for Tanzania." In *Christianity in Independent Africa*, ed. by Edward Fasholé-Luke, Richard Gray, Adrian Hastings and Godwin Tasie, 503-515. Bloomington: Indiana University Press, 1978.

Magesa argues that Vatican II, together with the World Council of Churches, has advocated a conservatism that discourages activism. Magesa compares the conservatism of the World Council of Churches to the activism of the Arusha Declaration. See 104-105. He concludes that Tanzanian Christians are edified more "in the praxis of *ujamaa* than in the traditional *loci* of God's presence" (p. 503). That Tanzanian Christians, according to Magesa, find *ujamaa* more edifying than official church positions indicates the relevancy of liberation theology for Tanzania. For, Magesa, then, an *ujamaa* theology——see 389——is produced from a praxis consistent with the platform of the Arusha Declaration. Here, social and religio-cultural analyses, tempered by the gospel, are tested in an activism that eschews vulgar reform.

391 Magesa, Laurenti. "African Culture and Spontaneous Prayer." In *African Christian Spirituality*, ed. by Aylward Shorter, 109-111. Maryknoll, N.Y.: Orbis Books, 1980.

According to Magesa, traditional African prayer is improvisational, spontaneous, and free. Western prayer, by contrast, is officious and formulated. Magesa does not depreciate the latter in order to glorify the former. He advocates "the middle road"——both prayer modes are legitimate and are to be employed appropriately. African Christians, he holds, are to use the traditional mode of prayer in effusive, intuitive response to the faith of the church. Western prayer may be adopted in less melismatic circumstances. In focusing, then, on prayer, Magesa argues that Christian liturgy must be meticulously examined "to see the relevance of its symbols, gestures and idioms to Africa" (p. 111).

392   Makhaye, M.M.   "Sickness and Healing in African Christian Perspective."   In *Relevant Theology for Africa*, ed. by Hans-Jurgen Becken, 158-162. Durban: Lutheran Publishing House, 1973.

Sickness in traditional Africa, whether psychosomatic or actual, was often thought to be the result of a specific misdeed of the afflicted, who had incurred the ire of the ancestors. See 206. The priest-diviner's task was to identify the offended ancestor and prescribe and direct the sacrifice commensurate with the trouble. See 275. Priest-diviners also identified and battled witches. According to Makhaye, then, much of African traditional religion was functional in that it sought to maintain and safeguard health and wholeness, fecundity and fertility——states witches sought to destroy. For Makhaye, the traditional African orientation toward sickness and healing is perfected in Christianity. Christianity, he argues, reveals a structure in which God intends finally to triumph over all forces that deny humans fullness of life. This fullness is "guaranteed" by way of the sacrifice of Christ, himself the embodiment of God's salvific purpose. Christ not only ultimately vanquishes death, but also defeats the forces that undermine sanity. Thus Makhaye argues that Christianity can thrive in the rich field of traditional religion. "All means that effect healing are of God," asserts Makhaye. There is no reason to forbid Africans from exploring traditional modes which promote their mental and physical well-being; but such modes must not contradict the gospel.

393   Ma Mpolo, Msamba.   "Symbols and Stories in Pastoral Care and Counseling: The African Context." *Bulletin of African Theology* 6,11 (January-June 1984): 39-56.

Ma Mpolo seeks to clarify the relations between "African theology and African pastoral care." Here, argues Ma Mpolo, it is critical to appreciate the psychological violence done to Africans when Christianity alienates them from the legacies of their ancestors. See 308, 334, 345, 366. When theological reflection is brought to bear on that problem, the following question is raised: "Can we... say that the symbolic role of the ancestor has set up new liberating possibilities in which are mingled together the God in us and the God who wears the image of our humanity and reveals himself in this very symbol of reconciliation, celebration and continuity?" (See p. 42.) Ma Mpolo appears to believe so.

394   Mayatula, V.M.   "African Independent Churches' Contribution to a Relevant Theology." In *Relevant Theology for Africa*, ed. by Han-Jurgen Becken, 174-177. Durban: Lutheran Publishing House, 1973.

Mayatula, a member of the African Independent Churches Association (AICA), asserts that the independent churches embody true African theology in that they exemplify the themes of liberation and indigenization. See 046, 141, 330. According to Mayatula, the independent churches are liberating and believe that God is love and justice. Love here translates into the celebration of Africanity, as seen, for instance, in the honor paid to the ancestors. See 366. Justice has to do with the refusal to acquiesce in the position that Christianity gives sanction to the oppression of South African blacks.

395   Mbiti, John.   "The Ways and Means of Communicating the Gospel." In *Christianity in Tropical Africa*, ed. by C. G. Baëta, 329-350. London: Oxford University Press, 1968.

Mbiti asserts that Christianity, in coming to Africa in the 19th Century, encountered static cultures. The task of inculturation, he argues, is to pierce that cycle of "deteriology" through the injection of a Western eschatology that is biblical, translated into Africans' vernacular, proclaimed from the pulpit and explained in catechisms. See 396. He envisions, then, a "'mass inoculation' with the Gospel." In that way, asserts Mbiti, "Christians could...'baptize'...traditional rites, and give them a Christian blessing" (p. 334). Acculturation is also a factor in African theology, for Mbiti. According to Mbiti, "more attention should be given to kinship ties and household structures of African people, in presenting the Gospel to them....their keen sense of community and kinship relationships should be grafted into the new and eschatological community of the Body of Christ, with him as the Head" (p. 338). See 415-416.

396 Mbiti, John. "Eschatology." In *Biblical Revelation and African Beliefs*, ed. by Kwesi Dickson and Paul Ellingworth, 159-184. Maryknoll, N.Y.: Orbis Books, 1969.

This essay is related to Mbiti's book on the subject. See 397. Consistent with the methods of the old guard, Mbiti compares and contrasts "African eschatological ideas" with Christian eschatology in order to draw out their correspondences. His basic position is that Africans traditionally have had virtually no sense of the future; they have had, however, a sense of the present, and an awesome sense of the past which——as macro time——pulls the present and the nominal future into itself. Time for the African, asserts Mbiti, is "a composition of events"——which explains the radically diminished sense of the future. This, according to Mbiti, makes traditional religion static rather than dynamic, natural rather than revelatory. Christian eschatology, however, *is* dynamic and revelatory; its dynamism is revealed by the Holy Spirit, who bestows faith in Christ. In Christ, asserts Mbiti, this age and that to come overlap. And so, for Mbiti, "The eschaton must invade the African world, not to destroy or colonize but to fulfil, to inject into its cosmology Christian realties." For Mbiti, then, inculturation means that Christianity overwhelms African eschatology in sublating the burdensome past to the liberating future. African "deteriology" is swallowed up in Christian teleology. A nominal acculturation also occurs in the process, according to Mbiti. He claims the African belief in the fullness and reality of the spirit world would resuscitate the vitality of the New Testament spirit world demythologized by the Enlightenment.

397 Mbiti, John. *New Testament Eschatology in an African Background*. London: Oxford University Press, 1971.

See discussion in Chapter three; and 396.

398 Mbiti, John. "Some African Concepts of Christology." In *Christ and the Younger Churches*, ed. by C.F. Vicedom, 51-62. London: SPCK, 1972.

Mbiti explores issues related to African christology. See 395. He wishes to gain insight into an African understanding of the humanity of Christ, which he explores in terms of the birth, baptism and death of Jesus, as well as analogous African *rites de passage*. According to Mbiti, Africans' rites of passage reveal their well-developed sense of kinship. Rites related to birth, transition into adulthood, marriage, and death——all anchor a people to common progenitors, who symbolize a people's identity. This fact, argues Mbiti, explains Africans' interest in the genealogies of the gospel. Mbiti substantiates this claim in his examination of the African independent churches, particularly the Aladura, or praying, churches of Nigeria. See 063, 137, 183, 225, 234.

399 Mbiti, John. "African Theology." *Worldview* 16 (August 1973): 33-39.

Mbiti examines African theology, with a focus on the views of white missionaries as well as the Africans themselves. Bengt Sundkler is one of the white missionaries he discusses with apparent admiration and respect. See 258. The outstanding African theologians he discusses are: Harry Sawyerr; (see 476-480); B. Idowu (see 356-357); and Charles Nyamiti (see 445-448). Mbiti's discussion of them serves as a foil for his old guard definition of African theology as a theology of inculturation, which is opposed to a theology of liberation. For Mbiti, the African theologian's primary task is to understand the transcultural meaning of the gospel in terms of African culture.

400 Mbiti, John. "Our Savior as an African Experience." In *Christ and Spirit in the New Testament,* ed. by B. Lindars and S. Smalley, 397-413. Cambridge: Cambridge University Press, 1973.

According to Mbiti, study of the independent churches reveals that Africans are basically interested in redemption from all that would destroy fecundity. "Savior," like the title *Christus Victor,* suggests Jesus' power to promote fecundity. Titles such as Messiah, Christ, the Son of David, however, do not strike a responsive chord in Africans. See 308. For Mbiti, then, inculturation would be greatly facilitated if proselytizers would build on the African preoccupation with fecundity and teach a doctrine of atonement that would feature the Classic Theory——Christ as Victor.

401 Mbiti, John. "Some Reflections on African Experience of Salvation Today." In *Living Faiths and Ultimate Goals: A Continuing Dialogue,* ed. by S.J. Samartha, 108-119. Geneva: World Council of Churches, 1974.

Mbiti examines the traditional African understanding of salvation and its implications for African theology. As in his major work on eschatology and African values——see 396, 397——Mbiti focuses on the Akamba. He reveals that missionaries to the Akamba often defined salvation through autochthonous idioms that conveyed a message different from what the missionaries intended. So Kikamba (i.e., Akamba) words used to explain salvation hardly conveyed the transhistorical implications of Christian soteriology. Rather, they conveyed Zahan's view that Africans are stubborn earth-dwellers. See 282. For the Akamba's sense of salvation signifies a deliverance from forces which impede the fecundity of the earth and the fertility of marriage. See 349. Modes of sacrifice employed to effect such harmony do not correspond to the imputation of an eternal righteousness that justifies sinners before God. Indeed, asserts Mbiti, traditional modes of sacrifice have nothing to do with original sin (construed as either traducianism or creationism). The challenge for African theologians, asserts Mbiti, is to plant a Christian soteriology in African soil without uprooting the traditional significance of salvation embedded there. For, Mbiti, "Christianity has come to African peoples to bring more abundantly what in their daily life they felt and needed most. It has come to legitimize their case and to bring an extended understanding, scope and applicability of salvation" (p. 115). Mbiti also notes that the christianization of African concepts of salvation would heighten Africans' awareness of the socioeconomic and political ramifications of human sin. Here, we see that Mbiti, though a member of the old guard, was at least aware of the relevance of the theme of liberation for Africa. He writes that "Christians in Africa and elsewhere...can only understand salvation in the context of political liberation——and who can blame them? Yet," he writes, "the Church in Africa as a whole, has not begun to take seriously the liberation dimension of salvation" (p. 118). As examples of the need for liberation, Mbiti refers to tribalism (micro-nationalism), corruption, economic exploitation, and the like. See 403.

402 Mbiti, John. "Some Current Concerns of African Theology." *The Expository Times* 87 (March 1976): 164-168.

Mbiti focuses on African theology as a written rather than an oral theology. See 407-408. Written theology is produced by white missionaries and the Africans themselves.

As a written discourse, African theology entails biblical theology, pastoral theology, political theology——i.e., black theology——and dialogical theology. Each of these explore problems related to inculturation and acculturation. Each of the subdivisions of African theology concern problems regarding the tension between Christian faith and African realities.

403 Mbiti, John. "Theological Impotence and the Universality of the Church". In *Mission Trends No. 3: Third World Theologies. Asian, African and Latin American Contributions to a Radical, Theological Realignment in the Church*, ed. by Gerald H. Anderson and Thomas F. Stransky, 6-18. New York: Paulist Press; Grand Rapids: Wm. B. Eerdmans, 1976.

According to Mbiti, the axis of Christianity is shifting from the North to the South——a shift that necessitates new paradigms consistent with the experiences and values of Third World people. To demonstrate this need, Mbiti tells a story of an African scholar. Educated abroad, well-versed in several languages——including Greek and German——this scholar is estranged from his native tongue, with which he struggles upon returning home. At his "welcome home" party, one of his aunts, stricken to the ground, screams; at which point the estranged scholar frantically requests that she be taken to the hospital. He is told that she is possessed by an offended ancestor and that his theological education is quite useless if he is not equipped to deal with this religious issue. The scholar, writes Mbiti, looks frantically to Bultmann, who has demythologized the whole thing. But nothing in Eurocentric tradition is relevant to this African context. For Mbiti, then, traditional theology, i.e., Eurocentric theology, is beset with a serious contradiction: the universality of the kerygma (gospel) is truncated by a definition of theology that is exceeding narrow. Mbiti, in this essay, also indicates the importance of social analysis in regard to the search for more relevant paradigms. He notes African's preoccupation with survival in contexts sated with the oppression of the masses. He writes: "Racism, segregation, ethnicism, nepotism, corruption——these are national ills which afflict every country in Africa. What is the theology of race, of corruption, of nepotism?" (See p. 11.) Mbiti also notes the importance of religio-cultural analysis; he asserts that African theologians must go beyond reified concepts, like African personality and authenticity, in order to attain substantial deliberations on "theology of culture." In "Theological Impotence and the Universality of the Church," Mbiti clearly shows his awareness of issues related to liberation. See 401.

404 Mbiti, John. "An African Answer." *Concilium* (October 1977): 88-90.

Mbiti ponders the central question of this issue of *Concilium*: " Why did God make me?" According to Mbiti, the question would not ordinarily be posed to an African. "In an African setting," he explains, it would be considered very rude or curse-worthy." According to Mbiti, the question signifies an impertinence, tantamount to a child asking his parents "Why did you bear me?" Still, Mbiti ventures to answer the question in terms of African mythology, and in a style similar to that of *Concepts of God in Africa*. See 203. That is, in the final analysis, he argues for a necessary correspondence between African values and Christian faith. The two together answer the question, "Why did God make me?" For Mbiti, "The insights from African religion and the basis of...Christian faith lead [one] to reject the notion that death can have the final say over life" (p. 90). God makes us so that we can enjoy eternal life.

405 Mbiti, John S. "The Biblical Basis in Present Trends of African Theology." *Africa Theological Journal* 8,1 (1978): 72-85.

See 408.

406 Mbiti, John. "An African Views American Black Theology." In *Black Theology: A Documentary History*, 1966-1979, ed. by Gayraud Wilmore and James Cone, 477-482. Maryknoll, N.Y.: Orbis Books, 1979.

Mbiti——despite his awareness of the need for liberation——provides added insight into the old guard's alienation from liberation theology. See 401, 403. He assumes that the black theologies of North America and South Africa constitute a different species from African theology. While, according to Mbiti, the black theology of South Africa bears some relation to African theology,

the concerns of Black Theology differ considerably from those of African Theology. The later grows out of our joy in the experience of the Christian faith, whereas Black Theology emerges from the pains of oppression. African Theology is not so restricted in its concerns, nor does it have any ideology to propagate (p. 481).

Mbiti thus reduces black theology to caricature and obfuscates the prevalence of an ideology of independence. Indeed, Oduyoye, Éla and Mveng——as well as Buthelezi, Tutu and Young——show clearly that Mbiti's definition of African theology is exceeding narrow. See 457, 338, 437, 524, 525, 602, 606, 609.

407 Mbiti, John. "'Cattle are Born with Ears, Then Horns Grow Later': Towards an Appreciation of African Oral Theology." *Africa Theological Journal* 8,1 (1979): 15-25.

According to Mbiti, the oral theology of African Christians embodies an authentic theology——not unlike that of the oral stage of the gospel——and awaits organization in writing. What is more, Mbiti argues that evangelization, and the attendant conversion it invites, is effective in Africa largely because Africans, still largely illiterate, respond readily to orality. Indeed, Africans listen and retain information with impressive facility. Africans, claims Mbiti, are acutely attentive to sermons, which are emblematic of the distinctiveness of African theology. Mbiti also classifies prayers, hymns, songs and conversations as oral sources revelatory of an Christian faith rooted in popular culture.

408 Mbiti, John. "The Biblical Basis for Present Trends in African Theology." In *African Theology en Route*, ed. by Kofi-Appiah-Kubi and Sergio Torres, 83-94. Maryknoll, N.Y.: Orbis Books, 1979.

Mbiti broadly defines African theology as "theological reflection and expression by African Christians." African theology, for Mbiti, is eminently biblical, and has three dimensions: written, oral, and symbolic. Written theology is produced by an educated elite; oral theology, by the masses; and symbolic theology, through art. Mbiti focuses throughout on written theology, with attention to: Dickson (see 322-327); Sawyerr (see 476-480); Fasholé-Luke (see 345-348); Pobee (see 468-469); Kato (see 374); and Modupe Oduyoye (see 210-220). They substantiate Mbiti's claim that the Bible is the foundation of African theology. (Mbiti reveals that Kato was about to reconsider his sharp critique of him when Kato drowned in 1975.) According to Mbiti, the theme of liberation is supported biblically, but "African discussion of liberation" has little scriptural foundation. See 406. Another source indicating the relation of the Bible to African theology is the independent churches. See 046, 141, 142, 330. According to Mbiti, "The Bible gives [those churches] the basis for establishing close ties with the African traditional world" (p. 89). See 208. Mbiti notes that African traditional religion is yet another source of African theology, but claims that much of the work in this area assigns the Bible a small role. See 227.

409 Mbiti, John. "The Encounter of Christian Faith and African Religion." In *Theologians in Transition*, ed. by J.M. Wall and Martin E. Marty, 53-59. New York: Crossroads, 1981.

Mbiti rehearses a leitmotif of his *oeuvre*——African traditional religion is essentially monotheistic and well-equipped to function as a stepping stone to Christianity. See 200-204. See also 410.

410 Mbiti, John. "The Encounter of Christian Faith And African Religion." In *Third World Liberation Theologies,* ed. by Dean Ferm, 199-204. Maryknoll, N.Y.: Orbis Books, 1986.

Mbiti recounts his up-bringing in the Christian faith and asserts his commitment to the church. He reveals he has never been able to tear his ancestors from his Christian heart. See 366. His central thesis in that regard is that the old Africans——due to the providence of God——have always known the Creator. See 203. For Mbiti, then, God's revelation has been more extensive than the Bible would suggest. Mbiti does not undermine the Bible's authority. Indeed, he wishes to define a hermeneutic that would substantiate his focus on New Testament eschatology. See 396. If, he argues, African conceptions of God and biblical conceptions of God "are two wavelengths," they are not contradictory wavelengths. Their correspondence involves their necessary movement toward each other in the broad dynamism of salvation history. He records the fact that the proliferation of Christianity in Africa, especially "the southern two-thirds" of the continent, is due to the Pan-African phenomena——African traditional religion. African traditional religion has facilitated Africans' acceptance of the gospel and is thus an essential mode of general revelation.

411 Milimo, John. "African Traditional Religion." In *A New Look at Christianity in Africa,* 9-13. Geneva: WSCF Books, 1972.

Milimo, a Tanzanian, asserts that the study of African traditional religion serves as prolegomena to African theology. Milimo, however, appears to be more politically orientated than others of the old guard in that he links African traditional religion to African socialism——i.e., Tanzanian *"ujamaa"* and Zambian "Humanism." See 102-106; 066-070. According to Milimo, however, the closeness of human community valorized in traditional life——i.e., *ujamaa* itself——breeds paranoia. Goodwill often dissimulates enmity. For Milimo, the consequences of this paranoia are that individuals are persecuted as witches, and nature (the forest) is believed to be sated with malice. See 224. The incestuous implications of the tension between goodwill and enmity, asserts Milimo, is implied in African myths of human estrangement from God. As those myths correspond to biblical accounts of the Fall, African traditional religion is the "African Old Testament." See 325.

412 Milingo, E. *The World in Between: Christian Healing and the Struggle for Spiritual Survival.* Edited by Mona Macmillian. Maryknoll, N.Y.: Orbis Books, 1984.

Milingo, former Archbishop of Lusaka, Zambia, was recalled from Africa and placed under the direct supervision of the Vatican. In Zambia, Milingo had embarked upon a charismatic ministry that bore a remarkable resemblance to the ministries of the independent churches. See 141-142. He engaged in healing, struggled against malevolent forces and acknowledged, *and affirmed*, the reality of the ancestors. See 334, 341. After much controversy and many accusations against him, he was "given an appointment as Special Delegate to the Pontifical Commission for Migration and Tourism. As such he is in charge of the spiritual care of migrants, refugees, and Christian tourists and is directly responsible to the Holy Father" (p. 137). His new appointment is a benign form of punishment. The church did not——perhaps cannot——tolerate "his outspoken criticism of the Missions" (Ibid). What is more, his grounding in popular culture threatened the bourgeois orientation of the church hierarchy. See 331. Milingo's story is a revelation of the church's hostility to acculturation as well as its truncated sense of inculturation.

413 Mosha, Raymond S. "The Trinity in the African Context." *Africa Theological Journal* 9,1 (April 1989): 40-47.

According to Mosha, Hebrew monotheism and "communitarism" have influenced the Christian doctrine of the Trinity. The Trinity, then, has as much to do with anthropology as it does theology. See 389-390. Indeed, argues Mosha, good theology is always the product of the dynamism of the anthropology explicating it; it would thus be wise for Africans to investigate ways in which their cultures bring fresh insights into the oxymoron, "three in one." While Mosha concedes that the theistic notion of three Persons in one God does not reflect of an African religious view, the "communitarian" aspect of African society——the concept of family, as well as African holistic understandings of the cosmos——provides a basis from which to understand the creativity that emerges from "perichoretic" tensions between unity and diversity.

414 Mosothoane, E.K. "The Message of the New Testament Seen in African Perspective." In *Relevant Theology for Africa*, ed. by Hans-Jurgen Becken, 55-67. Durban: Lutheran Publishing House, 1973.

According to Mosothoane, the New Testament proclamation that Christ is the Savior neither condones nor condemns traditional African values. It is up to the theologian him or herself to define the relation of the gospel to a context. Referring to the reappropriation of the New Testament in Europe——specifically the theologies of Bultmann, Barth, and Tillich——Mosothoane argues that the on-going reinterpretation of the gospel defines the dynamism of the history of Christian thought. Why, he asks, should eyebrows raise when Africans deepen that history in terms of their own experience (faith)? According to Mosothoane, attempts to deny Africans their place in the sun truncates an appreciation of the gospel's transcontexual, indeed ubiquitous, implication——ultimate salvation for all. None whom God elects are denied "heaven"; and a *gracious* God does not mandate that a people live in alienation from their ancestors as they seek the way to heaven. See 308, 334, 366. Indeed——and here he indicates the reciprocity between acculturation and inculturation——blacks "need to use African concepts for the creation and development of an African Christian theology and for the full effective communication of the Gospel to Africans" (p. 63). Mosothoane's example of how acculturation would work involves the New Testament meaning of the poor. They are principally the *harmatōloi* or sinners——"people of immoral life who, because they were immoral, were also contemptible outcasts" (p. 61). In africanizing the notion of *harmartōloi*, and in drawing on the work of both Mbiti (see 395-410), and Tempels (see 261-262), Mosothoane argues that evil in traditional Africa is coincident with the diminution of vital force. Wicked necromancers are responsible for such diminution. See 224, 411. According to Mosothoane, then, the poor are witches and others who gratify themselves in gross wickedness. In sum, inculturation would bear fruit as Africans come to see that the atonement pulls in its train the forgiveness of even the most despised——i.e., "the poor"——of traditional society.

415 Mulago, Vincent. "Nécessité de l'adaptation missionnaire chez les Bantu du Congo. In *Des prêtres noirs s'interrogent*, ed. by A. Abble, et al., 19-40. Paris: Les Éditions du Cerf, 1956.

Mulago marvels over the fact that a third of the population of the Congo had, after only half a century, become Roman Catholics. The uniqueness of this event causes Mulago to ask: Is this phenomenal movement toward Christianity complete? Is it deeply-rooted in the African's soul, or is it simply an expression of the general europeanization of the black continent? The answer to this question rests, in part, in the realization that African Christians do not shake their ancestral values. Mulago argues that there is something profound in these values, and this profundity has to do with the stoic doctrine of the *logos spermatikos*. The diffused logos——as a form of general revelation——is embedded in "pagan" phenomena; but much of this phenomena must be uprooted as it is inimical to Christian monotheism. Only those elements that may be christianized are acceptable; that is, they must be adaptable and sublated to Christian faith. According to Mulago, such *adaptation*——since it is but the mystical extension of the incarnation——is sanctioned by the Roman Catholic Church. See 418.

416 Mulago, Vincent. "Le pacte du sang et la communion alimentaire. Pierres d'attente de la communion eucharistique." *Des prêtres noirs s'interrogent*, ed. by A. Abble, et al., 171-188. Paris: Les Éditions du Cerf, 1956.

Mulago examines the amicable relations among the Banyarwanda and the Bashi, on the one hand, and the Banyarwanda and the Barundi on the other. Despite wars among them, these Africans are often interrelated through the blood pact, which joins two distinct races——Hamites and Bantu. (One wonders, however, how significant the covenant is, given the internecine conflicts of Rwanda and Burundi. See 376.) Mulago defines this essential "give and take situation" in terms of *force vitale* or *courant vital* or *la communion-participation*. See 261-262. According to Mulago, this vital current is discovered in every meal or drink that is shared, in every gift. But we reach the quintessential exchange——*le paroxysme du réalisme*——*dans le pacte du sang* when we really give ourselves to our neighbors, become fused with them in reciprocal drinking (*s'entre-boit*). Here we experience a profound *communitas*——see 273——and actualize vital participation. The blood pact, then, is *the* expression of human community. Through it individuals eat and drink as one, as if fused together, enjoying a reciprocity that is the truest expression of the gift of one's self to the neighbor. All events which build community revel in this vital principle. Having defined the religious significance of the blood pact, Mulago explores its correspondence to *les mystères de l'Eglise*. Specifically, Mulago investigates the relationship of the blood pact to *le sacrement des sacrements*——the Eucharist. For Mulago, the Eucharist is a mode of God's gracious immanence; it establishes a vital exchange between Christ and his disciples; through this exchange, one is redeemed and the community itself, uplifted. Somewhat like the relationship between the blood pact and its communal meal, the Eucharist also makes eating and drinking integral to flesh torn and blood shed in the act of reconciliation. The correspondence, asserts Mulago, makes conditions fertile for *adaptation* (inculturation). See 415. The gospel invites Africans to know salvation through the autochthonous stepping stones to Christian faith. For Mulago, Providence has decreed that the Bantu must receive the unique bread that has descended from the sky.

417 Mulago, Vincent. *Un visage africain du christianisme: L'union vitale Bantu face à l'unité vitale ecclésiale.* Paris: Présence Africaine, 1962.

See discussion in Chapter three of this bibliography.

418 Mulago, Vincent. "Christianisme et culture africaine: Apport africain à la théologie." In *Christianity in Tropical Africa*, ed. by C.G. Baëta, 308-328. London: Oxford University Press, 1968.

In this essay on Christianity and African culture, Mulago seeks to avoid two extremes: (1) *a priori* assumptions that Eurocentric theology——*que l'on baptise trop facilement Théologie universelle ou mondiale*——is normative; and (2) a superficial *adaptation*, based on a reified *négritude*——*africanisation superficielle, basée sur une sorte de romantisme de 'l'âme africaine', de 'l'âme bantu'* (p. 308). For Mulago, meaningful africanization must be biblical and correspond to the incarnation. He asserts there is fertile ground for such *adaptation* because of (1) the African belief in a Supreme Being and (2) the relation of that belief to *union vitale*. *Union vitale* is a force rather than an alliance——it is an *a priori* field which is the "stuff," both visible and invisible, of existence. Its primary symbol is blood which signifies a people's connection to the first ancestor——*l'ancêtre fondateur tomba du ciel*——and thus to God. See 334. Mulago argues that there is a likeness between "vital union" and the Trinity, since both heighten the complementarity between community and oneness (as in *perichoresis*). Thus, the Bantu participate in perfect union only when they are christianized. Mulago's essay bears the influence of Tempels and Kagame. See 261-262; 369-370.

419 Mulago, Vincent. "Vital Participation: The Cohesive Principle of the Bantu Community." In *Biblical Revelation and African Beliefs*, ed. by Kwesi Dickson and Paul Ellingworth, 137-158. Maryknoll, N.Y.: Orbis Books, 1969.

Influenced by the work of Tempels——see 418——Mulago examines the values of Bantu people in terms of an ontology reminiscent of the notion of the "Great Chain of Being." Mulago calls this chain vital participation, which signifies the links between: life and death; the living and their ancestors; the visible and the invisible. The dominant symbols of this continuum are blood and land. See 196, 417. So vital participation has a metonymic dimension, namely the vertical succession of the living from the dead. Vital participation also includes a metaphoric dimension, namely the horizontal exchange of properties of the group and "its belongings." The unity of vertical and horizontal relationships——it bears reiteration——is signified in symbols. According to Mulago, vital participation is consummated in the church, in which there is an analogy between the Triune God——defined particularly in christological and pneumatological terms——and Bantu culture.

420 Mulago, Vincent. "Le langage de l'Eglise missionnaire." *Bulletin de théologie africaine* 1,1 (janvier-juin 1979): 35-56.

Mulago ponders the relevance of 1 Corinthians 14:36. He asks in general: *La parole de Dieu a-t-elle chez vous son point de départ? Etes-Vous les seuls à l'avoir reçue?* For Mulago, the question indicates that the gospel is not the property of one particular culture. Rather, each culture must make God's Word its own in order to realize the diversity of Christian experience. The problem of inculturation, then, is to indigenize the universal gospel, that is, *de le transposer, sans la moindre trahison de sa vérité essentielle* (p. 35). In other words: *Si l'Eglise est transcendante, si elle n'est ni occidentale ni asiatique ni africaine, et si, malgré cela, partout elle est chez elle; si elle est la Mère aussi bien des orientaux que des africaines et des occidentaux, c'est signe qu'elle universelle* (p. 38). Such universality in diversity requires that there be African theologies.

421 Mulago, Vincent. "La famille et la mariage africains interpellent l'Eglise." *Bulletin de théologie africaine* 4,7 (janvier-juin 1982): 17-40.

According to Mulago, the central role of the family, which includes the ancestors, must make its way into African Christianity. According to Mulago, *le problème délicate est de savoir assumer tout ce dynamisme familial dans les perspectives de la modernité et surtout dans l'esprit du Christ* (p. 18). One such problem is whether polygamy, a traditional institution, may be christianized. Less problematic, asserts Mulago, is the possibility of christianizing incest, which had fortunately been only theoretical among the BaKongo. See 185, 198, 199, 238. Such problems do not diminish the fact that marriage, for Mulago, is at the heart of the struggle for inculturation. That is, the correspondence between Christianity and African values involves reverence of the nuptial love that is a metonym of both the unity of the church and the unity of Bantu culture. See 310, 416.

422 Mushete, Ngindu A. "Unity of Faith and Pluralism in Theology." In *The Emergent Gospel*, ed. by Sergio Torres and Virginia Fabella, 50-55. London: Geoffrey Chapman, 1978.

Ngindu Mushete examines the problematic relation between unity and pluralism in the church. Unity, he argues, is an eschatological gift in Jesus Christ; pluralism signifies the diverse ways Christians appropriate that gift through the particularity of their cultures. "Far from being in opposition," asserts Ngindu Mushete, "unity and pluralism complete and complement one another in a kind of reciprocal causality: communion of faith, diversified teaching" (p. 51). For Ngindu Mushete, African theology partakes of that holy communion through the diverse vessels of black culture.

423 Mushete, Ngindu A. "The History of Theology in Africa: From Polemic to Critical Irenics." In *African Theology en Route*, ed. by Kofi Appiah-Kubi and Sergio Torres, 23-35. Maryknoll, N.Y.: Orbis Books, 1979.

Ngindu Mushete discusses: (1) "Missionary theology," (2) African theology, and (3) black South African theology. Missionary theology, asserts Ngindu Mushete, involves christianization of the heathen. Those who would christianize the heathen sought to uproot African culture, as if they could create a *tabula rasa*. According to Ngindu Mushete, subscribers to that theology had no sense of the implications of general revelation and thus failed to perceive the presence of God in non-Christian modes. Where missionaries employed that theology, they have produced sickly imitations of their own cultures. A better approach is that of Vatican II, particularly given one of its major themes: The church is one by virtue of its diversity. Ngindu Mushete divides African theology into two types, both of which oppose, more or less, the missionary theology: the theology of *adaptation*——see 416, 418——and "a more critical African theology." *Adaptation*, he reveals, is a continuum of missionary theology in that it seeks to overcome, rather than be enriched by, African culture. With reference to Mulago——see 415-421——Ngindu Mushete asserts that *adaptation* produces a Christianity that is only ostensibly African. Critical African theology, however, entails a more rigorous endeavor which seeks to probe the structures of Christian faith and African religion. Black theology, for Ngindu Mushete, involves an appreciation of the struggles of African people of the United States and South Africa. Ngindu Mushete criticizes black North American theology for its dependence on European models. For Ngindu Mushete, *African* theology, in its critical mode, is best equipped to divest black theology of its dependence on European consciousness. See 609.

424 Mushete, Ngindu A. "La théologie africaine. De la polémique à l'irénisme critique." *Bulletin de théologie africaine, 1,1 (janvier-juin 1979):* 69-98.
    See 423.

425 Mushete, Ngindu A. "L'inculturation du christianisme comme problème théologique." In *Combats pour un christianisme africain: Mélanges en l'honneur du Professeur V. Mulago*, ed. by A. Ngindu Mushete, 9-19. Kinshasa: Faculté de Théologie Catholique, 1981.

For Ngindu Mushete, a critical African theology is open to the aspirations of the African people, and thus effects the incarnation of the gospel in Africa. See 423. Ngindu Mushete discusses the problem of inculturation in terms of three areas. (1) The transmission of the gospel: the transmission of the gospel is hindered by *certaines manifestations d'un triomphalisme euro-centrique et le certains associations à des intérêts séculiers.* He cites Tempels as an example of such triumphalism. See 209, 261. (2) The role of the church in the process of colonization: the role of the church, asserts Ngindu Mushete, is to reject colonization. The church, moreover, must be diverse, and seek an understanding of its diversity in terms of contrasting hermeneutics. (3) Perspectives on a new age of mission: the human and religious experiences of the African people are *the* loci of a new missiology that appreciates African traditional values. These values are integral to a hermeneutical freedom that is God-given and eschatological.

426 Mushete, Ngindu A. "Le rôle des intellectuels chrétiens dans la pensée de l'Eglise." *Bulletin de théologie africaine* 3,6 (juillet-décembre 1981): 219-232.

   According to Ngindu Mushete, the African church must nurture Christian intellectuals, who have an important role to play within the laity. See 311. Their significance is heightened by the lack of ordained clergy. In Africa this issue is acute and is similar to the state of the primitive Church——*situation de diaspora d'une minorité dans un monde plus ou moins étranger à l'influence chrétienne* (p. 226). As Christianity is strange to many Africans, the issue of inculturation is a critical one, asserts Ngindu Mushete. Christian intellectuals, by virtue of their expertise and important function within the church, are critical to the goals and aspirations of inculturation since they are equipped to make Christianity intelligible to the laity. For Ngindu Mushete, intellectuals will analyze the theanthropological (*théandrique*) moorings of the church. Theanthropology concerns not only an examination of African values, but also a critique of *certaines manifestations d'un triomphalisme euro-centrique et certaines associations à des intérêts séculiers* (p. 229). See 425. What is more, Christianity here is a religion beside others: God is not *un préalable inscrit dans une seule tradition, exclusive, intolérante et conquérante*. In sum, inculturation involves the eschatological possibilities emergent from the tension between Christian faith and African traditional religion. Ngindu Mushete also asserts that the struggle for liberation is as indispensable for the African church as the struggle for inculturation. *C'est dans ce contexte que l'Eglise doit trouver une manière adéquate d'annoncer l'Evangile, de proclamer la primauté du Christ libérateur* (p. 231). See 253.

427 Mushete, Ngindu A.   "L'Afrique à la Vᵉ Conférence de Théologiens du Tiers-Monde." *Bulletin de théologie africaine* 4,3 (janvier-juin 1982): 135-141.

   Ngindu Mushete, representing the African contingent at the 5th conference of EATWOT, held in New Deli in 1981, discloses the issues that were discussed. The conference, entitled *"L'irruption du Tiers-Monde: Questions à la théologie chrétienne,"* sought to prepare EATWOT theologians for a discussion with First World theologians, which was held in 1983. The Africans made their Pan-African connection clear in terms of these themes: (1) socioeconomic realities and the attendant political situations; (2) cultural, ethnic and religious conceptions of the world; (3) Christian presence and engagement; (4) the influence of Western theology and the progress of inculturation and contextualization. According to Ngindu Mushete, the Africans are agreed that colonialism and capitalism are on-going problems that reveal the oppression propagated by both the elite and the Western church. The Africans, reports Ngindu Mushete, were also worried about the shortcomings of the North-South dialogue and the deterioration of the terms of exchange. These problems exacerbate the problems Africans have regarding inculturation. Despite these problems, Ngindu Mushete asserts: *Un discours théologique est né qui avance inexorablement, avec le mouvement général de la libération totale de l'Afrique.* Ngindu Mushete also reports that Africans insisted that *l'Association oecuménique des théologiens africains* (AOTA)——see 437——is not a wing of EATWOT. He closed by noting that AOTA has recommended the organization of a seminary focused on the role of women in the church and society. AOTA has also recommended that minority groups, such as those of the African Diaspora, become members.

428 Mushete, Ngindu A. "La VIᵉ rencontre de théologiens du tiers-monde." *Bulletin de théologie africaine* 5,9 (janvier-juin 1983): 131-132.

Ngindu Mushete summarizes the events of the sixth meeting of EATWOT, which, convening in Geneva, Switzerland, constituted an encounter between Third and First World theologians. See 427. The theme of the event was *pratique de la théologie dans un monde divisé*. At Geneva, writes Ngindu Mushete, the epistemological breaks from the North (*les déplacements*) were valorized. According to Ngindu Mushete, the great achievement of Geneva will have been to clarify the meaning of liberation. Liberation, explains Ngindu Mushete, is not to be interpreted exclusively in Latin American terms. See 314-315. African have something profound to contribute to definitions of liberation too: *Les théologiens africaines ont largement contribué à éclaircir le concept de pauvreté. Ils parlent de plus en plus de pauvreté anthropologique* (p. 132). See 437.

429 Mutiso-Mbinda, John S. "Liberation and Mission in Africa." *Africa Theological Journal* 8,2 (1979): 45-55.
According to Mutiso-Mbinda, the church——if it is to be relevant to African realities——must be involved in the liberation struggle of the African people. This struggle is primarily against neocolonialism——see 004, 097——which entails the legacy of missionaries, who tried to strip Africans of their heritage in order to make them imperial subjects. Mutiso-Mbinda makes extensive use of the ideas of Frantz Fanon. For Mutiso-Mbinda, moreover, Africa must be edified by its religious heritage if it is to produce an African theology equipped to define the meaning of liberation.

430 Muzorewa, Gwinyai H. *The Origins and Developments of African Theology.* Maryknoll, N.Y.: Orbis Books, 1985.
Muzorewa provides an account of African theology in terms of its essential sources——the Bible, African traditional religion, and the independent churches. He also examines the historical background of African theology. This background is essentially that of the movements for independence, which are tied to African nationalism and rediscovered today in terms of the problem of neocolonialism. See 429. He notes that African theology's development will be hindered without a substantial focus on liberation.

431 Muzzanganda, Aloysius Lugira. "African Christian Theology." *Africa Theological Journal* 8,2 (1979): 50-61.
According to Muzzanganda, African traditional religion is the essential basis for African Christian theology. Indeed, for Muzzanganda, it is not possible to exclude African traditional religion from discussion of either Christianity or Islam in Africa. What is more, traditional religion is so essential to African identity, that it is correct, asserts Muzzanganda, to discuss African theology without substantial reference to Christianity or Islam. Muzzanganda concludes with a discussion of several sources of African theology. Included are the Bible, the African religions, and the independent churches.

432 Mveng, Engelbert. *L'art d'Afrique noire: Liturgies cosmique et langage religieux.* Yaounde: Éditions CLE, 1974.
See discussion in Chapter Three of this bibliography.

433 Mveng, Engelbert. "L'art d'Afrique noire: Liturgies cosmiques et langage religieux." *Bulletin de théologie africaine* 1,1 (janvier-juin 1979): 99-104.
See 434.

434 Mveng, Engelbert. "Black African Art as Cosmic Liturgy and Religious Language." In *African Theology en Route*, ed. by Kofi Appiah-Kubi and Sergio Torres, 137-144. Maryknoll, N.Y.: Orbis Books, 1979.

According to Mveng: "Black art is essentially a *cosmic liturgy* and a *religious language*...[that] establishes a permanent link between the *destiny of humanity and that of the cosmos*" (p. 137). See 494. African art approximates the "essential thing"——the conviction that life conquers death. What is more, black art is the acculturative "stuff" out of which African theology is fashioned. According to Mveng, moreover, christology is but an attempt to convey the reality of Christ in terms of the anthropology of a specific context. He argues that whereas Eurocentric theologies focus on the Word-made-flesh, Africans prefer to talk about the Word-made-man. For Mveng, African emphases on the *humanity* of God are consistent with ancestral values in which the mystery of God involves the primacy of man and purveys the conviction that life is the victor over death. Indeed, what inspires liturgy, argues Mveng, is not theology, but life's struggle with death, which takes poetic form in religious art. In sum, African Christians should forge a Christian idiom deeply rooted in the tradition of black art, for "black art is both religious language and a cosmic liturgy" (p. 142).

435 Mveng, Engelbert. "L'Association oecuménique des théologiens africains en l'an 100 des Eglises africaines." *Bulletin de théologie africaine* 3,5 (janvier-juin 1981): 132-136.
Mveng, executive secretary of the Ecumenical Association of African Theologians (AOTA), defines the Association in terms of its goals and programs. The goals of the Association include: unification of African Christians regardless of language, region and confessions; promotion of an African theology; and assistance of African churches according to their socio-historical context. According to Mveng, a significant sign of the Association's growth and development is the growth and development of the *Bulletin de théologie africaine*. Mveng also takes a white scholar to task; this scholar asserts there is nothing, *ou si peu de chose, dans les traditions Asiatiques et Africaines, qui correspond à une préparation évangélique proche des catégories judaïques, hellénistiques ou Romaines* (p. 134). In response to that scholar, Mveng agrees that God's incarnation in the matrix of the first century cannot be gainsaid. But to assume that one is to understand the implications of the incarnation solely in terms of the first century misses the point. For Mveng, the incarnation is a sign of contradiction, of discernment, that puts all humankind in question and makes it imperative for all to choose or reject Christ. Africans who choose Christ do so within the modes of their culture——which does not diminish the historicity of the incarnation. Indeed, asserts Mveng, AOTA plans to institute an ecumenical center in Jerusalem, which attests to Africans' edification by the Jewishness of Christ.

436 Mveng, Engelbert. "Un visage africaine du christianisme pour une ecclésiologie africaine." In *Combats pour un christianisme africain: Mélanges en l'honneur du Professeur V. Mulago*, ed. by A. Ngindu Mushete, 133-135. Kinshasa: Faculté de Théologie Catholique, 1981.
Mveng contrasts Mulago's work to Pope Paul VI's *Lumen Gentium*. Both texts, asserts Mveng, herald new vista in Roman Catholic ecclesiology and are quite similar at first glance. According to Mveng, Mulago's work contains much that would edify the Western church, propped up as it is by an imperial structure. The church, as it is, tends to truncate an understanding of the scope of salvation because of its Eurocentrism. (*On comprend...pourquoi la gestation de l'Eglise a été et demeure une administration de type impérial.*) That kind of Church, asserts Mveng, cannot grow in Africa. Neither can the African church assume——as does its European counterpart——that its ecclesiology is normative. Nonetheless, he argues, the African church, committed to unity in diversity, must forge ahead with its quest for African ecclesiologies.

437 Mveng, Engelbert. "Récent développements de la théologie africaine." *Bulletin de théologie africaine* 5,9 (janvier-juin 1983): 137-144.

Mveng sets the context of African theology in terms of the death pangs (*l'agonie*) of the OAU. See 092. According to Mveng, its slow death *est le résultat direct des luttes fratricide qui déchirent l'Afrique.* Indeed, Africa is being chopped up by wars and apartheid. This structure of violence makes it necessary to focus on the issue of liberation. According to Mveng the continent's struggle for liberation has reached the breaking point. Africa, on the one hand, suffers direly from the need for political, economic, and cultural liberation. On the other hand, the continent seeks liberation from the outside pressures responsible for the death pangs of the OAU. What is more, blacks desire liberation from the oppression of Southern Africa. Africans seek deliverance from the oppressive realities of micro-nationalism and jingoism (*libération du tribalisme et des nationalismes étroits*)——to say nothing of the struggle for human rights, and the oppression deriving from the disingenuous promises made to the masses at the advent of "independence" (*grande déception des masses devant les promesses non tenues des indépendances politiques*). According to Mveng, Africa's situation is so grave, that one *should* think that the continent is the victim of a cynical, Western conspiracy. Mveng reports that the United States——under the pretext of protesting against the Cuban troops in Angola——had been covertly supporting South Africa in order to block the independence of Namibia. Although Namibia is now independent and the Cubans are leaving Angola, Southern Africa still provides evidence of the West's complicity in the underdevelopment of Africa. African theology, writes Mveng, must also be discussed in terms of *l'Association oecuménique des théologiens africains* (AOTA). See 435. AOTA is linked to EATWOT, though the two organizations have a strained relationship. Under the auspices of AOTA, reports Mveng, African theologians have identified six issues revelatory of the agenda of African theology: (1) the critique of Eurocentric theology; (2) the problem of theological method, explored in works such Boulaga's *Christianity without Fetishes*, (see 307); (3) the need for a conference o ' the meaning of the gospel; (4) The option for the poor: *C'est le coeur même de la problématique d'une théologie de la libération* (p. 141). Here Mveng makes a distinction between material poverty (*pauvreté réelle*) and ideological poverty (*pauvreté idéologique).* Both are inextricable and must be understood in terms of anthropological poverty (*pauvreté anthropologique*)——the total negation of Africa's humanity, which has Pan-African implications. (5) The theme of liberation is the fifth issue Mveng discusses. (6) The sixth issue concerns hope. He claims that a global consciousness is rising with respect to the dignity of the oppressed. In closing, Mveng claims that the Holy Spirit is at work in Africa, preparing the way of liberation.

438 Mveng, Engelbert. "Third World Theology——What Theology? What Third World: Evaluation by an African Delegate." In *The Irruption of the Third World: Challenge to Theology*, ed. by Virginia Fabella and Sergio Torres, 217-221. Maryknoll, N.Y.: Orbis Books, 1983.

Here Mveng explores tensions within the Ecumenical Association of Third World Theologians, tensions which indicate that Africans are the step-children of the organization (though Africans are largely responsible for EATWOT's creation). "Evidently," writes Mveng, "Africa is not taken seriously. Even in the Third World itself, in an association of theologians, Africa remains the everlastingly marginalized——not to say forgotten!——continent" (p. 218). Mveng is appalled at the dangerous and prevalent assumption that Latin American theology is synonymous with liberation theology. The irony here is that such assumptions within EATWOT re-introduce the problem of Western hegemony into an organization that has sought liberation from that hegemony. According to Mveng, EATWOT appears to be coming increasingly under the control of Latin Americans, who, in giving pride of place to social analysis, threaten to undermine the religio-cultural analyses so integral to African and Asian theologies. In this regard, Mveng asserts the critical significance of *pauvreté anthropologique* (see 437):

Strange, is it not, that in the immense literature that we have on the poor today, Africa is always looked down upon and derided? There is a type of poverty that I call, "anthropological poverty." It consists in despoiling human beings not only of what they have, but of everything that constitutes their being and essence——their identity, history, ethnic roots, language, culture, faith, creativity, dignity, pride, ambitions, right to speak...we could go on indefinitely (p. 220).

For Mveng, then, it is a fact——exceeding sad——that EATWOT is depriving itself of the voices of those who constitute, more so than any other people, the underside of history.

439   Mveng, Engelbert.   "Conférence inaugurale: L'Afrique du sud, un lieu théologique." *Bulletin de théologie africaine* 6,12 (juillet-décembre 1984): 203-210.

Mveng addresses the Yaounde conference on The Church and Black Theology in South Africa.   See 339.   He asserts that the meaning of the gospel is liberation and the hermeneutical task is to identify nuances of the biblical focus on liberation.   That being the case, he asserts that South Africa today appears to be the theological context *par excellence*.   For Mveng, South Africa is the context in which one can study the distinction between theology and its antithesis.   Apartheid, he argues, perverts Christian faith and is *en route* to becoming a monstrous idolatry as yet unequalled in the history of humankind. See 288.   Nazism and other satanic bigotries pale beside apartheid, argues Mveng. Apartheid, he asserts, is a totally anti-Christian anthropology that denies the biblical message of the universal fatherhood of God, the unity of the human race, *de la fraternité humaine, et du salut apporté à les hommes par le seul et unique Sauveur, Jésus Christ* (p. 204).   Apartheid contradicts the incarnation——the soteriological ramifications of which prohibit racial separation.   The fact that apartheid also upholds racial supremacy makes it all the more egregious from a christological perspective.   According to Mveng, apartheid is far worse than atheism: *il est...un anti-christianisme idolâtrique* (p. 205).

440   Mveng, Engelbert.   "A Cultural Perspective." In *Doing Theology in a Divided World: Papers from the Sixth International Conference of the Ecumenical Association of Third World Theologians, January 5-11, 1983, Geneva, Switzerland*, ed. by Virginia Fabella and Sergio Torres, 72-78. Maryknoll, N.Y.: Orbis Books, 1985.

"The problem," asserts Mveng, "is that the dialogue of divided Christians, for centuries now, has never been able to pierce the walls of arrogance of [the white world's] cultural bastions" (p. 73).   The antidote to this problem requires theologians, across the board, to de-europeanize themselves.   Only de-europeanization will abolish the hubris that makes dialogue essentially a monologue——one in which whites speak to the Third World "in terms of annoyance, demand, and arrogance——not of dialogue."   "Thus the problem of inculturation...is posed for us, first and foremost, in terms of 'deculturation.'   The gospel must be de-westernized and restored to the peoples of the Third World," argues Mveng.   See 312.   For Mveng de-europeanization alone facilitates the option for the poor, which is at the heart of the gospel.

441   Mwoleka, Christopher.   "Trinity and Community." In *Mission Trends No.3: Third World Theologies. Asian, African and Latin American Contributions to a Radical, Theological Realignment in the Church*, ed. by Gerald Anderson and Thomas Stransky, 151-155. New York: Paulist Press; Grand Rapids: Wm. B. Eerdmans, 1976.

Mwoleka, a Tanzanian, begins his essay with an assertion of his commitment to *ujamaa*——a species of African socialism defined, in part, by Julius Nyerere.   See 102-106.   Mwoleka's sense of the theology of *ujamaa* is based on an analogy between the Trinity and African communalism.   See 389-390, 411.   Thus *ujamaa*——a Swahili word meaning "unity"——is an indirect witness to the Christian doctrine of the Trinity, in which Persons are freely bound in an indivisible oneness.

442 Mwoleka, Christopher. "Trinity and Community." In *African Christian Spirituality,* ed. by Aylward Shorter, 117-125. Maryknoll, N.Y.: Orbis Books, 1980.
    See 441.

443 Ntakarutimana, E. "Les Eglises d'Afrique annoncent-elles l'Eglise de demain?" *Bulletin de théologie* 5,9 (janvier-juin 1983): 145-146.
    Ntakarutimana reflects on a conference held in Kinshasa in 1982. The conference considered the diversity of the African church——the anglophone, the francophone, and the independent and historical churches that comprise both languages. According to Ntakarutimana, the African churches, despite their financial, cultural and pastoral problems, are the hope of the continent and perhaps even of the world. Indeed, he reminds us, two-thirds *de l'Eglise appartiendront...au Tiers Monde* by the 21st century. *Les poids des Eglises africaines,* writes Ntakarutimana, *dans deux générations sera donc considérable* (p. 146).

444 Ntumba, Tshiamalenga. "Philosophie et cultures africaines. Clarification et projet culturel des sociétés africaines." *Bulletin de théologie africaine* 5,10 (juillet-décembre 1983): 239-250.
    The words "philosophy and cultures" in the title of Tshiamalenga Ntumba's essay are emblematic of his intention to draw out the generic implications of the juxtaposition of the singular and the plural. According to Tshiamalenga Ntumba——see 209——the plural signifies a certain empiricism while the singular, a certain idealism. For Tshiamalenga Ntumba: *le pluriel souligne diversité comme facticité tandis que le singulier anticipe l'unité comme idéalité.* Tshiamalenga Ntumba claims that the conjunction "and" in his essay's title has serious implications as well: Is it not the case that philosophy signifies a tautology——*une certain forme de culture?* Whether that be the case, all things cultural, he argues, are not, *ipso facto,* philosophical. Thus: *On n'oppose...pas le même au même et la conjonction 'et' dans 'philosophie et cultures africaines' se justifies* (p. 240). This is particularly so if Philosophy (*singulier*) transcends culture and philosophies. Tshiamalenga Ntumba argues that his reflection on the meaning of African culture does not constitute Philosophy. Rather, he is in quest of a theory of language pertinent to the cultural and socioeconomic struggles of African people. He argues for a symbiosis between African culture and technology——a technology that eschews the implements of destruction forged by the West. Africa's task, for Tshiamalenga Ntumba, is to forge technological and ideological tools out of its own matrix in order to serve, not subjugate, humankind.

445 Nyamiti, Charles. *African Theology: Its Nature, Problem and Methods.* Kampala: Gaba Publications, 1971.
    Nyamiti argues that the field of African theology needs to be widened. Its expansion would be contingent upon whether theologians divest themselves of the assumption that Christian revelation should be defined solely by way of philosophy. In focusing on philosophical issues, one assumes it is necessary to construct an African metaphysics that, based on traditional religion, would be the philosophical foundation of African theology. See 176. According to Nyamiti, such a conception is too narrow, and has tended to be little more than prolegomena. See 448.

446 Nyamiti, Charles. *The Scope of African Theology.* Kampala: Gaba Publications, 1973.

Nyamiti explores issues he set out in *African Theology: Its Nature, Problem and Methods*. See 445. He argues that the present narrowness of explorations of African theology will be overcome in: the recognition of the vastness of the subject; the theologian's recognition of his/her limitations; the pastoral approach. These caveats will enrich the discipline because they guard against tendencies to pigeonhole African theology. According to Nyamiti, African theology will be grounded nonetheless in African traditional values. These reflect a worldview in which life is an organic field with dynamics conditioned by the energies emanating from diverse entities, such as humankind, ancestors, God. The challenge to African theologians is to draw out the implications of questions such as: "How can the African dynamic and vitalistic approach to reality, spiritual world-view, anthropocentrism, and sense of communal solidarity serve to prove the existence of God, of human liberty and immortality, or of the validity of the moral law?" (See p. 18.)

447 Nyamiti, Charles. "Approaches to African Theology." In *The Emergent Gospel*, ed. by Sergio Torres and Virginia Fabella, 31-47. London: Geoffrey Chapman, 1978.

According to Nyamiti, African theology is as old as the history of Christianity in Africa. The "conscious efforts to build up such theology" is recent, however——"not earlier than the 1960s" (p. 33). (*Des prêtres noirs*?) Nyamiti reveals that the formal presentation of African theology involved prolegomena and then the essential stage, *adaptation*. See 423. He defines *adaptation* as "the application of the general principles of theological renewal to concrete cases, either by an effort to solve particular African problems (e.g., polygamy, ancestral cult) with Christian principles, or by attempting to adopt African elements into Christian theology" (p. 33). Bracketing the monophysite traditions of Ethiopia and Egypt, Nyamiti asserts that there are three types of African theology. (1) The speculative school, distinguished by "systematization and philosophizing," is made up of the francophone, Roman Catholic scholars. (2) The social and biblical school is pragmatic and accentuates the Bible in its exploration of cultural ("ethnological") and social issues. (3) The militant school——black theology——is found primarily in South Africa and, like its North American sibling, is a theology of liberation. Nyamiti argues that the three schools overlap despite their distinctiveness. An essential similarity is that "their characteristics are determined by Western culture rather than by African cultures" (p. 32). He also contends that African theologians——often reifying themes as if they were without nuance throughout the continent——tend to focus on the positive aspects of tradition, thereby ignoring practices which are as abominable as they are archaic. In concluding, Nyamiti argues that *adaptation* requires "the manipulation of all the cultural and historical themes in the African world——both the traditional cultures and the political and economic circumstances in the modern phase of Christianity's world wide development" (p. 44).

448 Nyamiti, Charles. In "The Theological Value of African Tradition." In *African Christian Spirituality*, ed. by Aylward Shorter, 104-106. Maryknoll, N.Y.: Orbis Books, 1980.

In this excerpt from *The Scope of African Theology*——see 446—— Nyamiti asks whether the industrialization of Africa renders traditional religion obsolete. As industrialization in Europe led to a loss of so-called primitive values, would not the same phenomenon occur in Africa? Nyamiti's point, however, is that Africa is not a carbon copy of Europe. "Hence," he writes, "a cultural element is not necessarily to be despised as 'primitive' because Westerners no longer have it" (p. 104). For Nyamiti, ancestral values are indispensable if one would forge an African theology; and both, for Nyamiti, are quite suited to the ethos of post-modernity.

449 Nyom, B. "Prière biblique et prière négro-africaine." *Bulletin de théologie africaine* 3,6 (juillet-décembre 1981): 155-218.

According to Nyom, Old Testament prayer is both personal and collective, but focused on obedience to God. Another significant aspect of Old Testament prayer, argues Nyom, is its Semitic anchor in this world, which distinguishes it from Greek dualism. God's righteousness, then, has no application other than what pertains to "flesh and blood." Nyom argues that dimensions of Jewish prayer are foundational to Christian prayer. Christian prayer, *la prière néotestamentaire,* deepens the tension between the individualistic and the corporate dimensions of prayer. Neither must be ostensible; each must emerge from a profound humility before God. The one who evinces such humility, asserts Nyom, is Christ. Thus Nyom asserts that *la prière chrétienne est d'abord une expression de foi, une communion au mystère humano-divin du Christ Jésus.* Bantu religion, he argues, corresponds to Christian prayer by virtue of its embodiment of the tension between the individual and the collective, as well as its celebration of the victory of life over death. See 434. Traditional Bantu religion must be christianized, but its predisposition to Christian truth itself facilitates its christianization.

450 Obeng, E.A. "Inroads of African Religion into Christianity: The Case of the Spiritual Churches." *Africa Theological Journal* 16,1 (1987): 43-52.

Obeng examines the African independent—or spiritual—churches. See 046, 137, 234, 330. His aim is to examine areas of contact between them and the traditional religions of Ghana and Nigeria. He thus focuses on the relation between traditional ritual and the liturgy of these churches. He argues that the dancing and the clapping, which complement possession by the Holy Spirit, are not unlike the dynamics of autochthonous rituals, in which possession trance is a distinguishing characteristic. Healing in these churches is also practiced in the traditional way. The prophet or prophetess has dreams or visions, given by the "spirit," through which one identifies the cause of the illness. Then, candles, oil, and/or water are used in performance of the healing process. Water is a traditional symbol of healing. Unlike the mission churches, the independent churches do not consider polygamy a sin; and, women tend to assume leadership, though churches follow the patriarchal customs of the ancestral community for the most part. Obeng concludes that the spiritual churches have africanized Christianity to the brink of syncretism. See 227.

451 Obeng, E.A. "Syncretism in West African Christianity? The Case of the Spiritual Churches." *Africa Theological Journal* 17,2 (1988): 106-177.

Obeng suggests that devotees of the independent churches do not see themselves as syncretistic, but as purveyors of traditional values unopposed to Christian faith. Indeed, the africanization at work in these churches is indispensable if it removes the alienation that had been purveyed by the historic churches.

452 Oduyoye, Mercy Amba. "The Value of African Religious Beliefs and Practices for Christian Theology." In *African Theology en Route,* ed. by Kofi Appiah-Kubi and Sergio Torres, 109-116. Maryknoll, N.Y.: Orbis Books, 1979.

Oduyoye focuses on African traditional religion in terms of "traditionalists"——Africans "who hold to the traditional religious beliefs and practices of their forbears to the exclusion of missionary religions" (p. 109). Although those ancestral beliefs have been weakened in the wake of colonialism(s), "the missionary religions together with modern technology have proved inadequate to [African] needs" (p. 107). The acculturative nature of these conditions makes the African context fertile for what Oduyoye calls a "creative syncretism." (Here, Oduyoye indicates her later definitions of acculturation and inculturation. See 458.) For Oduyoye, such syncretism——which, given the clash of cultures, involves the de-europeanization of Christianity——must quicken if African theology is to be more than a petrified relic of Western theology. What is more, "creative syncretism," according to Oduyoye, has every reason to bear fruit because Christianity and African traditional religion are quite similar. See 041. In both, she argues, humankind is not unlike an *axis mundi* that concentrates the meaning of creation as sacred time. In both, humans have vitiated their central position in alienating themselves from God. Additional correspondences, asserts Oduyoye, are emphases on: community; the holistic view of the person; the dignity of women; theocracy; "covenant-making"; reconciliation; *rites de passage*; and liturgies, as exemplified in the independent churches. According to Oduyoye, moreover, African religion is quite soteriological. This fact promises that the ingenious mixture of Africanity and Christianity will yield rich nuances in the understanding of salvation.

453 Oduyoye, Mercy Amba. "Naming The Woman: The Words of the Akan and the Words of the Bible." *Bulletin of African Theology* 3,5 (January-June 1981): 81-97.

Oduyoye, here Vice-President of the Ecumenical Association of African Theologians——see 437-438——examines Akan myths that clearly show the traditional subordination of women to men. According to Oduyoye, there is a correspondence between the African traditional oppression of women and the oppression of women found in the Old Testament. Both evince the depth of sexism in human culture. In the words of Oduyoye: "The folk-tales and myths [I] have surveyed lead one to see the way in which female characters' socialization produces the mentality that sees nothing wrong with the limited participation of women in society" (p. 94). In regard to the Bible, argues Oduyoye, critical exegeses——born from feminist hermeneutics of suspicion——would deprivilege biblical patriarchy in discovering the presence of the dissimulated voices of women and laying, therefore, the foundation of non-sexist discourse. According to Oduyoye, then, myths must be created that "stimulate what ought to be the concept of balance in human relations. This has got to be examined, and effected in order to correct the super-ego of the male and the political indolence as well as the self-preserving cunning acceptance of the female" (p. 96).

454 Oduyoye, Mercy Amba. "In the Image of God. A Theological Reflection from an African Perspective." *Bulletin of African Theology*, 4,7 (January-June 1982): 41-54.

Oduyoye puts her definition of acculturation into practice as she uses African myths to define the *imago Dei*. She recounts that both the Igbo and Akan tell tales in which the human soul confers with God regarding its destiny. See 133, 144, 139, 222. Both people, writes Oduyoye, believe they are co-creators with God. Igbo, for instance, have an aesthetic tradition called *mbari*, in which collectivity takes precedence over individuality and thereby extends the memory of sacred time. (Sacred time here may be understood in terms of *communitas*. See 247, 273.) The intention of *mbari*, explains Oduyoye, "is to renew the positive creative powers in the community and thereby return things to the way they were when God first created" (p. 43). Still, traditional myths are vitiated by sexism. Traditionally women are placed in a caste that would derive them of the fullness of God's image. It is at this point that inculturation proves redemptive. According to Oduyoye, the gospel reveals to Africans that, "The image stamped on us is God's not the male's....None except Christ is a model" (p. 53).

455 Oduyoye, Mercy Amba. "Feminism: A Pre-Condition for a Christian Anthropology." *Africa Theological Journal* 11,3 (1982): 193-208.

Oduyoye examines male images that tend to control conceptions of God; her argument is that God transcends male/female categories. Oduyoye rejects the assumption that women should be subordinated to men in the Church: the church, as the body of

Christ, is, essentially, neither male nor female. Thus, Oduyoye argues for an anthropology that affirms the maleness *and* femaleness of the image of God.

456 Oduyoye, Mercy Amba. "Reflections from a Third World Woman's Perspective: Women's Experience and Liberation Theologies." In *Irruption of The Third World: Challenge to Theology*, ed. by Virginia Fabella and Sergio Torres, pp. 246-255. Maryknoll, N.Y.: Orbis Books, 1983.

Oduyoye begins this essay with an Akan fable——a fable not unlike that of Adam and Eve——that indicates the opposition and complementarity of woman and man. Her point is that unity without diversity diminishes human community and, in this case, dissimulates male hegemony under the banner of (pseudo) homogeneity. Indeed, Third World women would enrich the church if they were not marginalized by men of both the First and the Third Worlds, and by white women. The fact that men——within the contexts of EATWOT and AOTA——do not accord women the fullness of the integrity granted to them by God indicates, to Oduyoye, that Third World theology has yet to be edified by its own "underside."

457 Oduyoye, Mercy Amba. "Who Does Theology? Reflections on the Subject of Theology." In *Doing Theology in a Divided World: Papers from the Sixth International Conference of the Ecumenical Association of Third World Theologians, January 5-11, 1983, Geneva, Switzerland*, ed. by Virginia Fabella and Sergio Torres, 143-149. Maryknoll, N.Y.: Orbis Books, 1985.

Theology, she argues, is not an intellectual pursuit devoid of engagement in real-life struggles. Indeed, Oduyoye employs a quote from Luther which draws out the implications of her assertion: "Not reading and speculation, but living, dying, and being condemned make a real theologian." Real theologians today, she argues, are "third way" theologians. According to Oduyoye, the third way involves an interdisciplinary approach to theology, one in which pride of place is given to social analysis. Religio-cultural analysis is also involved in this interdisciplinary approach.

458 Oduyoye, Mercy Amba. *Hearing and Knowing*. Maryknoll, N.Y.: Orbis Books, 1986.

Oduyoye explores the relation of African theology to other EATWOT theologies. She then discusses the history of Christianity in Africa. Her central thesis is that theology perishes when it becomes irrelevant to the people. She thus posits that Christianity in "medieval" Nubia perished——nearly without a trace——in its encounter with Islam because it was essentially captive to the Coptic Church further North and out of touch with the struggles of the Nubian people. According to Oduyoye, a relevant theology, truly contextualized and indigenized, may appear somewhat heterodox to those on the outside. Heterodoxy, however, may in fact be a mark of vital theology. Indeed, Oduyoye argues that African theologies in touch with the people's realities have always been somewhat heretical to imperial theologies. Here she cites the example of the Donatist Church as well as the independent churches of recent times. In examining the history of mission in Africa, Oduyoye notes the alienation Eurocentric theologies have wrought in Africa. In discussing current trends in African theology, she lifts up the work of Baëta, Kato, and Idowu. Baëta, she thinks, correctly champions the way of liberation in African theology, but incorrectly eschews the epistemic values of African primal religions. (Oduyoye prefers the term primal religions to African traditional religions, as the latter suggest static phenomena.) Oduyoye sees little value in Kato's narrow fundamentalist position, in which both liberation and africanization are rejected. See 374. She notes Idowu's *Toward an Indigenous Church* as an early paradigm of the study of africanization and christianization. See 356. For Oduyoye, then, African theology must embody both a commitment to the praxis of liberation and the study of Africa's primal religions. In this regard, Oduyoye forges her useful definition of acculturation and inculturation. Acculturation pertains to the efforts of "Africans to use things African in their practice of Christianity"; "inculturation [refers to] the manifestation of changes that have come into the African way of life as a result of the Christian faith." This definition serves her discussions of a doctrine of God and the Exodus very well. As Africa's most known feminist theologian, Oduyoye concludes her book with a critique of the sexist values of both African traditional religion and African theology. See 454, 456. Her argument is that any view which sublates women to men truncates the fullness of the *imago Dei* redeemed in Christ. See 454.

459 Oduyoye, Mercy Amba. "The Value of African Religious Beliefs and Practices for Christian Theology". In *Third World Liberation Theologies,* ed. by Dean William Ferm, pp. 240-247. Maryknoll, N.Y.: Orbis Books, 1986.
  See 452.

460   Okolo, B. "Liberation Theology and the African Church." *Bulletin of African theology* 4,7 (January-June 1982): 173-188.
  The Christian meaning of liberation in Africa, asserts Okolo, is made clear through inculturation. This is to say, the gospel takes root in Africa as it plows through and uproots the injustices that oppress the poor, creating free space for them to reap the gifts of racial and economic justice. While liberation is to be defined in African terms——coincident with African realities and in accordance with African cultures——Latin American theology has great heuristic value for African theology. See 314-312. Particularly edifying here is the discovery that liberation involves a praxis in which theology is the second step. See 352. For Okolo, the essential and critical step toward God's kingdom——and inculturation therefore——is the activist's commitment to struggle with the poor against the inhumane and ungodly structures that oppress them. See 331, 483.

461 Onibere, S.G.A. Osovo. "Christian Reactions to Indigenous Religion in Nigeria: The Ancestor as a Case-in-Point." *Bulletin of African Theology* 3,5 (January-June 1981): 81-87.
  Onibere examines a problem that the old guard featured in their discourse——are the ancestors worshipped or revered? See 161, 178, 479, 485. In re-examining that issue, Onibere refers to the work of Parrinder and Idowu. See 229-231; 177-179. For both scholars, argues Onibere, linguistic evidence suggests that Africans, such as the Yoruba and the Ashanti——see 145, 206——distinguish ancestor worship from that of the divinities. Although Idowu concludes that such worship is not true worship——but veneration in fact——Onibere asserts "that the ancestors are worshipped and not venerated" (p. 58). On that ground, he also takes Fasholé-Luke to task for assuming that the cult of the ancestors can be christianized in terms of the communion of saints. See 345, and 334. For Onibere, such christianization would be possible only if the saints were worshipped——an impossibility for him. What is more, argues Onibere, "opinion is divided among Christians in respect of the veneration of the Saints, which practice is virtually peculiar to Roman Catholicism. For Fasholé-Luke to base his argument on this is nothing short of forcing the issue" (p. 59). For Onibere, then, the ancestors have no place in Christian theology in Africa——except as a *praeparatio evangelica.* According to Onibere: "Anything that is not along this strain of thought probably smacks of unbiblicity [sic]."

462 Onibere, S.G.A. Osovo. "The Phenomenon of African Religious Independency: Blessing or Curse on the Church Universal?" *Africa Theological Journal* 10,1 (1981): 10-26.

Onibere examines the rise of the independent churches and the significance of this phenomenon for the church universal. See 046, 137, 141, 208, 330. For Onibere, these churches developed in response to the racism rampant in the historic churches. They represent the attempt of African people to maintain their dignity and embody the best of African traditional values that have been modified by Christianity.

463 Onwu, N. "The Hermeneutical Model: The Dilemma of the African Theologian." *Africa Theological Journal* 14,3 (1985): 145-160.

Onwu discusses the problem of the translation of biblical words into the African vernacular. Indeed, he argues, the fact that African and biblical idioms are asymmetrical exacerbates problems related to African theologies. Use of European languages is also problematic because they have been the discourse in which God and Christ have been confused with Western colonialism. What is more, the assumption that African languages are more faithful to biblical truth than European ones may be a reproduction of Eurocentric confusion. See 294. In that regard, Onwu criticizes the work of James Cone. See 532-544. Onwu concludes that the Cross-Resurrection event empowers African theologians to confront neocolonialism.

464 Parisot, Jean. "Vodou et christianisme." In *Des prêtres noirs s'interrogent,* ed. by A. Abble, et al., 213-258. Paris: Les Éditions du Cerf, 1956.

According to Parisot, Haitian Vodun is the syncretistic relationship of "paganism" and Catholicism. Nonetheless, Vodun, he argues, has its own religious integrity, as does its "pagan" prototype in Dahomey. See 288. While, asserts Parisot, Vodun is a so-called primitive religion, it bears an essential likeness to Platonism. Platonists, like devotees of Vodun, hold that there is a Supreme Being from which all being is derived. Both hold there are spiritual entities created by the Supreme Being——the gods or the divinities (*loas*). The biblical Hebrews, moreover, are depicted as exhibiting religious behavior not unlike that discovered in Haitian Vodun: '*Au temps de Samuel, il sont des enthousiastes; ils se réunissent ou vivent par troupes. Ils exécutent des exercices bizarres, sortes de danses religieuses au son d'instruments de musique, tambourins, cymbales, luths* (p. 222). In these vibrant dances of the possessed, in Vodun as well as in the Old Testament, there looms *le Bon Dieu*. Indeed, the relation between Vodun and the Old Testament should pave the way for the christianization of neo-African religion. What should also pave the way, asserts Parisot, is the correspondence between the Roman Catholic saints and angels, on the one hand, and the *loas* (divinities) of Vodun on the other. The power of the memory of Africa helps to explain the sublation of Roman Catholicism to Vodun. What is more, the Europeans and their priests, who enslaved the Haitians, were no exemplars of Christianity; and that too helps explain the persistence of ancestral religion. The shortcomings of the church, then, only fortified the favored position of Vodun among the masses. According to Parisot, Christianity will only take root in Haiti if religious see that inculturation is a task *qui consiste à enraciner l'Eglise dans le terrain psychologique, ethnologique, et cultural des peuples* (p. 242). Not unlike Mbiti, Parisot claims that Vodun, and other African religions, constitutes——under informed supervision——a *praeparatio evangelica*. For Parisot, then, it is proper for Haitian music, stripped of its "pagan" content, to be christianized, i.e., *de christianiser ces airs en y adaptant des paroles orthodoxes*.

465 Parratt, John. "African Theology and Biblical Hermeneutics." *Africa Theological Journal* 12,2 (1983): 88-94.

Parratt explores the significance of biblical hermeneutics that would facilitate the development of an African theology. He emphasizes oral traditions, themselves constitutive of African self-understanding, and thus gives pride of place to African religious traditions. According to Parratt, in addition, biblical kinship paradigms correspond to African ones. He contends that this correspondence can edify the struggle for authentic African theologies insofar as they strengthen the quest for autochthonous hermeneutics.

466 Penoukou, E.J. "Avenir des Eglises Africaines. Questions et réflexions." *Bulletin de théologie africaine* 4,7 (janvier-juin 1982): 189-204.

Penoukou begins his essay with an account of a young man who vociferously takes the church to task for its irrelevance: *Une Eglise de...d'incapables, des vendus...!* Penoukou concedes the prophetic element here. The African church, as statistics verify, is growing; but the church is in crisis. Indeed: *l'Eglise a-t-elle encore en Afrique des chances réelles d'avenir?* An answer to the question requires an inquiry into the problem of neocolonialism. Penoukou holds that a recital of the litany of colonial wrongs will do nothing to remedy the situation. An answer to the question also requires an examination of inculturation. Here, the challenge is to find the *communitas*——see 247, 273——in the encounter between Africanity and Christianity. On the one hand, the African heritage is critical for the de-europeanization of the Christian faith; on the other hand, the faith itself must be so strongly rooted as to check proclivities of *les prophètes de fortune* who use African culture in a way that obscures the God of the oppressed. Penoukou goes on to delineate ten points that suggest the road to a vital future. He also suggests the role African bishops should play in the struggle. In any case, Penoukou argues that the African Church will have a future only if it is true to both African realities and the gospel.

467 Penoukou, E.J. "Avenir des Eglises africaines. Questions et réflexions (suite et fin)." *Bulletin de théologie africaine* 5,10 (juillet-décembre 1983): 193-204.

Inculturation, asserts Penoukou, signifies the insertion of the Christian message into the totality of a culture——such that the gospel joins with *ses modes de penser, d'agir, de vivre; avec ce qu'on est et aspire à être* (p. 193). Indeed, the task of the African church is to understand, to express, to communicate, to celebrate its piety in African style. This, he explains, has nothing to do with *un retour aux pratiques traditionnelles.* According to Penoukou, too many African Christians are essentially pagan. See 227. Inculturation among them is only ostensible; it is also ostensible when sewn in racist resentment (as is the case in South Africa). If the ground is clear of benightedness and racism, however, Christianity will root itself in the deep soil of Africanity, asserts Penoukou. According to Penoukou: *Au total l'Africanisation du christianisme concerne l'homme africain actuel; il n'en demeure pas moins que cet homme doit être rejoint aux racines profondes de ce qui lui donne finalement sen et valeur* (p. 198).

468 Pobee, John S. *Toward an African Theology.* Nashville: Abingdon, 1979.

Pobee's discussion of African traditional religion focuses on the Akan. See 131. He would like to see them develop an African christology. After discussing elements such as *mogoya, sunsum, ntoro* and *kra*——see 155, 477——Pobee concludes:

> In our Akan Christology we propose to think of Jesus as the *okyeame*, or linguist, who in all public matters was as the Chief, God, and is the first officer of the state, in this case, the world. This captures something of the Johannine portrait of Jesus as the Logos, being at one and the same time divine and yet subordinate to God.... Jesus as a chief is human and shares common humanity with the rest of mankind (p. 95).

Thus an Akan anthropology, modified by incarnation doctrines, is a critical epistemological fount for a theology in touch African realities. Pobee concludes his work with a chapter entitled "The Ethics of Power." Here he explores issues pertinent to liberation in Africa. He asserts that Christ demands that one act ethically in a world assailed by evil. Such action does not exclude revolution. The christological imperative, however, is that of service, regardless of the means. "To achieve this, writes Pobee, "the man of power should be primarily concerned not with his own dignity but with selfless and self-sacrificing devotion to his fellow men. As the Akan put it, *oku no ho ma ne man*——he kills himself for his nation" (p. 155).

469 Pobee, John S. "Political Theology in the African Context." *Africa Theological Journal* 11,2 (1989): 168-175.

Here Pobee focuses upon the development of a political theology relevant to the political, economic, and religious situations of Africa. Every political theology should have these fundamental tenets: a confession of the sovereignty of God; an anthropology based on the *imago Dei*; and final judgment——the righteousness of God's wrath. For Pobee, the cross is central to a political theology because it exemplifies the way in which God has walked the true path to liberation.

470 Randall, Frances. "African Proverbs Related to Christianity." In *Mission Trends No. 3: Third World Theologies. Asian, African and Latin American Contributions to a Radical, Theological Realignment in the Church*, ed. by Gerald H. Anderson and Thomas F. Stransky, 181-191. New York: Paulist Press; Grand Rapids: Wm. B. Eerdmans, 1976.

Randall, during missionary work among Kenyan peoples, discovered that their aphorisms, and other modes of folk culture, agreed with Scripture. A primary correspondence, according to Randall, is Exodus and the traditional assessment of the British "Pharaohs." For Randall: "African theology will keep on developing as long as it can speak about the act of loving and living in its own context" (p. 188).

471 Sacrin, A. "Théologies en dialogue. En marge d'un congrès." *Bulletin de théologies africaine* 4,7 (janvier-juin 1982): 299-300.

Sacrin reports on a conference, held in Italy, that focused on the challenges posed to the church by the secularized world. Prominent among the African theologians in attendance were V. Mulago and A. Ngindu Mushete. See 415-419; 422-425. Sacrin notes the surprising interest Italians take in African affairs and that Africans *ont remarqué un certain nombre de problèmes communs à l'Italie et à l'Afrique*. According to Sacrin the Africans showed in diverse ways that *la théologie africaine est effectivement en marché*.

472 Said, Wa Dibinga. "An African Theology of Decolonization." *Harvard Theological Review* LXIV (Oct. 1971): 501-524.

Said defines "types" of African theology, one of which is "Ethiopian"; it encompasses, for him, both the historic churches and the so-called "Zionists" churches. See 258. According to Said, the "Ethiopian" theology signifies: (1) the recapture of the land; (2) the end of all Eurocentric institutions and symbols ("whitianity"); (3) the alliance among revolutionary movements (i.e., Mau-Mau); (4) the recognition of black Sainthood (i.e. Kimpa Vita in the Congo); (5) the quest for a liberating biblical religion. Said also discusses the African theology of decolonization. Here emphasis is on the liberation of the oppressed from "spiritual-socio-politico-economic colonialism, imperialism and neocolonialism" (p. 518). Said prefigures, then, a theology not unlike that of the new guard, which draws close in praxis to black South African theology.

473 Sanneh, Lamin. "A Christian Reflection on Religion and Politics." *Bulletin of African Theology* 4,7 (January-June 1982): 202-212.

The contradictions that confront Africans require their critical vigilance, argues Sanneh. As they are both Western and non-Western, he asserts, Africans must "take a fresh look at inherited political institutions." Thus, Sanneh examines the notion of the sovereignty of the state, and critiques the religious ideas that lay beneath the idea of sovereignty. According to Sanneh: "The sanctity of the political compact that existed between the ruler and his subjects, and which therefore had the character of a limited contract, derived from the sanctity of the Creator's act on which the notion of sovereignty was irrevocably constructed" (p. 211). The implications of his conclusion for Africans today: "...religious abdication in politics is an illusory thing, and on that basis the Christian stake in the current ferment in political and religious circles [is] incontestably clear" (p. 212).

474   Sanon, A. "L'humanité de l' Eucharistie." *Bulletin de théologie africaine* 4,7 (*janvier-juin* 1982): 123-134.
    Like Éla——see 340——Sanon asks, rhetorically, whether the point of the Eucharist is to hold to a static representation of the elements. Although wafers and wine, as metaphors of flesh and blood, are thought by the West to be universal, they do not fit the African context. According to Sanon, eucharistic elements should reflect the reality of the people. Then none would ask: *Quelle est cette pâte blanche?* Why is it reserved for special occasions when food is so scarce? According to Sanon, Christ transforms edible materials——it does not really matter which——such that they become his body and blood. On that basis, Sanon asserts that Africans should use the more accessible *grain——C'est la pâte de mil bien localisée, 'zonfa', c'est la nourriture* (p. 124). For him, the point is *dans la volonté du Christ désireux de manger avec les hommes de tous les pays en touchant leurs conditions primordiales de vie* (p. 127).

475   Sastre, Robert. "Liturgie romaine et négritude." *Des prêtres noirs s'interrogent*, ed. by A. Abble, et al., 153-170. Paris: Les Éditions du Cerf, 1956.
    Sastre wonders whether the black can be a Christian *sans renoncer à sa négritude?* Sastre argues that *négritude* signifies a profound religious orientation which may be summed up in one word——celebration. Although his assessment of *négritude* (celebration) involves an appreciation of the past, Sastre asserts that *négritude* is a present reality that must be related to the spread of Roman Catholicism among Africans. He asks himself what can be done to better correlate *négritude*, on the one hand, and the Roman Mass on the other. According to Sastre, the correspondence between *négritude* and Catholicism can only be the agreement between two modes of celebration. In juxtaposing the two, Sastre employs a phenomenological method, specifically one influenced by Van der Leeuw. Here, the meeting point is the idea of repetition, of renewal. For Sastre, however, *la liturgie romaine* is given pride of place in this encounter. The Roman Catholic liturgy, for Sastre, calls the African to purification, to decantation, and to pacification. According to Sastre, something must die in the Africans so that the best in them may live in fullness of life. What would die, implies Sastre, is not *négritude*; *négritude*, as celebration, has an essence——*une verdeur, un suc*——which can revive what is too staid in the Catholic ritual.

476   Sawyerr, Harry. *Creative Evangelism: Towards a New Christian Encounter with Africa*. London: Lutterworth, 1968.
    See discussion in Chapter three of this bibliography, and 478.

477   Sawyerr, Harry. "Sin and Salvation: Soteriology from the African Situation." In *Relevant Theology for Africa*, ed. by Hans-Jurgen Becken, 126-138. Durban: Lutheran Publishing House, 1973.

According to Sawyerr, salvation means that God has become incarnate in order to impute to sinners the gift of righteousness that is identical with God's grace. Soteriology, moreover, entails a biblical anthropology that holds that consummate grace redeems the whole person, her body and soul. This anthropology, taken from a Hebrew conception, is one in which *anthropos* is appreciated as the integration of body, soul and spirit. For Sawyerr, these three Hebrew nuances of human personality correspond to the tripartite structure of the Akan personality. See 155, 468. *Mogoya*, mother's blood or corporeality; *kra*, the soul which is itself an element in the diffusion of the Supreme Being; and *sunsum/ntoro*, the essence of individuality bequeathed through the father's semen——all can be christianized. Specifically, the Christian understanding of sin must correct and perfect the Akan notion of sin. The latter hardly reveals human deformity and thus cannot convey the salvific significance of the Christ event. Drawing on the work of Placide Tempels——see 261-262——Sawyerr argues that the traditional concept of sin has been tantamount to the misuse of *force vitale*. Quintessential evil, then, is the work of witches, who seek to disrupt the harmony of the community, thus making people less powerful and more susceptible to misfortune, disease, and death. For Sawyerr, the protagonist of *Things Fall Apart* exemplifies one who enjoyed the fullness of force. See 132. Okonkwo falls, however, due to insidious forces. Okonkwo——the African *par excellence*——attempts to expunge his troubles by way of sacrifices or other expiatory acts prescribed by priest-diviners. Sawyerr holds that Okonkwo exemplifies the extreme alienation of traditional people. For Sawyerr, Africans must come to accept that the omnipotent Christ has irreversibly restored the balance of the cosmos——such that all malevolent forces have been rendered impotent. Salvation here is total——the African, posits Sawyerr, would know that all of the nuances of his essential self participate in Christ, who is both sacrificial victim and high priest.

478   Sawyerr, Harry.   "Jesus Christ——Universal Brother." In *African Christian Spirituality*, ed. by Aylward Shorter, 65-67. Maryknoll, N.Y.: Orbis Books, 1980.
       This excerpt is taken from Chapter Eight of Sawyerr's *Creative Evangelism* (see 476). Sawyerr focuses on the humanity of the God-man. Christ's true humanity, asserts Sawyerr, should serve as a basis for explaining Christianity to the "pagans." Here, the church is depicted as the great family and Christ, the elder brother. This approach to inculturation, argues Sawyerr, is far more edifying than the christianization of "chieftainship." See 468. The latter is far too functional and thus truncates an *essential*——i.e., *trinitarian*——understanding of the Person and work of Jesus Christ. When Jesus Christ, however, is seen as the first-born among many, one has attained insight into the soteriological meaning of the incarnation (which strikes a responsive chord among Africans). According to Sawyerr, African traditional religionists are ridden with anxiety regarding necromancers, demons and death, and seek comfort through "pagan" ritual and sacrifice. See 477. When Africans, asserts Sawyerr, recognize that Christ has defeated all demonic forces, they will be freed of the illusion of a world beset by myriad, malevolent forces.

479 Sawyerr, Harry.   "Living and Dead in Fellowship with God. In *African Christian Spirituality*, ed. by Aylward Shorter, 130-134. Maryknoll, N.Y.: Orbis Books, 1980.
       At first glance, it may appear that Sawyerr succumbs to the universalism that Kato ascribes to him. See 374. Sawyerr, though, writes: "We may rightly and in all humility postulate that, on the final day of judgment, 'God shall be all in all', and pray that all men may have come to grasp his unspeakable love" (p. 134). Sawyerr posits this; he does not *assert* it. Thus, in this excerpt from *Creative Evangelism*——see 476, 478——Sawyerr explores the ostensible correspondence between the ancestors and the *sanctorum communio*. See 334, 345. The analogy is rooted in a christology that proclaims that the living and

their ancestors are now joined in a covenant made possible through the incarnation and the atonement. While Sawyerr's assertion that Africans have no evidence for "worship" of their ancestors is strange——as if Christians have "evidence" of the resurrection and the incarnation——he argues that Christian eschatology is broad enough to include even "pagan" ancestors within the resurrection community. According to Sawyerr, then, "the prayers of African Christians might, in the providence of God, lead us to the salvation of their pagan ancestors" (p. 132). Although Sawyerr posits that the ancestors may be included in the Kingdom of God, he forbids the practice of libation.

480 Sawyerr, Harry. "What Is African Theology?" In *A Reader in African Christian Theology*, ed. by John Parratt, 12-28. London: SPCK, 1987.
    This essay, published originally in *Africa Theological Journal* in 1971, explores the historical development of African theology. With reference to Idowu's *Towards an Indigenous Church*——see 356——Sawyerr notes that African theology is related to the idioms, African personality and *négritude,* and was presaged by persons such as James Johnson (see 007); Samuel Crowther (see 109); and Edward Blyden (see 016-018). He notes that the independent churches provide clues as to what is implied by an African theology, though "it is unlikely that the advocates of African theology can truly use [them] as their yardstick" (p. 20). See 227. For Sawyerr, African theology must be based on the few correspondences between the gospel and African traditional religion. The yardstick that determines how far such analogies go is systematic theology. African theology, he asserts, in addition, should have little if anything to do with the black theology of the United States; but it should be unqualifiedly ecumenical.

481 Sebahire, Mbonyinkebe. "Les intellectuels africains et l'Eglise: interpellations et attentes." *Bulletin de théologie africaine* 3,6 (juillet-décembre 1981): 273-275.
    Sebahire challenges African intellectuals to interpret the historic and present role of the church in light of its two-fold charge to: (1) edify humans as to their responsibility to God; and (2) respond to the problems confronting Africa. Above all, intellectuals are not to become jaded and purvey a spirit inimical to what a philosopher from Zaire calls *l'anti-liberté*. According to Sebahire, African intellectuals should deplore the injustice that would censure progressive thought; and the church must hold intellectuals accountable in that regard. To that extent, *il lui faut théologie chrétienne africaine qui réconcilie les dimensions de l'Incarnation et de la Rédemption* (p. 274).

482 Sebahire, Mbonyinkebe. "Théologies du péché et du salut en dialogue. A propos du symposium de Bonn." *Bulletin de théologie africaine* 5,10 (juillet-décembre 1983): 322-329.
    Sebahire recounts the salient issues discussed at an international symposium held near Bonn in 1982. The most significant issues were *faute, réconciliation et salut dans la théologie occidentale et dans la théologie africaine,* especially as defined in Zaire. A question here was the extent to which African values can open up new insights into the distinction between sin and salvation. Sebahire notes that communication between Africans and Germans was strained, as the latter were often perplexed by the African's grounding in the realm of the invisible——*de sa relation au corps et au monde 'bigarré et 'curieux' des Ancêtres, des Génies et des Esprits* (p.322). According to Sebahire, the ancestors constitute the keys to an African soteriology and eschatology based on the here-and-now. That is, *L'outre-tombe est souvent pensé en termes de 'vie d'ici-bas'* (p. 325). Indeed, life beyond the grave makes sense traditionally only in terms of the ancestors. See 308. After discussing the Germans' papers, Sebahire concludes that the dialogue edified both sides.

483   Segundo, Juan Luis.   "The Hermeneutic Circle." In *Third World Liberation Theologies*, ed. by Dean William Ferm, 64-93. Maryknoll, N.Y.: Orbis Books, 1986.

Like Gutiérrez and Dussel——see 352, 331——Segundo is heuristically related to African theologians. In this excerpt from his seminal *The Liberation of Theology*, Segundo defines a hermeneutic of suspicion that liberates theology from white supremacist and bourgeois moorings. According to Segundo, the oppressed have concluded that the dominant caste and classes do theology in a way that legitimatizes injustice. Realizing that Christianity is nothing by itself——but always bears the impress of an ideology——the oppressed are empowered to reread the Bible and reinterpret Christian tradition in a way pertinent to their situation. For Segundo, as for many new guard theologians, the hermeneutics of the oppressed are truer to the gospel than that of their oppressors. According to Segundo, in addition, the black theologian, James Cone, is an outstanding example of one who completes the hermeneutic circle. For Segundo, Cone's work, notably *A Black Theology of Liberation*——see 541——exemplifies an authentic epistemological break with theologies that fail to focus on the problem of human oppression.

484 Sempore, S. "Conditions of Theological Service in Africa: Preliminary Reflections." In *Christianity in Independent Africa*, ed. by Edward Fasholé-Luke, Richard Gray, Adrian Hastings and Godwin Tasie, 516-530. Bloomington: Indiana University Press, 1978.

According to Sempore: "The two-fold reaction against colonial domination and missionary hegemony has taken two roads...the cultural ideology of *négritude*, and...that of *adaptation* as a theological concept applicable to the whole African church" (p. 517). In regard to *adaptation*, Sempore cites the seminal *Des prêtres noirs s'interrogent*. See 475. According to Sempore, the two foci of African theology become credible only if they are sharpened and thus transformed by way of religio-cultural and social analyses. For Sempore, creative African theologies are produced by service-oriented, loyal, and critical theologians committed and responsible to the oppressed of Africa.

485 Serote, S.E. "Meaningful Christian Worship for Africa." In *Relevant Theology for Africa*, ed. by Hans-Jurgen Becken, 148-154. Durban: Lutheran Publishing House, 1973.

According to Serote——as opposed to Kenyatta, Idowu and Bujo——Africans have worshipped their ancestors. See 461. The ancestors, to whom Africans have appealed in their quests to maintain cosmic, as well as individual, harmony and health, are the keys to an understanding of traditional religion. Serote holds that while Africans were mostly bound to their ancestors, there loomed beyond them a Supreme Being. The remoteness of that Being, as compared to the closeness of the ancestors, is an indication that Africans need the gospel if they are to commune with the true God. The fact, moreover, that Africans have "worshipped" the ancestors is, for Sarote, a sure sign that they have not really known God. Sarote does not think, however, that Africans should be torn from the roots of their "personality"; rather, he has the hope that this African personality will "be permeated, flavored and redirected Gospel-wise" (p. 149). In short, Sarote proposes that ancestor "worship," *inter alia*, be christianized——such that the dead are remembered in an African way, but are not worshipped. See 479.

486 Setiloane, Gabriel. "I Am an African." *Mission Trends No. 3: Third World Theologies. Asian, African and Latin American Contributions to a Radical, Theological Realignment in the Church*, ed. by Gerald Anderson and Thomas Stransky, 128-131. New York: Paulist Press; Grand Rapids: Wm. B. Eerdmans, 1976.

Professor Setiloane's prose is reminiscent of the style and content of *négritude*:
They call me an African:
African indeed am I:

Rugged son of the soil of Africa,
Black as my father, and his before him;
As my mother and sisters and brothers, living and gone from
this world.

"I Am an African" implies his central thesis: that the traditional African conceptions of God are more than equipped to express the tension between the aseity and the knowability of God. See 487.

487 Setiloane, Gabriel. "How the Traditional Worldview Persists in the Christianity of the Sotho-Tswana." In *Christianity in Independent Africa*, ed. by Edward Fasholé-Luke," Richard Gray, Adrian Hastings and Godwin Tasie, 402-414. Bloomington: Indiana University Press, 1978.

Here Setiloane reiterates his assertion that Sotho-Tswana conceptions of God are far deeper in their implications than Christian conceptions of God. According to Setiloane, the Sotho-Tswanas' deep conceptualization of God explains why they find continuities between ancestral godliness and Christianity. Both convey the imperative to love God fervently. Sotho-Tswana values, however, such as those regarding marriage and the ancestors, must de-europeanize Christianity——the key to which is the "indigenous understanding of the workings of divinity" (p. 408). Throughout, Setiloane brackets the word religion, as it signifies a Western orientation irrelevant to Africa. "Religion," asserts Setiloane, implies attempts to define God——attempts far too profane for the Sotho-Tswana. According to Setiloane, even the word *God* pales in comparison to the word *Modimo*.

488 Setiloane, Gabriel. "Where are We in African Theology?" In *African Theology en Route*, ed. by Kofi Appiah-Kubi and Sergio Torres, 59-65. Maryknoll, N.Y.: Orbis Books, 1979.

Setiloane posits that "the breakthrough with regard to the traditional Western theology occurred at the World Council of Churches meeting on mission and evangelism at Bangkok in 1972" (p. 59). There, asserts Setiloane, Africans called for a moratorium. See 316, 371. Another important development, asserts Setiloane, was "the conference on Christianity in post-colonial Africa held in Jos, Nigeria...August 1975" (p. 60). *Christianity in Independent Africa* is the volume containing the papers delivered at that conference. See 390, 484, 487. He cites John Kibicho's paper in particular; Kibicho's views are similar to Setiloane's. Both men assert that an African sense of the aseity of God is far more profound than a European sense. See 378-380. For Setiloane, moreover, African theology is at a crossroads, beyond which awaits a true African christology. According to Setiloane, the structure of traditional religion renders the Chalcedonian sense of the incarnation irrelevant, since it defines God's immanence in terms that run counter to traditional concepts of the mystery of God. An African christology, however, would entail no sacrifice of theological integrity——the redemptive being and action of Christ would not be diminished. But the issue is whether Eurocentric consciousness should dictate the orientation of African theology. Indeed, Setiloane criticizes black theology for its dependence on that consciousness.

489 Setiloane, Gabriel. *African Theology: An Introduction*. Braamfontein: Skotaville Publishers, 1986.

Setiloane's definition of African theology serves as a foil against those who prefer black theology to African theology. According to Setiloane, African theology

claims authenticity and validity for itself and the African Traditional
Religion as arising out of the same Source. It accepts that there is a
difference in conceptualizing and verbalizing Reality as a result of the

geographical, chronological, cultural situations and contexts of the various people concerned. It further contends that Reality becomes more real to any person and people when verbalized to them in the context, and myth which is second nature to them: for we each see and hear through our cultural eyes and ears (p. 320).

For Setiloane, then, it is entirely unnecessary to see God——or Christ——in Western terms, as certain black theologians tend to do. See 488. Neither is it necessary to understand African theology as a liberation theology in the conventional way. That is, liberation need not be understood in terms of social analyses that expose the contradictions of a "socio-political context." Rather, liberation in African theology pertains to freedom from "the imprisonment in the vaults of Western conceptualism and discourse, from cerebration and pseudo scientific-ness" (p.45).

490   Shorter, Aylward. *African Christian Theology: Adaptation or Incarnation.* Maryknoll, N.Y.: Orbis Books 1977.

Shorter explores African theology in terms of the distinction between *adaptation*——see 447, 484——and incarnational theologies. The former, characteristic of the views defined in *Des prêtres noirs s'interrogent*, constitute the superficial attempt to inculturate Christianity in African contexts. See 415, 416, 475. A deeper rooting of Christianity, however, is conveyed in an incarnational theology. Here African theology is essentially African *and* essentially catholic. For Shorter, then, African traditional religion, in the scope of an incarnational theology, is more than a *praeparatio evangelica*. African traditional religion "paves the way for the Christianity of the future, which hopefully will be more universal" (p. 159). Here, African traditional religion is not something to be overcome, but is essential to ecumenicity.

491   Shorter, Aylward. "Man and His Integral Development." In *African Christian Spirituality*, ed. by Aylward Shorter, 15-20. Maryknoll, N.Y.: Orbis Books, 1980.

Shorter examines the problem of christology in African theology. He notes the ways in which African theologians have favored a from below approach——that is a method which gives primacy to human experience in the definition of Christ. According to Shorter, the Africans favor a christology that focuses on the *a posteriori* "givenness" of the incarnation, which makes the God-man every person's sibling. Like Bujo——see 308——Shorter discusses Christ as the ancestor; but docetic implications, suggests Shorter, make "ancestor christology" problematic. See 583. According to Shorter, ancestors are primarily spirit (hence the docetic implication). For Shorter, it would be better to see the Father, the first Person of the Trinity, as the ancestor, which would be commensurate with certain traditional religions. Christ, then, would be Elder Brother.

492   Shuuya, I.K. The Encounter between the New Testament and African Traditional Concepts." In *Relevant Theology for Africa*, ed. by Hans-Jurgen Becken, 47-54. Durban: Lutheran Publishing House, 1973.

Shuuya asserts that Africans have traditionally believed in God, and, like Mbiti, he lists many African names of the Supreme Beings. See 203. For instance, he records epithets of the Shona God, *Mwari*——"the Supreme Being, the God of the cosmos, the God of fertility," etc. Thus, he provides an index which substantiates his claim that a central feature of African traditional religion is its monotheism, a feature which corresponds to Christian Scripture.

493   Sidham, Swailem. "The Theological Estimate of Man. In *Biblical Revelation and African Belief*, ed. by Kwesi Dickson and Paul Ellingworth, 83-115. Maryknoll, N.Y.: Orbis Books, 1969.

Sidham's interpretation of African traditional religion is focused on the Nilotes, and dependent upon the work of Tempels (see 261-262). This is curious since Tempels did not focus on the Nilotes, who are significantly unlike the Bantu, on whom he did focus. See 169. Nonetheless, Sidham notes that African intellectuals were forced to reconsider traditional religion, despite earlier attempts to marginalize it. Reminiscent of Abraham and Davidson——see 131, 031——Sidham argues that life-sustaining, traditional values are indispensable today, given the life-threatening crises of the Continent.

494 Sofola, Zulu. "The Theatre in the Search for African Authenticity." In *African Theology en Route*, ed. by Kofi Appiah-Kubi and Sergio Torres, 126-136. Maryknoll, N.Y.: Orbis Books, 1979.

Sofola asserts that despite efforts to root Christianity in Africa, it is still potted in its European vessel. Given that comic predicament, how "can Christianity be authentically *rooted* in African soil?" He tackles that problem in terms of African theatre. Theatre, he argues, is a living metaphor of a people's culture. It is grounded in a traditional structure, the constitutive parts of which are interdependent, but singly free; fixed, but transmutable. See 384. Life, the subject of African art, is the struggle to return to the "Supreme Essence" that, diffused in human souls, Itself returns in the souls' cycles of death and rebirth. Such cycles form the most supple processes through which the unborn become the living, grow old and die to return with the intent to thrive. In sum, works of artists, such as Wole Soyinka, embody, for Sofola, dimensions of this "African cosmic view." Ola Rotimi's *The Gods Are Not to Blame*, however, is misconceived——still-born because it essentially adapts Oedipus Rex to an African context. Here, africanization is ostensible——fundamentally, the thing is Greek. Sofola argues that much African theology is like the work of Rotimi.

495 Sprunger, A.R. "The Contribution of the African Independent Churches to a Relevant Theology for Africa." In *Relevant Theology for Africa*, ed. by Hans-Jurgen Becken, 163-173. Durban: Lutheran Publishing House, 1973.

According to Sprunger, theology in Southern Africa will continue to be irrelevant if it does not investigate the goings-on in the independent churches. These churches represent the Christianity of the masses; a theology which ignores them is out of touch with the faith of most Christians of Southern Africa. Sprunger classifies these churches as either Ethiopian, prophetic/pentecostal or messianic movements. The Ethiopian churches display a notable continuity with the historic churches, while the latter two——especially the messianic movements that "do not fit the traditional definition of a Christian Church"——are more in line with African traditional religion." See 258-259. The prophetic/pentecostal churches, for Sprunger, represent authentic African Christianity. These churches provide examples of a faith directed by the Spirit, rather than by the letter of dogma. Thus they edify African theologians as to what an African pneumatology might be. These churches also provide a dynamic paradigm of the meaning of Christian community. For Sprunger, the independent churches, imbued with missionary zeal and committed to apostolicity, radiate tolerance and thus a spirit of ecumenicity. Their worship is joyful, and their piety, infectious. The independent churches also emphasize healing——a dimension of Christian witness all but lost to the Western Church. In sum, Sprunger holds that independent churches, since they "consist of eighty percent Biblical theology and twenty percent African spirituality," are indispensable contexts for the study of inculturation.

496 Stadler, P. "Approches christologiques en Afrique." *Bulletin de théologie africaine* 5,9 (*janvier-juin*) 1983: 35-50.

Stadler notes that a film on Jesus of Nazareth made a sizable impact on the region near Kimpese. The film, for Stadler, raises the issue of inculturation, since it implies the question——how should Jesus be depicted in Africa, i.e., among the BaKongo? See 185, 198, 199, 238, 263. This question is critical, he argues, as christology is central to systematic theology. Stadler defines christology as follows: *La christologie est une réflexion systématique sur Jésus Christ à partir des sources bibliques, notamment du Nouveau Testament* (p. 37). Stadler goes on to say that christology valorizes the historical Jesus without compromising the salvific import of the incarnation, crucifixion, and resurrection. Christology, then, has little to do with a Jesus that fits the spaces of a secular historiography. According to Stadler, African investigations into christology have been modest; but the need for such inquiries is acutely felt. To substantiate his claim, Stadler quotes African theologians such as Gabriel Setiloane and John Mbiti. See 488-489; 398, 400. Stadler notes that African christology should be influenced by hermeneutics derived from studies of the African independent churches and African traditional religion. See 495. Stadler also refers to the works of James Cone and Alan Boesak, who assert that an African christology must focus on the identity of Christ as one of the oppressed. See 517-522; 532-544. Here, the claim that Christ is the savior is inextricable from his historical identity as an oppressed Jew. Jesus is also to be understood as the perfect man, whose true humanity may be expressed through African idioms, such as those related to rites of initiation. Here Stadler quotes Mbiti. See 398-403. According to Stadler, African women, such as Mercy Oduyoye——see 452-459——are especially likely to advance a christology that may indigenize Christian soteriology.

497 Tabard, R.T. "L'Eglise catholique romaine en Afrique." *Bulletin de théologie africaine* 3,5 (janvier-juin 1981): 61-71.

Can one be *catholique romain et africain*? Yes. It is not necessary, argues Tabard, for Africans to be Roman. See 475. According to Tabard, catholicity signifies the tension between the universal and the particular. He writes: *Dire l'Eglise 'catholique', c'est dire qu'elle n'est pas sectaire, repliée sur elle-même, qu'elle ne peut pas se contenter d'un particulier, mais qu'elle est tournée vers les autres particuliers* (p. 62). Catholicity, then, for Tabard, is contingent upon the celebration of diversity. On the model of the Trinity, the world will be one to the extent that it revels in diversity. Work toward that end is dependent upon the valorization of a cultural relativity in which distinct species of Christianity are celebrated. Diversity, asserts, Tabard, also demands a faithfulness to the structure, or essence of being——*c'est-dire celle où vit le Christ* (p. 63). Tabard's understanding of Christ carries eschatological implications that caution the church against its apotheosis. All the same, for him, the christianization of the world is the responsibility of the church.

498 Tempels, Placide. "Catéchèse bantoue." *Le bulletin des missions* 22 (1948): 258-279.

"Catéchèse bantoue" is an example of the theological foundation of Tempels' Bantu philosophy. See 261-262.

499 Thetele, Constance Baratang. "Women in South Africa: The WAAIC." In *African Theology en Route*, ed. by Kofi Appiah-Kubi and Sergio Torres, 150-154. Maryknoll, N.Y.: Orbis Books, 1979.

Ms. Thetele examines feminist issues in South Africa, with a focus on the independent churches. With reference to the work of Adrian Hastings——see 045-048——Thetele argues that the rise of the independent churches must be seen as a response to the agglutination of mission churches alienated from the masses. See 061. The Women's Association of African Independent Churches (WAAIC), asserts Thetele, has emerged from those churches and indicates the revolutionary path characteristic of them. The WAAIC is the sister organization of the African Independent Churches Association (AICA). The revolutionary implications of both organizations are that they express blacks' realizations that "the dictates of their oppressors" are not "God-given" (p. 154). More specifically, Thetele asserts that the WAAIC and AICA "have not allowed invasion to alienate them from the spirit of their own culture and from themselves" (p. 154).

500 Thiam, Joseph. "Du clan tribal à la communauté chrétienne." *Des prêtres noirs s'interrogent*, ed. by A. Abble, et al. 41-56. Paris: Les Éditions du Cerf, 1956.

Thiam wonders whether Christianity can be enriched by African traditional values. In responding to that question, Thiam focuses on the boundaries of Senegal, particularly *la Basse-Casamanu*. According to Thiam, the informed missionary recognizes that Africans are profoundly spiritual and will therefore gravitate to Christianity. Here, Thiam utilizes the myth of African communalism. Whereas, he holds, the European is an individualist, the African is immersed in a cosmic and social milieu that makes it imperative for him to valorize ancestral traditions and pass them faithfully to his descendants. The Africans' devotion to the group——both visible and invisible——lays a foundation for their openness to the church. This same devotion, however, asserts Thiam, also poses problems because it is rooted in values that are a bit archaic. It would appear, then, that the work of the priest is to uproot (*déraciné*) problematic aspects of traditional culture as he penetrates the society. For Thiam, however, the paganism of the West——*communisme, laïcisme*——is far worse than so-called African paganism. Insofar as Christianity bears the influence of those godless values, he argues, Africans must return to a more spiritual base. And so he reiterates that the traditional magnification of community provides arable ground for Christianity. What is more, writes Thiam, if the gospel has taken root among the Jews, why can it not take root in Africa? Thus he asserts: *L'adaptation du christianisme, sa capacité d'Incarnation dans un milieu donné, telle est la pierre de touche de son universalité* (p. 55). Who can rule out——he asks in closing——that the African Christian will not exemplify, once again, the mystical communion characteristic of the apostolic age?

501 Thompson, P.E.S. "The Anatomy of Sacrifice: A Preliminary Investigation." In *New Testament Christianity for Africa and the World: Essays in Honor of Harry Sawyerr*, ed. by Mark E. Glasswell and Edward W. Fasholé-Luke, 19-35. London: SPCK, 1974.

Thompson, Sawyerr's former student, discusses the implications of Canon Sawyerr's thesis that there is a correspondence between traditional immolation and biblical sacrifice. Indeed, the late Sawyerr, asserts Thompson, held that this correspondence is the "'open sesame' of the heart of the African to Christian teaching" (p. 19). See 241. According to Thompson, however, Sawyerr does not see the disparity between the two modes of sacrifice. Thompson argues that biblical sacrifice is orientated to the past while African sacrifice looks to the future. Indeed, he argues, Old Testament sacrifice differs from that in the New, though both must be appreciated in terms of the legacy of the biblical kingdoms. By way of Old Testament exegesis, principally source and rhetorical criticisms, Thompson argues that sacrifice is a dynamic mode that should not be reified in static terms. Still, definite patterns emerge. For Thompson, a fundamental pattern of Old Testament sacrifice is that it is offered *after* the Deity has intervened on behalf of humankind. Here, sacrifice is two-dimensional since it signifies a vertical and a horizontal orientation. The vertical, i.e., the burnt offering with its ascending smoke, is consecrated to God, while the horizontal, often a cereal offering, signifies a eucharistic element in which the covenant between God and humankind is accentuated. What is more, Thompson argues that sacrifice was never really the leitmotif of the Old Testament. Historically, he posits, sacrifices were "part of ethnic tribal religion which did not feature in original

Yahwism" (p. 35). Traditional African sacrifices, however, are central to African culture. African sacrifices are supplied to restore or to bolster a harmony between the visible and the invisible worlds and is forward-looking in that sense. In short, Thompson argues that there is little correspondence between African and biblical sacrifices.

502 Tshibangu, T. "The Task of African Theologians." In *African Theology En Route*, ed. by Kofi Appiah-Kubi and Sergio Torres, 73-94. Maryknoll, N.Y.: Orbis Books, 1979.

Bishop Tshibangu of Zaire notes that *Des prêtres noirs s'interrogent* is seminal to the study of African theology as it signified a fruition of the planting of the Christianity in Africa. See 475, 500. He then delineates specific obligations of African theologians. (1) They must be spiritually committed. (2) They must be rigorously intellectual. (3) They must be committed to "the ongoing process of their society." (4) They must be involved in the life of the church. Related to these obligations, asserts Tshibangu, are specific tasks: (1) to understand and appreciate African traditional religion as the ground from which African theology grows; (2) to integrate social analysis into theology (with black South African theology serving as the paradigm); (3) to contribute to the dynamic quest to clarify and resolve "the theological options that have not been solved by the churches."

503 Tshibangu, T. "Abbé Mulago (Vincent). Jubilé sacerdotal." In *Combats pour un christianisme africain: Mélanges en l'honneur du Professeur V. Mulago*, ed. by A. Ngindu Mushete, 289-291. Kinshasa: Faculté de Théologie Catholique, 1981.

Tshibangu notes that Mulago is a pioneer of African theology. (*Un des promoteurs de la théologie africaine, il a développé plutôt pour sa part davantage une théologie des "pierres d'attente," de l' "adaptation."*) See 415-421.

504 Tshibangu, T. "L'Eglise et les droits de l'homme." *Bulletin de théologie africaine* 5,9 (janvier-juin 1983): 5-20.

According to Tshibangu *la Déclaration Universelle des Droits de l'Homme*, proclaimed by the United Nations in 1948, is but another revelation of the God-given Truth that the abuse of humankind is a misanthropy identical, in essence, with the contempt for God-in-Christ. For Tshibangu, then, the church, above all other institutions, must always be at the cutting edge of movements that seek to safeguard the rights of human beings. The church must affirm the essential truth of Genesis, *qui déclare que l'homme est fait à l'image de Dieu....Ceci exprime la participation voulue de l'homme à Dieu, fondement essentiel des droits et de la dignité qui appartiennent à l'homme* (p. 7). The human link to God essentially upholds the sacredness of the *imago Dei——tous les hommes sont égaux en noblesse, dignité et nature, sans distinction de race, et de religion...tous ont donc les mêmes droits et devoirs fondamentaux* (p. 10). Again, the one who fully reveals this equity is Christ, claims Tshibangu, who is, quintessentially, *la dignité de l'image de Dieu*. The gospel, then, impels the church to a praxis that opposes all that would deny human beings fullness of life. This praxis is eschatological, but nonetheless entails *la réalisation du bonheur de l'homme, poursuivre avec effort sur cette terre* (p. 13).

505 Tshibangu, T. "Un concile africain, est-il opportun?" *Bulletin de théologie africaine* 5,10 (juillet-décembre 1983): 165-178.

Tshibangu discusses the heightened interest in and critical reflection on the propriety of an African Council. The issue itself is a ramification of Vatican II and crystallized at a synod of bishops held in Rome in 1974. A seminal document in that regard was *Les Déclaration des Evêques Africaines*. AOTA has decided to devote its energies to a determination of the scope of such a council. Provisionally, the council would address: the general African situation; doctrinal issues; liturgy, spirituality, and pastoral concerns; the church and contemporary African society.

506   Ukachukwu Manus, Chris.   "2 Cor. 10-11:23a. A Study in Paul's Stylistic Structures." *Bulletin of African Theology* 5,10 (July-December 1983): 251-268.

Ukachukwu Manus examines Paul's "literary skill" in order to draw conclusions regarding higher criticism and its relevance to African Bible students. Paul's style and content are analogous to those of African writers, such as Chinua Achebe. See 132-134. That is, both Paul and Achebe reveal that "literary style and form are indexes of a style of life."   That generic observation allows Ukachukwu Manus to argue that Paul's work——entailing the hellenization of Christianity——is a fitting paradigm for the africanization of the gospel.

507   Utuk, Efiong S.   "An Analysis of John Mbiti's Missiology." *Africa Theological Journal* 15,1 (1986): 3-15.

According to Utuk, Mbiti's missiology is based on the Trinity——the economic implications of which are seen in terms of the incarnation and the Holy Spirit (who empowers missionaries to proclaim the *kerygma*). See 395-403. Utuk reveals, in addition, that Mbiti focuses on the communal dimensions of Christian faith which correspond to African values. For Mbiti, Utuk claims, the church must build upon the African kinship ties and household structures that sublate individuals to the group. When, however, there is a conflict between the ancestors and Christ, Christ is the authority. In answering the question, "What is the purpose of mission according to Mbiti?" Utuk notes Mbiti's assertion that the goal of mission is evangelism and social action. According to Utuk, evangelism, for Mbiti, is "an act of proclaiming Christianity's universality and cosmicity." For Mbiti, evangelism in Africa demands unity among mission societies, church groups and denominations. See 061, 063. In short, Mbiti's ecclesiology——according to Utuk——is based upon the belief that the church must serve Christ and thus execute the will of God on earth.

508   Uzukwu, E.   "Christian Liturgical Rites and African Rites." *Bulletin of African Theology* 4,7 (January-June 1982): 87-110.

After considering types of rites, from the patristic period to the present, Uzukwu concludes that ritual diversity is fundamental to Christianity. Should one deny Africans the free space to play their own liturgical game, he/she would be unfaithful to Christian faith. Since inculturation, moreover, is the means by which Africans attain indigenous liturgies, inculturation is a necessity in Africa.

509   Uzukwu, E.   "Africa's Right to Be Different, Part II: African Rites in the Making." *Bulletin of African Theology* 4,7 (January-June 1982): 243-276.

Uzukwu examines various types of liturgical experiments in Africa, which indicate the diversity of commitments to inculturation. Inculturation, he asserts, has nothing to do with *adaptation*. See 490. Inculturation explores liturgical possibilities that go beyond the facile *adaptation* in which there was no "grappling with the traditional religious ideas, [and which accommodated] the externals of African life...without coming to terms with the fundamental spirit generative of these externals" (p. 247). An example of inculturation is the attempt to africanize baptismal ritual in terms of Mossi initiation. Another example is Zairian efforts to africanize the Eucharist. See 366-367. "Zairian composers have made a genuine effort to translate the local churches' faith-experience into ritual. A translation which keeps the Zairian world, in all its dynamism, in healthy dialogical tension with the living Jewish-Christian tradition" (p. 274).

510   Uzukwu, E.   "Igbo Spirituality as Revealed in Igbo Prayers." *Bulletin of African Theology* 5,10 (July-December 1983): 205-222.

Uzukwu explains that traditional Igbo prayer joins the petitioner to the invisible——i.e., the spirit world replete with ancestors, deities and the Supreme Being (*Chukwu*). According to Uzukwu, prayer signifies the "awareness among the Igbo that dynamic interaction with the spiritual originators and allies of the community precedes and founds any other action in the community [and] constitutes the basis for studying Igbo spirituality" (p. 211). See 360. Uzukwu takes issue with Robin Horton's thesis that traditional religion is a science——a theory that is closed. See 174-175. Uzukwu argues that Igbo religion is more practice (action) than theory, and more open than closed. Quoting Wole Soyinka——see 494——Uzukwu holds that theorists like Horton "bypass the code on which this [African] world view is based, the continuing evolution of tribal wisdom through an acceptance of the elastic nature of knowledge as its one reality, as signifying no more than reflections of the original coming-into-being of a manifestly complex reality" (p. 214). For Uzukwu, Igbo spirituality, examined through traditional prayer, is a vital and dynamic orientation, and a fitting field for inculturation.

511 Verdieu, E., and P. Ondia. "Sacerdoce et négritude." *Des prêtres noirs s'interrogent*, ed. by A. Abble, et al., 83-110. Paris: Les Éditions du Cerf, 1956.

The authors examine the implications of *négritude* for the priesthood. They hold that a black priest is first and foremost a priest. Only secondarily is he black——*sa négritude ne lui ajoute rien* (p. 84). Because of the implications of the incarnation, however, *négritude* must be taken seriously, assert Verdieu and Ondia. *On peut dire en toute vérité que le Christ n'est étranger a aucun groupement humain; au contraire, il se fait semblable à chacun* (p. 86). It is the black priest who gives Christ his African visage. So *négritude* is not to be purged——as if a *tabula rasa* were possible. Indeed missionaries must build on what exists. Only in that way do persons learn that *qu'il y a du spirituel dan le temporel, et qu'avec ce temporel on peut faire de l'éternel* (p. 93). Still, only that which agrees with the gospel can be christianized. What is more, the authors contend that African culture is too enigmatic at present to be the epistemological underpinning of theological education for Africans (let alone European missionaries). Verdieu and Ondia conclude by charging black priests to be in solidarity with one another and with the Catholic Church.

512 Verryn, T.D. "Rites of Passage." In *Relevant Theology for Africa*, ed. by Hans-Jurgen Becken, 139-148. Durban: Lutheran Publishing House, 1973.

According to Verryn, rites of passage are fundamental transitions that define the essentials of communal and individual life. Each passage involves: a break away from one's former position; a crossing over into the new position; and a re-incorporation into the matrix of traditional life. Analogously, argues Verryn, the entire continent of Africa is involved in the passage from "small-scale, rural, agricultural society to large-scale, urban, industrial, pluralistic, and individualistic society" (p. 144). Consequently——he assumes——the traditional rites of passage will be discarded as they will have little significance in the new matrix. Thus, Africans will be thrust into an era without a structure equipped to provide meaning in the wake of tremendous change. According to Verryn, the church may take the place of traditional rites of passage, and thus give stability in times of crisis. Christianity both supplies rites that give meaning to individuals as they mature, and connects them to a community. Baptism, communion, marriage, and funerals "dramatize the giving up of a previous status, the crossing over to a new one, and the integration into the new" (p. 145).

513 Wambutda, D.N. "Savannah Theology: A Biblical Reconsideration of the Concept of Salvation in the African Context." *Bulletin of African Theology*, 3,6 (January-December 1981): 137-154.

Wambutda joins the issue of contextualization with a focus on salvation. Biblically speaking, salvation signifies that humankind is reconciled to God; and salvation pertains to both spiritual and physical dimensions of life. Salvation is thus concrete and knowable in space and time. For Wambutda, then, reconciliation with God pulls in its train a liberation from earthly realities that would truncate the fullness of the life that God intends humans to enjoy. The Savannah——emblematic of "most of the arable land on the continent of Africa"——is thus the contextual symbol of the concreteness of salvation offered to Africans in Christ. The Savannah signifies that famine, corruption, and fascism are offenses to God and antithetical to salvation. *A fortiori*, salvation is to the Savannah as oppression and alienation are to the desert.

514 Zoé-Obianga, Rose. "The Role of Women in Present-Day Africa." In *African Theology en Route*, ed. by Kofi Appiah-Kubi and Sergio Torres, 145-149. Maryknoll, N.Y.: Orbis Books, 1979.

Within the context of the Cameroon, Madame Zoé-Obianga defines the Christian struggle to raise the consciousness of the young to a heightened appreciation "of their...living and dynamic culture." Christians must also raise the consciousness of African women to the level of feminist assertiveness. According to Zoé-Obianga, the African church is woefully backward with regard to women's struggle for a full humanity.

9

Black South African Theology: Sibling of the New Guard

515 Becken, H.J. "Towards a Relevant Theology for Africa." In *Relevant Theology for Africa*, ed. by Hans-Jurgen Becken, 3-7. Durban: Lutheran Publishing House, 1973.

Becken sets the context for the entire volume, which constitutes the papers delivered at a consultation held at Lutheran Theological Seminary, Mapumulo, Natal. See 392, 394, 414, 477, 524. According to Becken, theology is contextual——see 513——so it is more appropriate to speak of theologies; but these have the Bible in common, and more specifically, a christocentric understanding of the Bible. For Becken, the Bible attests to the revelation of God in Christ, and is the center of an ecumenism that is forged out of theological diversity. Becken's definition of ecumenism betrays a far too positive assessment of white missionaries in Africa. He attends to neither the missionaries' relation to colonialism nor the church's role in erecting a theology of imperialism. What is important for Becken is that white missionaries planted Christianity in Africa. For Becken, in addition, theology in Africa is comprised of African and black theologies. African theology is the attempt to produce an autochthonous theology, rather than an indigenized Western theology. Black theology, on the other hand, is seminally influenced by its African-American counterpart, and is "a situational approach to theology which takes its point of departure from the sociological situation in which 'Non-Whites' find themselves in South Africa" (p. 7). He notes that black theology is a fruit of the Black Consciousness Movement, a legacy of Steve Biko. See 013-015. In comparing the two theologies, Becken reproduces the error of the old guard in assuming that black South African theologians have more in common with African-Americans than with Africans outside of South Africa.

516 Bennett, Bonita. "A Critique on the Role of Women in the Church." In *The Unquestionable Right to Be Free: Black Theology from South Africa*, ed. by Itumeleng J. Mosala and Buti Tlhagale, 169-174. Maryknoll, N.Y.: Orbis Books, 1986.

Bennett recognizes that women's oppression constitutes a transcontextuality in that women are oppressed regardless of their social location. Socialist critique, she argues, heightens one's awareness of the strength to be drawn from the broadness of women's oppression. Such critique also facilitates a criticism of bourgeois churches. According to Bennett, a feminist hermeneutic——produced from the ideological suspicion intrinsic to social analysis——discovers the Jesus on the side of women. This Jesus, absent in the exegesis of males, raises the consciousness of women regardless of their class. See 452-459.

517 Boesak, Alan. *Farewell to Innocence: A Socio-Ethical Study on Black Theology and Power*. Maryknoll, N.Y.: Orbis Books, 1977.
See the discussion in Chapter Four of this bibliography.

518 Boesak, Alan. "Coming in out of the Wilderness." In *The Emergent Gospel*, ed. by Sergio Torres and Virginia Fabella, 76-95. London: Geoffrey Chapman, 1978.
Boesak asserts that black theology is a product of the Black Consciousness Movement. See 519. Consistent with the legacy of Steve Biko——see 013-015——Boesak defines Black Consciousness as "a discovery, a state of mind, a conversion, an affirmation of being (which is power)." Identifying ways in which black South African theology is historically tied to African-Americans, Boesak notes the historic relation of Bishop Henry McNeal Turner to black South Africans. See 122. According to Boesak, in addition, black theology and African theology are "two aspects of the same theology, two dimensions of the same existential and theological experience" (p. 86). See 524, 606. To pigeonhole black theology——to bracket it when talking formally of African theology——is to truncate theological dimensions of the African experience. Boesak also asserts that black theology is a contextual theology, the dynamism of which may be studied in terms of situational ethics. See 515. Black theology's prophetic edge, then, is proportionate to the level of injustice it must oppose. Prophesy here, moreover, is always measured in terms of its agreement with the Word of God. While Boesak asserts he is a servant of the Word, he argues that James Cone——see 532-544——comes perilously close to deifying blackness in spite of the Word. For Boesak, the Word of God is ubiquitous; Christ speaks to myriad contexts simultaneously. Despite his diversity, the Word is One; and the diversity of the hearers of the Word indicates the dynamism of the revelation of the one Jesus Christ. To assume, then, argues Boesak, that the Word of God speaks solely to this group as opposed to that one is to theologize in static terms. Boesak, however, agrees with Cone that reconciliation between blacks and whites is nothing without justice. Still he argues that Cone's work has lacked social analysis in that regard. Boesak concludes his essay with a Sotho proverb that captures the meaning of black theology for him. "*Motho ke motho ka batho ba bang...*: One is only human because of others, with others, for others" (p. 93).

519 Boesak, Alan. "Liberation Theology in South Africa." In *African Theology en Route*, ed. by Kofi Appiah Kubi and Sergio Torres, 169-175. Maryknoll, N.Y.: Orbis Books, 1979.
Boesak notes that the Black Consciousness Movement produced black theology, and that both seek to abolish apartheid. Like Tutu, Boesak asserts that black theology responds to the problem of theodicy, which has been resolved with the help of Black Consciousness. See 599-605. "Through Black [C]onsciousness," he writes, "Black people discover that they are children of God and...have rights to exist in this world" (p. 170). For Boesak, the Bible, particularly Exodus, is a fundamental source for black theology. Here, Black Consciousness is the paradigm of suspicion, which allows black theologians to define the theme of Christian faith——"God is on the side of the oppressed"——in a way appropriate to their context. Showing his awareness of the new guard's perspective, and indicating his sense of black theology's relation to African theology, Boesak notes that liberation and africanization go together. They complement each other——such that focus on one without the other truncates the development of theology in Africa.

520 Boesak, Alan. *Black and Reformed: Apartheid, Liberation and the Calvinist Tradition*. Edited by Leonard Sweetman. Maryknoll, N.Y.: Orbis Books, 1984.

Black and Reformed is a compilation of Boesak's sermons, writings, and speeches, in which he explores his identity as a black theologian in the Calvinist tradition and reiterates his commitment to black and white reconciliation.

521 Boesak, Alan. "Black and Reformed: Contradiction or Challenge?" In *Third World Liberation Theologies: A Reader*, ed. by Deane William Ferm, 272-284. Maryknoll, N.Y.: Orbis Books, 1986.
This excerpt from the book——see 520——is a speech Boesak delivered in October, 1981. Boesak addresses the ostensible conflict between the neo-Calvinism that legitimizes apartheid and his membership in the Dutch Reformed Church——a church that has defined itself in terms of a certain neo-Calvinism. How, he asks, can one be about black liberation in South Africa and remain a member of the church that has heaped abominations on the heads of the black oppressed? For Boesak, it is necessary to make a distinction between the Reformed tradition and its deformation by racist whites in South Africa. Calvin's genius——itself a product of the Reformation——was to bring out the aseity and knowability of the *Word of God*: a mysteriousness and concreteness that negate the necrophilic values of apartheid. (It is precisely on this point that Jerry Mosala takes Boesak to task. For Mosala, the Word of God is as equivocal as the social locations of theologians. What is more, the Reformed tradition, transmitted as it is by Eurocentric consciousness, is barely——if at all——equipped to found an epistemological base for *black* theology in *Africa*. See 572-578.)

522 Boesak, Alan. "Liberation Theology in South Africa." *Third World Liberation Theologies: A Reader*, ed. by Deane William Ferm, 265-271. Maryknoll, N.Y.: Orbis Books, 1986.
See 519.

523 Buthelezi, Manas. "Theological Grounds for an Ethic of Hope." In *A New Look at Christianity in Africa*, 72-80. Geneva: WSCF Books, 1972.
According to Buthelezi, a life without hope is tantamount to death. Hope is the gospel——the witness to an abundant, meaningful life that is true to Christ, and which is revelatory of how one should act ethically in the world. For Buthelezi, hope is that dimension of faith which allows Christians to overcome the destructive as they gravitate daily toward the creative——Christ Jesus. What is more, argues Buthelezi, Christian hope is constituted by the body of Christ, the church. The church is called to be supremely ethical, despite the hopeless, destructive side of life. So the Christian body, flayed for the sake of righteousness, follows an ethical path endured in faith and hope. What is more, hope is the spiritual gift that sustains and quickens the oppressed in their resistance to cruelty. Cruelty, for Buthelezi, is devoid of charity and subjects the other to poverty. Cruelty is *apartheid*. For Buthelezi, Christian ethics in South Africa enables the oppressed to live hopefully and creatively despite destructive apartheid.

524 Buthelezi, Manas. "African Theology and Black Theology: A Search for a Theological Method." In *Relevant Theology for Africa*, ed. by Hans-Jurgen Becken, 18-24. Durban: Lutheran Publishing House, 1973.
Why, he asks, is white response to *African* theology less ridden with consternation than white response to black theology? See 518, 606. According to Buthelezi, African theology seeks to repair the bridge between ancestral values and Christian theology. Yet African theology too often becomes the project of white missionaries alienated from the peoples' ancestors. According to Buthelezi, these white missionaries find African theology a fitting vehicle for their obsolete theology. What is more problematic——even insidious——asserts Buthelezi, is that African theology is too easily *adapted* to apartheid,

a primary goal of which is to contain surplus labor in the homelands through the promotion of vulgar tribalism. See 118. Black theology, on the other hand, is more relevant than African theology to the oppressed of South Africa. While investigating the implications of religio-cultural analysis, black theology examines the contradictions of race and class, which a certain African theology too often dissimulates. For Buthelezi, black South Africans must be edified by black theology.

525 Buthelezi, Manas. "An African Theology or a Black Theology." In *The Challenge of Black Theology in South Africa*, ed. by Basil Moore, 29-35. Atlanta: John Knox Press, 1973.

For Buthelezi, African theology differs methodologically from black theology. African theology is ethnographic; black theology is anthropological. In regard to the former, Buthelezi examines the work of Placide Tempels and Bengt Sundkler. See 529. Of the two, he finds Sundkler's work the most edifying. Still, the ethnographical approach is unsatisfactory because Africans are reduced to "epistemological entities" which are static. Here one assumes——contrary to the position of Fanon——that culture has always the translucidity of custom. See 034. The anthropological method, however, renders the truth of the black situation as it deals with living realities rather than a reified past. Here one takes into consideration both African culture and the socioeconomic crises that influence it. For Buthelezi, then, black theology in South Africa, given its anthropology, is at once a theology of liberation *and* africanization. Black theology, moreover, without deifying black culture and politics, signifies an attempt to be faithful to the gospel. Yet, the gospel, despite its transcultural meaning, can only be interpreted according to the *cultural* and *socioeconomic* particularity of a people. Indeed, black theology reflects the faith of an *African* people afflicted by *apartheid*.

526 Buthelezi, Manas. "Theological Grounds for an Ethic of Hope." In *The Challenge of Black Theology in South Africa*, ed. by Basil Moore, 29-35. Atlanta: John Knox Press, 1973.

See 523.

527 Buthelezi, Manas. "The Theological Meaning of True Humanity." In *The Challenge of Black Theology in South Africa*, ed. by Basil Moore, 93-103. Atlanta: John Knox Press, 1973.

True humanity, for Buthelezi, signifies a "socio-ethical" praxis that seeks the abolition of the contradiction between the oppressor and the oppressed. According to Buthelezi, this praxis entails theological reflection on the practice of love for the other, who is analogous to God's perfected image in Christ. Where the other is despised, as in South Africa, where whites despise blacks, there is *false* humanity. Buthelezi argues that the African, prior to her christianization, knew that true humanity is practiced by virtue of a prudent respect for the other. Given the correspondence between African values and faith, argues Buthelezi, one must find the proper threshold between Christianity and ancestral mores.

528 Buthelezi, Manas. "Daring to Live for Christ." In *Mission Trends No.3: Third World Theologies*, ed. by Gerald Anderson and Thomas Stransky, 176-180. New York: Paulist Press; Grand Rapids: Wm. B. Eerdmans, 1976.

Buthelezi begins his essay with the conviction that Christians must attempt to be Christ-like. On that basis he claims that all Christians are humane; a racist Christian, an inhumane Christian, is an oxymoron. This is seen clearly in the behavior of white supremacists, who claim to be Christians. For Buthelezi, moreover, the oppressive suffering in which blacks often acquiesce is also inhumane and therefore unChristian.

Redemptive suffering, however, which lifts the oppressed to the spirituality of liberation, is Christian and thus quintessentially humane.   According to Buthelezi, the Black Consciousness Movement has theological meaning precisely because, through it, blacks have been able to see that unmerited suffering is redemptive.   Redemption here is related to blacks' revolutionary assertion of their humanity.   True Christianity, then, is found among the black oppressed, who know, in large measure, what justice is because they have suffered from injustice.   Their unjust oppressors, on the other hand, practice anti-Christianity (what Mveng calls *un anti-christianisme idolâtrique*. See 439.)

529 Buthelezi, Manas. "Toward Indigenous Theology in South Africa." In *The Emergent Gospel*, ed. by Sergio Torres and Virginia Fabella, 56-75. London: Geoffrey Chapman, 1978.
      Buthelezi argues that no theology is naked——each is clothed in the array of its culture. According to Buthelezi, this truth has been dissimulated by Western assumptions that "theology is European." For Buthelezi, blacks who assume that theology is European are woefully misguided. Buthelezi credits John V. Taylor——see 260——with being one of the first Europeans to document blacks' suspicion that the hermeneutics of the missionaries served colonialism rather than Christ.   Buthelezi also notes Bengt Sundkler——see 258-259——who has also recognized that African theology cannot be European.   Buthelezi notes Tempels' work as well——see 261-262——though he finds Tempels too paternalistic.   Still, Taylor, Sundkler and Tempels all exemplify the "ethnographic approach." See 525. As the ethnographic approach has been integral to the quest for inculturation, reasons Buthelezi, inculturation itself has become a specious enterprise.   Here Buthelezi calls to mind Fanon's dictum, "culture has never the translucidity of custom." See 034. Many inculturationists assume that African culture constitutes the relics of the past. The dynamism of such culture is lost because those who would do the indigenizing are alienated from the masses where African culture develops. Then too, argues Buthelezi, missionaries take up the task of inculturation to maintain their essentially untenable position in a post-colonial context, and to satisfy their Eurocentric neuroses. See 524. Buthelezi asserts that missionaries, in returning to a secularist Europe, found their theologies hopelessly out of date. Hence, they returned to Africa, reproducing obsolete theology. For Buthelezi, an *African* theology eschews such theology in favor of an anthropology true to itself. See 525.   In South Africa, reveals Buthelezi, such anthropology——i.e., blacks' self-definition——has nothing to do, really, with what Dosseh and Sastre call *propagande missionnaire*. See 329. In sum, Buthelezi exemplifies a way in which the Black Consciousness Movement indelibly influenced black theology. See 515, 518.

530 Buthelezi, Manas. "Toward Indigenous Theology in South Africa. In *Third World Liberation Theologies: A Reader*, ed. by Deane William Ferm, 205-221. Maryknoll, N.Y.: Orbis Books, 1986.
      See 529.

531 Chikane, Frank. *No Life of My Own*. Maryknoll, N.Y.: Orbis Books, 1988.
      Frank Chikane is a hero of the anti-apartheid struggle and a prophetic figure within the South African church. Here, he shares his understanding of the Christian faith and the terrifying suffering this faith has helped him withstand. Repeatedly detained and tortured, under constant surveillance by the Security Police, and recently nearly poisoned to death, Chikane virtuously upholds the prophetic banner of liberation while exemplifying a pastoral dimension of black theology.

532 Cone, James. *Black Theology and Black Power*. New York: Seabury, 1969.

This seminal volume emerged at the dusk of both the Black Power and Civil Rights movements. Yet, one might say that *Black Theology and Black Power* emerged at the dawn of the Black Consciousness Movement. See 515, 518. A classic text in the genre of liberation theology, *Black Theology and Black Power* exemplifies the significance of Segundo's liberation of the hermeneutic circle. See 483. Cone, as Segundo shows, having been suspicious of whites' hermeneutics, examines the meaning of Scripture and tradition through the grid of black experience. He thus arrives at (an)other hermeneutic that undermines, on a certain level, Eurocentric thought. By way of his black hermeneutic, Cone identifies the gospel with black power. European theologians and intellectuals——such as Karl Barth, Paul Tillich, and Albert Camus——are reread in the light (or opacity) of the hardness of the black experience and are "blackenized" in order to facilitate Cone's break from theologies that tacitly legitimize racism.

533 Cone, James. *The Spirituals and the Blues*. New York: Seabury Press, 1972.

Cone's first two books——see 532, 541——had been critiqued by other black North American theologians, who argued that his books were only ostensibly black. Underneath, they asserted, his theology was Eurocentric and thus in the mode of Barth, Tillich, Bultmann and Bonhoeffer. His method was not really derived, they argued, from the exteriority——see 331——of blackness, but from an Eurocentric epistemology in which human existence was radically, and neo-orthodoxly, negated *and* affirmed by God in Christ. *The Spirituals and the Blues* is an example of Cone's early attempt to give more weight to the black experience by way of a religio-cultural analysis of black music.

534 Cone, James. "Black Theology and Black Liberation." In *The Challenge of Black Theology in South Africa*, ed. by Basil Moore, 48-57. Atlanta: John Knox Press, 1973.

As in his *A Black Theology of Liberation*——see 541——Cone explains that a source of black theology is black history. Black history links black theology to Africa; Africa, in turn, provides a point of reference for the expression of black power. According to Cone, black power and the African heritage have been militant expressions that valorize blackness. See 535. For Cone, moreover, the God of black freedom is the biblical God who "spoke by the prophets" and is incarnate among the oppressed, who bear the cross of unmerited suffering.

535 Cone, James. *God of the Oppressed*. New York: Seabury Press, 1975.

Although Cone's work seminally influenced the black theology of South Africa, the continent of Africa played a fairly minor role in his first two books. He tended to employ scholarship that ignored the continuum of African culture in the Americas. For instance, in *Black Theology and Black Power*, Cone claimed that slavery obliterated African culture, though Melville Herskovits had already written the significant *The Myth of The Negro Past* and Du Bois, "On The Faith of the Fathers," and *The Negro Church*. In subsequent texts, however, Cone explored the memory of Africa in slave culture and was thus careful to link black theology to Africa. See 533, 538. In *God of The Oppressed*, Cone deepened his exploration of the African heritage (without diminishing the significance of the Bible and the history of Christian thought for black theology). He analyzed the sociology of knowledge; examined modalities of African-American culture; critiqued Richard Neibuhr's *Christ and Culture*; and exegeted select biblical themes.

536 Cone, James. "A Black American Perspective on the Future of African Theology." *Africa Theological Journal* 7,2 (1978): 9-19.

Cone examines John Mbiti's position that African and black theologies are radically dissimilar. See 406. Cone acknowledges that Mbiti's view has been conditioned by an African context that differs from the black North American context. For Cone, however, common concerns demand that black North American and African theologians confer with one another. According to Cone, the quest for liberation from European and Euro-American domination, and faith in Jesus Christ, should draw Africans and African-Americans together. Cone, moreover, offers a critique of the old guard and thus bears an affinity to the new guard, who agree with him that African theology must serve the poor. See 338. He also recognizes that African theology edifies black theology as to the theological significance of popular culture. See 331.

537 Cone, James. "A Black American Perspective on the Future of African Theology." In *African Theology en Route*, ed. by Kofi Appiah-Kubi and Sergio Torres, 176-188. Maryknoll, N.Y.: Orbis Books, 1979.
>   See 536.

538 Cone, James. "La signification du ciel dans les negro-spirituals." *Concilium* 143 (1979): 77-91.
>   Cone extends his interest in black music by focusing on the eschatological significance of the sky in black spirituals, spirituals that Dr. W.E.B. Du Bois called the "sorrow songs." According to Cone, the sky has symbolized African-Americans slaves' attempt to liberate their minds from *des valeurs établies de la société blanche, rendant les esclaves noirs capables de penser par eux-mêmes et d'agir par eux-mêmes* (p. 85). For Cone, this struggle for liberation is inextricable from a this-worldly faith in the righteousness of God.

539 Cone, James. "What is the Church? A Black Perspective." *Bulletin of African Theology* 5,9 (January-June 1983): 21-34.
>   According to Cone, the church is an eschatological community and its ultimate destiny transcends sociological categories. Ecclesiologies, however, too often eschew a social analysis that would guide Christians in their mandate to uphold the gospel. Such analytical weakness contributes to the church's lack of credibility and indicates that it lives perilously close to a kind of ecclesial Docetism. That is, the church's failure to deal with social crisis suggests that Christ was not a true man, but a spook god with relevance only to a far away, enigmatic spiritual world. Paradigms of the sociology of knowledge indicate that spook god and its other-worldly orientation are signs of the church's sanction of the oppressive order. Indeed, the institutional church——as is indicated in social analysis——is too often part of a hegemonic bloc that must be opposed by the true Church. The true Church shuns the static identification of the gospel with a hegemonic order. The Spirit, argues Cone, directs this eschatological orientation, and requires the Church to serve humankind, and especially the poor and oppressed.

540 Cone, James. *For My People*. Maryknoll, N.Y.: Orbis Books, 1984.
>   Cone reviews the history of black theology, with specific focus on its emergence from the Civil Rights and Black Power movements. As in *My Soul Looks Back*——see 542——Cone casts a critical eye on the black theology he essentially defined. He examines black theology's lack of social analysis in its early years, as well as its insensitivity to the oppression of black women. Particularly pertinent for the study of African theology is his discussion of Third World theologians. Here, he focuses on EATWOT, an organization to which he belongs. See 089, 344, 352, 438. Cone's discussion of EATWOT's theological method is particularly clear and useful.

541 Cone, James. *A Black Theology of Liberation*. Rev. ed. Maryknoll, N.Y.: Orbis Books, 1985.

A revised edition of his second book: here Cone identifies black history and experience, and Scripture and tradition as cardinal sources of black theology. For Cone, those sources enable a reinterpretation of select, but interrelated, aspects of Christian doctrine. Thus Cone offers a systematic theology that is defined by the particularity of black consciousness. His doctrine of God, christology, and eschatology embody a black perspective, the content of which is biblically based, in dialogue with the history of Christian thought, and vociferously opposed to theologies that fail to inquire into the problem of human oppression.

542   Cone, James. *My Soul Looks Back.* Nashville: Abingdon Press, 1982. Reprint. Maryknoll, N.Y.: Orbis Books, 1986.

In autobiographical style, Cone casts a critical eye on the development of black theology. He notes how black theology lacked an analysis of political economy in the United States, and thus failed to examine the material base of white supremacy. Cone also discusses black theologians' failure to recognize the correspondence between white supremacy and black males' mistreatment of black women. Cone concludes that black theology must be globalized by Third World theologians. See 540.

543   Cone, James. *Speaking the Truth.* Grand Rapids: Wm.B. Eerdmans, 1986.

What is pertinent here is Cone's revelation of his impressions of the trip he made to South Africa. His exposure to the injustice of apartheid deepened his position that liberation *is* the gospel and not epiphenomenal to the gospel. His trip also heightened his intolerance for "professional theologians and church leaders (black and white) who view the matter otherwise" (p. 168).

544   Cone, James. *Malcolm and Martin and America: A Dream or a Nightmare?* Maryknoll, N.Y.: Orbis Books, 1991.

Cone comes full circle here, so to speak: he returns to the legacies of the men who embodied the essences of the Black Power and Civil Rights movements, both of which gave impetus to his ground-breaking *Black Theology and Black Power.* See 532. He concludes, in part, that the legacies of both men are invaluable to anyone who would put African-American experience in historical perspective. What is more, in examining the two men, Cone exemplifies the critical importance of social analysis in black theology.

545   Crawford, Robert G. "Black Liberation Theology in South Africa and Liberation Theology in Latin America." *The Expository Times* 101,11 (August 1990): 329-334.

According to Crawford, black theology is distinguished by two phases: (1) that defined by Buthelezi, Moore, and Boesak; and (2) that defined by theologians such as Mosala, Mofokeng, and Tlhagale. See 517-520; 527-530, 565-568. Unlike Latin American theology, "phase one theology" lacks a social analysis defined in socialist terms. "Phase two theology," however, valorizes social analysis, and is thus not unlike Latin American theology. (Crawford posits that the Latin Americans are more advanced than the Africans in matters related to the *praxis* of liberation. His view here appears specious.) Crawford argues wrongly that black theology, now in its second phase, favors the "non-racialism" of the United Democratic Front (UDF). He thus forsakes the black nationalism of the Azanian People's Organization (AZAPO)——progeny of the Black Consciousness Movement. It would appear, then, that Crawford believes that black theology——like Latin American theology——sublates race to matters of political economy. Yet, he makes the outrageous claim that black theology——like its North American counterpart——is essentially racist since it excludes Afrikaners, another "oppressed group." Here, he reifies oppression to such an extent that one loses sight of the fact that the Afrikaners are one of the most excessively racist people in the world. He also condemns black theology——as well as Latin American theology——for its (alleged) propensity to violence. He does not examine the violence of the South African government, or that of the Latin American matrix.

546 Dlamini, Timothy. "The Role Swaziland Churches Should Play in the Liberation of South Africa." *Journal of Black Theology in South Africa* 2,1 (May 1988): 43-47.

Dlamini explains that the words "Swaziland Churches" signify "three existing Christian Church Organizations:...the Swaziland Conference of Churches, the League of Swazi Churches, and the Council of Swaziland Churches." He goes on to explain that the *League* of Swazi Churches constitutes independent churches, that have emerged in opposition to socioeconomic and cultural alienation. The Swaziland *Conference* of Churches constitutes the historical churches, which he defines as "Conservative Evangelical Churches." The *Council* of Swaziland Churches is comprised of historical churches more liberal than the evangelical churches, including Catholics, Anglicans, and Lutherans. According to Dlamini, the totality of the Swaziland churches should, as an ecumenical body, facilitate the "liberation of South Africa." One way to do this, he argues, would be for Swaziland clergy to make a preferential option for the poor in order to "set a good example to clergy in South Africa, who have turned out to be ivory towers and to live in ecclesiastical cocoons" (p. 46).

547 Dwane, S. "The Significance of the Homoousios in Patristic Thinking and in Our Time." *Journal of Black Theology in South Africa* 2,1 (May 1988): 53-59.

Dwane examines the peculiar subordinationism and monarchianism of the arch-heretic, Arius. Arius's view that the logos was a creature——neither truly God nor truly human——threatened the developing soteriology of the early church. Had Arius won at Nicaea, "perichoretic" doctrines of the Trinity and the idiom, "hypostatic union," would have had little historical precedent. Dwane argues that the *homoousion*, "established" at Nicaea and clarified further at Constantinople and Chalcedon, defines Christ as an eternal Being, who is fully and truly as much God as the font of the Godhead, the Father. The significance of the *homoousion* today, argues Dwane, is the legacy of oxymoron it embodies. If one is to appreciate that Christ is both God and human, he/she must forego static dualism for the sake of a dynamic union in which humanity realizes itself in its antithesis (God). What is most relevant here is that the righteousness of God is revealed in the pathetic brokenness of Jesus, tortured on the cross. Indeed, God himself——the incarnate Son *homoousious* with the Father and in hypostatic union with the man Jesus——"knows what it is to suffer pain, anguish, and rejection" (p. 59). For Dwane, then, the *homoousion* today means that God is on the side of the oppressed.

548 Goba, Bonganjalo. "Corporate Personality: Ancient Israel and Africa." *The Challenge of Black Theology in South Africa*, ed. by Basil Moore, 18-28. Atlanta: John Knox Press, 1973.

Goba examines the analogy between Nguni traditional people——i.e., Zulu, !Xhosa, Swazi, Ndebele——and the Hebrews of the Old Testament. He argues that biblical culture corresponds to the cultures of the Nguni. See 294. According to Goba, the Israelites saw themselves as a corporate personality——a unit, an organism, a society——in which the individual was both subordinate to and the metonym of the group. Corporate personality, in addition, signified the macrocosm, i.e., the Two Kingdoms, as well as the microcosm, i.e., the family. Family relationships were reckoned patriarchically and the father figure was the dominate symbol of the nation's personality. Similarly, one finds African people for whom the term "corporate personality" is pertinent. Here, one should see "corporate personality" in temporal terms. Drawing on the work of Mbiti——see 200——Goba implies that African time flows counterclockwise——simultaneously and dynamically, backward and forward.   The living and their ancestors converge in a spiralling circle——they meet at the thresholds of death and rebirth.   Both the ancestor and the infant, then, concentrate the meaning of corporate personality because they are the foundation and posterity of the race.   According to Goba, both the Old Testament and Nguni senses of corporate personality are indispensable for a theology that is black, by virtue of its Africanity, and Christian by virtue of its biblical base.   These African and biblical values signify that corporateness entails an anti-capitalistic ethic.   For Goba, this ethic received its highest and inimitable expression in Christ.

549   Goba, Bonganjalo.   "Toward a Quest for Christian Identify: A Third World Perspective." *Journal of Black Theology in South Africa* 2,2 (November 1980): 31-36.
      Goba argues that Third World Christians signify a liberating faith only if they have undertaken the necessary task of de-europeanization. See 440. Setting his remarks in the context of EATWOT——see 540——Goba implies that de-europeanization demands revisions of a hermeneutic circle "that gives clear direction or inspires action." See 483. In Africa, this hermeneutic circle involves social and religio-cultural analyses that are integral to black and African theologies. On the one hand, new guard theology reveals the indispensability of critical study of acculturation and inculturation——both of which heighten exegetical suspicion.   On the other hand, black theology slices the laminated socioeconomic context, in order to uncover layers of political deformities inimical to the gospel.   The two theologies, held together in critical reflection, edify one engaged in liberating praxis. For Goba: "This praxis-centered theological approach which arises out of our commitment redefines who we are in the struggle and at the same time is based on our faith" (p. 36).

550   Goba, Bonganjalo.   "The Black Consciousness Movement: Its Impact on Black Theology." In *The Unquestionable Right to Be Free: Black Theology from South Africa*, ed. by Itumeleng J. Mosala and Buti Tlhagale, 57-70. Maryknoll, N.Y.: Orbis Books, 1986.
      For Goba, black theology has emerged from the black struggle and reflects the identity of the black community. Although Goba valorizes Black Consciousness in its relation to black theology, both modes of reflection are static for him if unaccompanied by a revolutionary activism.   In drawing out the implications of that praxis, Goba refers to Fanon. See 034-035. Fanon places the following before the black theologian: (1) "the rural base of the revolution; (2) the nationalistic character of the revolution; and (3) the fundamental problem of violence in revolutionary process." According to Goba, each of Fanon's points challenges the theologian to test the relevance of black theology at the grassroots——what Cabral calls the substratum of national culture. See 023-025.

551   Goba, Bonganjalo.   "A Theological Tribute to Archbishop Tutu." In *Hammering Swords into Plowshares: Essays in Honor of Archbishop Mpilo Desmond Tutu*, ed. by Buti Tlhagale and Itumeleng Mosala, 19-22. Grand Rapids: Wm.B. Eerdmans; Trenton: Africa World Press, 1987.
      Goba expresses his profound appreciation for the critical ministry of Bishop Tutu, a pillar of the anti-apartheid struggle and pioneer in the construction of black South African theology.   According to Goba, Bishop Tutu helped to lay a indispensable Pan-African epistemology in his seminal "Black Theology and African Theology: Soulmates or Antagonists?" See 602. Here Tutu explains that the distinction is a bit specious as black South African theology is an *African* theology.

552 Kretzschmar, Louise. *The Voice of Black Theology in South Africa.* Johannesburg: Raven Press, 1986.

A decent introduction to the "Freedom charter wing of black South African theology." Kretzschmar, a white South African, surveys the history and major themes of black South African theology in the ANC vein. A major flaw of the text is Kretzschmar's neglect of the AZAPO wing of black theology. See 565-568, 572-578.

553 Kunnie, Julian. "Christianity, Black Theology and Liberation Faith." In *The Unquestionable Right to Be Free: Black Theology from South Africa*, ed. by Itumeleng J. Mosala and Buti Tlhagale, 153-167. Maryknoll, N.Y.: Orbis Books, 1986.

Kunnie argues that the most insidious ramification of apartheid is that blacks have internalized white supremacist values. Black Consciousness, however, raises the African's self-esteem and is thus indispensable for a revolutionary faith. The union of the two——without confusion——gifts blacks, argues Kunnie, with "the sense of unwavering and fearless determination to extirpate the evil powers besetting [their] nation" (p. 163). Only this resolve, drawn from the structures of Africanity and Christian faith, is powerful and whole enough to heal black minds——such that they overcome their fear of death and confront apartheid.

554 Lamola, J.M. "Towards a Black Church: A Historical Investigation of the African Independent Churches as a Model." *Journal of Black Theology in South Africa* 2,1 (May 1988): 5-14.

According to Lamola, only the African Independent Churches (AIC) have attempted to establish "a Black Church." See 046, 258. The AIC emerged from blacks' refusal to accept the alienating Christianity of the white settlers. What is more: "The AIC Movement is a symbol of African religious boldness and novel theological creativity, a step toward the construction of an authentic black religion for Africa of the twentieth century" (p. 5). For Lamola, the independent churches, despite the fact that they contain central elements for black theology, have reactionary tendencies. That is, they have not "developed liberatory leadership and administrative structures" (p. 6). Neither, asserts Lamola, have these churches overcome a certain tribalism. To that extent, the independent churches have not reached their potential. Finally, Lamola distinguishes the Ethiopian churches from the Zionist. See 472. The Ethiopian churches have more continuity with the historic churches than do the Zionist churches; and the Ethiopians are more formally related than the Zionists to the more secular Pan-African movement (that has itself been called "Ethiopianism"). Both churches, however, as examples of "independency," constitute a fertile field——the plowing of which will lead to "a revolutionary idiom of our time and into projects for the transformation of black life in oppressive South Africa" (p. 13).

555 Lediga, S.P. "A Relevant Theology for Africa: A Critical Evaluation of Previous Attempts." In *Relevant Theology for Africa*, ed. by Hans-Jurgen Becken, 25-33. Durban: Lutheran Publishing House, 1973.

Lediga argues that theology reflects the values and struggles of *a* people. In South Africa, theology embodies values that accentuate the distinction between blacks and whites. Calling to mind the thesis of Imasogie——see 364——Lediga argues that the worldview of the black African is significantly different from the worldview of the white Westerner. The African has more respect for the numinous than the Westerner; and it follows, then, that African traditional religion is assimilated by Christian theology in Africa, but is "unclean" in Europe. So one finds in Africa certain ecclesial emphases uncommon in Europe——namely those embodied in the African independent churches. According to Lediga, African Christianity——as found in the independent churches——is a conduit to healing and wholeness, and must be appreciated in terms of a traditional Bantu structure. While Lediga argues that the independent churches exemplify the power of acculturation in Africa, he also notes the necessity of inculturation in his affirmation of the tautological relation of Christian identity to the Trinity. To this extent he is unlike Setiloane, who argues that Christian dogma is unequipped to render the sense in which non-Christian Africans have appreciated the aseity of God. See 487-489.

556 Mabona, Mongameli. "Black People and White Worship." In *The Challenge of Black Theology in South Africa*, ed. by Basil Moore, 104-108. Atlanta: John Knox Press, 1973.

According to Mabona, the Christian, despite the post-modern secularism that equates Christianity with illusion, must assert that Christian faith is actual, even though it is transhistorical. That faith is transhistorical does not mean, for Mabona, that it is ahistorical. Indeed, faith, he argues, eschews tendencies to be "misled by mystifying symbols or shimmering expectations" (p. 108). According to Mabona, then, black Christians must challenge apartheid in terms of Black Consciousness.

557 Maimela, Simon S. "The Implications for Theology of the Contemporary South African Understanding of War and Peace." *Africa Theological Journal* 14,3 (1985): 194-201.

For Maimela, the "just war" paradigm, traceable to Augustine, does not apply to South Africa. This just war theory legitimizes a state's right to self-defense; but the Pretoria regime has no such right. According to Maimela, "peacemaking and justice," not secular authority, should determine theological reflection on a government's involvement in war——and Christ is the model of such reflection.

558 Maimela, Simon S. "Current Themes and Emphases in Black Theology." In *The Unquestionable Right to Be Free: Black Theology from South Africa*, ed. by Itumeleng J. Mosala and Buti Tlhagale, 101-112. Maryknoll, N.Y.: Orbis Books, 1986.

Maimela asserts that black theology involves an appreciation of both God's transcendent freedom and the implications of that freedom in regard to apartheid. He thus assumes a correspondence between one's option for the black oppressed and God's own option for the poor. In doing so, Maimela argues that black theology valorizes the "this-worldly" dimensions of salvation. Integral to black theology is a study of socioeconomic contradictions that challenge Christian praxis. Christian praxis is the pursuit of justice——a fruit of justification and sanctification. See 561. Indeed, black theology, in Maimela's view, is a mode of the pneumatic, daily struggle against "Old Adam"——namely apartheid. In sum, black theology, in its epistemological break from "apartheid theology," overcomes the stasis of sin in a dynamic movement toward the eschaton.

559 Maimela, Simon S. "Archbishop Desmond Tutu——A Revolutionary Political Priest or Man of Peace?" In *Hammering Swords into Ploughshares: Essays in Honor of Archbishop Mpilo Desmond Tutu*, ed. by Buti Tlhagale and Itumeleng Mosala, 41-60. Grand Rapids, Michigan: Wm.B. Eerdmans; Trenton: Africa World Press, 1987.

Maimela praises Bishop Tutu for his virtuous and prophetic leadership in the anti-apartheid struggle. See 551. According to Maimela, Tutu exemplifies that a true priest must be political in contexts of vulgar injustice. As these contexts——such as the one dominated by white South Africans——are incapable of reform, the true priest is necessarily revolutionary. For Maimela, then, Bishop Tutu is undoubtedly a revolutionary political priest. Tutu's position, however, is incomprehensible apart from his essential vocation as a man of peace. His political values——epiphenomenal to his Christian faith——serve God's Spirit, who moves Tutu's irenic heart to embrace a revolutionary praxis of peace.

560 Maimela, Simon S. "Theological Dilemmas and Options for the Black Church." *Journal of Black Theology in South Africa* 2,1 (May 1988): 15-25.

Maimela begins his essay with a reflection on an EATWOT conference——see 438——he attended in 1987. The conference, for Maimela, revealed that Africans, despite a rich religious heritage, "have been turned into beggars in the realm of religion" (p. 15). Yet, according to Maimela, Africa has played an indispensable role in the development of both Christianity and Judaism, and should once again assume a position of authority in the current affairs of both. In Africa, however, despite the fact that the church is made up mostly of blacks, "the leadership is largely in White hands." According to Maimela: "The Black church is thus a colonized and dominated church theologically and culturally because it has inherited all the theological slogans and expressions from our White mentors" (p. 16). This Eurocentric flaw is found in black theology, argues Maimela, and is the greatest sign of the impoverished condition of black Christians. Such *pauvreté*——see 428, 437, 440——has both cultural and economic implications. Uncritically, the black church holds to bourgeois aspirations that can only reproduce black alienation from the path of self-definition and independence. To break from that condition, one must blackenize notions of sin and salvation, argues Maimela. Far more edifying than Lutheran and Reformed conceptions of sin and salvation in that regard are those related to African traditional religion. Here, African traditional religion would redefine orthodox doctrine. Here, sin and salvation are appreciated in terms of a traditional focus on communal democracy, which edifies one in regard to the quest for peace *and* justice. "In the light of this anthropology"——see 529—— explains Maimela, "sin and evil in the African context are thought to consist in the human attempt to destroy, to diminish and to threaten the life of one's fellows" (pp. 21-22). The quickest route, then, to a theology of justice, is the upward path of ancestral culture. A *black* theology, then, will necessarily be one in which pride of place is given to African culture as the hermeneutic center of liberating praxis. See 288.

561 Maimela, Simon S. "Faith that does Justice." *Journal of Black Theology in South Africa* 3,1 (May 1989): 1-14.

Maimela discusses Luther's definition of solafidianism and assesses its relevance for South Africa. He argues that "justification by faith alone" is of tremendous value to Christians who face apartheid. Maimela, himself a Lutheran pastor, argues that Luther's search for a gracious God is not unlike the searches of South Africans also saddled by ecclesial structures whose laws are oppressive, alienating, blasphemous. According to Maimela, Luther's great insight——gleaned from the writings of Paul and Augustine——"[is] that resources to life do not reside in human hands...rather access to life depends on the merciful God who gives it to those who dare to believe in God, the Savior" (p. 5). In the context of apartheid, Luther's dictum, *sola fide,* helps the oppressed to recognize that true authority rests in Christ, not white supremacists. Indeed, white supremacy is a contradiction of the faith that God is no respecter of persons. All are sinners and worthy only because Christ has imputed God's (alien) righteousness to them. Such justification, by faith alone, carries the imperative for "proper righteousness." The justified——sanctified with God's Spirit——*must* forsake the flesh of apartheid and act ethically according to the gospel.

562 Maimela, Simon S. *Proclaim Freedom to my People: Essays on Religion and Politics*. Braamfontein: Skotaville, 1989.

Maimela examines the contradictions of the South African churches, the most egregious of which are typified in terms of "the problem of the color line" (Du Bois). This problem makes social analysis critical, for such analysis uncovers the hypocrisy of ecclesial institutions that thrive in the necrophilic values inimical to Jesus Christ. For Maimela, black theology (and the social analysis integral to it) is indispensable if new life is be raised from the oppressive context of South Africa. Black theology exposes the contradictions inimical to Christian faith and thus edifies the South African Church regarding the meaning of God-in-Christ: the triune God is no respecter of persons, but is especially attuned to the distress of the black oppressed.

563   Makhathini, D.D.L. "Black Theology (I)." In *Towards a Relevant Theology for Africa*, ed. by Hans-Jurgen Becken, 8-13. Durban: Lutheran Publishing House, 1973.

According to Makhathini——a lecturer of Old Testament and Prorector at the Lutheran Theological Seminary——a Christian has at least three cardinal virtues. (1) A Christian is wise to the extent that he/she takes history seriously; and history reveals that human beings are first and foremost sinful creatures. So, a Christian is a *sagacious realist*, who accepts the pain that comes to him/her as a result of a commitment to justice in an unjust world. (2) Christians are prudent because they refuse to be pigeonholed; prophetic stances a Christian takes will always appear problematic to the provincial. Christians are thus *judiciously inconsistent*. (3) Christians, he writes, are courageous by virtue of a radicalism that confronts the status quo prophetically. For Makhathini, those three virtues are embodied in black theology.

564   Makhathini, D.D.L. "Black Theology (II)." In *Towards a Relevant Theology for Africa*, ed. by Hans-Jurgen Becken, 14-17. Durban: Lutheran Publishing House, 1973.

Here the author continues his discussion of black theology, but with a focus on hermeneutics. Makhathini, in a way relevant to Segundo's definition of the hermeneutic circle——see 483——advises black theologians to reread the gospel in terms of the edifying suspicions derived from black experience. While Makhathini's work here shows that black South African theologians were exploring hermeneutical problems in the early seventies, one finds a more edifying paradigm of the hermeneutic circle in the work of Jerry Mosala. See 572-578.

565   Mofokeng, Takatso. *The Crucified among the CrossBearers: Towards a Black Christology*. Kampuen: J.H. Kok, 1983.

Mofokeng examines the relations between black theology and the Black Consciousness Movement (BCM). He explains that Black Consciousness facilitated a critique of the superstructures of apartheid——a critique that gave impetus to the emergence of black theology. Here, black theology is defined in terms of a christology that valorizes the incarnation as the event whereby God is "inculturated" on the side of the oppressed. God's humanity is further interpreted through a liberation of the *theologia crucis*——such that one attains a heightened awareness of the correspondence between black suffering and the cross. Mofokeng employs Jon Sobrino's christology as a foil for his own christology. Although Sobrino's from-below-approach is critical in the praxis of liberation, Mofokeng concludes that crucifixion is far too sublated to resurrection in Sobrino's work. For Mofokeng, "The crossbearers of our time have a right to resurrection in their lifetime." Far more useful for Mofokeng is Karl Barth's high christology, because it enables discovery of the "eternal now" of the resurrection. In the resurrection of the Royal Man, the "nothingness" of sinful humanity——which is something and not nothing——is negated. True liberation is thus granted to a fallen, but saved, humanity. The Christ-event, then, argues Mofokeng, is the *structure* of all that is true and virtuous in liberation struggles everywhere. See 563. Indeed, the integrity of the black struggle against apartheid is that it is essentially God's own movement in history. According to Mofokeng: "Anthropologically, in the entire incarnation unto death, or the entire history of the cross of the son of God, God creates and empowers the poor and the weak to become active subjects of their own history" (p. 258).

566 Mofokeng, Takatso. "The Evolution of the Black Struggle and the Role of Black Theology." In *The Unquestionable Right to Be Free: Black Theology from South Africa*, ed. by Itumeleng J. Mosala and Buti Tlhagale, 113-128. Maryknoll, N.Y.: Orbis Books, 1986.

For Mofokeng, the Black Consciousness Movement (BCM), more so than any other movement, exemplifies "the epistemological break" from the Eurocentric mores of the oppressor. See 013-015, 518, 519. Black theology, a fruit of the BCM, is, he argues, the most vital Christian expression in the history of black resistance. In black theology, the relation between Black Consciousness and Scripture produces edifying hermeneutics to the extent that they advance the liberation struggle of the black oppressed. For Mofokeng, moreover, the liberation struggle is a christological event. Christ, he asserts, "is the event of creation of the black struggling community as a comprehensive subject" (p. 126). Here, blackness corresponds to God's true humanity, revealed still in the torn flesh of unmerited crucifixion. See 565.

567 Mofokeng, Takatso. "Black Christians, the Bible and Liberation." *Journal of Black Theology in South Africa* 2,1 (May 1988): 34-42.

The Bible, writes Mofokeng, symbolizes God's redemptive way in history; yet the Bible also signifies man's oppressive way in history. That is, the Bible, for many Africans, has been a metaphor of alienation rather than salvation. In the tragedy of the coming of the white man to Africa, the Bible has been exchanged for black people's land. Indeed, the Bible itself reflects an internal contradiction: one can find verses that signify liberation or legitimate oppression. See 572-578. Mofokeng argues that the Bible is to be reread in the light of its liberating messages, which are based on the incarnation, as explicated by the methodology of the underside.

568 Mofokeng, Takatso. "Black Theological Perspectives, Past and Present." In *We Are One Voice: Black Theology in the USA and South Africa*, ed. by Simon Maimela and Dwight Hopkins, 105-126. Skotaville Publishers, 1989.

Mofokeng discusses sources and methodological issues integral to black theology. These include the independent churches, African traditional religion, the Black Consciousness Movement, as well as the "epistemological privilege of the poor." Mofokeng gives pride of place to the PAC values that complement the nationalism of the black proletariat. See 039. Here, one——given the myopia of "prolet-aryanism"—— notes that Marxism, while of heuristic value, must be de-europeanized and thus africanized. For Mofokeng, the anti-apartheid struggle is against racist capitalism and for the nationhood of the black oppressed. This struggle is, for him, consistent with the reign of Christ.

569 Moila, M. "The Role of Christ in Jon Sobrino's Liberation Theology: Its Significance for Black Theology in South Africa." *Journal of Black Theology in South Africa* 3,1 (May 1989): 15-22.

Moila asserts that Sobrino's christology is yet another example of the distinction between the one Christ and the many christologies. See 565. Christ, that is, in Sobrino's christology, has a transhistorical (eschatological) significance——the meanings of which are conditioned by diverse historical contexts. According to Moila, moreover, Sobrino's christology, as opposed to many others, "is more appropriate for [the] situation in South Africa and has enormous implications for Black Theology" (p. 15). This is because his is a liberation christology. Sobrino argues that God's true humanity makes appreciation of the historical Jesus imperative. The historical Jesus, the "visibility" of God's incarnation, reveals the correctness of the liberationist's claim that God is on the side of the oppressed. As Moila explains, "Jesus for [Sobrino] is the way to liberation and because of this he says liberation theology is concentrated in christology....Christology begins "from below rather than from above" (p. 19). For Moila, there is a profound and radical correspondence between the one Christ and the many historic contexts of the poor, who correspond to the historicity of the incarnation. Moila concludes that Sobrino's "Christology is significant for Black Theology in that it demands that faith be...concrete and effective and...transmit its efficiency to the oppressed" (p. 22).

570 Moore, Basil. "What is Black Theology?" In *The Challenge of Black Theology in South Africa*, ed. by Basil Moore, 1-10. Atlanta: John Knox Press, 1973.

Moore asserts that the term black theology was coined in the United States and has been seminally influenced by the work of James Cone. See 532-542. Still, the content of the theology in South Africa has little to do with the United States. Black South African theology has to do with apartheid——a white supremacy distinct from that found in the United States. Moore reveals that black South African theology emerged in opposition to the status quo that sought over time to alienate the middleclass from the masses in order to entrench apartheid. According to Moore this technique was employed by liberals who lost ground in the 1970s due to the emergence of the Black Consciousness Movement. Black theology, a product of Black Consciousness is, in part, the rejection of "the false, bourgeois multi-racialism." Consequently, black theology is the outcome of an epistemological break with theological values that legitimize the status quo.

571 Mosala, Bernadette. "Black Theology and the Struggle of the Black Woman in Southern Africa." In *The Unquestionable Right to Be Free: Black Theology from South Africa*, ed. by Itumeleng J. Mosala and Buti Tlhagale, 129-134. Maryknoll, N.Y.: Orbis Books, 1986.

Bernadette Mosala confronts the fact that liberation has been defined in male terms, despite the glaring reality of the oppression of women. She wonders whether men are equipped to do justice to black women's oppression, and concludes that women themselves must take responsibility for a feminist discourse in theology.

572 Mosala, Itumeleng J. "The Biblical God from the Perspective of the Poor." In *God and Global Justice: Religion & Poverty in an Unequal World*, ed. by Frederick Ferré and Rita H. Martaragnon, 160-168. New York: Paragon House, 1985.

Mosala explores his contention that theology reflects the social conditions of the theologian. The *ambi*valence this implies regarding the "haves and the have-nots" implies as well the distinct "Gods" of the rich and the poor. "In point of fact," writes Mosala, "the two Gods stand in antithetical relationship to each other, reflecting the struggles between the rich and poor" (p. 160). Poverty, explains Mosala, is a condition that the dominant group perpetuates as totally as it can; and such totalization is carried out through a certain hegemonic use of the Bible. The oppressed, however, must read the Bible and do theology by way of new hermeneutics, the designs and methods of which are related to liberation. For the God of the poor, Mosala asserts, cannot "be suppressed in the biblical texts." Still, "this is not necessarily the dominant God of the Bible" (p. 166). Mosala's point is that the oppressed must do exegesis in such a way that the Bible itself becomes a plane of struggle between the rich and the poor. Within the context of black South Africa, "the biblical God [is understood] in such a way that God is the supreme ancestor, while Christ is the *Nyanja* (Diviner)." See 381. "The metaphysical God and Christ of missionary theology would not do since they are extrahistorical" (p. 166). Here,

Mosala indicates that culture is fundamental to the new hermeneutics of liberation, bringing to mind a negation of what Mveng calls *pauvreté anthropologique*. See 437, 438.

573 Mosala, Itumeleng J. " The Relevance of African Traditional Religions and Their Challenge to Black Theology." In *The Unquestionable Right to Be Free: Black Theology from South Africa*, ed. by Itumeleng J. Mosala and Buti Tlhagale, 91-100. Maryknoll, N.Y.: Orbis Books, 1986.

Mosala argues that African traditional religions reveal the historic contradictions of pre-colonial societies. To the extent traditional religions mirror African realities, argues Mosala, they also provide the essential tools for political resistance and systemic change. According to Mosala, African traditional religions today indicate the point where Europeans truncated Africans' autochthonous development. As domination always involves alienation of the oppressed from their culture, the struggle for liberation must valorize autochthonous culture in order to effect de-europeanization. Concomitantly, the struggle to discover the upward path of African culture requires a *re-Africanization* (Cabral). See 023-025. For Mosala, African traditional religions constitute the cultural essences which authenticate black and African theologies as praxes that reject the totalizing path of Europe.

574 Mosala, Itumeleng J. "The Use of The Bible in Black Theology." In *The Unquestionable Right to Be Free: Black Theology from South Africa*, ed. by Itumeleng J. Mosala and Buti Tlhagale, 175-199. Maryknoll, N.Y.: Orbis Books, 1986.

That the black theologies of South Africa and the United States have been captive to alienating hermeneutics is the central argument of Mosala's edifying work. See 572, 578. Here again he puts forward his central argument, making the convincing case that black theology has been crippled by an epistemological contradiction. Black theologians have taken a polemic stand against white bourgeois theology only to use a principle integral to that theology. "Black theologians," writes Mosala, "condemn White people's view of God and Jesus Christ as apolitical and above ideologies on the one hand, but maintain a view of scripture as an absolute, non-ideological Word of God which can be made ideological by being applied to the situation of oppression" (pp. 177-178). Mosala, however, breaks from that cul-de-sac by way of a new hermeneutic that he produces from an exegesis of Micah. Thus he probes polysemous Scripture and excavates biblical valences relevant to the material conditions of the black oppressed. "This means," Mosala explains, "that not only is the Bible a product and a record of class struggles, but it is also a site of similar struggles acted out by the oppressors and oppressed, exploiters and exploited of our society even as they read the Bible" (p. 196-197).

575 Mosala, Itumeleng J. "Ethics of the Economic Principles: Church and Secular Investments." In *Hammering Swords into Plowshares: Essays in Honor of Archbishop Mpilo Desmond Tutu*, ed. by Buti Tlhagale and Itumeleng Mosala, 119-129. Grand Rapids: Wm. B. Eerdmans; Trenton: Africa World Press, 1987.

Mosala deepens his analysis of the material conditions that "thingify" the black oppressed of South Africa and elucidates further his hermeneutical approach to the Bible. Here, Mosala examines the pre-colonial cultures of African people and valorizes their essential humaneness. Such cultures empower black hermeneutics of suspicion. See 573. He writes: "It is [that traditional "Bantu"] economic *morality* which Black Theology wants to base itself upon in its struggle for a new South Africa" (p. 123).

576 Mosala, Itumeleng J. "The Implications of the Text of Esther for African Women's Struggle for Liberation." *Journal of Black Theology in South Africa* 2,2 (November 1988): 3-9.

Mosala distinguishes liberation theology from a theology of liberation. Liberation theology, he argues, is Latin American; the theology of liberation signifies movements of other Third World people, who are also struggling to liberate themselves from imperialism. Mosala argues that the confusion of "liberation" with "of liberation" may lead one to acquiesce in the hegemonic strivings attributed to Latin American theology. See 438. According to Mosala, to lump Third World theology under the umbrella, "liberation theology," is to give pride of place to Latin America. According to Mosala, "The mistake is made mostly, though by no means exclusively, by white radical people who identify culturally more with the European descendants of Latin America than with Third World people" (p. 3). Mosala then goes on and discusses a rereading of Esther, which is emergent from black women's struggles. "Not only," he writes, "will this hermeneutics refuse to submit to the chains imposed on it by the biblical exegetes of apartheid or those of the liberal humanist tradition including its black and liberation theology versions, but it will contend against the 'regimes of truth' of these traditions as they manifest themselves in the text of the Bible itself" (p. 5). Here exegetical suspicion bears fruit in: (1) the assertion that Esther is a foil for sexist ends; (2) the conclusion that Esther betrays women's struggle in valorizing "a national struggle." Mosala ends with the iconoclastic refrain of his scholarship: "...oppressed communities must liberate the Bible so that the Bible can liberate them. An oppressed Bible oppresses and a liberated Bible liberates" (p. 9).

577 Mosala, Itumeleng J. "Prospects for the Future and Building of Alliances." In *We Are One Voice: Black Theology in the USA and South Africa*, ed. by Simon Maimela and Dwight Hopkins, 139-149. Braamfontein: Skotaville Publishers, 1989.

Mosala explores the relationship between the black theologies of South African and the Unites States. Once again, he puts forward his imperative for critical hermeneutics of the working class. Focusing on the South African context, he concludes his essay with a question that reveals his commitment to hermeneutics of suspicion: "Now the question is: black people have chosen to use the Bible and Christianity to get the land back; but can they get the land back and keep the Bible and Christianity?" (See p. 148.)

578 Mosala, Itumeleng J. *Biblical Hermeneutics and Black Theology in South Africa*. Grand Rapids: Wm. B. Eerdmans, 1989.

See discussion in Chapter four of this bibliography; and 572-577.

579 Motlhabi, Mokgethi. "Black Theology and Authority." *The Challenge of Black Theology in South Africa*, ed. by Basil Moore, 119-129. Atlanta: John Knox Press, 1973.

White supremacy, argues Motlhabi, is, in large measure, a diabolical force in South Africa because its power is exerted in the subliminal realm of myth. Here, the cruel greed of the white settlers is dissimulated in myths of black inferiority; whites propagate a hegemonic ideology from which they profit as they pauperize blacks. "This," asserts Motlhabi, "is authoritarianism" (p. 121). For Motlhabi, such fascistic authority is de-mythologized in the valorization of traditional culture. This culture, he claims, has much to teach black theology. See 573. Here, Motlhabi is reminiscent of Cabral. See 023-024. That is, the popular culture of the oppressed yields the alternative values conducive to the liberation of black consciousness. See 575. For Motlhabi, those values are indispensable for a *black* theology that is as Christian as it is African and as African as it is Christian.

580 Motlhabi, Mokgethi. "Black Theology: A Personal View." In *The Challenge of Black Theology in South Africa*, ed. by Basil Moore, 74-80. Atlanta: John Knox Press, 1973.

According to Motlhabi, the true Church lives its faith in the world through a praxis that seeks justice and peace. Like Pityana——see 591——Motlhabi argues that black theology is the theology of the true Church in South Africa. Black theology, through the particularity of Black Consciousness, reiterates the biblical claim that God is no respecter of persons. Black theology also indicates the contemporary implications of the view that God is historically——as in *heilsgeschichte*——on the side of those who suffer. *A fortiori*, black theology witnesses to the inclusivity of the true Church. While its transhistorical destiny is significant for Motlhabi, an exclusive focus on the eschaton would truncate an appreciation of Christian redemption. The commitment to praxis, however, brings to light the fullness of the true Church's eschatological vision of the already *and* the not yet.

581 Motlhabi, Mokgethi. "The Historical Origins of Black Theology." In *The Unquestionable Right to Be Free: Black Theology from South Africa*, ed. by Itumeleng J. Mosala and Buti Tlhagale, 37-56. Maryknoll, N.Y.: Orbis Books, 1986.

Motlhabi highlights the Pan-African dimension of black theology. For Motlhabi, black theology, in its broad connotation, is a transatlantic and transcontextual discourse pertinent to the United States and South Africa. Here the trajectories of the Black Power and Civil Rights movements and the Black Consciousness Movement form a crossroads, the center of which is the common ground of "Pan-Africa" (Du Bois). Indeed, a seminal source of black theology in South Africa is the work of James Cone. See 532-544. Other sources Motlhabi identifies are the African independent churches and African traditional religion. Motlhabi concludes his essay with the assertion that black South African theology has been concerned with "prolegomena." Now, he argues, is the time to "get on with it," so to speak, and *do* black theology.

582 Mpunzi, Ananias. "Black Theology as Liberation Theology." *The Challenge of Black Theology in South Africa*, ed. by Basil Moore, 130-140. Atlanta: John Knox Press, 1973.

The challenge of black theology, asserts Mpunzi, is to define its vision of a humane society, the structure of which would avoid both elitism and the thingification of the many. As important to Mpunzi as structure is attitude——an internal orientation that constitutes the individual's commitment to a new humanity. Black South Africans, argues Mpunzi, must be internally free before they can abolish apartheid.

583 Muzorewa, Gwinyai H. "A Quest for an African Christology." *Journal of Black Theology* in South Africa 2,2 (November 1988): 24-30.

Muzorewa examines Charles Nyamiti's work on christology. See 445-448. Here, the essential acculturative issue is the ancestors. The essential "inculturative" issue is the incarnation. Christ, by virtue of his true humanity, is the prototype of human beings. He is, in the Barthian sense, the supralapsarian, (proto)ancestor——existing always in the Son's "heart." It is by virtue of this "*the*anthropology" that the African sense of the ancestors is a fitting field for the planting of christology. See 426. Here, argues Muzorewa, one approaches the insights of the "word-man" school of the patristic period. That is Christ——and, "perichoretically," the Father and the Spirit——reveals God "himself" as the ancestor (especially if one considers the *genus majestaticum*). See 242. "Ancestrology" is even more compelling when one considers that the ancestors signify life after death. See 324. The correspondence between the ancestors and resurrection leads Muzorewa to claims that "ancestrology simply opens a window through which we can catch a spiritual glimpse of the nature and person of Jesus Christ" (p. 29) Muzorewa, however, argues that ancestrology does not commend the confusion of Christ with the cult of the ancestors.

584 Ngcokovane, Cecil Mzingisi. "Ethical Problems, Options and Strategies Facing the Black Church Today." *Journal of Black Theology in South Africa* 2,1 (May 1988): 26-33.

Ngcokovane asserts that the crises of apartheid force South African Christians to consider their participation in violence. Critical in that regard is the distinction between the overthrow of an oppressive *system* and the vindictive destruction of human lives. Justice and vengeance are not identical and only the former edifies the consideration of violence. "Because black South Africans do not see white South Africans as their enemies, but their oppressors," writes Ngcokovane, "it is almost inconceivable that a revolutionary strategy can work in South Africa" (p. 32) Ngcokovane argues that change will come "through dialogue."

585 Ngubane, J.B. "Theological Roots of the African Independent Churches and Their Challenge to Black Theology." In *The Unquestionable Right to Be Free: Black Theology from South Africa*, ed. by Itumeleng J. Mosala and Buti Tlhagale, 71-90. Maryknoll, N.Y.: Orbis Books, 1986.

Ngubane holds that blacks have africanized Christianity and thus divested it of its Eurocentric trappings, making it relevant to the aspirations of the masses. This is particularly true of the "Zionist" churches. See 554. Ngubane makes a very useful distinction between africanization and indigenization. Indigenization pertains to autochthonous leadership within the church. Africanization, on the other hand, "implies taking into consideration the culture of the people of Africa, their thought-patterns, their beliefs and their world view when creating structures and forms of the church" (p. 79-80). See 509. According to Ngubane, black theology and the independent churches are complementary. Black theology gives the independent churches insight into post-modern paradigms; the independent churches edify black theology regarding "the grass roots level of the ordinary people" (p. 82).

586 Ntwasa, Sabelo, and Basil Moore. "The Concept of God in Black Theology." In *The Challenge of Black Theology in South Africa*, ed. by Basil Moore, 18-28. Atlanta: John Knox Press, 1973.

The authors examine the image of God taught to Africans by missionaries. In doing so, they question the validity of Western theology for the oppressed. Ntwasa and Moore determine that Western, triune, conceptions of God convey God's omnipotence, omniscience, and so forth. This Western god is, essentially and economically——both in himself and in his revelation in history——a white male. Western theology, then, is essentially a product of Eurocentric male consciousness; it is as racist as it is sexist, and betrays itself as such in the assumption that white male rule is tantamount to Christian faith. Black theology, however, in its assertion that God is black, seeks to make blackness a symbol of God's identification with the despised, the poor, and the oppressed. In this way, the conception of God as Person is less bigoted; it transcends racism in opposition to racism as a rule of thumb. In black theology, then, God is a relational God rather than a God of apartheid; a God of love rather than a God of misanthropy; a God of freedom as opposed to a God who legitimates the oppressive order.

587 Ntwasa, Sabelo. "The Concept of the Church in Black Theology." In *The Challenge of Black Theology in South Africa*, ed. by Basil Moore, 109-118. Atlanta: John Knox Press, 1973.

A black ecclesiology, for Ntwasa, must distinguish itself, at the outset, from a white ecclesiology that has historically defended white supremacy. One of the most pernicious aspects of that ecclesiology is the cultural violence it has committed against blacks. Here cultural violence is manifest in blacks' self-hatred. For Ntwasa, blacks' lack of self-esteem is the deformity of apartheid. Black theology, however, is the well-proportioned product of self-esteem; it is the spirituality that enables blacks to seek to abolish apartheid. As white Christians have yet to evince commitments to black liberation, the black church must maintain and magnify its vision of liberation as the mark of the true Church, asserts Ntwasa. See 580

588 Ntwasa, Sabelo. "The Training of Black Ministers Today." In *The Challenge of Black Theology in South Africa*, ed. by Basil Moore, 141-146. Atlanta: John Knox Press, 1973.

Ntwasa laments the fact that theological education in South Africa is not contextual. Thus educated blacks, while decently equipped to read biblical languages and Eurocentric theologies, are barely——if at all——equipped to minister to their oppressed constituency. They are too often trained by scholars with neither academic nor existential knowledge of the black poor. For Ntwasa, blacks who would serve the church must be edified by the black community and unswervingly committed to its liberation.

589 Obijole, Olubayo. "South African Liberation Theologies of Boesak and Tutu——A Critical Evaluation." *Africa Theological Journal* 16,3 (1987): 201-215.

Obijole seeks to evaluate the theologies of both men in order to assess their viability in light of the struggle for liberation. See 517-522, 599-605. Obijole concludes early that neither challenges capitalism and that each is thus out of step with the struggle for authentic liberation in South Africa.

590 Omoyajowo, Akin. "An African Expression of Christianity." In *The Challenge of Black Theology in South Africa*, ed. by Basil Moore, 81-92. Atlanta: John Knox Press, 1973.

Referring to Oosthuizen's work——see 227——Omoyajowo asserts that the church has faced the problem of its irrelevancy from its tenure in North Africa to the present. Here Omoyajowo means the established church as opposed to the so-called heterodox, Donatist church. The established church, writes Omoyajowo, is too Eurocentric to be relevant to Africa; *African* Christianity is found in the independent churches. According to Omoyajowo these churches are trinitarian, but reveal an African structure related to divination. While such a juxtaposition is possible, one suspects that many of these churches are not as "orthodox" as Omoyajowo claims.

591 Pityana, Nyameko. "What Is Black Consciousness?" In *The Challenge of Black Theology in South Africa*, ed. by Basil Moore, 58-63. Atlanta: John Knox Press, 1973.

Pityana argues that Black Consciousness corrects the damage done by whites who——disgracing Christianity——attempted to teach blacks self-hatred. According to those whites, traditional culture and the Black Consciousness that upholds such culture are anti-Christian. For Pityana, those whites, in their own hatred, did not essentially love the neighbor; but Africans, who valorize their blackness, have insight into the meaning of such love. Their black theology, then, facilitates both love of the neighbor and an appropriate respect for traditional culture——both of which negate white bigotry. In sum, black theology affirms the humanity of blacks without negating the humanity of whites, especially whites gifted with the insight of *metanoia*.

592 Rabothata, A. "How Far Can Christians and Non-Christians Work Together in Social and Religious Spheres?" In *Relevant Theology for Africa*, ed. by Hans-Jurgen Becken, 178-180. Durban: Lutheran Publishing House, 1973.

Rabothata, like Mbiti, discusses the disappointment Africans experienced when their literal understanding of missionaries' teaching of the "last things" was contradicted by the on-going delay of the apocalypse. See 396, 397. Their disillusionment with Christian eschatology led many Africans to abandon Christianity as an impotent religion. Those that remain Christian frequent priest-diviners, who promise relief from psychological and physical afflictions. The failure of Christianity to provide meaning for African people can also be seen in the proliferation of independent churches. For Rabothata, the church must be willing to coexist with traditional religions, which do not wane in the light of Christianity, but tend to wax. Such cooperation would be a sign that the church is up to the challenges that confront it in revolutionary times.

593   Sebidi, Lebamang. "The Dynamics of the Black Struggle and Its Implications for Black Theology." In The Unquestionable Right to Be Free: Black Theology from South Africa, ed. by Itumeleng J. Mosala and Buti Tlhagale, 1-35. Maryknoll, N.Y.: Orbis Books, 1986.
        Sebidi surveys the history of black struggle in terms of four phases: (1) the !Khoisan; (2) the tribalistic; (3) the nationalistic; and (4) the Black Consciousness. (1) The !Khoisan, the aboriginal "bushmanoid" people of the Cape, lost their land to white settlers who, in the seventeenth, eighteenth, and nineteenth centuries, also (2) subdued the Bantu people dispersed further north. (3) In the twentieth century, black resistance, no longer distinguished by the traditional militarism of the Zulu nation or the diplomacy of Mosheshe, took on the character of liberal moderation. That orientation, forced by the hegemonic collusion of Afrikaner and English-speaking whites, was characteristic of the African National Congress (ANC), though the unionism of Clement Kadalie was perhaps more radical than the ANC. (4) The Black Consciousness phase may be said to be a return to the alterity of the so-called "tribalistic" phase, though its leadership had, like that of the ANC, been westernized. Thus does Sebidi discusses the historical factors that have produced black theology. The dominant factor is the Black Consciousness Movement. See 566. He asserts that two prevailing trajectories have emerged from that history: (1) the race-analyst position, and (2) the class-analyst position. The first trajectory makes blackness, both chromatically and culturally, the symbol of struggle. Indeed, blackness is a metonym for the land. The second trajectory makes the contradictions among peasants, workers, and the bourgeoisie dominant. Sebidi argues that black theologians must incorporate both positions.

594   Setiloane, Gabriel. "About Black Theology." In A New Look at Christianity in Africa, 66-71. Geneva: WSCF Books, 1972.
        Setiloane argues that black theology did not emerge solely in the United States. African theology is itself a black theology. That is, the relationship among Christian exegesis, post-modern thought and black experience was made clear in Africa in 1962——before American definitions of black theology emerged. For Setiloane, then, black theology signifies that whites' oppression of African people is not Christian. Black North American theology is but a species of black theology. It is a liberation theology emergent from political struggle. African theology, however——understood here as a form of black theology——is a theology of culture and is produced "in an atmosphere of physical freedom and comparable calm" (p. 69). According to Setiloane, black North American theology is too focused on the pain of blackness——the modalities of sorrow; the justified bitterness emergent from unabated, unnatural grief. See 406. For Setiloane, black North American theology should also reflect the transcendent spirit of black folk—— the exuberant sophistication of their jazz as well as their sorrow songs.

595   Setiloane, Gabriel. "Civil Authority——from the Perspective of African Theology." Journal of Black Theology in South Africa 2,2 (November 1988): 10-23.
        Black theology and other liberation theologies, argues Setiloane, have tended to reduce African theology to caricature in insisting that it be radicalized for the sake of African liberation. It is true, he asserts, that African theologians have tended to focus on a cultural problematic; but that should not indicate a lack of interest in liberation. Indeed,

Setiloane asserts "that when African Theology reaches the stage of theologizing in that area [i.e., liberation], the outcome will make the preoccupations of the other theologies appear like a Sunday School picnic" (p. 10). According to Setiloane, African tradition has it that an unjust civil authority is to be overthrown by any means necessary.

596 Sizwe, M. "The Christians Political Responsibility (or the Christian Attitude to the State)." *Journal of Black Theology in South Africa* 2,1 (May 1988): 48-52.

Sizwe demands that Scripture be reread in order to determine the New Testament foundation of clergy opposition to the state. He thus examines Romans 13: 1-7. "Let every person be subjected to the governing authorities." He concludes that the meaning of the text——once exegetical suspicion has been applied——is "obey God, not the government." The upshot of this for him is that clergy activists, such as Frank Chikane——see 531——reveal that temporal authority is to be obeyed only in compliance with God's commandment to love the other. "When," writes Sizwe, temporal authority "abuses this trust, it is the duty of God's prophet [i.e., Chikane] to tell them so, and to point out to them the limits of their authority" (p. 49). For Sizwe, then, Christian duty demands disobedience to and prophetic denouncement of unjust laws.

597 Tlhagale, Buti. "On Violence: A Township Perspective." In *The Unquestionable Right to Be Free: Black Theology from South Africa*, ed. by Itumeleng J. Mosala and Buti Tlhagale, 135-151. Maryknoll, N.Y.: Orbis Books, 1986.

Tlhagale investigates the implications of the township violence that escalated in the 1980's and brought about the state of emergencies that intensified the structural violence on which apartheid has thrived. For Tlhagale, township violence is epiphenomenal to the more ugly violence of the Pretoria regime. Indeed, truly liberating theology, argues Tlhagale, must break from the duplicitous norms regarding violence. Why is the oppressors' violence tolerated but the violence of the oppressed anathematized? A certain exegetical suspicion here produces a new hermeneutic that adjudicates among species of violence by way of a critical use of Scripture. That Jesus appears to be non-violent makes his legacy nearly useless to the oppressed in a revolutionary situation. The scandal of his irrelevance leads, Tlhagale explains, to a rereading of Scripture——such that Christ himself demands the abolition of apartheid *by any means necessary*. See 572-578. The establishment of justice and peace may require violence as a last resort. Township violence is the sign that time is running out in South Africa regarding non-violent change.

598 Tlhagale, Buti. "Nazism, Stalinist Russia, and Apartheid——A Comparison." In *Hammering Swords into Ploughshares: Essays in Honor of Archbishop Mpilo Desmond Tutu*, ed. by Buti Tlhagale and Itumeleng Mosala, 265-278. Grand Rapids, Michigan: Wm. B. Eerdmans; Trenton: Africa World Press, 1987.

Tlhagale notes the similarities among Nazi Germany, Stalinist Russia, and apartheid South Africa. According to Tlhagale, there is little difference between the three. For Tlhagale, moreover, it is imperative for Christians to follow the Tutu's lead regarding the problem of fascism. In the vanguard of Christians who oppose fascist regimes, Tutu exemplifies the role they should play in struggles against economic and racial injustices.

599 Tutu, Desmond. "Some African Insights and the Old Testament." In *Relevant Theology for Africa*, ed. by Hans-Jurgen Becken, 40-469. Durban: Lutheran Publishing House, 1973.

Archbishop Tutu, the highly politicized priest and a leader of the anti-apartheid movement, discusses the negative image of Africa embodied by many missionaries. These assumed that blacks were either without religion or devotees of the devil. In examining those racist opinions, Tutu refers to *African Ideas of God*, edited by Edwin Smith, and

Placide Tempels' *Bantu Philosophy*. See 156, 163, 254, 256, 261-262. Africa's negative image, asserts Tutu, is but Eurocentric propaganda. See 329. Indeed, this negative image is integral to the missiology that Boulaga calls cruel and alienating. See 305-307. *A fortiori*, missionaries were contemptuous of a modality of the *imago Dei*——i.e., the alterity of Africanness——which is an organ of God's graciousness. (On alterity, see 331.) For Tutu, the African *visage* of the gospel may be seen, in part, in the independent churches. Indeed, it is regrettable, asserts Tutu, that the chauvinism of whites prevents them from seeing the correspondence between African culture and the Bible. See 294. Whites' condescension and paternalism toward Africans persist, reveals Tutu, with the result that black theology is indispensable if South Africans are to witness to the gospel.

600 Tutu, Desmond. "Viability." In *Relevant Theology for Africa*, ed. by Hans-Jurgen Becken, 34-39. Durban: Lutheran Publishing House, 1973.

Tutu's sense of "viability" signifies, in part, the self-contentment of the Western bourgeoisie, who, relishing their capital, delight in the fact that the imperial superstructure is "viable." For Tutu, privileged members of the Third World, who tend to reproduce, on a smaller scale, the obscenity of Western "contentment" must beware of that "viability." For the most part, however, viability, for Tutu, entails African self-reliance and the community it builds. That is, self-reliance is an admirable goal; but self-aggrandizement is mired in the "viable" decadence of Western values. According to Tutu, Black Consciousness——see 593——and black theology call for a viability that draws from African traditional, as opposed to Western capitalist, values. As an example of this viability, Tutu cites the Arusha Declaration and its ideology, *ujamaa*. See 102-106. In terms of the theological implications of "viability," Tutu notes the necessity of appreciating the New Testament image of the church as the body of Christ. See 416.

601 Tutu, Desmond. "Whither African Theology." In *Christianity in Independent Africa*, ed. by Edward Fasholé-Luke, Richard Gray, Adrian Hastings and Godwin Tasie, 364-369. Bloomington: Indiana University Press, 1978.

Tutu argues that the themes of liberation and africanization are inextricable because cultural repression is but a manifestation of socioeconomic oppression. According to Tutu, missionaries stressed discontinuities between traditional religion and Christianity because of a vulgar tautological view that assumes that salvation comes by way of Europe alone. Tutu, however, asserts——and in a way reminiscent of Bajeux——that the African traditional cosmos and that of the Bible are quite similar. See 294. The correspondences between Old Testament religion and traditional African religion are sure signs that African signs and symbols can convey biblical convictions with integrity. Yet, argues Tutu, African theology is nonetheless prey to "a too facile and cheap alliance between culture and Christ" (p.368). African traditional religions have their share of elements opposed by the gospel. What is more, Tutu implies that "culture has never the translucidity of custom" (Fanon). See 034. Culture, as Fanon and Cabral have shown, is dynamic. See 023-025, 035, 529, 550, 595. For Tutu, then, the anthropological dilettantism of bourgeois theologians and the current social and religious realities of the African poor are significantly different. Indeed, Tutu critiques the mores of the old guard who failed to respond prophetically to the *l'agonie*——see 437——of the black continent.

602 Tutu, Desmond. "Black Theology and African Theology: Soulmates or Antagonists?" In *Black Theology: A Documentary History, 1966-1979*, ed. by Gayraud Wilmore and James Cone, 483-491. Maryknoll, N.Y.: Orbis Books, 1979.

Tutu examines the old guard's contention that black and African theologies are radically dissimilar. Specifically, he challenges Mbiti's views——see 406——and notes that "African theology has failed to produce a sufficiently sharp cutting edge." For Tutu, moreover, black South African theology *is* an African theology; and its North American sibling may also be said to be an African theology (if one subscribes to a Pan-African definition of blackness). See 606, 609. At any rate, Tutu holds that the two——or perhaps one should say the three theologies——are soulmates. All of them, he argues, "are bound to mother Africa by invisible but tenacious bonds."

603   Tutu, Desmond.   "The Theology of Liberation in Africa." In *African Theology en Route*, ed. by Kofi Appiah-Kubi and Sergio Torres, 162-169. Maryknoll, N.Y.: Orbis Books, 1979.

Tutu argues that African theology should be a theology of liberation. His essay reflects his thoughts shortly after the murder of Steve Biko. See 013-015. Although certain scholars have held that African *liberation* theology pertains to South African theology alone, Tutu argues that the theme and the praxis of liberation are relevant to the entire continent. "Independence" has not obliterated the suffering of the poor in Africa. See 334-341. For Tutu, theologies that do not address the poors' suffering are not biblical, for the Bible indicates that God is on the side of the poor. Tutu concludes that African theologians who bracket the theme of liberation also truncate the gospel.

604   Tutu, Desmond.   "The Theology of Liberation." In *Crying in the Wilderness: The Struggle for Justice in South Africa*, ed. by John Webster, 34-36. Grand Rapids: Wm. B. Eerdmans, 1982.

Tutu asserts the indispensability of liberation theology for a church that would be edified by its faith. According to Tutu, faith entails the pneumatic knowledge of the "God of the poor, of the hungry, of the naked, with whom the Church identifies and has solidarity" (p. 36). See 603. This church, for Tutu, is the true Church——the anti-apartheid church.

605   Tutu, Desmond.   "Black Theology and African Theology: Soulmates or Antagonists." In *Third World Liberation Theologies: A Reader*, ed. by Deane William Ferm, 256-264. Maryknoll, N.Y.: Orbis Books, 1986.

See 602.

606   Young, Josiah U.   *Black and African Theologies: Siblings or Distant Cousins?* Maryknoll, N.Y.: Orbis Books, 1986.

A study of the similarities and differences among black and African theologies. Young focuses for the most part on the old guard, though he notes the emergence of the new. Looking critically at the histories and dominant themes of both theologies, Young identifies the theologians who embody the values of an incipient Pan-African theology. See 602, 609.

607   Young, Josiah U.   "African Theology: From Independence to Liberation." *Voices From the Third World* 10,4 (December 1987): 41-48.

Young elucidates the distinction between the old and new guards and valorizes——with a focus on Éla, Oduyoye and Boulaga——the new guard's synthesis of themes related to liberation, inculturation, and africanization. According to Young: "The new guard's synthesis of liberation and africanization signifies the intrinsic relation between a truly autochthonous struggle for political self-determination and cultural integrity" (p. 47).

608   Young, Josiah U.   "Zama Azefani." In *We Are One Voice: Black Theology in the USA and South Africa*, ed. by Simon Maimela and Dwight Hopkins, 127-138. Braamfontein: Skotaville Publishers, 1989.

Young draws on the analogies between the two theologies, and argues that their futures are inextricable given the fact that black theologians of South Africa and the United States share profound similarities that evince the transatlantic reality of a Pan-African theology.

609   Young, Josiah U.   *A Pan-African Theology: Providence and the Legacies of the Ancestors*. Trenton: Africa World Press, 1992.

A *Pan-African Theology: Providence and the Legacies of the Ancestors* blends certain perspectives of African-American and African theologians. Young draws on the views of Éla, Oduyoye, Mveng, Adoukonou, Boulaga, and Cone in a sustained analysis of Pan-Africanism as a praxis of struggle and mode of African spirituality. He argues that Pan-Africanism is indispensable for blacks who reject the alienation wrought by white supremacy and desire to grow in Afrocentric commitments to the black poor of Africa and Diaspora. Examining the legacy of seminal black clergy of the nineteenth century as a critical principle, Young offers a constructive model that assimilates African values which de-europeanize black Christians who seek the meaning of their continuity with Africa. By way of a Pan-African approach to both social and religio-cultural analyses, Young makes a case for a liberation theology uniquely suited for the task of furthering the solidarity of the black oppressed on both sides of the Atlantic.

Index of Names

Index refers only to the entry numbers of the bibliography.

Index of Titles

Index refers only to the entry numbers of the bibliography.

Index of Subjects

Entries refer to both page numbers of Part One; *and* numbers of annotated entries in Part Two. The distinction is as follows: p. 12; 003.

About the Author

JOSIAH U. YOUNG III is Professor of Systematic Theology at Wesley Theological Seminary. He has published extensively on black and African theologies.